ACROPOLIS FROM EAST

A History of Greece

BY

CYRIL E. ROBINSON

METHUEN & CO LTD

11 NEW FETTER LANE · LONDON EC4

This book was first published June 20th 1929
It has been reprinted ten times
Ninth edition 1957
Reprinted 1960, 1962 and 1064

folio   attached

amum
amured
amuped

foim
from
from

9.4
CATALOGUE NO. 2/7129/6

PRINTED AND BOUND IN GREAT BRITAIN BY
BUTLER & TANNER LTD, FROME AND LONDON

PREFACE *Shows*

DURING the last twenty or thirty years the whole
field of Greek History has been the subject of
much patient and intensive research, carried on
by classical scholars, excavators and archaeologists. Not
merely has new light been shed upon old problems, but
fresh aspects of Hellenic life, economic and social in particular, have been studied as never before. The results of
such study and research have hitherto been widely scattered among various periodicals, pamphlets or monographs ;
but the publication of the Cambridge Ancient History has
lately brought a part of them at least within the more
convenient compass of a connected tale. That work,
however, is not primarily intended for the reading of
younger students, and its many volumes would make it,
in any case, unhandy for their use. I do not feel, therefore,
that any apology is needed for this attempt to retell the
story of Greece in the light of our new knowledge.

In doing so I have not thought fit to overload these pages
with the discussion of controversial matter, but rather I
have tried to present (with such occasional caveats as
uncertainty may demand) those conclusions which upon
the whole appear most probable. It has been my aim,
moreover, while introducing as much picturesque and
illustrative detail as is permitted by the limits of my space,
to keep clear the general outlines of historical developments,
economic, social, artistic and intellectual no less than
political or military. Two or three chapters have been
devoted mainly to a description of Greek literature, Greek
art, Greek religion and Greek thought. For it is after all
in these no less than in political and tactical developments
that the significance of Greece to the modern man resides.
It seems impossible to neglect those telling anecdotes of
Herodotus or those masterly descriptions of Thucydides

v

which, however trivial or unimportant in themselves, have justly become a recognized part of traditional Greek history. But the fact remains that the teaching of Socrates and Plato, the dramatic genius of Aeschylus and Euripides, or the artistic skill of Pheidias and Praxiteles, deserve as much attention, to say the least of it, as the story of Gyges' ring or of the beleaguerment of Plataea.

To keep an even balance between so many divergent claims is a problem difficult enough ; nor is it any easier to determine what emphasis or proportion should rightly be assigned to the various epochs of the narrative. The prehistoric period and the subsequent formation and evolution of the more important states clearly demand a more than cursory description. But partly because, when we come to the fifth and the fourth centuries, our knowledge is at once more detailed and less dependent on conjecture, partly because the interest of those centuries makes a more obvious appeal to modern minds, I have tried to develop their story at somewhat greater length. Nor do I think that any justification is required for an attempt to carry the tale briefly into Hellenistic times. It is impossible to understand the full importance of Greek thought and Greek art to the world, unless we realize that the Greek spirit did not die at Alexander's death in 323 B.C., but on the contrary that it was then for the first time spread over an area not only vast in extent, but also of vast significance to the subsequent history of the civilized world. To leave unnoticed the debt of Rome to Greece would be as serious an omission as to neglect the debt of historic Greece to the Homeric Age. Nor should we do full justice to our Hellenic heritage if we failed to realize the part it played in the evolution of Christianity itself. Within the compass of such a book as this, it is impossible (apart from occasional allusions) to place Hellenic history in its true relation to the general trend and wider movements of the Mediterranean world. But it would be a serious error to treat that history as a mere isolated episode, springing, as it were, out of nothing and ending again abruptly in a vacuum. For the Spirit of Hellas—much changed no doubt and under different guises—has lived on through the ages. It is still alive to-day.

I must not conclude this preface without acknowledging my very great debt to Professor J. L. Myres, to Mr. C. W. M. Cox, of New College, Oxford, and to Mr. M. Holroyd, of Brasenose College, Oxford. Without the assistance of their criticisms and suggestions this book would be much less accurate and much less comprehensive than it is. Such errors, however, as may have crept into its pages must lie at the Author's door. To Mr. R. H. Dundas, of Christ Church, Oxford. I am also indebted for a most helpful revision of the proofs. Finally acknowledgment is due, for permission to use their photographs, to M. F. Boissonnas, of Geneva (chiefly the scenic photographs) ; to M. Alinari, of Florence (for the sculpture) ; to Messrs. Fleming, of London, and M. Calavas, of Paris, for two reproductions of Greek vases ; and to the Hellenic Society for what remains.

For the Diagram Sketch of Ancient Athens, reproduced here as an endpaper from my book *The Days of Alkibiades*, I am beholden to its publishers, Messrs. Edward Arnold and Co.

C. E. R.

WINCHESTER,
April, 1920

PREFACE TO NINTH EDITION

VIEWS upon Greek Pre-history have recently undergone so drastic a change that a complete recasting of the chapters here concerned has seemed called for ; and two of my one-time pupils, now members of the Winchester College Staff, have been good enough to undertake the task of rewriting them. It has been most admirably done ; and the debt which I owe to Mr. Colin Badcock and Mr. John Stow will be felt also, I am sure, by all future readers of this book.

C. E. R.

OKEHAMPTON,
January, 1957

CONTENTS

PART I

PART II

MAPS

ILLUSTRATIONS

* Photos : Alinari, Florence.
† ,, Boissonnas, Geneva.
‡ ,, Hellenic Society.

Mountain Ranges or Peaks

Hilly or Mountainous Country

Plains

40 Miles

PHYSICAL MAP OF GREECE

PART I

CHAPTER I

LAND AND PEOPLE

UNDER a sunlit atmosphere of startling clearness and on a sea incredibly blue the limbs of Greece and her attendant islands spread strangely gaunt and grey. The contours, angular and lively, are unsoftened by other vegetation than a close growth of sallow scrub. The bones of the land show bare. And yet, behind such appearance of bleak monotony—and herein lies the secret of the country's charm—there is concealed a rich variety of contrast and surprise. In rare nooks of shelter among the sterile rock you will find starry clusters of delicate spring flowers, blood-red anemones, pale hyacinths and the ghostly asphodel. So, too, between the stark ridges of this mountain waste—two-thirds perhaps of the entire peninsula —run narrow strips of level, fertile plain where fig and pomegranate and even the orange ripen, and where corn is cut in June between the olive groves. Even the clear weather has moods of sharp rebellion. Brief winter snows will cover the landscape, to melt at the coming of noon ; and the spring or autumn sky will grow dark with sudden tempests which swell the slender trickle in the broad, parched river-beds to a frantic and roaring spate. And, as the land, so were its ancient people—a curious compound of conflicting elements. In the Greeks, the hot-blooded passionate temper of the South was always strong ; and, when the thrill of life was on them, they would abandon their bodies to a reckless impulse for wild dance and drunken rout. Yet what chiefly distinguished them from other peoples was their more habitual self-restraint. The luxurious softness of Oriental culture they honestly despised ; and it was the stricter discipline of their insignificant

1

armies which enabled them twice to conquer the invading Persian hordes. Their men continued the practice of athletic exercise well into middle age ; and in their art they were especially remarkable for a scrupulous avoidance of excess. It is natural to explain these traits in the Greek character by reference to their climate and their land ; for there was enough of cold in winter to fortify and brace where the heats had threatened to relax, and the winning of sufficient soil to cultivation involved them in seasonal rather than continuous toil, which allowed long intervals for leisure or amusement. The influence of their physical environment, however, was greatest in the sphere of politics. Never till Rome conquered her did Greece become one State. The mountain-barriers which divided plain from plain made free and easy intercourse impossible ; so the folk of the various plains—as Thebes and Attica above the Isthmus, Corinth, Argos and Lacedaemon south of it—remained jealously separate and independent. Such isolation, though the source of futile and destructive quarrels, had one result for good. The narrow local patriotism which it engendered proved a matchless training in the art of civic life. Every free-born Greek was himself a politician. The conduct of public affairs, if not always directly under his control, was transacted at any rate close under his eyes and reacted swiftly on his daily life. So political thought was vigorous ; self-government developed in a congenial soil ; and experiments were made in the realm of pure democracy which have ever since been the wonder of the world.

Not all Greek states, however, were equally progressive. Those which, like Thebes and Sparta, lived mainly by the tilling of the land, were conservative and backward. Athens, on the other hand, which carried freedom furthest, took readily to the sea. This can have been no accident ; for foreign intercourse and maritime adventure are apt, as in Elizabethan England, to breed free habits and keen wits. The Greeks for the most part were great mariners, plying the Levant and the Black Sea for commerce and flinging out numerous settlements on neighbouring coasts.

VALE OF TEMPE

SCRUBLAND IN ATTICA

Nor is it fanciful to trace here the partial source of that restless, inquisitive spirit which was the peculiar genius of their race. Herodotus, their historian, was a great voyager and had ransacked every corner of the then known world. It was among Ionian traders of the Asiatic seaboard that arose the first dim inklings of philosophic thought; and, above all, it was in Athens at the hey-day of her maritime supremacy that Hellenic culture was carried to its most consummate pitch. No people ever surpassed the beauty of her sculpture or her buildings. In literature she established models which poets and prose writers of almost every age have followed; and the inquiry then begun concerning the deepest truths of life gave such impulse to philosophy as will outlast time itself. When at the close of our own Middle Ages men had more than half forgotten how to think, it was the rediscovery of the old Attic authors that inspired Renaissance scholars to renew the quest for truth. And the influence of Greece is with us yet. Not merely have we drawn from her much of our daily language, most of our literary forms, and even—in the last resort—that mental attitude towards the world around us of which natural science is the latest fruit; but, more than this, as often as new problems and new theories may perplex us, there are still abundant lessons and sure guidance to be drawn from the profound, clear-sighted wisdom of this marvellous folk. Over material things, it is true, they held no great mastery. They were not, like the Romans, efficient engineers. They can scarcely be credited with a single invention of outstanding practical utility. But they understood, as few have understood it, the art of living life. They never, as we often do, mistook mere means for ends, nor expected the apparatus of material wealth to bring happiness to mankind. A simplicity there was about their daily habits, severe as the landscape of their native hills; but side by side with this simplicity there grew in them a zest—rich as the vale under the naked mountain—for the noblest joys and the fairest visions that can delight the spirit of man.

CHAPTER II

EARLY DAYS

THE Greeks' own mythology, as we know, was rich in legend fancifully recalling the picturesque incidents of their earlier days. But these stories tell us nothing of the real beginning of the tale, and it has been for modern scholars and archaeologists to piece together their deductions and give an account of what probably occurred. It was in about 2000 B.C., it is now widely agreed, that the Greek-speaking people first entered, like the Angles into Britain, the land to which they were to give their name. Coming into Greece from the north, they found already in possession an Aegean folk. Of these people all we need say is that they were bronze-users, their pottery was still made by hand, and they have left us traces of their language in such non-Greek terminations as *-nth*, *-ns*, *-ss*, which survive for example in *hyacinth*, *Corinth*, *Tiryns*, *Larissa* and *thalassa*.

Soon after their arrival, we see the Greeks split into two groups. One moves into Epirus, and remains segregated in that extremely rugged and mountainous district. We shall not hear of them again until we come to speak of them six or seven centuries later as the Dorian invaders of southern Greece. The other group passes into Thessaly and on into the south, and this is the group with which we are immediately concerned. They are to become the people whom Homer later calls Achaeans, and who create the civilization of ' golden Mycenae.' Of this civilization which lasted for five centuries (1600–1100 B.C.), the first and not the least brilliant of the creations of Greek genius, much is known with certainty, and with an account of it and its discoverer any history of the Greeks must properly begin.

4

MYCENAE—FIRST PERIOD (Shaft-graves)

Mycenae stands on a rocky knoll, dominating the rich Argive plain which slopes down to the sea twelve miles distant. It must have struck the Achaeans as they made their way south from the isthmus as an ideal place to settle. Certainly by 1600 B.C. Mycenae was the centre of a flourishing civilization.

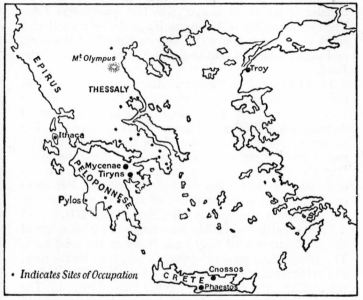

MAP TO ILLUSTRATE CENTRES OF EARLY AEGEAN CIVILIZATION

For our knowledge of this civilization we are indebted to Heinrich Schliemann. Born in 1822, the son of a small-town Lutheran minister, Schliemann was fascinated as a boy by the tales his father told him of the Trojan War and by the romance of archaeology. Forced to leave school at the age of fourteen and enter a grocer's shop as an apprentice, he still did not lose the love of learning. Then one evening a drunken miller came into the shop and recited a hundred lines of Homer. 'From that moment,' writes Schliemann, 'I never ceased to pray to God that by His grace I might yet have the happiness of learning Greek.'

His prayer received an almost miraculous answer. Leaving the grocer's shop, he became in rapid succession a messenger-boy, a clerk, a merchant, a millionaire. In the process he taught himself fifteen languages, among them ancient Greek. He was now ready to fulfil the ambition of his childhood and devote his life and wealth to searching for remains of the Homeric age. His first quarry was Troy. Trusting implicitly in Homer as his guide, he unearthed a series of cities one above the other on the hill of Hissarlik, and satisfied himself that one of these was the Troy of the *Iliad*.

Then he turned to Mycenae. Here his guide was Pausanias, the antiquarian and traveller of the second century A.D. Pausanias had said that he had seen the grave of Agamemnon and others within the walls of Mycenae. For various reasons most scholars did not then believe that this meant the existing walls of the citadel; Pausanias must, they thought, be referring to another later wall, all traces of which were lost. But Schliemann followed Pausanias exactly, as he had followed Homer at Troy, and began to dig just inside the famous Lion Gate (Plate III).

Tons of earth and rubble were removed by his army of Greek labourers until they came down to the solid rock. There they found six shaft-graves going down into the rock, and in them nineteen bodies and a treasure of gold and silver richer than even Schliemann could have dreamed. The men had golden masks on their faces, the women gold diadems on their brows, the children were wholly wrapped in gold. Beside the bodies lay swords, daggers, drinking-cups, rings, toilet-boxes, all in gold and silver. And the treasure was not only fabulously rich; the objects were beautiful too. Lively scenes were depicted on the sword and dagger blades, the cups were adorned with figures, the diadems were embossed with intricate patterns. In all the craftsmanship was superb, and the artistry of the design and liveliness of the conception showed that here was a culture at the classical stage, mature, vigorous, controlled, effortless.

Schliemann, still trusting Pausanias, believed that these were the graves of Agamemnon and his family. When he lifted the gold mask from the face of a buried king who had died in his prime, he sent a telegram to the King of Greece —' I have gazed on the face of Agamemnon.' But later evidence has shown that these shaft-graves are in fact to be dated in the sixteenth century, three hundred years before the Trojan War.

Pausanias had spoken of another group of graves outside the citadel wall, and these were discovered in 1951 by accident, during repairs to a tomb nearby. They belong to the same period as Schliemann's graves, and contain treasures only slightly inferior to his. In the sixteenth century, then, Mycenae was indeed rich in gold.

But such riches and artistic refinement are a far cry from the rude culture of the Achaeans who entered the stage in 2000 B.C. From some source they must have received an education, and this, we now know, had come about through their contact with a people who enjoyed a civilization and a culture infinitely more advanced than their own.

CRETE—THE MINOAN PERIOD

The home of this civilization was in Crete, and around its discovery by Sir Arthur Evans there hangs a romance as great as that attending the adventures of Schliemann at Troy and Mycenae. Arthur Evans had gone to Cnossos in Crete in the spring of 1894, hoping to find there the clue to an early system of writing which intrigued him. By 1899 he realized he was uncovering a whole civilization, hitherto unheard of, and stretching back in time far beyond the founding of Mycenae. Happily Evans, like Schliemann, had both wealth and leisure. In the course of his long life, working slowly and more scientifically than Schliemann, he was able to excavate his site completely, restore some of the crumbling remains, and sort out and publish his findings, financing the greater part of the undertaking from his own resources. Discovery and deduction on such a scale can seldom have been achieved by any single man.

Of the civilization in Crete before 2000 B.C. there is not much to tell. Little is known of the origins of the islanders, who certainly were not Greek by race or language. It seems that they were akin to the peoples who lived in western Asia Minor and in the coasts and islands of the Aegean before the coming of the Greeks had brought Indo-European [1] stock and language to those parts. Scholars, unable to be more exact, have given to the culture of Crete the name ' Minoan ' after her fabled King Minos. By 2800 the use of bronze was beginning there, and Crete was passing out of her stone-age culture already more than a thousand years old. By 2000 B.C. palatial residences were being built upon the hill of Cnossos in the north of the island and at Phaestos in the south. Other arts besides the builder's flourished at this time. Pottery was made on the wheel, and its black glaze surface decorated with bold designs in red, white and orange. House walls were richly frescoed in motifs drawn from nature ; here sea-animals frequently occur, lending weight to tradition's story that Cnossos was once a ruler of the sea. Perhaps the most charming example of a Minoan artist's

---

[1] The Greek language has many cousins—Sanskrit, the ancient tongue of Hindustan, Latin, which early migrants carried to Italy, German, and through German considerable portions of our own mixed speech. These languages are known as Indo-European. Their kinship may be illustrated by such a word as Sanskrit *pitâ*, Greek πατήρ, Latin *pater*, German *vater*, English *father*.

PLATE III

(a) The Throne Room in the Late Minoan Palace at Cnossos is here shown in its restored condition. Note the restored frescoes on the walls, and the simple but dignified design of the throne itself. (b) The Lion Gate forms the chief entrance to the Citadel of Mycenae. Note the squared stones, the monster block which forms the lintel of the gate, and the lion effigies carved on the triangular slab which surmounts it. The Sacred Circle, containing the shaft-graves, lies just within this gate and on the right hand as one enters.

THRONE ROOM, CNOSSOS

LYON GATE MYCENAE

work at this period is a fresco of a monkey arranging a vase of crocuses he has picked. All this Cretan art may well have owed something to the yet older civilization of the Nile Valley. Certainly there were close connexions with Egypt, where Cretan potters found a ready market for their coloured wares two hundred miles across the sea—an easy journey on the summer winds. Possibly colonists (and certainly copper) from the Nile had already reached Crete ; and on a likely interpretation of evidence from Egypt, the Pharaohs once drew tribute from the Cretan kings, and later came to respect them as their equals and even fear them as their foes. Writing too, which was known in Crete in this early period, consisted of picture-symbols not unlike Egyptian hieroglyphics and perhaps originally derived from them. In the years between 2000 and 1600 this early picture-writing gave way to a syllabic script, known to scholars as Linear A. Its language is unknown, and too little of the script has come to light to make complete decipherment likely.

Suddenly about 1600 some strange upheaval occurred, and the palaces at Cnossos and Phaestos were partially destroyed. Most probably an earthquake, such as Evans himself experienced at Cnossos, was the cause, for no signs of fire or an invader's violence appear upon the walls. But this destruction was not the end of the story. Out of the wreck a new and more splendid epoch came, and a yet grander palace grew on the ruins of the old. From this time Cnossos dominates the whole island, and from its buildings, their decorations and store-rooms much can be deduced of Cretan life in what is called the Late Minoan Period.

There are frescoes showing ladies in styled gowns gossiping as they watch some function. Whatever it is they are attending they seem to find each other's fashions more interesting than the scene. So indeed they may have been, for their pannier skirts and leg-o'-mutton sleeves and clinging corsages cut low might be the creations of some modern Paris salon. Bulls form the motif of many more frescoes. There is a remarkable picture, cartoon almost, of a young man doing a hand-stand vault from the horns of a bull and over its back, for all the world as though the charging animal were a Swedish horse. A girl waits to steady him as he lands. There is a gaming-board for playing some game like draughts, made in ivory inlaid with gold, and chequered with blue paste and silver foil. There was a small theatre to accommodate four hundred or so. This was no doubt used for dancing ; it is too small for bull-fights, though these, if the interest the frescoes show in bulls is anything to go by, must also have been held. The palace itself is unwalled ; the dangers of war seem to have been remote from the minds of this pleasure-loving people. Covering a total area of five acres, the palace had a throne-room (Plate III), public halls, a grand staircase of five flights, light-wells balustraded with those curious upside-down pillars that are characteristically Cretan, an ingenious drain device for running off rain-water (the drain follows the turns of the main staircase, dropping through a series of scooped troughs that check the flow sufficiently to steer it safely round the corners), immense numbers of rooms and labyrinthine passages handsomely frescoed with gay scenes of contemporary life, vast storage-jars for goods and rooms for official records. The palace is in fact not merely the residence of a royal family, however rich. The scale is too large. It is the site of a civilized court life and the administrative centre of a considerable empire. The arts of building and decoration as well as those of store-keeping and accounting are well developed. Here lived a carefree people, immensely rich and with a taste for elegant amusement. Wealth seems to be based on trade and on tribute received from subject peoples, certainly in Crete and perhaps overseas as well.

PLATE IV

A view taken from inside the so-called Treasury of Atreus, showing the shaft-entrance by which the subterranean tomb is approached, and the domed roof which gives its name to this type of ' Beehive Tomb '. The dome is not built upon the principle of a true arch ; for its stones are laid *horizontally*, each tier projecting slightly over the tier below it.

TREASURY OF ATREUS, MYCENAE

This is the civilization from which Mycenae learnt her refinement, and whose influence shaped the pattern of Mycenaean art. The valuable things found in the shaft-graves at Mycenae, the jewelled daggers, the beads and seals, the golden masks and the pottery, are undoubtedly of Cretan design. Crete therefore plays a vital part in the story of Greek development ; for those who settled too far north in Greece to feel the educating influence of Cretan contact, remained without art or order ; the Mycenaean cities of the south on the other hand learnt both to an astonishing degree, and to the story of their achievement it is now time that we should return.

MYCENAE—SECOND PERIOD (Bee-hive Tombs)

Of the buildings at Mycenae in the early period (1600–1500) few traces remain—only isolated lines of wall beneath the later palace and fragments of frescoes strikingly similar to those found at Cnossos. The massive fortifications with walls six yards thick which can be seen in Plate III, and the great bee-hive tombs, of which the finest is shown in Plate IV, were built a century or so later. These made the setting for the great events of which we read in the Greek poets. ' It was on these walls that Clytemnestra's watchman stood waiting for the beacon to announce the fall of Troy ; through this Lion Gate that Agamemnon and Cassandra passed to meet their death ; perhaps at one of these bee-hive tombs that Orestes made an offering to his father's shade before passing into the citadel to kill his mother.

We have now come to the first distinct figure in Greek history—Agamemnon, king of men, whose exploits we read in the Homeric poems. They tell a romantic story : how Menelaus' wife, the lovely Helen, eloped with Paris the young Trojan prince, and how Menelaus' brother, Agamemnon of Mycenae, intent on her recovery, gathered a large Greek host ; how the warriors both from Thessaly and the Peloponnese assembled at Aulis and were there detained by winds from sailing, until Agamemnon, to appease the gods, had sacrificed his daughter Iphigeneia ; how once arrived at Troy, the Greeks sat down for nine weary years of warfare underneath its walls ; how Achilles, their great hero from Thessalian Phthia, there met and slew in single combat Hector the Trojan champion ; how at last the town was taken by the trick of the wooden horse and Priam's lordly citadel went up in flames ; how Agamemnon returned to meet death at the hands of his unfaithful wife, and how Odysseus wandered for ten years before he returned to Penelope.

Homer wrote his poems some five hundred years after the events he described, and if the *Iliad* and *Odyssey* were still our only evidence for this period, we should have little idea what was fact and what was fiction, which details of the background-picture had been faithfully preserved by tradition and which were drawn by Homer from his own time.

But evidence has recently come to light which has immensely increased our knowledge and has in many ways strikingly confirmed the picture which Homer had given us. There have been fruitful excavations of thirteenth-century houses at Mycenae ; at Pylos the palace of Nestor or his immediate successors has been brought to light and shown to be the headquarters of a powerful kingdom. But the outstanding archaeological event of the twentieth century has been the decipherment of the so-called Linear B script by a young Englishman, Michael Ventris.

Some two thousand clay tablets in this script had been found in Cnossos by Sir Arthur Evans. In 1939 and 1952 a thousand more came to light at Pylos, and a number have been found in private houses excavated at Mycenae. Isolated examples have occurred at Tiryns, Thebes, Orchomenos and Eleusis. The script was therefore in widespread use in the Heroic Age and its decipherment was clearly vital for an understanding of the period. But in the fifty years that followed its appearance, though many useful facts were discovered—that the tablets were mostly inventories, that the script was syllabic (one sign for *ta*, others for *te*, *to*, etc.), that the language was inflected, that certain words were probably place-names and others names of men and women, and so on—the actual interpretation of the signs and recognition of the language written were as elusive as ever.

In 1934 Ventris, while a schoolboy of thirteen, had heard Sir Arthur Evans lecturing on the script, and had resolved from that day that he would crack the cipher. After the war he became an architect, but he devoted all his spare time to working on the tablets. Finally in 1952 he realized his ambition and with the help of a young Cambridge philologist, John Chadwick, was able to reveal to the world that the Linear B tablets had been deciphered and that the language was Greek.[1]

But it must not be thought that even now it is an easy matter to understand any text in Linear B that is found. The spelling-system is clumsy and impressionistic and only records roughly the sound of a word, and the language itself is as different from classical Greek as Chaucer's English is from that of our own day. But in spite of these difficulties, many tablets have been given very plausible interpretations, and have provided us with a flood of miscellaneous information on Mycenaean life.

These bits of information we must now weave into the fabric of a narrative ; for thanks to the decipherment we are able to draw a new and more detailed picture of life in the Mycenaean centres of civilization. Most of the tablets that have been deciphered were found, as we have seen, at Pylos and Mycenae on the mainland of Greece, and at Cnossos in Crete. Leaving till later the question of how it comes about that Mycenaean documents are found in Cretan Cnossos, we shall draw a general picture of life in Mycenaean communities from the contents of all the tablets wherever found. For all are records of the same civilization, and all are written in what we may call Mycenaenan Greek.

Homer's story of the mustering of the Greeks to fight the Trojan War will give us a convenient starting-place for examining the structure of Mycenaean society. From all the great Achaean kingdoms came contingents of goodly men to swell the host at Aulis, and with them came their kings. Of these each held wide dominion, but over all

[1] A description of the decipherment process is given in an appendix at the end of this chapter.

Agamemnon of Mycenae stood out as pre-eminent. No Achaean was ashamed to look to Mycenae for a lead, for Agamemnon, Homer tells us, was 'kingliest among kings' and 'led folk far greatest in number'. This fits well with the evidence of archaeology which reveals a great palace at Mycenae with roadways radiating from its gate, and others at Tiryns and Pylos, but none so great as Mycenae's. The palace found at Pylos cannot indeed have been much inferior; here in Homer old Nestor ruled as king, and the Linear B tablets discovered in his archive room at Pylos tell us much of how life was organized within a Mycenaean kingdom.

The structure of society was undoubtedly monarchic. The tablets refer to a single ruler, the 'anax', or overlord. Immediately beneath him ranks an official called 'lawagetas', perhaps the leader of the war-host (the name being compounded of λαός and ἡγέτης). Like the king, he enjoys a special reserve of land and the services of a personal staff of heralds and messengers. We learn also of two aristocrat classes. There are folk called 'telestai', or men of *telos*, a warrior class owing their high social position to the fact that, in return for military undertakings, they have been made masters of land by the king. Another important class is that of the 'hepetai' or 'followers'. They form the court circle, the companions and gentlemen-attendants on the king, and are found commanding army detachments on special duties.

In a single word, the structure of society at the top is feudal.[1] Outside the town, the word βασιλεύς is used to refer to local princelings, chieftains in their own right, who

---

[1] Professor Palmer has drawn some interesting parallels with Germanic feudal society. He points to the parallel distinction between anax and war-lord, and king and duke. The word lawagetas when Latinized gives 'dux' and so our 'duke'. 'Baron', like telestes, means literally 'man of burden'—an astonishing resemblance; and 'hepetes' through the Latin 'comes' gives our word 'count'. He therefore sees the origins of the feudal idea stretching far back in time to some Indo-European cradle race and inherited from them by the Mycenaeans and by the feudal states of later western Europe.

no doubt form the council of the supreme king. The Pylos tablets mention twelve of them, and over such a council of twelve βασιλῆς King Alcinous was hurrying to preside in the sixth book of the *Odyssey* when his daughter Nausicaa stopped him to beg a favour. From Homer too we should expect to find slaves at work in Mycenaean society. So indeed we do, though on a scale far larger than anything that Homer mentions. At Pylos, 1,500 slaves are listed, a retinue thirty times the size of any to be found in the households of Homeric heroes. From the tablets and from Professor Wace's excavations at Mycenae a great deal has been revealed about an aspect of Mycenaean life of which we get no glimpse from Homer ; it is an aspect which would have had little interest for a compiler of heroic saga, for it concerns the existence of rich merchants living graciously outside the citadel of Mycenae, and within the towns of a highly specialized artisan slave class. The tablets are the palace ledgers ; they keep a detailed record of the amounts of raw materials, bronze, silver, gold, timber, wool and linen, handed out to artisans retained by the palace to be worked up into finished products. That the lovely examples of Mycenaean art were no amateur productions we may see from the formidable list of specialized trade-names that can be got from the tablets ; goldsmiths, masons, fullers, potters, bow-makers, unguent-boilers are among the craftsmen employed ; on the farms the jobs of herding sheep, cows and goats are all kept distinct ; in the house, women have their special duties as seamstresses, bath-pourers or makers of head-dresses.

Two questions present themselves. Where do all these slaves come from and what is done with the products of so many craftsmen ? To the second question trade is no doubt the answer. Archaeology knows that the Mycenaeans traded, and the tablets too show contact with Egypt, Cyprus and Phoenicia. As to the slaves, they must be the loot of raids. Women and boys predominate in the slave-lists ; like other raiders the Mycenaeans would kill the men and carry off the women and children. Further, from the names given to the slaves after their place of origin, we can guess the direction the slave-raids took ; Miletus, Cnidus, Lemnos, and Cythera are names so found.

Inventories of Mycenaean war-materials include swords, spears, arrows and chariots. A tablet from Cnossos speaks of linen for making a chiton and of bronze plates to be attached to it ; someone is making a uniform for a ' bronze-shirted Achaean ', and Homer's stock epithet is explained. Details of Mycenaean armour can be pieced together from what the tablets tell us, from pictures made by artists of the period and from Homer's somewhat muddled account. Customs no doubt were changing all the time and a variety of equipment was employed, and this accounts for the conflicting details that our sources give us. Great figure-of-eight shields with pinched-in sides, ' man-enveloping ' as Homer calls them, were perhaps the first article to go out of date, to be replaced by ' tower-like ' half-cylinders such as Ajax carried in the *Iliad*. The old and clumsy man-envelopers survived as military relics to be dedicated to the gods, just as in our own time a regiment laying up its colours recalls the days when standards were carried into battle. In a lion-hunt scene depicted upon a Mycenaean dagger both types of shield appear to be in use ; both can be seen too upon a silver vase decorated with a picture of a siege. Later still a round and handier shield replaced both types. Swords changed their shape too from the long and slender thrusting point to a broader blade, still pointed for the thrust, but with two cutting edges for the slashing stroke. Another glimpse of changing equipment may be won from a careful scrutiny of Homer. Three hundred chariots, so the tablets tell us, were stored at Cnossos, though Homer's battles know nothing of the use of massed chariots. Always they are used for the transport of a single warrior from one part of the battle to another. Yet just once, it has been pointed out, old Nestor, drawing on his endless reminiscences of former wars, bids his chariots be drawn up in massed array, ' for so ', says he, ' men of old used to sack walls and cities '.

The tablets tell us something new about the religious beliefs of these people, for they record offerings of country products and of gold, not to any remotely conceived principle of fertility in nature, but to the Olympian deities familiar in classical times—to Zeus, Poseidon, Hera, to Hephaestos, Lady Athena and Apollo. We hear of priests and priestesses in charge of the cults and of people called ' slaves of the gods '—no doubt dedicated persons of quite high rank, for they were able we know to lease land.

Tribute, carefully listed, comes into the Mycenaean capitals from subject townships. Proportion and addition sums on the tablets show that there was nothing haphazard about the assessment of what was due. At Cnossos 20,000 sheep appear among the annual tribute. At Pylos it was more varied. The goods so collected were no doubt redistributed by the palace either in the form of raw materials to be made up by workers, or as pay and rations. This explains the existence of the tablets ; it was necessary to keep accurate inventories of the amount of raw material on hand and the numbers on the pay-roll and ration-strength. One wonders very much who made these inventories and kept these elaborate accounts. Are we to think of yet another specialized calling, that of secretary ? Professor Webster, noticing echoes of the tablets' contents in the Homeric formulae,[1] suggests ingeniously that the scribes of the tablets were the forerunners of the poet-rhapsodes who are the source of Homer's material. But there is evidence that literacy was quite widely spread. In a private house at Mycenae thirty-seven tablets have been found written in six different hands.

From all this, then, there emerges a picture of a monarchical society with a feudal aristocracy, the wealth of the whole being based on agriculture. Below them there exists a highly organized retained manufacturing class, and the clerical staff of an elaborate bureaucracy. Outside this social nexus we find an independent merchant class living in prosperous dwellings. But Mycenaean life proper is lived in Homeric-style baronial halls in well-found cities with noble gateways, where courtyards stand and verandahs and a Great Hall ; and where there is feasting at sun-down after

[1] See page 29, and footnote.

the time of the loosing of the oxen ; where there is gold and chased cups, fine linen and fleecy wool, and ivory and honey and wine ; but where there is also efficiency and order and scrupulous accounting.

The authors of this stately way of life were no stay-at-homes. The tablets, as we have already seen, give some hints of trade connexions overseas ; archaeology can tell us more. Mycenaean pottery has been found as far west as Sicily and southern Italy. They drew supplies of copper from Cyprus, and, as dialect indicates, probably colonized the island. They exchanged goods with Egypt and appear to have established trading-settlements upon the northern coasts of Syria and the western sea-board of Asia Minor. But not only as traders were the Mycenaeans known abroad. A Hittite ruler, as his own records show (himself the ruler of the largest empire in western Asia and the rival of the Pharaohs), adopts a respectful tone when addressing some Achaean king. Clearly Mycenaean prestige is known in central Asia Minor, and the force of Greek arms felt around its edges. Some time before 1400 they raided Crete and took control of the island. We have mentioned already that tablets in the Linear B script have been found in enormous numbers in Cnossos. This must mean that at some time the Minoan empire fell before the power of her pupils from the mainland, and the administration of the island and the collection of tribute from its subject townships was conducted from Cretan Cnossos by Mycenaean Greeks. The new rulers bring with them of course the cult of their Olympian gods, and the Cnossos tablets record offerings to Lady Athena, to Ares, Apollo and Poseidon. It is not enough therefore to explain the existence of Greek tablets in Cnossos by supposing merely that the Minoan lords were employing Mycenaean clerks and secretaries to keep their records for them. Undoubtedly the new regime at the palace is Greek ; the mainland roving warriors have arrived and conquered. They add much to their mythology during their stay. Everyone knows the story of King Minos and the fearful Minotaur, half human and half bull, feeding on the blood of boys and girls in the dim recesses of the labyrinth built by Daedalus, the master-craftsman of the ancient world ; how the Greek hero Theseus, with the help of Minos' daughter Ariadne, entered the labyrinth, slew the monster and found his way out alive.

Another great oversea adventure of the Mycenaeans was the siege of Troy. Here we have only the half-light of tradition to guide us, illumined fitfully by the revelations of archaeology. So strong is the tradition, however, and so numerous the tales that sprang up around this event, that a man would need very weighty evidence indeed who sought to argue that no such war ever took place. Troy stood in a commanding position, controlling the entrance to the Hellespont. Upon a site so strategic many early cities had risen and fallen. Soon after 1300 the last of the important settlements rose on this spot upon the ruins of a predecessor which had enjoyed much contact with Mycenae before falling victim to an earthquake. This last city clearly was destroyed by violence and set on fire ; its conquerors did not settle in the land they had won, but departed leaving the inhabitants to build again, but never on so grand a scale. So much archaeology reveals, and does something to confirm tradition's story of the Trojan War. But who the Trojans were and why the Achaeans really fought against them remain obscure. We have seen that the Mycenaeans had trade interests in the Asia Minor coastline ; perhaps the interests of Troy ran counter to them. No doubt the citadel commanding the Hellespont was a tempting prize to any warrior folk on the make, who would feel the lure of the Black Sea trade-route leading to the riches of the Pontus. If this was the prize they sought, they never grasped it, for after victory the Mycenaeans never settled in the area. Nor indeed was their power in mainland Greece to last much longer. They soon must face in their homeland the menace of roving enemies from the north, whose power they will not be able to withstand. These are the Dorians.

APPENDIX

The Linear B Decipherment

At some risk of obscurity and great risk of over-simplification we must try to explain something of the technique employed by Ventris in his decipherment of the Linear B script.

His first step was to make a ' grid ', and to arrange in each horizontal line signs believed to contain the same consonant value (*ta, te, ti, to, tu*) and in each vertical column the signs with the same vowel value (*re, ne, pe, te, se*, etc.). The vital importance of this will become apparent later.

This grid had to be constructed before the actual phonetic value

te	ta	to	ti	tu
me	ma	mo	mi	mu
se	sa	so	si	su

FIG. 1.—A grid.

FIG. 2.—Examples of consonant equations.

The symbols underlined in each group are the ones to be placed in the same consonant line.

of any of the symbols had been discovered. How then could it possibly be known which different signs shared the same consonant or vowel value ?

There were a number of words on the tablets which were identical except for the final sign (Fig. 2). These it was seen were likely to be different inflexions of the same word (as in Latin DO-MI-NUS, DO-MI-NI). If that was so, the last sign of each word would contain

20

the same consonant but a different vowel. So they were put in the same horizontal line in the grid.

Now for the vertical vowel columns. Look at the two pairs in Fig. 3. In the second or inflected form of both words the same signs occur at the end. (Compare this with the Latin DO-MI-NUS, DO-MI-NO-RUM. CA-PTI-VUS, CA-PTI-VO-RUM.) The words, it was realized, must belong to the same declension, so the second-last signs of the inflected words share the same vowel. These could be put in the same vowel column in the grid.

By these and similar methods a fairly complete grid was built up after long months of patient examination and brilliant deduction. Not till this was done could the next step be attempted—the experimental substitution of phonetic values.

An American scholar, Alice Kober, had discovered in the Cretan tablets a series of words which appeared in different contexts in three different but closely related forms. Ventris guessed that

FIG. 3.—An example of a vowel equation

The symbols underlined are the ones to be placed in the same vowel column.

these were the names of chief Cretan cities and the masculine and feminine adjectives derived from them. The first sign of the first 'triplet' had already been guessed as A (its enormous frequency as an initial sign and rarity elsewhere in a word suggested that it was a plain vowel without preceding consonant, and as the commonest of such initial vowels it was most likely to be A). The obvious Cretan town to begin with A was Amnisos, the port of Cnossos. By guessing A-MI-NI-SO for the first word Ventris got possible values for the vowel columns A I O in the grid, and by reading off from the grid he was able to fill in the vowels (though not the consonants) for the remaining Cretan place-names. These now appeared as L*-*i-*o, *a-*i-o*, **-li-*o, *o-*o-*o.[1] Ventris at once saw them as Lu-ki-to, Pa-i-to, Tu-li-so, Ko-no-so; or Lyktos, Phaistos, Tylissos and Knossos, four of the most important Cretan towns.

---

[1] The 'l' value had already been guessed for reasons too complicated to be explained here.

2

With experimental values now for six consonant lines and all five vowel columns on the grid (thirty signs), Ventris started to apply them to the pattern of declensions which had already been analysed. He was surprised and delighted to find that these fell into line with the known *Greek* system of declension and specifically with its most archaic forms. (It must not be forgotten that Ventris had not known that the language was Greek, and indeed had not thought it likely that it would be.)

At this stage he called in Chadwick, an expert on Greek dialects, who had been working independently on Linear B for six years. Together, with the assumption now that the language was Greek, they soon found values for the majority of the eighty-eight signs used. Some of the guesses were wrong, but the grid ensured that a mistaken value could not be maintained for long, since each one involved a whole row of syllables with the same consonants and a whole column with the same vowel.

In July 1952 their results were published and enthusiastically received. But previous decipherers had managed to construct imposing systems out of the tablets they knew, which broke down when presented with new material. Ventris and Chadwick had the grid to control their deductions, so it was hardly likely that their reasoning could turn out to have been circular; but they were not entirely happy until they could get ' a decisive check with virgin material '. Then early one morning Chadwick was woken by the telephone. It was Ventris to say that at last the confirmation had come. A tablet had been found at Pylos *after the publication of their solution* which contained the following passage:

di - pa me-wi-jo qe-to-ro-we   I di pa me-wi-jo,

δεπας μειον τετρωες   I, δεπας μειον

cup small(er) with four ears   I, cup small(er)

ti - ri - jo-we   I, di-pa me-wi-jo a - no-we I

τριωες   I, δεπας μειον ανωες I

with three ears   I, cup small(er) without ears, I

FIG. 4

Each group of words when given Ventris' values was a perfectly intelligible Greek description of the pictograph which followed it. Here was confirmation indeed.

CHAPTER III

THE DORIANS

MYCENAEAN civilization had flourished for a long time. Schliemann's excavations revealed its wealth and artistic refinement at the beginning of the sixteenth century. The tablets show us its prosperity at the end of the thirteenth. During these four hundred years no violent hand seems to have been laid on any mainland centre. The palace at Pylos was without fortifications; at Mycenae there were, it is true, massive walls round the citadel, but we find richly furnished houses placed confidently outside them. Warlike activity there was in plenty, but it appears to have been entirely aggressive.

In about 1200 this immunity of the homeland comes to an end. Pylos was sacked and the site never again inhabited. At roughly the same time the houses outside the citadel at Mycenae were burned, and in one—' the House of the Oil Merchant '—we can tell that the storage jars of oil were deliberately broached to add fuel to the flames.

Where did the enemy come from ? We saw how when the Greeks first entered Greece one group passed into Epirus and remained there in rude isolation. While the Achaeans were coming under the influence of Crete and building the splendid fabric of Mycenaean civilization, the Dorians in Epirus remained as primitive and uncultured as they had been when they dwelt in the northern plains. Now pressure of population at home, or the lure of plunder, was bringing them out from Epirus in a series of raids on the fringes of the Mycenaean world.

Of the steps taken to meet this threat we get a glimpse from two tablets found at Pylos. The first is a document on the disposition of a coastguard and gives the names of the commander and his subordinate officers, the area to be guarded, and the numbers of men at their disposal. The second tablet records the dispatch of thirty rowers to Pleuron in Aetolia, at the mouth of the Corinthian Gulf. The two kingdoms are working together in the face of their common danger. But all their preparations were in vain. Pylos was captured, and suffered the fate she had herself dealt out to Cythera, Lemnos, Miletus, Cnidus and the other cities from whom she had taken her slaves.

Pylos was probably not the first to feel the Dorians' hand, though the first on the mainland. The great palace at Cnossos had been destroyed some years before. This destruction is generally placed in about 1400, but recently archaeologists have come to wonder whether this date is too early, and in this they are supported by the Linear B tablets. There is virtually no difference in either letter-formation or grammar between the tablets written in Cnossos before its destruction and in Pylos about the year 1200. Surely no language and writing could be so stable over a period of 200 years ? If the sack of Cnossos is brought down to 1300 or later it can perhaps be seen as an early raid by Dorians, and some confirmation of this view is to be found in the *Odyssey*. For Homer, who mentions Dorians nowhere else, says they are to be found among the peoples of Crete. There are traditions, too, of an early appearance of Dorians in Rhodes and in Halicarnassus.

First then, we may suppose, the attacks fell on the outer edges of the Mycenaean orbit. In 1200 a bolder and stronger thrust destroys the great mainland kingdom of Pylos, and an attack is made on Mycenae itself, which is only repulsed after the destruction of the town outside the citadel walls. Finally in about 1100 the great citadel itself, the heart of the whole system, is captured and destroyed by fire.

The Mycenaean age is now over. Of the period which succeeded it we know tantalizingly little. There seems to have been no immediate appearance of a different Dorian culture, no sudden break in artistic continuity. The transition in pottery from late Mycenaean to Geometric (see Plate V) is a gradual one, a steady decline in craftsmanship and inspiration. So we must not picture the Dorians as swarming over Greece in one mighty wave, sweeping away all that previously existed and substituting a complete new culture of their own. The process was a more gradual one. First the violent overthrow of the Mycenaean state, leading to the sort of confusion and chaos that might be expected to follow the sudden breakdown of a bureaucratic system (this would naturally be accompanied by a general degeneracy of the arts) ; then, when there was no longer any organized resistance to stop them, a gradual migration or infiltration of Dorians into the more accessible and desirable parts of Greece. Like the advance of the Anglo-Saxons across Britain after the removal of the Roman power, it would be a process of slow penetration. Tribes would filter down, resting for a while in some congenial plain, then moving on in answer to pressure from behind, or to the lure, perhaps, of still fairer lands ahead. Artistically these rude cousins of the Achaeans seem to have brought nothing of their own, and so we find much the same traditions as before continuing, in a degenerate form, in the areas they occupied. But the splendour has gone and the riches and the gracious living. Communications are broken down, trade ceases, the art of writing is lost. And Greece settles down into a Dark Age of 300 years, dark both because its history is wrapt in obscurity and because no light of art or culture seems to have shone upon it.

Dark and obscure though this period is, something must be said of the situation and events that followed the arrival of the Dorians. From our knowledge of which areas of Classical Greece spoke the Dorian dialect and which did not, we are able to deduce the pattern of the Dorian settlement. From the different dialects of the areas where Dorian was not spoken we can gather something of the movements of the people they displaced.

Of the Peloponnese all was Dorianized except Arcadia and Messenia. (We shall see later how the Pre-Dorian people of Messenia were subjugated by the Dorian Spartans just before 700 B.C.) Arcadia always escaped the main currents of Greek history, and here in classical times we shall find lingering on a Pre-Dorian dialect. The classical Arcadians

are in fact speaking a language directly descended from
Mycenaean,[1] and in their mountain fastnesses were least
affected of anyone by the Dorian arrival.

In the area north of the Corinthian Gulf, most of the north
and west (Epirus, Acarnania, Aetolia) was Dorianized before
the sea-raids began.　It is after all the area from which the

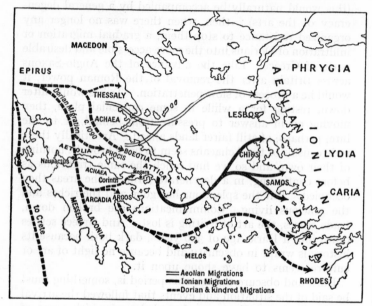

MAP TO ILLUSTRATE MIGRATIONS

invaders were starting.　In classical times this area, together with Locris and Phocis, still spoke a dialect which
was more or less Dorian.　Thessaly and Boeotia spoke a
mixture.　Attica and Euboea alone remained un-Dorianized,
and it was always the Athenian tradition and boast that they
were ' autochthonous ', their blood unmixed with the strain
of the invader.　This Athenian consciousness of being apart

[1] This dialect, found also in classical Cyprus (an area colonized
presumably by the Mycenaeans, and, like Arcadia, never touched
by the Dorians), is known as Arcado-Cypriot.

and distinct from a predominantly Dorian Greece was to play its part in later history as we shall see.

Though the greater part of the mainland of Greece was now in Dorian hands, this was not the limit of their movement. From the Peloponnese a stream of Dorian settlers flowed to the islands of the south Aegean, in the wake, no doubt, of earlier exploratory bands who had already touched on these parts. So it is that Cythera, Melos, Thera, Carpathos and Rhodes form an arc of Dorian territory straddling the sea-gap between the tip of southern Greece and the south-west corner of Asia Minor, where Cnidos and Halicarnassus are also Dorian areas.

The Dorians were not the only ones to move overseas. The pressure upon the limited resources of Greek soil caused by their arrival led to the emigration from Greece of many of its Pre-Dorian inhabitants. Two main streams of refugee emigrants can be discerned. From Thessaly and Boeotia Pre-Dorian Greeks emigrated to the northern shores of Asia Minor and formed that group of Asiatic Greeks known as the Aeolians. To the south of this settlement came emigrants from Attica and Euboea, forming the Ionian section of Asiatic Greeks. Into this refugee stream flowed Mycenaean Greeks displaced from the Peloponnese by the Dorians. These evacuated Greece via Attica, an area unmolested by the Dorians and probably an important centre of civilization during this period of disturbance in Greece.

These emigrations must not be thought of as a single mass trek to a new and unknown land. The process was no doubt a gradual one spread over two or three centuries ; the destination chosen had been known to the Mycenaeans since the thirteenth century, and they already had a foothold there. We need not trouble greatly about the distinction between Ionians and Aeolians, for the two groups merge into each other, and the general name ' Ionian ' comes to cover both groups and their settlements in all the Aegean islands except those in the south occupied by the Dorians.

In some such way as this the torch of Mycenaean enlightenment is carried, flickering but safe, out of the Dorian darkness to burn brilliantly again on the shores of Asia

Minor. So it was here, rather than upon the soil of Greece itself, that the future cultural pre-eminence which we associate so especially with the Greeks was to arise. And it was among the Ionians that the memories of their ancestors' deeds in the great days of Mycenae were enshrined in the immortal verse of the *Iliad* and *Odyssey*.

The date of the composition of these poems is now generally thought to have been about the middle of the eighth century. No predecessors of Homer survive, but it cannot be thought that Greek epic poetry sprang fully grown from a single poet's genius, like Athena from the head of Zeus. There must have been epic lays composed for many generations before Homer of which we have no record. Indeed some scholars, noticing variations in language between different passages in the poems and a number of inconsistencies in the customs they describe,[1] went so far as to declare that no such poet as Homer existed and that the epics as we have them are a patchwork of such early lays roughly sewn together by an undistinguished compiler. The more reasonable view is that Homer, like bards of other ages, had a copious poetic tradition on which to draw, a stock-in-trade of epithets, descriptive phrases, whole lines and even groups of lines describing common actions, which had been handed down from generation to generation of poets and added to by each generation. All these he used freely as they stood, not caring to impose any uniformity

[1] *e.g.* in some passages the digamma appears while it is absent in others. Sometimes the heroes are buried, sometimes cremated, and so on.

PLATE V

(*a*) A somewhat crude example of geometric vase. Note the ill-drawn human forms and the various patterns designed on the same strictly geometric lines. The decadence of such workmanship is strikingly illustrated by the contrast to (*b*), a piece of Minoan ware of obvious beauty and depicting a cuttle-fish. Cf. later vases, Plates VII and XIII.

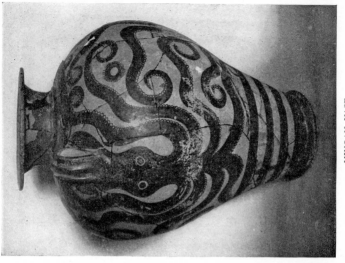

MINOAN VASE

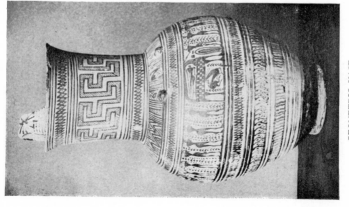

GEOMETRIC VASE

of dialect or consistency in the culture represented. We do not know for certain when this poetic tradition began. But the accuracy with which certain features of Mycenaean civilization, which do not survive its overthrow at the hands of the Dorians, are preserved in the poems suggests that it must go right back to the time of the Trojan War. One such feature is the use of the title Basileus to denote not a king but a princeling, which occurs quite often in the poems. In Homer's own day Basileus only meant king, and so it is frequently used in other passages. But in the Linear B tablets it always means a princeling, dependent on the great lord or Anax, a position which is only known in Greece in Mycenaean times. We can only presume, then, that when Homer uses the word in this sense he is making use of a formula which has its origin in Mycenaean times. So it is with the ' Man-enveloping ' shields, the bronze Chitons and all the other things which we know from archaeology to have been common in the days of Mycenae and unknown afterwards. They appear in Homer because they have survived in phrases which were first composed by bards who were themselves familiar with them.[1] But they appear alongside features unknown to the Mycenaeans, such as the use of iron for weapons and the practice of cremation, which Homer drew from later ages and from his own time.

We need not suppose that this poetic tradition was handed down in writing. It seems fairly certain that after the Dorian Invasion the Linear B syllabary died out and Greece became illiterate again until the appearance of the

[1] There are in fact remarkable similarities with Homer in the writings which actually survive from the Mycenaean epoch. The headings of two Linear B tablets are in hexameter rhythm, giving us the last three and the last three and a half feet respectively of the Homeric line. And Prof. Webster has drawn attention to the ' Inventory style ' of some of Homer's descriptions. Compare ' An axe, big, fitted to the hands, bronze, sharpened on both sides ' with a modern Army form ' Soap, scrubbing, plain white, troops for the use of.' This strengthens the view that the poetic tradition was already beginning in the days of Linear B.

new alphabet in about 800.[1] The phrases would be preserved in the memories of the bards and taught to their sons
or successors. But the *Iliad* and *Odyssey* themselves would
have been far too long to have been handed down in this
way (each is over 12,000 lines), and we must presume that
they were written down in the new alphabet, or dictated
to a scribe if the bard was really blind, as tradition tells us.

We have then a poet in the eighth century, composing in
Ionia, mainly in his own Ionic dialect, but making use of
formulae which originated in different dialects ; freely incor-
porating background colour from his own day, but at the
same time faithfully preserving certain features of Mycenaean life. Historically, then, and linguistically, the poems
are a hotch-potch, but artistically each is a unity and a
masterpiece such as has never been surpassed in any
language.

But the *Iliad* and the *Odyssey* were more to the Greeks
than just their oldest and finest poems. They occupied a
similar place in their education and in the background of all
their thought to that which the Bible occupies in our own.
Athenian schoolboys learnt great quantities by heart. We
are told that Alexander the Great slept with a copy of the
Iliad under his pillow and tried to model himself on Achilles.
Poets and artists alike turned to Homer for their subjects
and their inspiration. And, as he wrote of a time when
Greece was united against a foreign enemy, he helped to
promote a common Greek consciousness and so to soften the

---

[1] The Greek alphabet (and so our own which is derived from it)
is owed originally to the Phoenicians, who from their bases on the
Syrian seaboard spread their influence widely over the Mediterranean
area after Egyptian power declined in 1200 B.C. Discarding the
clumsy system of syllabic signs, which had been current in various
forms in the Mediterranean world for many centuries, they adopted
a much handier method of writing in an alphabetic script. This
script received its name from the first two Phoenician letters Aleph
and Beth (which can be seen in the Hebraic headings to the first
two sections of Psalm 119 in the Biblical version), or in their Greek
form Alpha Beta. We do not know exactly when the new writing
reached Greece, but the first examples of Greek written in that
adaptation of the Phoenician letters which we call the Greek alphabet
belong to about 750.

fierce rivalries and hatreds which had grown up between the small city-states.

For when the light of History shines once more upon Greece after the Dark Age, in place of a few feudal kingdoms, united perhaps in some form of allegiance to Mycenae, we find a multitude of small units, each so jealously proud of its independent existence, so prone to bitter feuds with its neighbours, that for a thousand years after the coming of the Dorians Greece remained a disunited and distressful country and the cockpit of interminable wars. The city-state was at once the pride and also the curse of Greece ; and concerning the lines on which such states were first formed and governed something must now be said.

Of the political and social conditions in Greece immediately after the overthrow of the highly-organized governments of the Mycenaean Age it must be confessed that we know nothing whatever. We can only draw on our imagination to picture perhaps a number of small settlements struggling in isolation to maintain their standard of living, until a wandering group of Dorians came and drove them from the best lands in the plain. We have seen that the Dorians brought nothing artistically ; it seems probable that they also brought nothing worthy of the name of political organization, and the history of political development in Greece must start again right from the beginning, as if the highly-developed Mycenaean systems had never existed. Groups of Dorian families would settle in small communities, in numbers perhaps equal to a large-sized village, with a simple patriarchal organization and in complete independence of their neighbours. In this primitive condition certain parts of Greece continued until much later times. At the zenith of Athens' greatness, for example, the Aetolian mountaineers of north-west Greece still lived in such scattered villages. But the influence of geography is strong. The narrow plains of which we spoke above, hill-girt, compact, in natural isolation from the outer world, formed ideal units for political association, and in time the communities in such plains were almost bound to coalesce. Hostile raids, too, would drive them to take concerted action for defence ; and in nearly every plain, as it so happened, there stood some natural outcrop of the rock to form a convenient citadel. Thus Athens had her ' Acropolis ', Argos her ' Larissa ' ; and hard by the isthmus there was the ' Acro-Corinth ', more a mountain than a hill. Such rocks would even from the earliest times form a ' city of refuge ' for the plain's inhabitants ; but before long this centralization for purposes of war led to centralization also for purposes of peace. The petty tribes composed their differences ; and the citadel, in effect, became the Capital. So the dwellers in the Argive plain were centralized round Argos, the Lacedaemonians round Sparta, the people of Attica round Athens ; and similar movements took place in nearly every plain in Greece. The centralization was primarily political and did not necessarily imply change of residence. Even in the fifth century we find a large proportion of the Athenian people still living at a distance in their scattered villages. But its importance was soon felt. Concentration makes for efficiency ; it means a wider outlook on administrative problems, less toleration of muddlers, and a readiness to break loose from the hide-bound custom of a narrow local life. The first to suffer from its searching influence was, of course, the king himself ; for it is clear that one person could no longer adequately fill the triple role of general judge and priest. At Sparta he lost much of his political authority, but retained his rank of generalissimo. At Athens the reverse occurred. A ' Polemarch ' or ' Warlord ' was created to command the host ; and the king remained a civil governor. Nor did even this degradation content the jealous nobles. The office from being an hereditary right was made elective ; and in 683 its tenure was limited to one year. What occurred at Athens occurred also sooner or later in the other states of Greece, the monarchy surviving in Sparta and Argos only and the half-barbarous Macedon. And as the power of the kings diminished and disappeared, so the power of the nobles grew. Aristocracy, in short, became the order of the day. Some states clung to it almost throughout their history. Even in those which arrived at a complete democracy, the partisans of the old order never quite abandoned hope ; and the perpetual clash between the ' Few ' and the ' Many ' remained the outstanding issue of Greek political life.

Such then was the political organization of the city-states of Greece when they begin to emerge from the Dark Age. In most of them a Dorian aristocracy was firmly in power, the citizen body of Dorian commoners possessing on the whole few rights, and the Pre-Dorian population possessing for the most part none at all. Among such states the one whose history is best known to us is Sparta ; and partly for that reason, partly because she was soon to play a leading role in Peloponnesian politics, our task must presently be to study more closely the details of her development.

CHAPTER IV

COLONIES, TRADE AND TYRANNY

I. COLONIZATION

THE fury of the Dorian Conquest is said to have reached its height about the year 1050. During the ensuing epoch, as we have already seen, the invaders settled down ; political combination within certain limited areas produced a more or less clear-cut arrangement of independent states ; and by the Eighth or Seventh Century the Map of Greece had assumed in general outline the recognized divisions of historic times. But the process of expansion was not as yet complete ; and during these two centuries fresh settlements were made on the surrounding coasts. The age of haphazard wandering was over ; but the age of colonization was now to come.

The motive which underlay this vigorous outburst of overseas adventure was half economic and half social. The soil of Greece, as we have remarked above, is very limited in extent ; and for the growing population of those narrow plains to produce the necessities of life was not by any means an easy task. In Asia Minor equally the fertile hinterland was barred against the expansion of the coastal Greeks by the powerful realm of Lydia. It was therefore not unnatural that the more adventurous spirits on both sides of the Aegean should have gone forth to seek a livelihood and home in other lands.[1] But there was another force at work besides the hungry stomach. Among Greeks, as it so happened, it was not the custom for a father's property to pass solely to his first-born. The land was divided up amongst all his sons, and the consequence is

[1] The Arcadian peoples cut off from the sea in the central fastnesses of the Peloponnese seem to have found an alternative in later times at any rate in seeking military service as mercenaries.

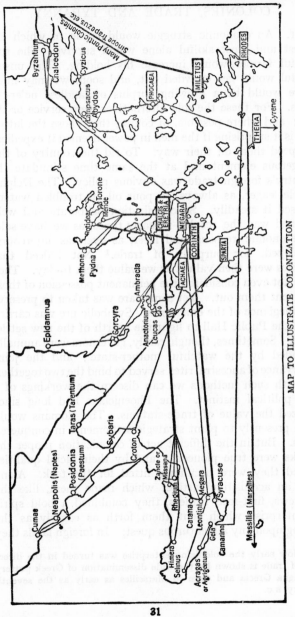

MAP TO ILLUSTRATE COLONIZATION

N.B.—When a line passes *through* one colony to another, it indicates that the first founds the second, e.g. Corcyra founds Epidamnus.

clear. An economic struggle would ensue in which the fittest and most skilful alone would survive. The successful farmer would increase his holding. The unsuccessful would get crowded out, and soon, we may infer, there would be a growing surplus of landless ne'er-do-wells. For these the sole alternatives were service or the sea ; and where possible, of course, they chose the latter. Nor is it surprising if the men in power deemed it expedient to speed them on their way. To rid the country of this dangerous element and at the same time stimulate the country's foreign trade was obvious policy. The Delphic Oracle, eager, as always, to pour oil on troubled waters, advised it steadily. So colonization deliberate and well-planned was the result—in early times, as we have said, for economic reasons, and later, as overseas intercourse developed, for purposes of trade.[1] Not indeed that colonies were then valued as we value them to-day. They were not even considered the permanent possession of those who sent them out. Yet some care was taken to preserve the allegiance of the emigrants. Symbolic fire was carried from the Public Hall to light the hearth of the new settlement. Sometimes, though rarely, governors were annually provided by the watchful mother-state ; and the joint observance of ancestral rites served to bind the two together. Beneath such methods we can discern the workings of a rare political instinct. The Phoenicians had long since realized the value of trade-stations. The Romans would learn presently to plant strategic settlements in conquered lands. But in the difficult act of colonization proper the Greeks were true pioneers ; and by their racial qualities indeed they were peculiarly fitted for the task. Along with an acquisitive instinct which made them, like the Hebrews, first-rate traders, they combined a bold spirit of enterprise which sent them forth as eagerly as the Viking upon any adventurous quest. In foreign lands they

[1] How early the colonizing enterprise was turned in the direction of trade is shown by the wide dissemination of Greek pottery in Magna Grecia and even in Marseilles as early as the seventh century B.C.

adapted themselves easily to an unfamiliar environment ;
but their natural strength of character and the compact
formation of their traditional City-states saved them from
absorption by surrounding peoples ; and though in early
days, at any rate, they seem to have intermarried with
the natives, their individuality was seldom merged.   Once
a Greek always a Greek ; and whether on the inhospitable
shores of Thrace or in the rich corn-lands of Sicily, the
same instinct for a well-ordered city-life, for intellectual
curiosity and artistic culture remained with them to mark
them as the true sons of Hellas.

The Aegean basin was an ideal cradle for a seafaring
race.   Its numerous creeks afforded excellent harbours.
Its scattered archipelagos supplied convenient halts.   Its
winds in summer, if not in winter, were calculable and set.
So, though the Greeks were at all times cautious sailors,
ill at ease if carried out of sight of land and, whenever
possible, spending the night ashore, yet they took to the
water with a natural zest.   Foremost among the early
navigators of the Aegean we must place the Ionians of the
Asiatic coast.   The wealth of the Lydian hinterland found
an outlet through their harbours ; and in particular the
wool from upland sheep farms formed a special stock-in-
trade with the merchants of Miletus.   This city took a
leading part in the planting-out of colonies ; and the Black
Sea region, which offered special facilities for flax and
corn and metals, was her chosen sphere.[1]   Byzantium
at its entrance was subsequently founded by Athens'
little neighbour Megara (660).   But the Milesians planted
Cyzicus on the south of the Propontis, and Abydos in the
Narrows, securing access to outposts at Sinopê and other
places in the Black Sea itself.   Meanwhile over in Greece
an equal vigour was displayed by the two townships
of Euboea, Eretria and Chalcis.   Aptly placed to serve the
mainland shore with cross-Aegean traffic, they drove a
prosperous trade.   But the story of their long-drawn struggle
for the Lelantine Plain which lay between them, proves

[1] Corn was grown to the north of the Danube basin, timber, flax
and metals were produced from the southern shore.

at least that neither had sufficient home-land to supply its needs ; and this may well account for their colonizing vigour. As other mercantile states such as Corinth, Megara and Miletus were perhaps drawn into the war, it seems likely that the conflict extended into a competition for colonial sites and other commercial advantages. What at least is certain, is that both Chalcis and Eretria sent forth settlers, like Miletus, to establish many off-shoots. One area which they planted was the North Aegean group of three peninsulas, henceforth named Chalcidice after the chief parent state. Nor was this the only or the most important fruit of the Euboeans' enterprise. First among Greek peoples they turned their attention to the more distant West. In early times they settled men at Cumae in the neighbourhood of Naples, and so entered on trade relations with Etruria beyond. To Sicily also they sent numerous parties, and there the north-eastern shores were dotted with their colonies —Messana, Naxos, Catana and others. The native inhabitants of Sicily were, like those of Southern Italy, a backward race ; and a golden opportunity was waiting there for emigrants from Greece. After the Euboeans the city that made most use of it was Corinth. A unique position on a central Isthmus enabled her traders to look both east and west. So we find that she too planted a town, called Potidaea (609), on the south-west prong of the Chalcidic trident ; but her chief effort was made in the west. The island of Corcyra, a handy port of call, she colonized betimes (735). From thence the trade-route passed to the heel of Italy and so to Sicily beyond (for few Greek mariners would risk a wider passage), and on the east Sicilian coast Corinth could claim a town one day destined to be the greatest in the island—Syracuse (735). The Corinthians, in fact, soon supplanted the Euboeans in the trade of Magna Grecia [1] ; and these westerly activities made them in later

---

[1] Magna Grecia is the name given by the Romans to the Greek settlements in Italy and Sicily. It was probably the early Italian colonists that first gave the name of Graei or Greeks to the inhabitants of the home-land who amongst themselves were never known by any other name than Hellenes.

days the foremost rivals of Athenian sea-power. A still bolder spirit of adventure carried Ionian traders of Phocaea even further west to settle at Massilia (or Marseilles) in Southern Gaul (600), and, beyond that, past the Pillars of Hercules, to trade with Tartessus in Spain, and, some say, even to the tin mines of our own British Isles. It was only the growth of Carthaginian power in the Fifth Century which prevented a later and more extensive exploitation of this Atlantic trade.

Space fails to tell of the other colonies which during the Eighth and Seventh Centuries were planted out by Greeks. The map will show how South Sicily was further peopled by emigrants from Rhodes, how adventurers from Thera reached North Africa and founded Cyrene on that distant coast, and how Sparta, though mainly occupied with the subjugation of Messenia, found energy to colonize Tarentum (705). Enough, however, has been said to show that by these efforts whole countries were drawn into the orbit of the Greek world. Though the original inhabitants did not, of course, disappear, it was a real repopulation : for from the nature of its inception it would seem that such enterprise was not, in the first instance, aimed mainly at trade. These men went out, like our own New England settlers, to find fresh homes to dwell in and fresh lands to till ; but, as with the New Englanders, their subsequent importance was undoubtedly commercial. The areas of expansion correspond, as we have said, with the trade routes most in vogue. Pontus in the north, and Magna Grecia in the west, were the fertile sources from which the Greeks' supplies were drawn. There was a third, however, which must not escape our notice. Levantine trade was mainly in Phoenician hands ; but Cyprus even in very early times had been inhabited by Greeks, and Cyprus was a half-way house to Egypt. Now most of the Pharaohs, it is true, were no friends to alien settlers ; but about the middle of the Seventh Century a new attitude prevailed. Psammetichus, the founder of the Delta dynasty, had won his throne by the aid of hired Greek troops, and the friendly monarch expressed his gratitude by opening his kingdom to their fellow-countrymen. On one of the Nile mouths Ionians from Miletus procured themselves a mart (640), and when in the Sixth Century Greek traders were excluded from other parts of Egypt, their port at Naucratis assumed a special importance as a centre of commercial intercourse. Even here, however, the Greeks, as was their habit, remained true to type. They kept their customs, built shrines to their own gods and refused to be absorbed. Indeed, nothing is more striking in the whole history of this colonizing movement than their persistent loyalty to Greek ideals. Connexion between colony and mother-country did not rest on any strong material ties. The settlers for the most part were self-governing. They resented interference. They acknowledged no obligation to lend military aid. But deep down in their hearts there was a sentiment immensely strong which forbade them ever to forget their home. The further they spread, the more conscious the Greeks became that they were a peculiar —we might almost say a chosen—people. All foreigners alike were to them 'barbarians'—men, that is, of an unintelligible tongue ; and a closer acquaintance with barbarian ways made them feel the priceless value of their heritage. They lacked, indeed, the stiff, exclusive temper which marked the Hebrew people ; but they had all the Hebrew's pride.

II. Economic Effects

It is not to be supposed that such colonial enterprise, involving as it did new maritime activities and a wider contact with the outside world, would leave quite unaffected the parent states of Greece. Throughout the range of history trade has always proved a vigorous solvent, breaking down the walls of obsolete tradition and opening the channels to rapid social change. And trade was now becoming, for better or for worse, no unimportant factor in Hellenic life. To the land-owning nobility, or to commercially minded members of their class, this meant, if they cared to use it, a new opportunity of wealth, and what is more important, of wealth in a new form.

For money had now come in ; and the old-fashioned method of exchange by barter had given way [1] to the use of metal discs, the quality and weight of which was officially guaranteed. The invention, it seems, was Lydian ; but the system of an authorized state-coinage spread through Ionia to the Aegean, where two standard currencies came quickly into vogue, one issued by the cities of Euboea above-mentioned, one by the prosperous little island of Aegina [2] (c. 680). The effect of this important innovation was to widen the interval between poverty and wealth. For money is easier to accumulate than goods ; and, so long as business was transacted by exchange in kind, it was not easy to amass an undue fortune. But once coinage was recognized as the medium of exchange, then hoarding became possible ; and not merely could the rich man multiply his riches, but the power he wielded through them was increased many-fold. There would come a bad harvest when the poor must borrow. The rich man, whose instinct was to hoard rather than lend his money, would part with it only on the best security, and, since the only security the poor peasant could offer was a lien on his home and his person, the rich creditor would thereafter hold the poor debtor at his mercy. Entangled in a mesh of debt, the wretched man would part first with his land, then with his household goods, and finally would barter away his freedom and become the rich man's slave. ' Unto him that hath shall be given ; ' and, as the wealth of the great landlords grew, so grew in like proportion the temptation to misuse it. For some while already, indeed, the ' Few ' had been exalted at the expense of the ' Many '. From Hesiod, the rustic poet of Boeotia, writing in the Eighth Century B.C. his poem ' Works and Days ', we have a doleful picture of oppression and distress. The character of the nobles has been changing. They are no longer, as in Homer's day, the ' shepherds of the folk '. They are ' the princes that swallow bribes.' Wealth rather than birth has now become the basis of their political supremacy ; and avarice has supplanted the neighbourly habits of the

[1] After intermediate stage of ingots valued by weight. [2] See p. 57.

past. This process of transition from the Aristocratic State to what we should call to-day the Plutocratic, was naturally hastened by the advent of a coin currency. Capitalists arose, if we may use a modern term, to organize production for the export trade ; and to meet the new demand for cheap industrial labour, a regular slave traffic was begun from overseas. The competition of slave labour placed the poor freeman in an even worse position than before ; and the lower he sank in the economic scale, the more was he at the mercy of the rapacious landlord class. Abuse of their political power was a natural concomitant of their economic predominance, and they tightened their hold. The cry of the oppressed went up ; but, when the oppressor was also the judge, no justice could be won ; and the very gods, as the Boeotian bard lamented, seemed to have vanished from the earth.

III. Tyrannies

For such an evil condition of affairs—one widely prevalent in Seventh-Century Greece—there were, in fact, a variety of cures. In agricultural states—Boeotia, for example—we find but little progress during the centuries which followed ; but the ruling class presumably avoided revolution by learning wiser ways. At Athens, on the other hand, as will presently be seen, the reforms of a great statesman healed the breach by hastening the passage to democracy. There was, however, one interesting development which in many states, and amongst them Athens herself, did much to break down the power of the aristocracies, and so pave the way for a more popular form of government, and this was the rise of the so-called Tyrants. This was not, it would seem, exclusively due to the Agrarian unrest, although that, as at Athens, was frequently the root cause. The country folk themselves were too helpless in the grip of their masters to raise any effective opposition. But with the steady increase of industry and commerce there had sprung up in the more progressive towns a growing class of merchants and skilled workers

who were less subservient to the aristocratic landlords
than the downtrodden peasantry. The quicker wits and
more independent status of this new urban middle class
inevitably inclined them to resent the existing oppression
and to welcome a remedy. And the remedy came with the
emergence of a leader. For the need called forth the man
—an individual more personally ambitious or more patriotic-
ally audacious than the rest, sometimes a member of the
aristocracy itself, sometimes an upstart from the proletariat
(in one instance the son of a butcher or a cook), but in
very many cases, so far as we can judge, a man who,
once in power, saw the advantages which might accrue
to himself, his partisans and his city from industrial or
commercial enterprise. In his attempt to overthrow the
existing order he proceeded, as he was bound to do, by
force. His coup, if successful, would be short and sharp.
With a body of retainers he would seize the citadel. The
discontented populace, and more especially the urban
workers, would rise at his appeal. The existing government would be arbitrarily cancelled, and he himself would
take sole charge of state affairs. Such a man, having won
his power by violence and retaining it without sanction of
legality, was called by the Greeks ' Turannos '—a word
borrowed, significantly enough, from monarchical Lydia.
The name fell later into evil odour ; for to Greek ideals of
law and liberty such unconstitutional procedure was fundamentally abhorrent. But, in our sense at least, the Tyrant
was not usually ' tyrannical '. Sometimes, indeed, his
character was brutalized by power ; and all know how
Phalaris of Sicilian Acragas was wont to roast his victims
in a brazen bull. But more normally, owing his elevation
as he did to the common people's favour, the tyrant
proved himself the people's friend. The nobles whom
he ousted from power, he did not of course spare ; and
indeed it was obviously dangerous to leave them long
at large. Banishment was a remedy more politic than
death, and a remedy more frequently employed. But a
significant tale is told of the Milesian Thrasybulus, who,
when asked for his advice by a nervous fellow-tyrant,

conducted the messenger into a neighbouring wheat-field, and, switching off the more prominent corn-stalks, bade him carry back that hint to the inquirer. Some safeguard, too, against possible rebellion was secured by such mutual understanding between monarchs. It was, in fact, a favourite policy with tyrants to form alliances with other monarchs. Polycrates of Samos had a close connexion with Amasis of Egypt, and other examples might easily be quoted. It was a common practice, moreover, to cement such external friendships by the bond of intermarriage. Thus Cleisthenes of Sicyon (c. 600–570) to take a well-known instance, invited noble applicants for his fair daughter's hand, and Herodotus tells the entertaining story of one gymnastic suitor, who thought to win the lady by the excellence of his dancing, but, unhappily for his ends, overdid the exhibition by mounting on a table, standing up upon his hands and ' gesticulating ' with his legs in air. High, irresponsible spirits and sumptuous living seem, on the whole, to have been a characteristic of these upstart monarchs and their families. They retained their power partly by maintaining a royal splendour which dazzled and impressed the public eye, partly by bettering, in whatever way they could, the lot of their middle-class partisans. So long as trade throve and employment was plentiful, their popularity was reasonably assured ; but it needed, above all, a strong personality to maintain a position which in the face of the exiled nobles' hostility was at best precarious, and which in the long run proved against the grain of the best political instincts of Greece.

Though unconstitutional monarchy was not a phenomenon confined to any single epoch or district, the Seventh Century was destined, for reasons already stated, to witness a regular crop of such tyrannies, especially in the cities of Ionia and of Central Greece.

For the frequent recurrence of tyranny in Ionia there was perhaps a special reason. The close proximity first of the Lydian and then of the Persian power made a strong and centralized government essential to the safety both of mainland and even of island states ; and the result was that tyranny was here a more common and more prolonged phenomenon than in European Greece. Among Seventh Century tyrants the most notable figure was Thrasybulus of Miletus (*c.* 620) the skill of whose government and the brilliance of whose court made him an almost perfect model of the type. But even his pre-eminence was eclipsed in the next century by Polycrates of Samos (*c.* 530). He organized a strong navy, made an alliance with Amasis of Egypt, and it has even been thought that his ambition centred on the overlordship of the Aegean archipelago. In any case his prosperity was a byword in Greece ; and all know the story of the ring which, to avert Nemesis, he flung into the sea, and which Fortune, unplacated by the sacrifice, returned to him in the belly of a fish, a complimentary present from its humble captor. Nemesis indeed came ; for he was captured by the Persians in 523 and met his end by crucifixion. This is not perhaps the time to speak of the Sicilian tyrannies, which in part at least owed their origin to a similar cause—the proximity of a menacing external foe, the Carthaginians. The magnificence of these Sicilian monarchs' courts, from Gelon and Hieron in the first half of the Fifth Century to Dionysius in the Fourth, surpassed anything ever known upon the Greek mainland. There, apart from the later rule of Pisistratus at Athens, of which more will be said anon, tyranny was confined to the Seventh Century and in particular to the states around the Isthmus, Corinth, Sicyon and Megara. Here, too, it would seem there was a special cause at work ; for in these states the descendants of the Pre-Dorian population much resented the oppression of their Dorian overlords and their discontent found a champion in the tyrant leaders. Cypselus, the founder of the Corinthian dynasty, was himself of Pre-Dorian descent. He was a man of peace, a promoter of his city's early colonizing efforts along the north-western shores of Greece ; and from him his still more famous son Periander inherited not merely a very powerful realm, but also a high tradition of artistic patronage. Periander (625–585) did much to encourage the development of a local school

of poetry, and by checking the importation of slave
assured skilled craftsmen of a better standing than they
enjoyed elsewhere. He is said to have planned, though
he did not accomplish, the digging of a ship canal through
the Isthmus, and to him in all probability may be attributed the fine pillars of a temple which still stand to mark
the site of ancient Corinth. Lavish expenditure on public
works was indeed a common feature in most tyrants'
policy. The building of a temple, an aqueduct or a harbour, besides giving employment to their artisan followers,
served also to magnify the city's reputation in the eyes of the
world. The same motive may perhaps be assigned to the
tyrants' peculiar interest in the promotion or institution of
public festivals. Cleisthenes of Sicyon (c. 600–570) appears
to have concerned himself greatly in championing Apollo's
shrine at Delphi ; and not merely did he there take a
prominent part in the founding of the famous Pythian
Games, but he also instituted a similar festival in his own
native city, just as Pisistratus of Athens, as will presently
be seen, promoted the great national festival of Athena.
By such a measure the tyrant's own fame was enhanced
and a new sense of civic solidarity was simultaneously
encouraged by the celebration of a ceremony in which all
alike could share. It provided a stimulus to the pride of
nationality, and gave the citizens, hitherto unprivileged
in the main, their first important lesson in the Rights of
Man. The truth is that the tyrants, like our own Tudor
sovereigns, were paving the way towards democracy.
Like the Tudors, they had broken down the monopoly
of power held hitherto by a narrow noble caste. Like the
Tudors, too, they rested their power largely on the sympathy
and support of a commercial middle class whose activities
they encouraged and whose national pride they deliberately fostered. But, like the Tudors, finally, they were
all the while awakening in their subjects a vigorous and
sturdy spirit of political independence which would one
day break the bonds and proclaim the gospel of self-
government.

The reign of the Tyrants was for the most part brief.

Some succeeded in handing on their power to sons who usually soon lost it. At Sicyon the dynasty lasted a hundred years ; but that was an exception.   More often the power gotten by violence was violently withdrawn. So the tyrants disappeared again ; and, although among the masses the memory of their benefactions seems to have lingered for a while, yet in later days their very name became an object of universal execration.   So deep had grown the sense that above the individual stood the duty of obedience to the law ; and, just as some poison which infects the system will summon into play its effective antidote, so here the experience of an unconstitutional régime let loose the latent forces which were to make the Greeks stand out as the first great protagonists of Freedom.

CHAPTER V

SPARTA

I. POLITICAL AND SOCIAL

AS we approach the year 600, the chronicle of events becomes both more precise and more connected; but although we can trace the development of history with greater minuteness than was possible before, we are driven simultaneously to narrow down its scope [1]; and partly by reason of their completer records, partly, too, for the striking contrast which the pair present, our attention will be focused more and more on the two rival states Athens and Sparta. Each claimed to represent a different branch of the Hellenic family; for Athens was of Ionian, Sparta of Dorian blood. Each, as time went on, asserted a hegemony over different parts of Greece— Sparta south of the Isthmus, Athens among the islands and the seaboard towns of the Aegean basin. And the rivalry thus begun led in the final issue to that prolonged and

---

[1] At the same time there is no *connected* history available until the time of the Persian wars. Evidence for the Seventh and Sixth Centuries must be pieced together from (a) episodes described by Herodotus (often in much detail), and Thucydides' sketch of early events; (b) contemporary literary fragments such as Tyrtaeus' or Solon's poems; (c) contemporary inscriptions, pottery, etc.; (d) historians of a much later date, e.g. Plutarch.

PLATE VI

(a) A typical view of olive trees taken in the vale of Sparta; but similar scenes may be found in almost any plain of Greece. (b) A view of the Vale of Sparta, the broad bed and strong stream of the Eurotas in the foreground; Mount Taygetus rising behind.

OLIVES AT SPARTA

VALE AT SPARTA

bitter struggle which is known to history as the Peloponnesian War.

The vale of Lacedaemon, in which the town of Sparta lay, nestles long and low and narrow between two massive ranges of inhospitable mountain, Parnon rising eastwards in gentle gradations of receding moorland, while, opposite, Taygetus towers beetling and abrupt with winter snows long lingering on its rocky spine. The stream of the Eurotas, unlike most of the Greek rivers, runs clean and strong among its fertile orchards ; and to the early Greek invaders coming down from the bleak north the country must indeed have seemed an earthly paradise. These Dorians' conquest of the Eurotas valley had probably been gradual ; but sooner or later, as we saw above, the whole existing population had passed under their heel.

During the long period which followed the Conquest the small district of Sparta became the centre of the valley's government ; but its only citadel was an unpretentious knoll unworthy to rank with the Acropolis of Athens or the Larissa of Argos, and the town itself was never fortified after the manner of most Greek capitals. The Dorian citizens lived scattered about the plain in various villages, and even in later times when the demands of the parade-ground drew the warrior males to the capital, there was no such concentrated city life as was to be found in other states. On the outskirts of the country, and in particular around the coast, were to be found out-settlements of mixed Dorians and Pre-Dorians, who had been sent afield soon perhaps after the Conquest, and who, with lapse of time and by reason of their distance from the capital, had lost their claim to citizenship and civic rights. These, the *Perioeci* or ' *Dwellers Round About* ', lived free of interference in their scattered villages. Some drove a prosperous trade. But they were not allowed to marry with the Spartan citizens proper ; and, as a mark of their subordinate status, they paid a heavy tax. By far the most numerous element, however, of the valley's population were the descendants of the old Pre-Dorian aboriginals who had been reduced at the Conquest to utter servitude.

These, the so-called *Helots*, were mere chattels of the soil, providing their Spartan task-masters with the product of their labour and compelled, if need be, to serve in war along with the citizen-force. They were the most down-trodden people in the whole of Greece ; nevertheless, as we shall see, their existence was a constant menace to the state's security, and the fear of them hung like a mill-tone around their Spartan masters' necks.

It was not, however, in the Eurotas valley only that this serf system prevailed. In the latter half of the Eighth Century, when other states were solving their economic problems by peaceful overseas expansion, Sparta had found her remedy in the military conquest of a neighbouring people. Beyond the high range of Mount Taygetus lay a plain somewhat similar in shape and at least equal in fertility to the Vale of Lacedaemon. Its inhabitants, the Messenians, were mainly drawn from the same stock as the Spartan Helots ; and when they came (*c.* 736–16) to be attacked by the Helots' warlike masters, they too succumbed, despite their vigorous resistance, to a similar fate. Their land was divided into lots and portioned out among the conquerors ; and their labour equally was requisitioned to provide for the mess-tables at Sparta. Two generations later, however, they rebelled (*c.* 650), and a stubborn war was waged under their legendary leader Aristomenes. It needed the martial strains of the patriotic poet, lame Tyrtaeus, to arouse the waning ardour of the Spartan host before the rebel stronghold on Mount Eira was reduced, and the dominion of Messenia was recovered (*c.* 630).

But the effort had been tremendous, and the moral of that struggle was not lost upon the victors. If they were to keep under permanent control a population of discontented serfs which outnumbered the free citizens by perhaps fifteen to one, then they must be ready against all emergencies, train themselves, boy and man, to a perfection of physical fitness and to a practised skill of arms, and become, in a word, a nation of professional soldiers. Now in the Seventh Century Sparta had not as yet attained to that incomparable military efficiency which was later to make her invincible in Greece.[1] There was nothing, indeed, to distinguish her citizens as more disciplined, more austere or more warlike than other kindred peoples. On the contrary, all the evidence goes to show that they were in these early days a pleasure-loving folk, much addicted to dance and song. In music they were to be reckoned as true pioneers. In literature the genius of Tyrtaeus, their patriot poet, ranked with the best ; and Alcman, the song-writer, though of Lydian extraction, found a congenial home in their midst. Their artists are known by archaeological evidence to have produced beautiful pottery and delicate ivory carvings. There was, in fact, if later writers are to be trusted, not merely high promise of aesthetic culture, but a positive tendency towards luxury and ease. And all this, with an effort of will-power which for its stern self-abnegation must surely be unparalleled in the history of the world, the Spartans now determined to put deliberately away. With the single object of making themselves an efficient fighting force they undertook a complete transformation of their entire social system, involving a change of life so revolutionary and so utterly opposed to the whole tradition of Greek character that it made them for ever afterward a people apart, an over-specialized and strangely one-sided product of a unique educational experiment, superb upon the battlefield, tough as steel, drilled to perfection, but utterly inartistic,[2] almost unlettered, with scarcely a thought beyond the one central business of their lives—the art of war. Such was the price which the men of Sparta paid to secure in perpetuity

[1] The following account of the course and chronology of early Spartan history is based on the theories advanced by Mr. Wade-Gery in the Cambridge Ancient History. The theories are largely due to the recent discoveries of British excavators at Sparta, but are much disputed.

[2] It would, however, be a mistake to suppose that Spartan art expired immediately after the Lycurgan reforms. Some of the most beautiful products of Laconian vase-painting date from the first half of the Sixth Century. After that, however, this side of the Spartan character seems to have decayed rapidly.

their domination of the rich farms of Lacedaemon and Messenia, and of the helotry who tilled them.

The author of this revolutionary change was according to the Spartans' own account a statesman named Lycurgus. Of his personality we know nothing. Even his date was traditionally placed at an epoch too remote to carry credence. It is possible that he was nothing more than a mythical hero under whose auspices the great reform was executed. In fact, the sole clear certainty about him is the existence of the system he is reputed to have founded. That many features of that system were copied from the institutions of Dorian Crete can hardly be disputed ; but that its introduction at Sparta must have been the work of some outstanding genius, seems equally beyond question ; and, since we do not know, and probably shall never know, his actual name, Lycurgus may serve as well as another.[1]

The constitution of Sparta, though the results of his reform did much to change its bias, was not in origin Lycurgus' work. Comprising as it did a monarchy, a council of elders, and a popular assembly, its form was manifestly derived from the simple political machinery of patriarchal days. But whereas in the evolution of most Hellenic states, one or other of these three elements succeeded in establishing a clear supremacy over the other two, at Sparta all three elements were retained in combination throughout her entire history.

So cautious and conservative was the temper of her citizens, and so conscious were they that in the constant presence of the Helot menace they could not like other Greek states afford the luxury of violent faction or political revolution. The result was that such constitutional changes as occurred in Sparta's history were of a very gradual growth and came into being without ostenta-

[1] The Spartans' own tradition placed the Lycurgan reform at a very much earlier date—perhaps with the intention of lending to it the dignity and glamour of antiquity. Similarly (if critics are right) the Book of Deuteronomy, published in Josiah's reign at almost exactly the same time, was ascribed by its compilers to the authorship of Moses.

tion, preserving the outward form at least of the old
traditional government. Nominally, then, Sparta was a
monarchy. But it was a dual monarchy. This duality
was not, as in the Roman consulate, the outcome of a
deliberate political device, it probably represented an early
amalgamation between the dynasties of two separate
tribal groups ; and the two crowns passed down by hereditary succession through the royal line of the Agiad and
Eurypontid families. But two Kings can scarcely enjoy
equal power, and the representative of one line or the other
was generally recognized as predominant. Even so the
royal prerogative was strictly limited. At home and in
peace-time the Kings were largely ornamental. Their
functions were in the main confined to religious ceremonial,
in which, like the Homeric chiefs of old, they filled the office
of high-priest. But they shared in the deliberations of the
Council, and a man of strong personality was able thus to
wield a considerable influence over state policy. If this
was so, however, it was chiefly because the policy of Sparta
was more often than not a policy of war. For with the
declaration of war the King came into his own. Once the
army was set in motion, he became supreme, marching at
the head of a personal bodyguard of three hundred picked
retainers, exercising a power of life and death over the
troops, and directing the campaign (under certain limitations hereafter to be noted) with absolute authority. But,
while viewed in the light of this war-time dictatorship the
Spartan constitution may appear monarchical, the wide
and important powers of the Council gave it an almost
aristocratic complexion. This Council or Gerousia consisted of twenty-eight elders, over sixty years of age,
chosen from the best blood of the country, and holding
office for life. In their hands was vested most of the
political, judicial and legislative power. It was they who
discussed and who virtually decided all matters of state.
For, though their decisions were submitted to the popular
assembly, it became at length a mere matter of form ;
and a law seems to have existed (though of doubtful date
and origin) expressly stating that, if the assembly ' voted

4

wrongly ', the Gerousia were under no obligation to accept the vote. It is apparent, therefore, that under the constitution of Sparta the citizens at large were meant to have little voice. The Apella, as their assembly was called, could not discuss the Gerousia's proposals. It could merely vote upon them ; and its wishes, as a rule, were ascertained by the childish method of simple acclamation, so that decisions rested, unless a count were demanded, upon the respective lung-power of opposing parties. Such at least was the situation at Sparta when her politics emerge into the light of clearer history.

With the Lycurgan reform, however, had come two important changes whereby the democratic element in the constitution was not merely given a much broader basis, but enabled ultimately to acquire a determining influence over affairs of state. For in the great reorganization which was to secure the Spartan predominance over the Helot population, it was found necessary, in the first place, to augment the number of enfranchised citizens. The peril of the Messenian War and the necessity of providing against the repetition of that peril involved the recruitment of new soldiers ; and the new soldiers would not unnaturally demand rights. So the franchise was widened. The three original tribes of which the governing class was composed were expanded into five ; and the old exclusive privilege of aristocratic caste was merged in a larger circle. Such a change could hardly fail to bring an increase of popular power ; and the second innovation of the Lycurgan reform worked in the same direction. This was the appointment of five Ephors or executive officials corresponding numerically to the five newly organized tribes. The office of Ephor was indeed an old one, going back to the Eighth Century at least ; its importance, however, was apparently but small until its transformation into this body of five. They were annually elected by the vote of the Apella ; and all citizens were eligible for election without distinction of blood. The office, in fact, was essentially democratic, and thus the Ephors came, like the tribunes at Rome, to be the recognized champions of the popular cause.

Their powers were confined, in the first instance, to administration of civil, as opposed to criminal, justice, and to the presidency of the Apella, whose meetings it was their duty to arrange. But within half a century these limits had been swiftly overstepped ; and it is not too much to say that the Ephors came thenceforward to be the chief power in the state. They could browbeat the aristocratic Gerousia, over which, it seems, they actually assumed the presidency. They often accompanied the King upon campaigns, where they kept a watchful eye on his conduct, and sometimes on his return even put him on his trial for actions of which they chose to disapprove. So Sparta, though in name a monarchy, and in form an aristocracy, came thus in the last resort under a more or less democratic control. Yet this did not lead, as at Athens and elsewhere, to an exercise of mob-licence, or even to an assertion of popular liberties. Public opinion at Sparta unswervingly maintained a strict subordination of the individual to the demands of state. The discipline of life which the Lycurgan system imposed remained for ever sacred. Obedience to its code was loyally given, not merely by the citizens at large, but also by the Ephors themselves, whose first duty it was to enforce its iron vigour ; and there lay a grim reality behind the curious edict which year by year, as they entered upon office, the Five were wont to issue to the populace—that all must ‘ shave their moustaches and obey the Laws.’

Discipline absolute and unquestioning was then the keynote of the Lycurgan system. Life at Sparta down to the smallest detail was henceforward organized for the single and deliberate end—military efficiency for the suppression of the Serf. The citizens were, in fact, a garrison in their own country ; and the stability of their political institutions was due to their conscious knowledge that the numbers of that garrison, compared with the numbers of the Helot foe, were perilously small. For at no time were the free Spartans numerous. Intermarriage with their subject peoples was forbidden them. Immigrants from other states were jealously excluded, so that there could be no fresh infusion of blood ; and, since the privilege of citizenship depended (as we shall see) on the observance of certain strict conditions, the tendency was for the citizen body to diminish rather than to grow. Early in the Fifth Century B.C. their number is computed at four thousand adult males ; while the total Helot population, including men, women, and children, ran to upwards of two hundred thousand souls. Such a disproportion was in itself sufficiently alarming ; and to restrict the further increase of the Helots, the Spartans had recourse to a barbarous expedient. There was a secret corps of youths, entitled the Crypteia, on whom was laid the duty of anticipating trouble by killing off in cold blood, and without undue fuss or noise, such Helots as showed too virile a character or were suspected of treasonable intentions. This method, however, merely served to minimize the danger. It did nothing whatever to remove it. And, if the ' garrison ' was to be ready against the last eventuality, there was nothing for it but to train and train. From his earliest childhood, therefore, the Spartan was subjected to the most rigorous discipline. If at birth he appeared weakly, he was quietly put out of the way as physically unfitted for the purposes of life. Those who survived the test were at the age of seven removed from home and mother to be drafted into 'packs ', where they lived together, played together, fed together and did their turn of ' fagging ' for an elder youth who acted as their ' prefect '. In the discipline they underwent there was indeed much to remind us of our own English Public Schools. The training of character and muscle was its outstanding feature. Everything was done to make the boys tough and hard ; and (though here, let us hope, the parallel is faulty) their mental development was sadly starved. But, if the little Spartan was no scholar, he was splendidly equipped to meet the buffets of life. He went barefoot in winter and clad in a single cloak. He played games which were a rude test of courage and endurance ; and, to develop his initiative, he was encouraged to augment the scanty rations provided him by stealing off the farms. In such escapades, moreover, it was a point of honour to avoid detection ; and all know the story of the youth who, when caught red-handed in the theft of a tame fox belonging to a neighbour, concealed the animal beneath his cloak and allowed it to lacerate his vitals rather than submit to the disgrace of a confession. Nor need we doubt the truth of such a tale, when we remember the ordeals through which these lads had passed. Once a year at the shrine of Artemis there was kept a custom, then highly esteemed, but horrible to us—a competition in endurance of the lash, voluntarily undertaken and ending not infrequently in death. Small marvel, then, that the Spartan grown to manhood was an incomparable warrior, inured to discipline and self-restraint ; nor did that discipline end with his minority.

Lycurgus' system was primarily a machine for manufacturing soldiers ; and much of the men's day, accordingly, was spent on the parade ground. But mere drill was insufficient for the reformer's purpose, and to secure the greatest measure of social unity he had endeavoured to remove, so far as possible, all diversity of interest between man and man. The adult Spartans, therefore, like the boys, were compelled to live a barrack life in Clubs or Messes. Home life there was none ; and it was only permitted to the young husband to see his wife by stealth. One consequence of this was to make the Spartan women more independent and self-assertive than in other parts of Greece. They were famous, as girls, for their athletic prowess ; as matrons, for a courage so stoical and unbending that the Spartan mother, it is said, preferred to see her son brought home from battle wounded and *on* his shield rather than scatheless and without it. It was their pride, in fact, to strengthen rather than in any way to undermine the discipline of their men-folk ; and it must have been largely due to the loyal support of the women that the whole Lycurgan system attained to a degree of Socialistic practice such as the world has never perhaps seen before or since. For in the life of the men's clubs all was shared in common, each member contributing a set quantity of food, provided either from the proceeds of the chase or from the fertile homesteads which his Helots tilled. The regular maintenance of such contributions was an essential condition of citizenship; and default involved disfranchisement. But apart from that there was no great inducement for the Spartan to worry his head much about this world's goods. Having enough and to spare for his own daily requirements, he had small need of money; and indeed, until in the Fourth Century luxuries began to find their way into the country, there was not much on which to spend it. Nevertheless, to safeguard the system still further against the insidious influence of wealth, Lycurgus had made two provisions. In the first place, his code absolutely forbade Spartan citizens to engage in any kind of commerce. In the second, it rendered the hoarding of money virtually impossible by limiting the currency to the use of cumbersome iron spits. These, since foreign coinage was jealously excluded, formed the sole legitimate medium of exchange; and a medium of exchange, thirty guineas' worth of which would have filled, as Plutarch says, a good-sized wagon, could not fail to be a barrier to all forms of financial enterprise. Thus, the Lycurgan institutions were completely unaffected by those influences which in other states most made for political change; and they were maintained for centuries with a rigid conservatism which, while admirably adapted to the end in view, found its inevitable result in stunting and stereotyping the whole national character. For the Spartan was different from other Greeks. Uneducated, inartistic and intellectually dull, though displaying on occasion a terse, sardonic wit, he presented the strongest possible contrast to the nimble-minded versatile Athenian. His mind worked in a groove, he shrank by instinct from risky or adventurous policies; and in nothing was the effect of his narrow upbringing more strikingly displayed than in the attitude he adopted towards the outer world. For from first to last, as we shall see, the policy of Sparta was abnormally self-centred and short-sighted. As a rule, she took small interest in affairs outside the Peloponnese; and although more than once in her history the call came to maintain the lead of the Greek world at large, she refused her opportunity and drew back once more into the selfish pursuits of her narrow local interests. For the truth is that Lycurgus' institutions, while producing many qualities which might make a nation great, had dried up at the source that precious spirit of initiative without which true greatness can never be achieved.

II. FOREIGN POLICY

Of the rôle played by Sparta in the affairs of Greece the dominating factor was her immense superiority in arms. The system of training which we have just described could hardly fail to produce a breed of formidable warriors ; and when, to supplement the relatively small number of her citizens, there were added large and well-trained contingents of both Perioeci and Helots, it was manifest that Sparta could command an army likely to make its mark in the battlefields of Greece. There was, however, another and still more potent reason for her prolonged military ascendancy, and this was more or less directly concerned with the new methods of fighting. The Messenian War, which, as we have seen, had revolutionized the social character of Sparta, had also revolutionized her tactics. Till then battles had been fought in the old haphazard style, each man taking his place in the *mêlée* as courage or opportunity might dictate, the nobility riding on horseback and often deciding the combat by their individual prowess of arms. But in the course of this war we discover a change. By an innovation first made, it would seem, by Euboeans a century earlier, the phalanx of *hoplites* or heavy-armed footmen now came into play, and about the same time it was also adopted by other peoples as well as the Spartans. By the new method all depended on the concerted onslaught of a close, well-ordered line. There was little open fighting ; and as the hills were over-rough for manœuvring in close order, the battles were invariably contested on the level of the plain. The hoplite's arming was much on the traditional Homeric pattern—bronze helmet, leather corslet, bronze greaves, shield of hide stiffened with metal, and spear. Such equipment presented a wellnigh impenetrable front, and a phalanx of these warriors, ranged elbow to elbow and (according to the general practice) in eight successive ranks, was a formidable weapon of offence. All depended, however, on maintaining that formation ; for, the shield-line once disrupted, it was hard to close the breach, and the hoplites' defensive armour was no adequate protection against flank-attack. Victory went, therefore, to the army better drilled in faultless dressing and accurate manœuvre ; and in this, as was but natural, the Spartans had an immense pull over their neighbours. For they alone possessed what we should call a standing army, and troops enjoying daily opportunity for parade-ground exercise were inevitably superior to the raw militia which in other states was hastily collected from scattered farms and villages when war should be declared. It was therefore little wonder that the professional soldiers of the Eurotas valley not merely won their wars, but established a hege-mony by force of arms over many surrounding peoples.

Sparta was not in early days, as she later came to be, the acknowledged leader of the Peloponnesian states. At the time of the Dorian Conquest it had been Argos, successor to the prestige and dominion of Mycenae, who had assumed the rôle of Dorian leadership. Over the north-eastern arm of the peninsula, including the smaller states of Sicyon, Epidaurus, Troezen and others, her first king, Temenos, had held a clear supremacy ; and to that supremacy, lost to her in the subsequent Dark Age, Argos ever afterwards looked wistfully back. To recover it remained the sole and central ambition of her foreign policy, dominating the imagination of her citizens, as the recovery of Alsace-Lorraine has in recent years dominated the imagination of France. During the first half of the Seventh Century, it is true, that ambition came near to fulfilment under the leader-ship of her famous monarch Pheidon (c. 690–650). With an Argive host, whose prowess the Delphic oracle extolled as the finest in the world, Pheidon 'reassembled the Kingdom of Temenos.' More than this, he made Megara his protégé and even pressed Corinth hard. The little island of Aegina also passed under his control, and there he established, it would seem, a mint, so that the Aeginetan currency, of which we spoke above, was in all probability the outcome of his genius; and to him, as we know, was attributed the authorship of the standard weights and measures employed throughout the Peloponnese. The eastern side of the peninsula was in fact at Pheidon's feet; and at one point even upon its western coast his influence was felt. For there he intervened to transfer from Elis to Pisa the management of the famous Olympic Games, now growing from a purely local celebration to an international affair, which drew athletes and spectators from Italy and Sicily as well as from the other parts of Greece, and thus served to promote much fruitful and friendly intercourse between the various members of the Hellenic family. Sparta's support was given, though ineffectually, to the rival claim of Elis; and with Sparta about this time King Pheidon measured his strength. At Hysiae (c. 668), in the plain of Thyreatis, then a bone of contention between the two hostile powers, he met her army and defeated it completely. This was a severe set-back to the ambitions of Sparta, who seems for the moment to have lost control over the whole eastern coast of her territory, the island of Cythera included [1]; and, though after Pheidon's death the realm he had built up fell rapidly to pieces,[2] Sparta was too much occupied with the Messenian Revolt of 630 and with the subsequent reorganization of her own institutions to push forward again for a while. When she did so, it was with the assurance of possessing a fighting force, trained under the method of the new Lycurgan discipline, and destined, as we have said, to prove ultimately invincible in Greece. Nevertheless in the first big war she waged during the Sixth Century, the results were disappointing.

---

[1] This extension of Argive power so far south may, however, refer to King Temenos' reign.

[2] Sicyon, Epidaurus and the other Dorian dependencies not merely asserted their independence, but in many of them were set up the anti-Dorian tyrants of which we spoke above (p. 41).

The Arcadian state of Tegea was its objective and proved a hard nut to crack. After thirty years of warfare (590–560) Sparta abandoned all hope of enslaving Tegea as she had formerly enslaved Messenia, and she accepted this neighbour city as a subject ally, possessing independent status, but bound to provide a military contingent in war-time.

The way was now clear for an advance on Argos, and in 546 Sparta made a second bid for the possession of the Thyreatic plain. When the Argives issued forth for its protection, a curious test of champions was arranged. The two main hosts withdrew leaving selected warriors—three hundred from each side—to fight the issue out. The contest was so bloody that every man was killed except a pair of Argives and a single Spartan. The former, deciding for themselves that they had won the day, marched off to Argos to announce their victory. The wily Spartan, however, stayed behind to spoil the dead, and finding himself in possession of the field, claimed the victory as his. So the dispute began afresh ; and a pitched battle ensuing, the Spartans beat their rivals handsomely. Thus Thyreatis was won ; but the victory meant far more to Sparta than the acquisition of fresh territory—indeed it was the last annexation which she was destined to make. What was infinitely more important, it removed from her path the only rival claimant to the leadership of the Peloponnese and she was free to build up the famous League which throughout almost her whole history remained grudgingly, but effectively, loyal to her. Security perhaps no less than love of power was the motive of its original formation. For Argos remained unforgiving and revengeful, brooding over the memory of her lost dominion and dreaming of its possible recovery ; and, though on every occasion when she might lift her head, the Spartans were watching cat-like to strike her swiftly down, yet it was obvious wisdom for them to keep her in isolation and to ensure that neighbouring states were their allies and not hers. So during the second half of the Sixth Century we find them extending the policy of alliance, begun already with Tegea, to the entire circle of surrounding states. The rest of Arcadia

joined them, Corinth and Sicyon swore alliance 'for ever';
even Megara came in. By the end of the century every
state in the Peloponnese except Argos and Achaea was a
member of the League. To call it a league, indeed, is
in the strict sense a misnomer. For its members were
bound by no ties to one another and their allegiance was to
Sparta alone. Its machinery was simple; and its object
almost exclusively confined to purposes of war. Common
policy was debated, when question of war arose, in a council of the members among whom Sparta, though of course
influential, possessed no more than one equal vote. No
tribute was levied, save for meeting war expenditure; but
each state was bound, when a joint campaign was called
for, to send two-thirds of its military force. In their
domestic affairs the allied states retained complete autonomy; but though she nominally refrained from open
interference, Sparta saw to it as far as possible that their
form of government should be one sympathetic to herself.
Oligarchies were, on the whole, both more dependable
and more in harmony with her own native institutions;
and to oligarchies accordingly she gave her full support.
Tyrants she regarded with comprehensible suspicion; for
not merely were their personal interests and ambitions
very liable to interfere with hers, but their patronage of
the lower orders was utterly opposed to her whole domestic
policy. Popular rule, indeed, more especially when it
meant the enfranchisement of artisans and tradesmen,
was her chief bugbear; and it is clear that the masters of
two hundred thousand serfs could ill afford to countenance
the infectious example of full-fledged democracy. That is
the true reason why in the process of time Sparta came
to see in Athens her foremost opponent and her most dangerous rival. For in these two states were represented
two political ideals which were diametrically opposed. In
the final clash of the Peloponnesian War towards the close
of the Fifth Century there came the testing issue between
Freedom and Enlightenment upon the one hand, and
Reaction and Ignorance upon the other. Nor can we but
feel that Sparta's triumph was a real tragedy for Greece;

for it meant that the meaner and narrower ideal had prevailed.

Nevertheless, the strange thing is that among the Greeks themselves there was always a strange veneration felt for Sparta. Even Plato, the great philosopher of Athens, was clearly a sympathetic student of her institutions. The manly self-restraint which marked her citizens no true Hellene could do other than admire. The marvellous perfection of their physical development made a strong appeal to a race devoted to athletic exercise. Above all, the complete subordination of the individual Spartan to the requirements of State-service, expressed with unique fidelity the current Greek conceptions of the political ideal. Within the narrow confines of these small self-contained communities there grew up a local patriotism the more intense for its very limitations. The constant demand made on the members of such states to defend their native soil taught them early to regard their own property and persons as the instruments and agents of the common weal. Nowhere perhaps more fully than among the Greeks was the doctrine of subservience to the state developed; and nowhere certainly, among the Greeks themselves, more fully than at Sparta. Yet the rival claim of Individual Liberty was also strong, though latent, in the Hellenic character. This force it was which, though in the ultimate issue it broke the bonds which held the City State together, was nevertheless to prove the greatest legacy bestowed by Hellas on the human race; and meanwhile, as we shall now see, it was to find its fullest and most vigorous expression in Sparta's future rival—the Democracy which presently was to be evolved at Athens.

CHAPTER VI

ATHENS

I. SOLON'S REFORMS

THE Seventh and Sixth Centuries, which saw Sparta first battling unsuccessfully with Argos, then more successfully with her own Messenian rebels, and finally rising, in the new strength of the Lycurgan institutions, to a predominant position among Peloponnesian states, had witnessed in Attica beyond the Isthmus a process of political development very widely different, but far more typically Greek. Athens' rise to prominence was by comparison much slower. It did not depend on supremacy of arms ; and it was due far more to the ready wits of her people than to any natural advantages the country possessed. For Attica was in truth a poor country. Its territory consisted of three wide stretches of level plain, divided by hills or mountain ranges and broken at intervals by outcrops of sterile rock—first the main central plain in which Athens herself stood, enclosed by Mount Hymettus to the south-east, Mount Pentelicus to the north-east, and by the much lower line of Mount Aegaleos to the north-west ; beyond the latter lay the Eleusinian plain, once an independent political unit, but long since annexed to the Athenian state ; south of Hymettus lay the third plain

---

NOTE ON PLATE I (*Frontispiece*)

The Acropolis seen from the east. In foreground is the stream-bed of the river Ilissus. In the middle distance and slightly to the left can be seen the surviving pillars of the Roman temple of Olympian Zeus, built on the site of Pisistratus' earlier edifice. On the Acropolis stand the ruins of the Parthenon.

stretching seawards in the direction of Cape Sunium, and much more broken than the other two. These plains, though affording ample space for cultivation, were never really productive. The olive and the vine flourished ; but

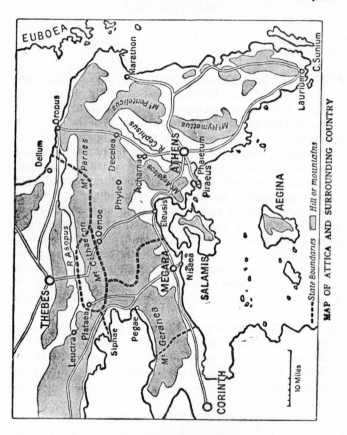

even before the abnormal growth of Athens' urban population, the product of the cornland barely sufficed for the needs of the inhabitants. The mountain country which enclosed the plains afforded grazing for goats and blossom for the bees. but little else. One great advantage indeed the Attic folk possessed in the admirable rock-guarded harbours adjacent to their capital, but the potentialities of these they were very slow to exploit. The result was that in early days the struggle for existence was severe and prosperity precarious ; nor was it till well on in her history that Athens began to take her rank among the foremost of Greek states.

Her political evolution had, down to the year 600, followed pretty normal lines. Concentration upon a common capital had taken place, as we have said, in very early days, the dwellers of the eastern shore and the hardy hillsmen of the mountain district having thrown in their lot with the peasant farmers of the central plain and agreed to form one state. For government henceforward all looked alike to Athens, set on that plain's broad level between the mountains and the sea. Her splendid rock, the famous Acropolis, afforded them a strong, capacious citadel ; and under the rock's north slope sprang up the nucleus of what later was to be incomparably the largest of Greek towns. As yet, however, the industrial enterprise which was to produce this consequence had scarcely begun at Athens. The bulk of her citizens still lived upon their farms ; and, if they came in to town at all, came in to market. Political power was vested, as we said above, in the hands of a landowning aristocracy, the ' High-born ' or ' Eupatrids '. From their ranks were yearly chosen the three Archons or executive officials—for civil administration, for religion, and for war. The Eupatrids composed, too, the celebrated Council of the Areopagus—a survival doubtless of the patriarchal ' elders ' ; and this now appears to have enjoyed complete control of both foreign and domestic policy.[1] The popular Assembly or Ecclesia, which was allowed perhaps to approve the choice of archons and give its feeble sanction to the Council's acts, was still a mere cipher in the State ; and the Few were in fact supreme.

The extreme impotence and servility of the Attic

[1] In historical times at any rate the Council was recruited from ex-magistrates.

populace was strikingly illustrated, towards the end of the Seventh Century, by the events of a famous *coup d'état*. At that time, as we have seen in a preceding chapter, tyranny was much in the air. Corinth, Megara and other neighbouring states had fallen under its spell ; and it was not unnatural that an attempt should be made also at Athens. It came from one Cylon, who had married the daughter of Theagenes, tyrant of Megara, and who, in his attempt to emulate his father-in-law's example, received from him a valuable backing of troops. With their aid he seized the Acropolis. That seemed an excellent start, but now it was that the backwardness of Athenian political development stood revealed. For nobody raised a finger in his support. There was, it would seem, no middle-class artisan faction to answer his call ; and the country-folk, we are told, even crowded in from the fields to assist in his suppression ; so strong was their tradition of subservience to the hated nobility. Thus aided, the Government soon succeeded in starving out his party on the hill. Seeing the game was up, the conspirators took refuge at Athena's shrine, and were only induced to quit it on a pledge expressly given that their lives should be spared. For greater assurance, however, they kept contact with the shrine by means of a rope to which they clung as they descended from the hill. The precaution was in vain. The rope was cut by the order of Megacles, the archon, and the suppliants were butchered—a blot on the honour of Megacles' family, the Alcmeonidae, which they were never afterwards allowed to forget [1] (*c.* 632).

The failure of Cylon's coup left the nobles still more powerful, and the peasantry, if anything, more down-trodden than before. But happily Athenians had a gift for compromise and about a decade later came a valuable concession. Hitherto the law of the land had been an unwritten law, and the aristocratic judges, who alone possessed the secret of its mysteries, had been able to expound and interpret it at will. Now about this time the art of writing, introduced perhaps some centuries before,

[1] See page 185.

was beginning to obtain a real hold among Greek peoples, and one not unnatural consequence was the demand for a written code. So in 621, according to tradition, the tabulation of Athenian law was entrusted to one Draco. The fruit of his labours was a stringent code in which the penalty for pilfering a cabbage-stalk was death, but not more stringent, so far as we can judge, than the prevailing custom of unwritten law. In relation to murder it marked one great advance by drawing a definite distinction between intentional and unintentional homicide ; and the summary methods of the family blood feud were now, at any rate, if not before, replaced by due legal procedure. To the helpless and ignorant peasantry, though they would scarcely seem to have much welcomed it, such an accurate definition of legal liabilities was an undoubted boon. It signalized a great step forward in their slow emancipation from the old, irresponsible control ; and the concession showed a spirit of forbearance in the nobles which appeared to augur happily for future social peace.

The fact is that moderation was of all man's moral qualities the Greek's chief ideal. ' Nothing too much ' was the motto inscribed above the doorway of Apollo's Delphic shrine, and the god's mild wordly wisdom had a sedative effect in these unsettled times. Even at Athens the bitterness of the struggle between rich and poor was destined, as we shall see, to find a peaceful issue ; and, if for the time being the rich were more than usually rapacious, it was because the unproductive nature of their country placed them at a real disadvantage in the competition for trade, and drove them almost inevitably to exploit their economic opportunities at the expense of the weak and the poor. So Attic history during these years reveals in their most unpleasant light all those abuses of the power of wealth which we described in a foregoing chapter. Extortionate usury began the evil work. Little by little the big landlords filched away his land from the small proprietor ; and finally, lacking the wherewithal to pay his debts, the poor bankrupt was forced to pledge the labour of his hands and become the bondsman of his creditor.[1] So heavy was the oppression and so deep the discontent that, as the Sixth Century opened, civil strife took overt form. Happily, however, when affairs looked critical, the spirit of compromise prevailed once more ; and there emerged a man whose far-sighted statesmanship (though he was himself perhaps hardly aware of its true significance) was now to point the way towards the ultimate solution through Democracy. Solon, the poet, sage and patriot politician, is perhaps the earliest figure in Athenian history of whose personality we can form some clear idea. Part of his writings have come down to us, couched naturally in verse, since prose was not as yet a normal method of literary expression ; and the story of his career, though somewhat overlaid by the legend-monger's fancy, gives us a consistent and picturesque impression of a man at once deeply imbued with an enlightened and inquisitive philosophy, and capable also of strong sagacious handling of practical affairs. Though by birth a noble, Solon appears to have interested himself in trade. He had travelled, it is pretty certain, in Ionia, and knew something of the intellectual movement there afoot. At Athens he was already an influential personage, trusted alike by noble and by peasant, when in 594 he was elected archon and embarked upon the urgent task of radical reform.

The problems confronting Solon were primarily economic ; and economic measures of redress were as a natural consequence his first concern. But these were no partisan measures ; and their author's chief claim to greatness rests on the temperate character of his reform. It would have been easy to yield to the peasantry's demand for a complete ' redistribution of land '. But this Socialistic remedy which would have thrown all Attica into a ferment and permanently estranged the noble landowners, found no favour with Solon. He was content to remove existing grievances without creating new ones. His first step was to cancel at a blow the liabilities of all who had been

[1] Some took a position analogous to the villeinage of medieval England, retaining their personal liberty, but paying *one-sixth* of the produce to their masters.

enslaved through debt, and to enact that for the future
no free Athenian citizen should be allowed to mortgage
his personal liberty. To redress, so far as possible, the
more glaring inequalities of wealth, Solon next proceeded
to limit by law the amount of land which any single
individual might acquire [1]; and he further endeavoured to
curb ostentatious extravagance by laying down a maximum
expenditure on funerals, or on public entertainments, or
even on the dowry of a wealthy bride. More important,
however, for the future of his country were his constructive
measures. Seeing that home-grown corn, though barely
sufficient for the nation's needs, was nevertheless exported
by profiteering merchants, he ordained that no Attic
produce should be sent abroad with the exception of the
olive—henceforth to be the staple of the country's foreign
trade. But agriculture alone would not, he saw, create
prosperity, and first among Athenian statesmen he directed
his fellow-citizens towards their future pre-eminence as a
manufacturing community. He ordained that every father
should teach his sons a craft ; and, since skilled workers
were none too numerous, he encouraged the immigration
of artisans from abroad—a policy which soon led to the
large foreign settlement of Metics or non-Citizens, concentrated in Athens and Peiraeus. In particular, we may note
that from this time onward the products of Attic potteries
began to rival those of Corinth, and before the end of the
century to oust them altogether. Solon was in fact the
founder of his country's future industrial prosperity and
the creator of her artisan class.

Such economic measures, though they marked a real
epoch in the development of Athens, were not, it would
seem, the whole or perhaps even the most important part
of Solon's work. Later generations clearly regarded him
as the original founder of their democratic institutions ;
and, though some doubt remains what precisely the
Athenian constitution owed to him, yet it is pretty evident
that he attempted to endow the populace with some sort

[1] This provision, of which a single statement by Aristotle is the
sole evidence, is, however, disputed by some historians.

of political power. Such an idea, we must remember, was hitherto unique in the history of mankind. No other peoples had, before the Greeks, even dreamt of such a system [1] ; and, familiar as we ourselves are with the practice of democracy, we must beware of supposing that in Sixth-Century Athens the principles of self-government could have been clearly or consistently visualized. Solon's reforms, at any rate, were extremely tentative and cautious. The aristocratic Council of the Areopagus he left with its sovereignty intact, and the archonship he confined as heretofore to the Eupatrid nobility. But he endeavoured to extend the limits of the franchise and entrust with some political responsibility those whose only part had hitherto been to obey. The lowest class of citizens were now for the first time admitted to the Ecclesia ; and a new Council or Boulê was set up, consisting of Four Hundred members and drawn from the ranks of all but the poorest class. The duty of the new Council was to prepare the business for the popular Assembly and to control its inevitable turbulence ; and, though it is clear that under Solon's constitution the aristocratic element was still to be predominant, yet equally is it clear that there was no intention, as at Sparta, for the democratic element to remain a mere empty show. The vital point was that the traditional prestige of the nobility was shaken. They were no longer the irresponsible masters of the State, but subordinate, like every other citizen, to the provisions of the great legal code which Solon himself drafted. This code of law, which over two centuries later was taken as the model for some of Alexander's colonies, was manifestly a masterpiece of social organization. Its enactments, together with a fixed schedule of fines and penalties, were duly engraven on pillars and erected for public study in the central Market Square ; and, though the Areopagites were appointed its official ' guardians ', the actual administration of the Code was placed in the hands of the people themselves. Not

---

[1] Athens was not quite first in the field ; for in this, as in so many spheres, Ionia led the way. Some sort of democracy existed, for instance, in Chios before the end of the Seventh Century.

merely was the right of prosecution granted to any free-born citizen who cared to undertake it ; but a genuine People's Court was now established in which citizens of every class were entitled to act as jurors.[1] To this Court or ' Heliaea ' appeal might henceforth be made from the decision of the archons ; and even the archons themselves, hitherto responsible to the Areopagus alone, were now bound on vacating office to render an account before this popular tribunal. How powerful was such a check on the conduct of officials is obvious enough. It was the very foundation of Athenian liberties ; and on the basis of this Solonian institution was built up, as time went forward, the jury-system which made the equity of Athenian justice famous throughout the entire Greek world.

Nevertheless, whatever the ultimate consequence of his reforms, Solon himself was too wise a man to hasten the process towards democracy unduly. It is doubtful even whether he aimed at more than to establish a certain equipoise of power and function, allowing to the populace just so much of privilege as they were competent to enjoy without abuse, and safeguarding the stability of his constitution by the twin ' anchors ' of the Areopagus and the Boulê, the former entrusted with the guardianship of the laws, the latter with the control of the popular assembly. Stability, however, was just what Solon failed to achieve for his country. His year of office over, he himself went off on his travels to Asia Minor and elsewhere. But no sooner had he turned his back than the old familiar troubles began to undermine his handiwork. The nobility, disgruntled by the curtailment of their power, resumed their old pretensions. The masses were disappointed by the slow effects of political reform ; and the peasant holders found it no easier than before to finance their agricultural undertakings. So the factions of Few and Many were soon at loggerheads once more ; and when Solon himself returned

---

[1] It is improbable, however, that this judicial body really counted for much in the Sixth Century. Certainly the elaborate organization of it into several courts dates from the time of Pericles, and some critics would wish to place its actual creation at that epoch.

upon the scene, he found discord at its height. Wishing perhaps to turn men's thoughts away from such selfish grievances, he endeavoured to stimulate their native pride to a task of external conquest. The island of Salamis, divided from the mainland by a bare mile or so of water, had long been coveted by Athens, but, despite a recent effort to achieve its capture, had been lost again to Megara. Solon now appealed in a patriotic poem for a renewal of the attempt :

> ' Arise and win you Salamis,
> The lovely island Salamis
> And wipe away your shame ! '

To this call of the statesman poet the Athenians rallied. War was declared on Megara ; and in 570 B.C. or thereabouts the coveted island was won.[1] But from this triumph, in itself so valuable to Athens, sprang a result far other than Solon had foreseen.

II. PISISTRATUS' TYRANNY

Chief among the heroes of this expedition was a certain Pisistratus, a man of large ideas and ambitious character ; and his success appears to have inspired him with the hope of yet greater things. He aimed, in fact, at tyranny ; but to accomplish his end, it was essential first to procure a following. Now one of the results of the Solonian changes had been to create a new class-division in Attica. The encouragement of industry had brought into being a commercial and manufacturing population, grouped mostly round the shore-side districts, and forming a political faction which came in consequence to be known as the ' Coast ' in distinction from their bitter opponents, the landowners of the ' Plain '. It was among neither of these, however, that Pisistratus found his party, but among another and less prosperous class, also the product of the Solonian reforms. These were the landless victims of the old serf-system who had been thereby restored to their

---

[1] There is, however, some doubt about the date. Some critics would put the conquest shortly before 600 B.C.

grazing farms on the hill-skirts but who lacked the financial resources to run them. They were a discontented body, ready to follow a leader who could hold out hopes of betterment ; and with the aid of these ' Hillsmen ', while Coast and Plain were at loggerheads, Pisistratus determined to seize the reins of power. One day in 560, when the Assembly was in session, he entered wounded and bleeding, the victim of an outrage planned, so he told the populace, by his enemies and theirs. On the proposal of Aristion— perhaps the very Aristion whose gravestone has been unearthed—he was voted a bodyguard, and thus equipped he proceeded forthwith to seize the citadel and proclaim himself master of the state. His tenure proved precarious ; for the parties of Plain and Coast made common cause against the tyrant, and next year he was forced to flee the land. Within a twelvemonth he turned up again, this time with a different ruse. He dressed up a woman (so the story goes) to represent Athena, and arriving with her in a handsome chariot, announced himself the goddess' nominee. To the majority in Athens even tyranny seemed better than the nobles' selfish rule, and they readily consented to receive him back. Again, however, he was ejected by the other factions and spent ten more years in exile. Then in 546 he returned once more to Athens, and this time he stayed for good until his death in 527. The fact is that he had made use of his exile to fortify himself with various friendships and alliances. He married an Argive wife and had Argive warriors to back him. He even struck up a connexion with Lygdamis, tyrant of Naxos, and Amyntas, king of Macedon. Thebans, Eretrians and Thessalians were in some way or other beholden to him ; and there can be little doubt that Pisistratus was a man of quite unusual charm or skill of address. The result was, at any rate, that he now possessed resources superior to his foes. Many of the nobles he banished into exile, the Alcmeonid family among the rest. He studied the interests of the common folk, preserved the outward forms of the Solonian constitution—while ensuring that his own nominees should always head the polls—and meanwhile by various measures of far-sighted policy raised the prestige of Athens to a height before unknown.

Hitherto, indeed, there has been little enough in the development of the city to foreshadow the great rôle which she would soon be called upon to play in the affairs of Greece. Immersed in domestic troubles, she had entertained no vision of a larger destiny ; and, if one man more than another may be said to have opened her eyes, it was Pisistratus. For with almost uncanny insight he seems to have struck out along the very lines which were later to be followed by another statesman of genius incomparably greater, but enjoying opportunities much greater too—the immortal Pericles.

To begin with foreign policy, it was Pisistratus perhaps who first may be said to have given Athens a foreign policy at all. He saw that, while other states had colonies so planted as to command Aegean trade-routes, his own country possessed none. Once, indeed, at the beginning of the century, she had seized Sigeum in the Troad, only to relinquish it a few years later. Yet there it was, if anywhere, upon the lines of the Black Sea corn-traffic, that Athens (never too certain of her own home-grown supplies) particularly needed to procure some more effective hold. Pisistratus reoccupied Sigeum ; and by a fortunate chance another opportunity of promoting Athenian interests in this region was equally afforded him. In the earlier days of his rule an appeal for Attic colonists had been sent, as it so happened, by the tribes of the peninsula which is now called Gallipoli, but was known to the ancient world as the Thracian Chersonese. What they needed, above all, was some man of character who would enable them to hold their own against their northern neighbours ; and a certain Athenian noble, named Miltiades, had volunteered for the mission. Hoping thus at a blow to be rid of a dangerous rival, and also to establish a valuable trade-link in the north, Pisistratus encouraged the enterprise ; and such was the success attending the bold policy that Miltiades and his settlers soon mastered the entire peninsula, and though at first they maintained their

Independence of the mother country, Athenian influence was thus firmly established in a quarter whence in later days she was to draw her chief supplies. Such a clear recognition of commercial opportunities would alone have proved its author a capable business man ; but this was not the end of Pisistratus' resources. During his years of exile he had somehow won a claim to the gold mines of Mount Pangaeus at the western end of Thrace. These, when in power at Athens, he continued to exploit ; and we may safely guess that further upon Attic soil itself he developed the working of the silver mines at Laurium, soon now to be a fruitful source of public revenue. With such financial backing it was possible to deal in a more thoroughgoing manner with the economic problems of the state, and in particular to set the peasant farmer more firmly on his feet. The confiscated property of exiled nobles was distributed to landless citizens. Loans were advanced to them on easy terms ; and, since with the aid of these the small holders were able to practise a more intensive cultivation and more especially to increase the area of their orchards, Pisistratus was not merely responsible for an agricultural revival, but was paving the way for the subsequent development of Athens' chief export—the olive.

That finance alone, however, will not make a great city, Pisistratus knew well ; and, like Pericles, he made it his deliberate aim to magnify his country in the eyes of other folk. He it was perhaps who earliest conceived the great ideal of making Athens leader of Ionian Greeks, as was Sparta of the Dorians. With such an end in view he undertook a ceremonial purification of the sacred island of Delos, a traditional centre of Apollo's cult much revered by Ionians on both sides of the Aegean and the scene of frequent gatherings akin to those that drew the Peloponnesians to Olympia. This stroke of policy, we can hardly doubt, was shrewdly calculated to emphasize and reinforce the old religious bond between Athens and Ionia. Nor here again, if this were so, was Pisistratus' instinct in any way at fault. For two generations later, when the Persian Wars were over and Athens came to organize her great defensive League of Aegean states and islands, Delos was chosen as the centre of the League and the place where its treasury was kept. Meanwhile, at home in Athens, Pisistratus had other schemes afoot which did much to bring the city into prominence. With the shrewd insight into human nature which most tyrants seem to have possessed, he set himself to encourage and develop those festal celebrations, half-religious rite and half public spectacle, which were so dear to the hearts of all Greeks. By transferring the cult of Dionysus from a local township to the capital and by instituting there a dramatic festival to be held in the god's honour, he inaugurated the performances of tragedy which in the following century were to be one of the city's chief glories and a medium for the genius of her greatest poets. More important still, it was he who did much to magnify, if he did not actually create, another festival held in honour of the city's patron goddess, Athena, and known as the Panathenaea. The magnificence of its pomp served to impress upon the citizens a sense of their state's increasing strength. The athletic contests which played a part in it drew competitors and sightseers from all over Greece ; and, as was typical of Athens' peculiar genius, the poetic art was here too given a prominent place. For competitions were held between Homeric ' rhapsodists ' or (as we should say) reciters ; and in organizing these Pisistratus performed a valuable service. He laid down the rules of such recitations, and there is good reason to believe, though indeed we have no certainty, that he was responsible for the issue of an authorized version of the two great epics which the whole Greek world came to consider as the authentic text. The climax of the Festival, however, was a procession of ascent to the temple of Athena on the citadel ; and, though this temple dated from times long before the tyrant, there is excellent evidence that he embellished it, adding perhaps the pillars which ran round the shrine's exterior, and the sculptured groups of marble figures which adorned its gable-ends. Nor were these the only monuments of his architectural zeal. He gave Athens a new fountain, known as the ' Nine Springs '—a handsome

benefaction to a town which badly needed a good supply
of water ; and under the south-east side of the Acropolis
he further planned the building of a magnificent temple
to Olympian Zeus. This scheme he never lived to see
completed ; and before the roof was added, the Athenian
people had regained their liberty. The gaunt columns of
the arrested work were left simply as they stood—a
memorial, as it were, of the tyrant's frustrated pride and
a warning to others who in future days might be tempted
to follow in his footsteps.

The overthrow of the tyranny did not occur in Pisistratus'
own lifetime. When he died in 527, Hippias and Hipparchus, his two sons, inherited the power, and for a time
at least ruled well. Trouble, when it came, began with
a plot which, though not itself of popular origin, made
none the less a great effect upon the public mind. Two
creatures of the court, Harmodius and Aristogeiton, had
conceived a grievance against the tyrant brothers, and on
the day of the Panathenaea they and a few companions
arranged to assassinate the pair. The coup in part mis-
carried ; for, impatient lest their secret should have been
discovered, they committed themselves to a premature
attempt and succeeded only in murdering Hipparchus
(514). Hippias was not touched nor his authority affected.
But alarmed by the event, he became more tyrannical,
and, as time went on, increasingly unpopular. The result
was that his brother's murderers were soon exalted in the
people's eye to the dignity of heroes. Later generations
indeed (though both Herodotus and Thucydides seem to
have realized the truth) regarded them as the liberators
of Athens. A statue-group was set up to their memory
in the centre of the town, and the ballad which was woven
round their bloody deed became the very war-cry of
democracy :

> ' In branches of myrtle my sword I'll enfold
> Like Harmodius and Aristogeiton of old ;
> By whose daggers the tyrant oppressor was slain,
> And Athens knew freedom and justice again.'

Meanwhile there were other influences at work to undermine the rule of the now ferocious Hippias. The nobles of the Alcmeonid family had not accepted their exile with equanimity and they were intriguing to accomplish their return. They had even enlisted the support of the priests at Delphi, whose temple they had helped to rebuild some years before, after its destruction by fire ; and the Pythian oracle had thus been made amenable to the furtherance of their design. Every time the Spartans came to ask the god's advice, they were put off with the same unvarying answer—' Go and free Athens first.' Such reiteration had the desired effect. The Spartans, as we have seen, were habitually suspicious of the effects of tyranny, and in 510 their King Cleomenes undertook an expedition to drive Hippias out. In this he was successful. The people were in sympathy. The exiled nobility returned, and Athens was once more free. Deliverance, however, had been bought at a high price. For the city was almost of necessity much dependent on her liberator, and it is possible that she was even compelled to join the Spartan League. But it was not for long. Cleomenes' calculation, when he restored the nobles, had been that the rich classes would resume their sway and the democratic movement, so distasteful to the Spartan, be permanently checked. But he had not counted on the Alcmeonids ; and that ingenious family, under Cleisthenes their leader, now came out as the champion of the populace. The other nobles, being overwhelmed by this novel combination, appealed for fresh assistance, and Cleomenes himself appeared once more to bring Athens back to heel. This time the people rose in wrath against such foreign interference. The Spartan band was cut off and blockaded in the citadel ; and, when after tame surrender they departed home, Athens was free at last to pursue her way unhampered. The hour of democracy had come (508).[1]

[1] This is the order of events according to Aristotle. But according to Herodotus the Reforms of Cleisthenes *preceded* Cleomenes' second invasion. The truth probably is that the creation of the new constitution took time, and that it was at any rate mooted before Cleomenes' arrival. Hence the surprising vigour shown by the democratic party in suppressing him.

III. CLEISTHENES' REFORMS

Cleisthenes, now the man of the moment, was happily a constructive genius of the highest order. By Solon Athens had been set upon the path towards democratic freedom ; but she had failed to make good her footing. Now, however, she was to receive a machinery of self-government which would last almost unchanged throughout her history and which was perhaps the most astonishing political achievement known to the ancient world. For Cleisthenes was no dreamer. As a practical reformer he understood the root-cause of the country's malady, and he cut deep to cure the deep-set troubles of the past. From the far-distant days of the patriarchal period, when the tie of blood was still paramount, there had come down a strong tradition of *Clan* loyalty, which was responsible in great measure for the more recent disorders. That a clan system promotes faction is obvious. The history of Scotland is one long illustration of its pernicious influence ; and in the internecine conflicts of Sixth-Century Athens it was the main source of strength to the contending leaders, who exploited for their own selfish purposes the loyalty of their clansmen. But, apart from the tie of blood, the tendency towards faction was further reinforced by the long-standing distribution of the people into four territorial tribes. These tribes had been taken as the basis of the existing political machinery. Thus, in the election of officials, the men of the Plain would vote together, so equally would the men of the Coast ; and the successful candidate could therefore hardly fail to be bound by local prejudice and to favour his own tribesmen against the other three. Seeing how disastrous were the effects of such a system, Cleisthenes made bold to sweep it clean away, and abolishing the old fourfold tribal division of Attica, he redivided the people into *ten* new tribal units. The basis of the redivision was still geographic ; for the tribes were severally composed of a certain number of small parishes or ' demes '. But since the demes which went to make up each tribe were of deliberate purpose scattered, some on the Coast, some in the city and its suburbs, and yet others in the interior of the country, the reform cut clean across the old territorial groupings on which the factions of the past were built.[1] And we shall never hear of Plainsmen or of Hillsmen or Coast-men again.

The chief importance, however, of the Cleisthenic regrouping was not merely that it destroyed the old territorial factions, but far more that it utterly undermined the traditional associations of blood which had given to the nobles, as clan-leaders, their overwhelming and disastrous hold. Henceforth a man's allegiance was to the state alone, and not to any individual; and since membership of a deme was now to be considered the basis of citizenship and civic rights, many who had previously been excluded from such privilege were now admitted to it—not merely of those who were Athenian born, but also the unenfranchised ' metics ' or alien settlers, whose introduction to the country had been one of the main achievements of the Solonian reform. The old blood associations were not indeed abolished. For the traditional family groups, known as ' phratries ' or brotherhoods, were permitted to survive. Every year a feast, called the ' Apaturia ', was held to celebrate their common ancestry; and before the members of his brotherhood every Athenian citizen was duly presented, for enrolment in early infancy, for formal scrutiny when he had reached eighteen, and again at the time of his marriage. But the significance of these gatherings was henceforth purely social and religious; and politically at least they ceased to count. For purposes of state the only unit recognized for the future was the deme. By his deme a man was known, as, for example, ' Demosthenes, Demosthenes' son, of the Paeanian deme '; and, though he might change his habitation, his hereditary deme remained unchanged. By demes the taxes were collected. From the deme registers were taken the names

[1] In each district the group of demes pertaining to a tribe was known as a ' trittys '. This artificial unit played, however, little real part in the working of the constitution and is hardly mentioned in Athenian literature.

of those entitled to attend the Ecclesia ; and in the demes again were chosen the candidates for the central Council or Boulê. This Boulê was of far greater power and importance than under the Solonian constitution ; and beside it the aristocratic council of the Areopagus, though still retaining considerable prestige and a general supervisory control, now took a definitely secondary place. It numbered five hundred members, not, as in Solon's system, four ; and under the Ecclesia, which was henceforth supreme, the Five Hundred were the chief organ of expressing the popular will. Its functions were various. It sat to hear reports from the archons, to interview the ambassadors of foreign states, to regulate finance and to prepare material for the Ecclesia's debates. The transaction of current business which was too trivial, or too urgent, to await popular discussion, was its peculiar province ; and a standing committee of fifty Councillors, changing from month to month, was constantly in session. Thus, the task of administration was placed at last in the hands of the citizens themselves ; and, although the poorest were still denied admission to the archonship, yet even the archons themselves were responsible for their acts to this democratic tribunal. In it all citizens, of whatever rank or station, were entitled to sit if over thirty years of age ; and since nobody was allowed to hold the office more than twice, it was probably even odds that some time in his life a man would become a member of the Council, and, inasmuch as the Five Hundred took turns as President, might even occupy for the period of one day a position of rare authority, and hold in his keeping the keys of the Acropolis itself. Socrates we know once held that proud position. and was able on that occasion to delay judicial proceedings against the generals of the battle of Arginusae. What a momentous part such an experience must have played in the political education of the individual citizen is scarcely to be exaggerated. The machinery of the Boulê was perhaps the master stroke of Cleisthenes' innovations. the very keystone of his democratic edifice.

But, if the Cleisthenic system pointed straight towards

full democracy, its democratic tendency was somewhat tempered by another institution which, though not in all probability his work, was yet a more or less direct development of his organization. This was the creation of ten ' Strategi ' or Generals. For efficiency now demanded that for military purposes some further organization should be evolved besides the single Commander-in-Chief or Polemarch ; and to command the ten tribal units of the Cleisthenic constitution were appointed these Ten Generals. Their duties at the outset were doubtless purely military ; but even so they would seem to have been a serious rival to the Polemarch, and in 487 an important change occurred which served to give their office a peculiar prominence. In that year it was ordained that in the interests of completer democracy the Archons and the Polemarch should no longer be chosen by a direct vote, but selected from among the people's elected nominees by the method of *casting lots*. Such a change clearly meant a considerable diminution of these magistrates' authority. An individual chosen in so chancy a fashion could not be relied upon for real efficiency ; and since no man was allowed to hold the office more than once, there could be no continuity of experience or of policy in its administration. To the position of the Generals, on the other hand, no such limitations were attached. 'They were elected by a direct vote, and their efficiency could thus be reasonably assured. The same man, too, was eligible for repeated re-election ; and on both scores it is plain that the office would carry more weight not merely than the Polemarch's command, but also than the civil archonship. So, almost from the outset, the generalship took on a political as well as a military importance. The leading member or President of the Ten became equivalent to what we may call the Prime Minister of Athens ; and it was in this capacity that Themistocles, Pericles and other statesmen in succession were able in a large measure to direct the whole policy of the city. As the needs and responsibilities of Athens grew, wide powers of administration were conferred upon the Generals. Foreign affairs were made their special province. They managed finance, and organized the food-supply. They became, in short, the chief executive of the state, carrying into effect the decrees of the Ecclesia, and in consequence exercising over it, as does our modern Cabinet over Parliament, a very considerable control. There was not, however, as in the modern Cabinet, any theory of joint responsibility. Each general was answerable to the Assembly alone, and was free to propose motions on his own initiative irrespective of his colleagues' agreement or dissent. Indeed, conflict of opinion between rival generals was frequent and inevitable. For, as was to be expected under a democratic constitution, they were drawn from the ablest and strongest personalities of the day : and, though these were at first mainly men of noble birth, yet, as education spread, the more intellectual and more ambitious of the middle classes began to find their way into office, and towards the close of the Fifth Century we find demagogues like Cleon the leather merchant, or Cleophon the lyre-maker, elected side by side with the aristocratic Nicias or Alcibiades the Alcmeonid. Such men were little likely to see altogether eye to eye ; and it is remarkable that the system should have worked as well as it did.

How far Athenian politics were removed from the modern conception of Party Government is clearly enough shown by what has just been said. The control of administration might alternate indeed between two rival statesmen or even possibly between two rival groups. But there was no recognized machinery for expressing the ebb and flow of popular opinions ; and Athens was never entirely free from the danger that party feeling, lacking the opportunity of constitutional satisfaction, might find vent in the violent methods of a *coup d'état*. That this danger was from the outset more or less clearly envisaged is proved by the provision of a curious safeguard, devised probably by Cleisthenes, and known as Ostracism or the ' Potsherd vote '. Once in a year, if the Ecclesia so willed it, a general referendum was taken of all the citizens whether any of their number should be banished from the state.

If more than six thousand votes were cast in all, the individual, denounced by the marjority went into exile for ten years. The original object of the institution was unquestionably to provide a precaution against tyranny ; but, when that risk had passed, it served subsequently to ease the dangerous clash between outstanding political leaders, and eventually towards the end of the Fifth Century it fell altogether into disuse. As a safety-valve against faction, it had indeed its uses, but it was upon the whole a very cumbrous and not perhaps a very necessary instrument. For the truth is that the machinery which Cleisthenes invented soon worked so well and so smoothly that strong measures were not needed. The Athenians learnt not to govern themselves merely, but to govern with restraint ; and, if under the stress of the Peloponnesian War they were to grow fickle and revengeful, yet in more normal times their policy was seldom a discredit to the great man who had first taught them to trust Democracy.

IV. ATHENIAN POPULATION AND COMMERCE

When we talk of the Democracy of Athens, there is, however, one important qualification of which it is necessary to take note. The government was indeed self-government by citizens, but not all the inhabitants by any means were entitled to that rank. First, there were the slaves, in later times at least almost as numerous as the citizens themselves. These had no rights at all, political or otherwise. They were simply the chattels of their freeborn owners ; and it has often been remarked that the Athenian democracy should rather be considered as an aristocracy of a half-leisured class enabled by this means to devote a portion of their lives to politics. The rapid growth of the slave population was doubtless due to the expansion of Athenian industries, which naturally demanded a proportionate supply of cheap and menial labour. To the same cause we may attribute the similar increase of another important element in the population, neither citizens nor slaves—the resident foreigners or ' metics '. For, unlike most states of Greece, and, above all, unlike the Spartans, the Athenians welcomed immigrants. Solon had given them facilities for obtaining civic rights. Many, too, were enrolled in Cleisthenes' new tribes. But in later times the opportunity of this privilege was barred to fresh settlers ; and from the middle of the Fifth Century onwards metics, though perhaps nearly a quarter as numerous as the citizens themselves,[1] were able to obtain no share in the country's government. Nevertheless their presence was from the first very valuable to Athens. It marked her out for what she was pre-eminently to be— a community of traders ; and already we can see her during the course of the Sixth Century groping forward to the fulfilment of her destiny.

It has already been noted how Solon had endeavoured to foster industry by encouraging instruction of handicrafts and by inviting the immigration of artisans from abroad. For manufacture, however, skilled workers are not alone sufficient, and a supply of raw materials is essential. And, as luck would have it, Attica possessed extensive beds of reddish clay extremely suitable to the production of fine earthenware. Especially since the era of the Solonian reforms this industry had steadily developed ; and the painter's art had made progress along with the potter's. At first the scenes depicted on the surface of the jars had been picked out in rich black lustre, the human figures and other accessory objects being shown as a black silhouette against the reddish ground. But from about 520 onwards the process was reversed, the background of the scenes being henceforth painted black and the figures standing out therefrom in the more appropriate and realistic hue of the jar's natural surface. Utensils of every kind were made, from common olive-oil jars to delicate drinking-cups and mixing-bowls. All were painted in an elaborate fashion, and no two were ever alike. Many of the painters

---

[1] Estimates of the Athenian population differ widely. The probable figures for 431 B.C. are :

50,000 . . . adult male citizens.
25,000 . . . ,, ,, metics.
55,000 . . . ,, ,, slaves.

signed their names, and though the vessels they adorned were intended solely for practical domestic purposes, the work often reached a perfection of draughtsmanship which has seldom, if ever, been equalled. The best work of Red-figure style was performed in the first half of the Fifth Century. But from 540 onwards Attic pottery found a ready market among foreign nations, especially in Etruria, Magna Grecia, Egypt and South Russia ; and the export trade thus started brought Athens swiftly into the foremost rank of mercantile communities. Even Corinth, whose pottery had hitherto been popular in the West, was forced out of the market, and, though she kept possession of the carrying-trade to those parts, she was already beginning to feel the menace of Athenian rivalry. Indeed, by the end of the Sixth Century Athens appears to have been conscious of her opportunity, and to have directed her foreign policy towards this end. In 506 a brilliant campaign against the Euboean town of Chalcis enabled her not merely to cripple an old rival, but also to annex and colonize a portion of the island.[1] For the first time, moreover, we hear hints of naval action ; for, if the evidence of an inscription is to be trusted, Athens seems to have made havoc of the Chalcidian fleet. At any rate, before many years were out we shall find her grappling with another commercial rival in Aegina ; and to the clear-sighted vision of Themistocles it was manifest that the future of his country lay upon the waters.

V. Sixth-Century Culture

The fact is that with the close of the Sixth Century Athens was entering upon a new phase of her existence.

[1] See below, page 90.

PLATE VII

(a) A Black Figure Vase, in which the pattern and bird forms are silhouetted in black lustre. (b) An example of the later Red Figure Vase where the black lustre fills the background, leaving the natural surface of the ware to represent the figures, etc. See also Plate XIII.

RED FIGURE VASE

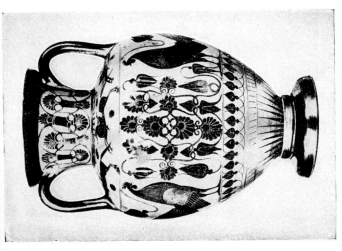

BLACK FIGURE VASE

A commercial and industrial activity which was one day to make her not merely the largest, but the most influential of Greek towns, was now definitely launched upon its course ; and alongside with this, as a natural and perhaps inevitable accompaniment, there was developed a new national spirit, bred of the free institutions of the Cleisthenic democracy. So during the succeeding century it was more and more the artisans and traders who set the tone and even dictated the policies of the state. And, though the ancient landowning nobility preserved for a while their weight of influence and right of leadership, yet the reforms of Cleisthenes heralded the swift decline and ultimate extinction of their old exclusive privilege. And with their disappearance something not to be recovered passed also away.

Despite the efforts of reformers and the interruption of tyranny the atmosphere of Sixth-Century Athens had remained predominantly aristocratic in tone, and one of the chief features or consequences of this aristocratic society had been a literary and artistic culture of unusual brilliance and charm. Of the fruits of that culture little indeed has come down to us beyond a fair quantity of exquisite pottery, a number of songs and other literary fragments, a battered remnant or two of architectural monuments, and perhaps a score or two of sculptured figures. Yet so individual and so distinctive was the genius of the period that from these alone we can gain a clear impression of a beauty incomparable in its kind, and displaying a youthful vigour from which the more mature and self-conscious work of the succeeding century seems under some aspects almost a decline. An aristocratic society, and an aristocratic society alone, could have produced such art. There is a light-hearted spontaneous vivacity about it which reflects the care-free spirit of men secure in their station, intent on making the most of life's opportunities, little troubled by its tragedies and problems, but, if concerned with these, meeting them with a level and unflinching gaze. Great gentlemen also these nobles must have been ; for the taste of the times is perfect tainted neither with vulgarity nor ostentation, restrained almost to a fault, condescending to no tricks or poses, and though far from complete mastery in technical accomplishment, yet in the highest sense refined.

Much of the poetry which has come down to us is, as might be expected, in the lighter vein—songs of love and wine and of the merrier sides of existence. Two writers stand out, neither of them Athenian born, but each brought to the court of Hippias by some accident of fate which drove them to leave their homes. Anacreon of Teos fled from the Persian Conquest of Ionia in 545 and visited many countries besides Attica. His strong, musical and withal quite simple verse attained such a vogue in Greece that later centuries gave rise to endless imitations of his style. His songs and elegies deal chiefly with passion and carouse, but, like the work of our best Elizabethans, they possess a stately dignity which seems to lift the theme. No better specimen could be found perhaps than this which even in prose translation reflects the author's vein : ' *Golden-haired Love, hitting me with a crimson ball, challenges me to play with a damsel shod with embroidered sandals. She comes from fair Lesbos, finds fault with my hair for being white, and yawns for some other prey.*' Simonides of Ceos was also a great traveller, and on Hipparchus' death he passed from Athens to other princely patrons in Thessaly and Syracuse. But he was no servile courtier. His profound and versatile genius commanded the respect of democrats as well as tyrants ; and his poems attained a celebrity which were to make him, at moments of national crisis or rejoicing, the recognized mouthpiece of Hellenic

---

PLATE VIII

One of the ' maiden ' figures, dedicated to Athena in the Sixth Century B.C., which after the Persian sack of 480 were built into the new terracing of the Acropolis. Note the ' archaic ' smile, the elaborate coiffure of draperies, and on the folds which fall down from the centre of the waist the slight traces of painted patterns. Cp. the advance of sculptors' skill in Plates IX, X and XI.

SIXTH-CENTURY MAIDEN

sentiment. His fame rested in large measure on the exquisite epitaphs he composed on the fallen heroes of the Persian Wars [1]; and these, together with other epigrams, of which he wrote a number, represent perhaps the Greeks' genius in its purest form. He was the embodiment of that virtue which they called ' Sophrosunê ' or Self-restraint, expressing patriotism without blatancy, pathos without sentimentality, and attaining loveliness with a touch so delicate and sure that no sense of strain or effort is perceivable. English translation can do but little justice to the magic of his style ; but this prose version of Professor Mackail may serve best to reproduce it. The lines were written in memory of the Spartans who fell at Plataea : ' *These men having set a crown of imperishable glory on their own land, were folded in the dark cloud of death ; yet being dead they have not died, since from on high their excellence raises them gloriously out of the house of Hades.*'

If the songs of the age stood alone, we should be able to form from them an adequate conception of the spirit of Sixth-Century Athens. But happily there has also survived enough of its sculptured handiwork to reinforce the same conclusions. When after the Persian sack of the Acropolis, the Athenians returned in 479 to undertake a complete reconstruction of the dismantled hill, they buried many statues among the foundations of the new terracing. These have been unearthed in comparatively recent times and in so fine a state of preservation that the bright, strong colours with which most of them were decorated seem as fresh as on the day when they were committed to the ground. They are mostly female figures, draped in delicate, elaborate garments which fall in straight firm folds. The features are set in a quaint but charming smile ; and not merely in these girl figures but also in the statues of naked, light-limbed athletes which date from the same epoch, there is an erect dignity of poise

---

[1] Recent literary criticism has, however, thrown considerable doubt upon the authenticity of many Epigrams ascribed by the ancients to Simonides. But if they are not all his, they were at least in his style

which exhibits the same self-reliant, care-free spirit already noted in the period's literature. The workmanship is indeed primitive. The anatomy is not invariably correct ; but the sculptor's touch is exquisite, his detail never crude. And one seems to see in the men and women he portrayed a proud, restrained but extraordinarily vigorous type, instinct with the conscious superiority of noble blood, but utterly free from snobbery, affectation or conceit. This early efflorescence of an aristocratic culture breathes, in short, an atmosphere of spring-like freshness. The succeeding epoch brought with it a maturer phase of art, a more complete mastery of technical skill, more profound intellectual conceptions, and a more serious philosophic attitude towards life. But, though the Fifth-Century masters of literature and sculpture attained a summit of perfection which was to be the envy and admiration of all posterity, yet midsummer is not springtime ; and somehow even in the most brilliant achievements of the Periclean democracy we miss the naïve, spontaneous grace of the earlier age. The imaginative energy of the Attic people could never perhaps have expanded to its full limits until political freedom was won ; but we must not forget that this very development towards democracy was itself the product of the aristocratic society which preceded it, and that not least among the triumphs of Sixth-Century Athens were the creative improvisations of Solon, Pisistratus and Cleisthenes, men drawn from its ranks and educated in its sane and dignified tradition.

PLATE IX

A head of a youth, of about 480 and perhaps a quarter of a century later than the ' maiden ' of Plate VIII. Note the painting of the eye-pupils—a device almost invariably adopted by Greek sculptors of every epoch. Note too the intricate arrangement of the hair. The Persians at Thermopylae were astonished at the care expended by the Spartans on the dressing of their hair. Cp. Plate XX, showing Fifth-Century sculpture at its best.

HEAD OF EPHEBE

VI. Sparta and Athens

Let us not, however, be mistaken about Athens. She had not at this time attained to the dominant position which she was presently to hold. In the realm of thought and literature, the Greek states of Asia Minor were far ahead of her ; and the leadership of Hellenic civilization lay still on the further side of the Aegean. Nor in Greece itself did Athens as yet count for much more than a second-rate power. Sparta, with all the weight of her Peloponnesian League behind her, dominated the southern horizon ; and under the forceful leadership of her great King Cleomenes (c. 520–489) she had been steadily growing in strength. Cleomenes, though Herodotus tends to belittle him, was clearly a man of very masterful and ambitious character. At home he appears to have asserted his royal prerogative against the growing interference of the ephorate ; and the country's foreign policy he dictated in a manner such as none of his successors could ever emulate. How pushful and high-handed that foreign policy could be, Athens had herself good cause to know. Once already, as we have seen, she had escaped from Cleomenes' clutches ; but he was not to be deterred by his failure of 508, and the next year we find him making yet another attempt against the new-won liberties of her young democracy. This time he called in the aid not merely of Boeotia, but also of the Euboean town of Chalcis from beyond the narrow strait. Athens was menaced, in fact, by a simultaneous attack from north and west and south ; and in this critical situation—as critical perhaps as she was ever called upon to meet—she showed a vigour and courage which gave ample proof, if proof were needed, of the inspiring influence of the Cleisthenic reforms. Their author,[1] indeed, had shown a lamentable lack of faith, and foreseeing the probability of a renewed attack, had stooped to crave the assistance of Persia. Before the envoys returned, how-

---

[1] Cleisthenes, though not specifically named by Herodotus, was probably the author of this pro-Persian policy. His disappearance from the stage seems to indicate his disgrace.

ever, opinion at Athens had changed ; and we hear no more either of alliance with Persia or of Cleisthenes himself. For the citizens had met the storm and had weathered it triumphantly. In a single day they defeated the Boeotians, crossed the strait into Euboea, and overthrew the men of Chalcis. The iron chains in which their captives were led home were seen on the Acropolis by Herodotus the historian ; and Chalcis itself was forced to submit to a settlement of Athenian citizens. But where, meanwhile, was Cleomenes ? The fact was that his advance from the south had been frustrated by an unforeseen obstacle. Corinth, the most important of his Peloponnesian allies, objected. She was a commercial city, and seeing in the growing strength of Athens a useful counterpoise to her own trade-rival Aegina, she had no wish to see the Cleisthenic democracy crushed. Her refusal to participate ruined the whole expedition, and Cleomenes was forced to retire without a blow (507). Nor was this the only occasion on which Corinth's inter- vention saved Athens : for three years later, when Cleomenes proposed at a League Congress to march again on Attica and restore the tyrant Hippias to the throne from which he had himself deposed him, it was the Corinthian veto which served to checkmate the extraordinary project (504).

Such ominous signs of disaffection within the ranks of her own League must clearly have given rise to nervousness at Sparta ; and her nervousness, as usual, took the form of fear concerning the attitude of Argos—still intent as ever on the recovery of a lost hegemony and watchful for the smallest chance of forming friends. Sparta could afford to take no risks ; and in 494, just ten years later than this last rebuff, Cleomenes led the Spartan army— unaccompanied on this occasion by other allied troops— into the Argive plain. There at Sepeia, near the ancient

---

PLATE X

One of the side pieces of the famous Ludovisi Throne, now in Rome. Date 475 (?) Note the skill with which the form is shown under the drapery, and com- pare with Plate XVIb.

FIGURE FROM LUDOVISI THRONE

hill of Tiryns, the two hosts lay for a while confronted ; and what followed was one of the most amazing episodes in the whole military history of Greece. The Argives, it appears, adopted the unwise system of imitating exactly the routine movements of their enemy. Seeing this, Cleomenes one day issued the order that when the herald sounded the fall-out for dinner, the Spartans were to remain at their posts ; and when the unwitting Argives dispersed to eat their rations, he launched a swift attack. It was a simple slaughter. The loss of six thousand men crippled Argos utterly, and not for a generation did she dare to raise her head.

By such a manifestation of Spartan strength the Peloponnese was instantly cowed. All disaffection in the League came to an abrupt end ; and the hegemony of southern Greece was now Sparta's beyond challenge. The truth is that we may see in Cleomenes a statesman who first perhaps in the history of the country conceived the idea of a united Greece. Such a union no doubt was primarily intended to promote the selfish interests of Sparta herself ; but, when all is said, it was Cleomenes' policy that laid the foundations of that concerted national resistance which alone was to save Greece in the coming invasion from Persia. For during these last years events had been moving on the further shore of the Aegean which were destined to bring at no very distant date the Asiatic conqueror to the European shore. In the hour of their great peril, therefore, it meant everything to the Greek peoples that they were able to look to Sparta for a bold patriotic lead. Even Athens, despite all that had happened in the past, was coming to recognize that claim to leadership. When in 491 the neighbouring islanders of Aegina threatened to turn vassals to the Persian King, it was she who appealed for Cleomenes' intervention ; and Cleomenes intervened. Nor was Sparta altogether to fail them, though her aid came too late, when in 490 the Athenians were confronted by the Persian host at Marathon. Thus the claim which Cleomenes made for his city was twice justified ; and during the Great Invasion of a decade later it was still more

gloriously upheld on the stricken fields of Thermopylae and
Plataea. Nevertheless it was on Athens, not on Sparta,
that was to fall the brunt of these successive onslaughts;
and it was well for her indeed that she had been spared
some years of respite to consolidate her new democratic
régime and to nurse her growing strength. To the little
state, barely emerging from a century of discord, without
any high tradition of arms, almost as yet without a fleet,
the coming crisis was in very truth a fiery trial. Yet there
are crises which will either make or mar the character of
a people; and, as for Elizabethan England the perilous
days of the Armada were a test of those high qualities
which, only through the victory then won, were enabled
to reach the full pitch of their development, so for Athens
equally the ordeal, though still more searching, was to be
perhaps still more fruitful in result. When it is over, we
shall find that she was beginning to realize her own true
greatness, and the city which not many years before had
suffered the high-handed intervention of a Spartan King,
will be already reaching forward to her future destiny as
the mistress of the Aegean and the acknowledged leader of
Hellenic culture.

CHAPTER VII

THE PERSIAN WARS

I. Ionia and Persia

IF, while following the fortunes of Sparta and Athens, we have hitherto touched but lightly on the progress of the Greeks of the Asiatic seaboard, it is not because their history lacked either interest or importance ; for in many ways they were far ahead of their less adventurous cousins of the European shore. The prosperous trade to which their numerous colonies had helped them, the bold policies pursued by their rich merchant princes (not a few of whom employed their wealth to maintain a tyrant's power), above all, perhaps, their closer contact with Oriental nations older and in some respects more experienced than themselves—all these advantages had led the Ionians on to a rapid and extraordinarily precocious evolution. In these insignificant and now half-forgotten cities it is not too much to say that the majority of the art-forms, and even very much of the philosophy and science of the Western world, took birth. The Dark Age which in Greece itself followed the Dorian Conquest had not, of course, affected in a like degree the seaboard towns and islands of the East Aegean, and among them the imaginative genius of the race now blossomed forth in an astonishing activity of literature and learning. Towards the end of the Seventh Century we find here individual writers who (if we except Hesiod and Archilochus) were the first to earn a true title to perpetual fame. Here the love-song became literature in the hands of the two Lesbians, Alcaeus, and the poetess of passion, Sappho (c. 600). Prose chronicles, though later in the field than verse, here flourished equally ; and at the end of the Sixth Century the Milesian Hecataeus was busy on the quest after historic truth. Miletus was, in fact, pre-eminently famous for the inquisitive temper of her citizens. There Thales, the first ' philosopher ', probed the dark mystery of what the world is made of, foretold the sun's eclipse in 585 B.C., and utilized so well his observation of the weather as to make a ' corner ' in the oil-presses. Thales had many followers ; and the practical nature of his own researches well reflected the general bias of Ionian thought. For these so-called philosophers were often more akin to scientists, and concerned with the study of matter rather than of mind. They worked out the elements of plane geometry some centuries before Euclid. They studied geology. They observed the stars. As biologists they even guessed at the law of evolution ; and some were so far advanced in materialistic reasoning that they explained away the Deity as atmosphere. True, Pythagoras (572–497), a citizen of Samos and later an emigrant to Italy, endeavoured to link up religious mysteries with mathematic law ; but the wiser of his followers abjured such fantastic fusion of piety and logic and reverted to the study of the natural world. The origin of creation, the composition of the elements, the process and significance of change—these long remained the central problems of Hellenic speculation ; and the Ionian instinct for rational inquiry was to prove a lasting stimulus to the search for abstract truth.

But, while in such free and vigorous exercise of their intellectual powers the Greeks of Asia Minor were sharply distinguished from their more superstitious and conservative neighbours of the ' barbaric ' Orient, yet it should be remembered also how much they were affected both for good and ill by their easterly environment. In the artistic forms adopted by their architects and painters we can clearly trace the handiwork of Egypt and Assyria ; Lydia, as we have seen, gave them their coinage ; nor was there ever absent the more insidious and unhealthy influence of Oriental luxury and vice. However vigorous in their early prime, the Ionian Greeks came to be a softer and less virile folk than the Spartans, the Argives, or even the

Athenians; and this was the more unfortunate since by their geographical position they were far more seriously exposed to the danger of political absorption. The most immediate threat came palpably from Lydia, whose kings were bound to covet the Aegean seaports. Nor indeed were the Ionians themselves capable of much opposition to such ambitions. Their numerous city-states were too jealous of each other for effective combination, though some of them were individually by no means to be despised.

Among the island cities Samos was by far the most powerful, attaining during the third quarter of the sixth century a position of great eminence under her famous tyrant Polycrates. Of this man's activities and ambitions enough has been said in a preceding chapter; but it is important here to note that thanks to his powerful rule Samos was able to maintain her independence for twenty years after her sister states of the mainland had already passed under the Persian yoke. Of these mainland cities Miletus was much the most prosperous and important. So great indeed were her resources that when the attack was pressed by successive Lydian monarchs, she alone was able to withstand the pressure. By the middle of the Sixth Century, when Sparta's power was at its height and Athens under bondage to Pisistratus, all the other Ionian cities had fallen beneath the heel of Croesus, by far the most wealthy and ambitious king who had yet held the Lydian throne (560–546). The calamity, however, was not a little lightened by the pro-Greek leanings of the conqueror. Croesus was plainly an admirer of Hellenic culture. At Ephesus [1] may still be seen the remains of sculptured columns which he caused to be erected in the shrine of Artemis. Towards the Delphic oracle he showed a special veneration and tried to win its favour by his lavish gifts. In fact, had subjection to the rule of Croesus been the worst fate in store for the Ionians, their history, and the history of Greece itself, would have followed very different lines. But another and a far more oppressive

[1] The best preserved is in the British Museum.

conqueror was already at the gate ; for Persia's hour had struck.

Before the coming of the Greeks and Romans the centre of civilization in the ancient world had lain in the Middle East ; and, while the swamps and forests of less clement Europe still seethed with barbarous chaos, empires of considerable culture and of enormous strength had arisen in the sun-scorched, fertile plains of Mesopotamia and the river Nile. Egypt, though as early as the Sixteenth Century extending her conquests to the Euphrates basin, had gradually weakened from internal troubles and through the hostile incursions of fierce, wandering hordes. The splendour of her Pharaohs was not indeed extinguished ; but by the end of the Thirteenth Century her empire fell away ; and its place was taken after some lapse of time by the monstrous domination of the Assyrian kings. The military prowess of these cruel Semitic dynasts won sway from the Caspian to the Syrian coast ; Egypt herself was humbled ; and the Bible tells us how the terror of Sennacherib's invasion was miraculously diverted from Jerusalem. But Assyria's supremacy was too tyrannical to last ; and in 612 she too went down before a combination of her subject peoples. Nineveh perished ; and the field was cleared for the rival pretensions of her two destroyers. The Chaldaeans of Babylon absorbed her western conquests from the river Tigris to the Syrian coast ; and their great King, Nebuchadnezzar, who led the Jews into captivity, surpassed in pomp and splendour all previous monarchs of the Orient. But Babylon's day was brief. The rival power of Media, now master over the eastern half of the Assyrian empire, was composed of sterner stuff. For the Medes were members, like the Greeks themselves, of the great Aryan family ; and among their vassal neighbours was a kindred tribe still more worthy to be scion of that vigorous stock. These Persians inhabited a hilly district north-eastward of the gulf which bears their name ; and here arose just fifty years after the Assyrian downfall a prince whose name must always rank among the great ones of the world. With the fables which were embroidered round the infancy of Cyrus (reigned 550–29) we are not here concerned; this much at least is certain, that he successfully challenged his suzerain's supremacy and substituted a Persian for a Median dynasty.[1] Before so ambitious and formidable a neighbour Babylon could not stand; the 'writing on the wall' foretold her doom; and in 539 B.C. the great fortress-town was captured and Cyrus thus became

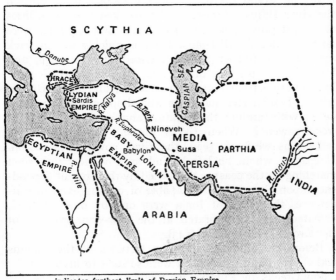

____ indicates furthest limit of Persian Empire

MAP TO ILLUSTRATE EMPIRES ABSORBED BY PERSIAN EMPIRE

Emperor, like the Assyrian Kings before him, from the Caspian to the Syrian coast. Indeed, in some directions his rule extended farther than did theirs. His eastern frontier stretched half-way to the Indus; and in the west —which is more closely related to the purpose of our story —he had swiftly pushed his conquests to the Aegean

[1] The Greeks themselves continued to call the Empire 'Median'; and in the coming struggle sympathy with the barbarian foe was known as 'Medism'.

shores. The realm of Media when first he took it over already abutted directly upon Lydia, the river Halys forming the boundary line, and between the two adjoining powers there had already in past years been considerable conflict. It is therefore not surprising that the Lydian monarch determined to try conclusions with the Persian upstart before his new-won empire should be solidified. Buoyed up by the Delphic oracle's ambiguous prediction that ' he would destroy a mighty empire if he crossed the river Halys ', Croesus had embarked upon hostilities and, as it proved, destroyed *his own*. For his arms were no match for the Persian. He was quickly driven back upon his capital at Sardis, reduced after a siege, and himself made prisoner in 546 B.C. The whole of his large kingdom thus passed into Cyrus' hands ; and for the coastal fringe of small Hellenic cities what hope could there now be of withstanding the greatest and most ambitious of world-powers ? When Cyrus himself turned back, to reduce, as we have seen, the rival power of Babylon, Harpagus, whom he left behind as governor, was soon marching on the coast. Weakened by their recent dependence upon Croesus and incapable of uniting even in self-defence, the cities of Ionia were one by one attacked, defeated, and incorporated in the new-won province of the Great Persian King (543).

Before we follow further the fortunes of the Ionians and the perils in which they were so soon to involve their fellow-Greeks in Europe, we shall do well to trace the progress of the giant dominion of which they had thus fatefully become a part. Cyrus himself did not long outlive his victory over Babylon ; and he fell in war against some outlying tribesmen in 529 B.C. His son Cambyses, though a wayward, unbalanced creature, depicted by Herodotus as half a lunatic, had none the less the energy to keep the realm together and even to add Egypt to its vast domain. After his suicide in 522 and the brief usurpation of an impudent pretender, the throne passed to a worthier successor of the royal house who proved himself well fitted to carry on the work of the great man

who founded it. Darius was his name; and for the
particular task awaiting him he possessed unrivalled genius.
That task was to organize an empire which by now extended
from the Aegean littoral to the Indus basin and from the
Nubian Desert to the Caspian Sea. For administrative
purposes this empire was now divided into twenty provinces,
each governed by a satrap in Darius' name. Great roads
were built and served, as in the Roman Empire, to knit
the whole together. Rapid intelligence and locomotion
were secured by a courier system so efficient that the
distance between Sardis and Susa could be covered in a
week; and confidential agents enabled the Great King
to keep a watchful eye upon his governors. The tribute
wrung by these out of his subject peoples served to keep
the royal exchequer duly filled; and though the Empire's
internal history was for the most part peaceful, yet countless
levies could be raised at need which, if poor in fighting
quality, were at least no less imposing than they were
picturesque. The real core, however, of the Empire's
military strength lay, by land, in the Persian guards who
were disciplined and sturdy fighters, and by sea in the
subject navies of Phoenicia. In the East their supremacy
was now unchallenged; for there was no rival power to
dispute it; and the desire of their master to show himself
also a warrior of ability soon induced him to undertake
an enterprise of Western conquest. About 516 Darius
bridged the Bosphorus and crossed over into Europe at
the head of a formidable host. Whatever his original
objective, he could make no real impression upon the
barbarous tribesmen of the Danube basin, and their
elusive horsemen, when he crossed the river, led him a
rare wild-goose chase over the Scythian steppes. It ended
in something very near to a real catastrophe. For the
Scythian tribesmen doubled round on Darius' rear
and bid fair to cut off his retreat across the Danube.
Had it not been for the staunchness of a certain Histiaeus
and other Ionian Greeks who had been left to guard the
boat bridge across the river and who refused to countenance the Scythians' suggestion that they should turn

traitor and break it down, the Persian army would hardly
have escaped from utter annihilation. Even as it was,
their retreat became a panic. Transport trains were
abandoned. Sick and wounded were left to their fate ;
and it was with infinite relief that they arrived to find
the Greek guardians of the bridge-head still loyal to their
alien master. Darius crossed with his army to the southern
bank, then himself made tracks for home. But he left
his general Magabazus to conquer the Thracian coastlands,
and the sole tangible achievement of the expedition was
the addition of this European outpost to his already
unwieldy empire.

Nevertheless the moral effect of the whole Scythian
fiasco had been profound. The Persian prestige was badly
damaged; and the revelation that the Great King was
not all-powerful served largely to encourage the same
Ionian Greeks, who had stood by him so loyally at the
Danube, to come out sixteen years later in open revolt.
However daring such a project may appear, it was not,
as the issue proved, a hair-brained effort. The revolting
Ionian cities took the generals of Darius six years to overcome. In the opening stages at any rate there was whole-
hearted enthusiasm among the rebels, and a unanimity
of action rare in the history of these jealous city-states.
Clearly the Persian rule was grievously unpopular ; and not
least among the causes of the discontent was the system
which Darius had adopted of establishing Greek tyrants in
the various cities to rule in his interest over their fellow-
countrymen. It was one of these tyrants, the Histiaeus
of Miletus above mentioned, who first served to give the
impetus to the rebellion. A man of restless and ambitious
character, he had obtained permission to extend his power
by a grant of land in Thrace. There his plan was to found
a Milesian colony ; but his operations awoke suspicion
in the mind of the Persian governor. He was recalled
to Darius' capital at Susa ; and so much did he resent
the injustice of this treatment that he determined to
take revenge by stirring up revolt among his Ionian
countrymen, and awaited his opportunity. Meanwhile,

his son-in-law, Aristagoras, who had succeeded him on the throne of Miletus, was also moving in the same direction. Having gained the approval of the Satrap of Lydia, he had attempted the conquest of the island of Naxos, had failed in his project, and fearing the anger of his Persian ally, had determined to cover his mistake by the desperate expedient of open rebellion. He found other Ionians willing ; and from Histiaeus at Susa he received an opportunely encouraging message. Herodotus relates with telling realism how the message was conveyed, branded for secrecy's sake upon the scalp of a faithful servant, who, when the hair had grown again, was sent down to Miletus with instructions that his head should be shaved. The story is one after the chronicler's own heart ; and we may well doubt its truth or importance ; but, be that as it may, the scheme went forward and Ionia was committed to revolt (499). The first step was to dethrone the pro-Persian tyrants and establish democratic governments in their stead ; and this was speedily done. The second was to procure, if possible, the co-operation of European Greece. This mission Aristagoras undertook in person, and he approached the Spartans first. Cleomenes, their King, was at the outset much impressed by the project, especially when shown a map of the world engraved upon bronze ; but when he learnt that the distance to Susa meant at least three months of marching, he rapidly changed his tone and told Aristagoras to quit Sparta by sunset. In Northern Greece the quest for allies was more successful. Eretria, the Euboean state, sent five ships, and Athens, fearful perhaps of Persia's championship of Hippias, and drawn by old ties of kinship to the Ionian cause, sent twenty.[1] Emboldened by the adhesion of these allies, the rebels struck their blow. In 498 they marched up country against Sardis—now the Persian governor's headquarters, as once it had been Croesus'—

---

[1] This policy seems to have emanated from leaders of the old aristocratic faction, now again in the ascendant. The policy of Cleisthenes, and presumably some of his fellow Alcmeonid politicians, had been, as we saw above, pro-Persian not anti-Persian.

occupied the city and burnt it to the ground. But this was the limit of their audacity; for, without more ado, they turned back home; and though the insurrection spread to Caria, to the Hellespont and even so far as Cyprus, retribution was at hand. Histiaeus indeed, who slyly volunteered to crush the rising, at once deserted to the rebels' side; but the Persian commanders could effect their purpose without aid from this volatile Greek. In 494 they appeared before Miletus; defeated the Ionian fleet off the neighbouring island of Ladê, then capturing the city after a long blockade proceeded to sack it utterly and massacre its male inhabitants. With this tragic collapse of its protagonist the rebellion petered out. Miletus could not be replaced, and its destruction was a cruel loss to the Greek world at large. For years the city had led the van of Ionian civilization. Its commerce and industry had made it one of the chief trade-centres of the Aegean basin. Its philosophers, poets and artists had given a lead which Greeks of other states and other times were fruitfully to develop; and the history of Hellenic culture might have followed very different lines, had not a career of infinite promise been thus rudely cut short. At Athens the news of Miletus' capture was received with consternation and horror. A poet, Phrynichus, who was rash enough to produce a tragedy upon the theme of its fall, was heavily fined for reviving so distasteful a topic. Feeling swung round against the withdrawal of help which had led to so dismal a conclusion, and the citizens perhaps began to have some inkling of their own impending peril. Their ships, it is true, had been withdrawn after the sack of Sardis; but, when Darius heard of the part they played in the impudent adventure,

---

PLATE XI

A bas-relief of Athena contemplating a pillar on which, it has been suggested, the names of fallen warriors are supposed to be written. Note the skill with which the falling folds of drapery are saved from mere conventionality by the touches of life-like variety. Date *c.* 450.

MOURNING ATHENA

he vowed to study revenge. Every night at supper, so the story goes, a slave was ordered to repeat three times 'Sire, remember the Athenians!' and to their bitter cost remember them he did. Those twenty ships, as Herodotus grimly remarks, were 'the beginning of troubles between the Barbarians and the Greeks'.

II. THE GREAT PERSIAN WARS

The noblest chapter in the annals of a fighting race is now immediately before us; we are come to the epic

MAP TO ILLUSTRATE PERSIAN WARS
N.B.—Compare also Physical Map of Greece)

years, and most happily for us their record is not merely continuous and full, but also upon the whole reliable. For, whereas hitherto the reconstruction of the narrative has been based largely upon the scattered references of various authors together with the fragmentary evidence collected from monuments, inscriptions and the like, we are now from the time of the Ionian Revolt onward able to take our information from a thoroughgoing and almost contemporary historian. Herodotus, a native of the Greek town of Halicarnassus, inherited to a high degree the inquisitive and philosophic temper of the Asiatic Greeks ; and when a generation after the Great Persian Wars' conclusion he undertook to chronicle its story, he set about his business in a most conscientious fashion. Exiled from his native town, he spent much time in wandering the world, settled for a while at Samos, then at Athens, and later at Thurii in Southern Italy, and meantime made frequent voyages to Egypt (perhaps Babylonia), Pontus and elsewhere. His material, no doubt, was in the main collected from the gossip and reminiscences of the folk whom he encountered ; but where records were available, it is certain that he used them and, though often he quotes the most fantastic fables, he seldom allows his critical faculty to sleep. His love of a good story inclines him to trace movements to the personal motives of his individual characters rather than to some profounder and more general cause ; and a grateful admiration for his Athenian hosts occasionally led him into rash acceptance of their somewhat biased versions of the truth. Yet his views are never narrow. He saw the Great War as a phase of the eternal conflict between East and West. In his endeavour to render the account complete he devoted nearly half his work to the histories of Lydia, of Egypt and of the Persian realm. Above all he possessed the poetic insight to discern the true magnitude of the Greeks' peril and to paint the high romance of their immortal victory. Nor was that victory to his view merely the triumph of his own beloved people over a barbarous foe ; it was a manifestation of the unseen providence which ever waits to visit wrathful vengeance on the presumptuous and the proud ; and, as we read his pages, we seem to be reading not a mere literal record of historic fact, but an inspired and awful epic, in which the springs of human destiny are laid bare to the eye, and the Great Powers which are the true masters of man's fate are seen to move like watchful and controlling spectres among the pigmy puppets of the historian's stage.

In 492—two years after the collapse of the Ionian rebels—came Darius' first attempt to punish the impudence of their European allies, Eretria and Athens. His son-in-law Mardonius was put in command of a powerful expedition; but coasting his way round the North Aegean littoral, he encountered a storm off the jutting rocks of Mount Athos; and so seriously was his fleet crippled that he was forced to turn back home. Two more years passed, and then, in 490,[1] a second expedition was in turn dispatched, some 140 vessels strong. This time its commanders, Datis and Artaphernes, avoiding the perils of the northern route and threading their way across by Naxos and the other Aegean islands, arrived safe off Attica, and after a diversion to Euboea, where Eretria was sacked, they proceeded to disembark upon the north-east coast in the Plain of Marathon, a narrow strip of marshy level lying between the mountain and the sea. Hither they were directed, so the story goes, by Hippias, the son and successor of Pisistratus the Tyrant, whom twenty years of exile from his native city had left but the more eager to recover his lost power, even by Persian aid; and his choice of a landing-place was based, it would appear, on a secret understanding with friends within the town. For faction was still rife in Athens; and the Alcmeonid family were once more playing a highly ingenious, but on this occasion by no means a creditable part. The democratic constitution which had been the handiwork of their old leader, Cleisthenes, was still in its infancy and still liable to be overthrown by the malcontent nobility. It seems, therefore, to have been the intention of some Alcmeonids, supported by Hipparchus, the tyrant's relative, to welcome back their old enemy Hippias, and thus even at the cost of treachery to perpetuate at once their own authority and also the

---

[1] Munro in the Cambridge Ancient History reckons the date as 491, but it seems best to adhere to the traditional date, as given by Herodotus.

predominance of their following, the democratic **mob.**
For among the lower orders the favours and indulgence
of the Tyrant house were still gratefully remembered,
and it well might be that the restoration of Hippias, while
destroying their political liberty, would at any rate secure
for them the upper hand against the detested nobles.
But though the idea found favour with some of the Alcmeonid faction (whose former leader, Cleisthenes, it will
be remembered, had strongly urged an alliance with
Persia), yet it so fell out that there had just arrived in
Athens a man of far different views. Miltiades (the
nephew and successor of that Miltiades who half a century
before had founded a colony in the Thracian Chersonese
and ruled it as a tyrant) had been forced by the barbarian
onset to abandon his inherited kingdom and make for
home.   Round him as a wholehearted antagonist of
Persia, now rallied at once the aristocratic opponents of
the Alcmeonids' treacherous scheme ; and in the coming
crisis he was to prove himself the heart and soul of the
national resistance.   After a bitter contest he was elected
to be one of the ten new tribal generals.   His pushful
character appears from this moment onwards to have
carried all before him.   Even Callimachus the Polemarch
and titular commander-in-chief seems to have bowed
to his decisions and he obtained almost a free hand in
directing operations when the time for fighting came.
On news of the enemy's arrival it was he who gave the
lead, and all hesitation vanished.   The armed forces of
the state were put in readiness to march.   A swift runner
named Philippides was sent off in haste to Sparta.   The
distance to that city was 140 miles ; we are told he covered
it within two days ; but the Spartans were keeping a

PLATE XII

A small bronze statuette of a Greek hoplite, now in
the Berlin Museum. It shows a plumed helmet,
breastplate, linen kilt and greaves—but the hoplite's
main defence lies in his shield. Cp. barbarian archer
in Plate XIII.

Luder

GREEK HOPLITE

festival. Religious scruple forbade them to abandon it and their force appeared in Attica too late to fight. Thus, but for a contingent from Plataea, their small neighbour,[1] the Athenians were left to meet the invader single-handed. Their citizen army, perhaps ten thousand hoplites strong, was marched out over the mountain which looks down on Marathon and encamped upon the foothills, commanding the road to Athens and in watchful expectation of the enemy's next move. They were certainly outnumbered, perhaps by two to one, and hoping for Spartan aid, they let several days go by in wise inaction. Then the Persians showed their hand. The plot with their friends in Athens was now ripe. The town itself was left defenceless by the departure of the army, which was, as we have seen, pinned down at Marathon and could not abandon its post without at once throwing open the road to Athens. If, while it was thus detained there, a part of the Persian army should re-embark on shipboard and round Cape Sunium, the Alcmeonids were waiting to admit them to the town. The moment for the coup had clearly come.

One of the chief motives, we are told, for the Persian disembarkation at Marathon had been that the plain was convenient for the manœuvres of their cavalry. That cavalry, in fact, constituted by far the most formidable menace to any force of Greeks. For they themselves had no means of countering the danger of encirclement with which it threatened them. Small wonder then that they clung to the shelter of the foot-hills and refused battle till they might secure at least some superiority of numbers. The situation was therefore dominated by the presence of the Persian cavalry ; yet the extraordinary thing is that in the engagement which was presently to follow, no mention whatever is made of this same cavalry. The inference is obvious. One day the Persians must have got tired of waiting and, resolving on a coup, must have re-embarked their cavalry on shipboard, pre-paratory to a voyage round Cape Sunium and a swift ride upon Athens. On the instant Miltiades sized up the situa-

---

[1] Plataea had seceded from Thebes and joined Athens in 519.

tion. From a military point of view it was critical enough, but simultaneously the most formidable portion of the enemy's force was temporarily out of action. On his advice the Athenians launched a swift attack. By a skilful arrangement they so reinforced their wings that, though the weakened centre suffered, they enveloped and rolled up the Persian line. The crash of the heavy-armed hoplites, advancing, so Herodotus declares, at the ' quick pace ', was more than the Oriental soldiery could stand ; and it was now, in fact, proved once and for all that the Persian infantry were no match for the Greeks. With their short spears, wicker shields, and quilted body covering, they could make but a feeble show against the long lances of the hoplite shield-line. The surprise deprived them even of the opportunity to deploy their more dangerous archers ; and, pluckily as they fought, none but a battered remnant succeeded in escaping to the ships. There a fierce tussle took place ; and the story is told how the brother of Aeschylus the poet, clutching the stern of a Persian galley, hung on grimly till his arm was completely severed with an axe. But the perils of the day were not yet over. As the battle drew to its end, and the Persian survivors had got safely to sea, there came suddenly the signal which they had long awaited. From the mountain-top above the plain of Marathon a shield was flashed ; it was an intimation from the pro-Persian party in Athens that the city was now ready for the coup. It was a perilous and anxious moment for the victorious army. They themselves were a twenty miles march or more away from Athens, and already the cavalry which had embarked that morning might be rounding Sunium. Miltiades' battle-worn heroes turned from the scene of the slaughter. All through the long afternoon and evening

---

PLATE XIII

A barbarian archer designed on the interior of a drinking vessel. It has been well said of the draughtsmanship of this piece, that ' no man could draw better, he could merely draw differently '.

BARBARIAN ARCHER

they raced against time ; and next day when the enemy fleet appeared in the offing, there were they at their posts. In the face of such defenders no landing was attempted, and Athens was saved.

It was a proud moment for the little town—and one long remembered among after-generations—when her people realized that they had met the army of the world's most powerful monarch and beaten it in fair fight. Their victory at Marathon, though they themselves scarcely knew it, marked the birth of their national greatness and, what was more, gave them courage to meet the even sterner ordeal which still lay ahead. But, if the whole citizen body participated in the fruits of that victory, it was to the aristocratic faction, in particular, that fell the chief share of its credit ; and it now remained to be seen to what end they would turn their twofold triumph, not merely over the enemy without, but also over political opponents within the town. Miltiades, their leader and the hero of the hour, was not a man to rest idle, and his plans were soon formed. Having obtained a free hand in the use of an expeditionary squadron, he sailed off without specifying his goal, to the island of Paros ; and, on the ground that it had lent treacherous aid to the enemy,[1] proceeded to lay its town under siege. What use he would have made of its capture we can only guess. It may well be that, had he come back to Athens victorious, he would have attempted to set himself up as tyrant. But the siege failed. Miltiades himself was wounded in the thigh, gangrene set in, and he returned home a dying man. His failure gave the Alcmeonids, discredited since Marathon, the opportunity of their revenge. They impeached the famous general for his unauthorized adventure, haled him into court despite his mortal sickness and succeeded in imposing on him a heavy fine which he never lived to pay. So the tables were turned, and the Alcmeonids had retrieved their position ; and as leaders of the popular party they appeared to have the game in their hands.

[1] Doubtless he wished to secure it as a precaution against a fresh Persian invasion.

In reality, however, the tide of democracy was now moving too fast even for their calculations. When in 487 it was decided that archons should henceforth be chosen by lot, it seems likely that some of them opposed the reform. In any case the leadership began to slip away from them ; and one by one their chief statesmen were ostracized, Megacles, Cleisthenes' nephew, in 486, Xanthippus, the father of Pericles, in 484, and finally Aristides, the colleague of Cleisthenes, in 482. It can hardly be doubted that this progressive decline in the Alcmeonids' fortunes was due to the growing self-assertion of the mercantile class [1] ; and at the head of this class there had recently emerged a new figure—not a noble masquerading as popular champion, but a commoner drawn from the ranks. This man was Themistocles, perhaps the most brilliant and arresting personality in the whole history of this keen-witted folk. The son of obscure parents, he does not seem to have received the education of well-bred gentlemen ; for he lacked the normal accomplishment of playing the harp. But he associated with professional teachers of political science and from boyhood had practised the study of rhetoric. He belonged, in fact, to a new type and a new age ; and, trained as he was to a business career, his appearance in the forefront of politics, hitherto the nobles' monopoly, was a striking symptom of the swift democratic evolution. To the problems of State he brought a mind not merely fresh in outlook, but singularly fertile in initiative and resource. There were numberless tales told of the quickness of his sallies and of his shrewd but somewhat underhand diplomacy. These, however, did but small justice to Themistocles' real genius. He was a statesman of the first order, and to his imaginative foresight the city now owed a new direction of policy

---

[1] Doubtless the ineffectiveness of their prosecution of the war against Aegina (see below) was also a contributory cause of the Alcmeonids' decline, Themistocles and his mercantile party wishing to push the campaign more hotly. For the ostracism of Megacles and also of Hipparchus in 487 the part they played in 490 was the more probable reason.

which not merely, as we shall see, paved the way for her own future ascendancy, but also proved the means of the salvation of Greece in the approaching struggle with Persia. It was Themistocles, in short, who made Athens a sea power. Already in 493 [1] he had begun a scheme whereby a new rock-guarded harbour, infinitely safer than the broad sandy bay of Phaleron then in use, should be developed at Peiraeus. The Persian invasion had delayed the work ; but in the years which followed, the opportunity arose for an even bolder departure. In 487 the Athenians had gone to war with the neighbouring island of Aegina, at that time by far the strongest of Greek naval powers. As their own fleet was insignificant, they had appealed for help to Corinth ; and Corinth, still intent on backing Athens against the commercial power of Aegina, had obligingly transferred to them a squadron of twenty sail, charging the nominal sum of five drachmae a ship, which works out at about half-a-crown. Even so, after a preliminary success, the Athenians had been worsted in battle, and, as hostilities dragged on in desultory fashion, suffered much from raids on their coast. In 482 a rich vein of ore was discovered in their silver-mines at Laurium ; and when it was proposed to expend the proceeds in distribution among all the citizens, Themistocles proposed that they should be applied to the construction of new ships. In a couple of years two hundred galleys had been put into commission, but it was not against Aegina that these were to be used. For now the Persian peril was once again looming large on the horizon ; and Themistocles' policy was to find its justification in a manner which few beyond its author can possibly have foreseen, and perhaps not even its author himself.

For meanwhile at Susa the disgrace of Marathon was not forgotten. Darius, indeed, had died in 486 B.C. ; but his successor Xerxes, after some demur, had resolved to execute his father's purpose and return to the attack. His preparations were lengthy, and (with all allowance

[1] Or possibly in 488.

made for Greek exaggeration) on a gigantic scale. It added a telling touch to the superstitious interpretation of his downfall that he even endeavoured to circumvent the elements and to vanquish Nature herself. Through the isthmus of Mount Athos, where his first fleet had been wrecked, he dug a ship canal. The Hellespont he bridged with boats, persisting in the project when storms carried it away and impiously cursing the unruly water which thus dared to oppose his will. The army which he mustered in the neighbourhood of Sardis was of unprecedented size. Herodotus, who clearly had access to some official census, reckoned infantry alone at 1,700,000 and the personnel of the whole expedition at just three times that number. Even of modern critics few would put the total at less than a quarter million ; and the provisioning alone of such a host was itself a portentous problem. Food depots were prepared along the projected route ; a powerful fleet of merchantmen was to follow stage by stage. The Phoenician navy, together with a pressed contingent of Ionian Greeks, was present in full force ; and it was an essential feature of the Persian strategy, dictated to some extent by their mutual dependence, that the army and the fleet should move in unison. Thus organized and led in person by the Great King himself, the unwieldy expedition set out from Asia into Europe, crossed by the bridge of boats, passed through the Thracian coast-lands, still held by Persian garrisons, and entering Macedonia stood thus upon the threshold of Greece. The very rivers encountered on the march were dried up by the watering of its men and beasts (480 B.C.).

Of such vast movements the Greeks themselves were not long ignorant ; and it was clear to all that they had now to deal with no mere passing danger of a punitive incursion, but with a scheme of permanent conquest. The nerve of many northern states was badly shaken. Thessaly and Boeotia were inclined to ' medize ' and accept the yoke from which escape seemed hopeless. Even the oracle of Delphi wavered, and ever after suffered in prestige for its prophetic failure to back the winning side.

Happily in the south there prevailed bolder counsels. Argos, indeed, still smarting from her late defeat by Sparta,[1] was a doubtful quantity. But the security afforded them by the defensible isthmus encouraged others to follow Sparta's lead and prepare for stern resistance. The fear, however, that the Persian fleet might turn their land position compelled them to seek naval succour where they could ; and an urgent appeal was sent to western states. Corcyra proved lukewarm, and her promise of help came to nothing. Gelo, the Tyrant of Syracuse, might have rendered yeoman service, but all his strength was now needed to meet a similar danger at home ; for an attack from Carthage was impending, and Sicily, in fact, was only saved by a remarkable victory at Himera, won (as tradition appropriately reckoned) on the selfsame day as Salamis.[2] So no naval succour came from the west ; and most crucial therefore was the attitude of Athens. There, most happily, courage was still high. The tempting voices of Hippias' supporters were now hushed. The mercantile class, backing the strong policy of Themistocles, was uppermost, and resolve was taken to resist the invader to the very death.

But though Athenian loyalty was welcome and the value of her fleet duly appraised, yet her actual adherence proved an awkward complication to the Allies' strategy. For, were the isthmus chosen as the point to be defended, Attica would meanwhile be overrun ; and some suitable position further north was therefore to be sought. Two suggested themselves. One—the most distant—was in the pass of Tempe among the mountains of Northern Thessaly, and thither the force was sent ; but an alternative inland route was discovered to be open to the Persians ; so seeing themselves in danger of being outflanked, the Greeks retired, and Thessaly was lost. The second position was more promising. The solid barrier of impenetrable mountain which protects Phocis and Boeotia on the north could only be circumvented by following the foreshore

---

[1] At the battle of Sepeia, 494 B.C. See page 90.
[2] See page 218.

along which the road skirted narrowly between mountain-cliff and sea. No alternative route here existed for an army,[1] and this narrow gateway, in which Persian numbers could not possibly be used, even a small Greek force might hold impregnably. To Thermopylae, therefore (for so the pass was named), a mixed force of allies was dispatched under Leonidas, the Spartan King. There were Thebans,

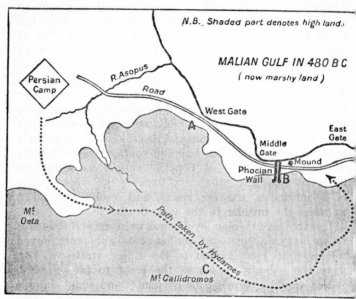

A GREEKS' FIRST STAND   B GREEKS' LAST STAND   C PHOCIANS' POSITION

MAP TO ILLUSTRATE BATTLE OF THERMOPYLAE

Thespians, Phocians and others in the host; and Leonidas himself brought with him a large auxiliary supplement of Helots, though of true Spartan hoplites he had but a

[1] There did, indeed, exist a route by the narrow ravine of the Asopus, by which subsequently a Persian detachment made its way to Delphi. It was not, however, suitable for the movement of a large army, which could have been held in check by a handful of men. It is of course probable that it was at this moment held by Greek troops.

bare three hundred. But if this small contingent of scarcely more than six or seven thousand was to hold the pass till reinforcements reached them, it was nevertheless essential that the Greek fleet should co-operate and guard their seaward flank. Happily the strait between the mainland and Euboea offered an excellent battle-ground ; for in these narrow waters Persian numbers could not tell, and the Greek fleet, in fact, did wonders. Posted at Artemisium and in close touch with Thermopylae, they not merely defied all efforts to dislodge them, but on more than one occasion they attacked the enemy when scattered at his moorings and inflicted heavy damage on isolated portions of his fleet. Weather, too, favoured them ; one severe storm wrought considerable havoc on the Persians while operating north of Euboea, and when they attempted to circumnavigate the island and come in on the Greek rear, they were badly mauled by another. Thus the naval strategy of which Themistocles undoubtedly was author proved so far justified, and it was not from any failure of the fleet that the tragic issue came.

The first phases of the struggle by land were not less promising. Regiment after regiment, Xerxes had hurled his troops on Leonidas' position, spurring their flagging spirits with the lash and finally engaging his crack corps, named the ' Immortals ', the pride and terror of the East ; but all in vain. Cooped on the narrow frontage and opposed by the serried shield-line of the Greeks, the Orientals suffered terribly. Corpses littered the road, and many fell into the sea. But Greek treachery found a way where Persian valour failed. Through the information of a local guide Xerxes learnt of the existence of a footpath scaling the mountains and debouching on the rear of the Greek position. Late one evening ' at the time of the lighting of lamps ' the Immortals took that path, surprised at dawn the Phocian outpost set to guard it, and, descending behind them, caught the Greeks as in a trap. Though a swift retreat might possibly have saved him, Leonidas resolved to stand his ground ; and, keeping the Thebans, the Thespians and his own three hundred Spartans, he sent the others back—to meet presumably the menace on his rear. If that were so, they ill performed their mission ; for we hear of no engagement and the jaws of the trap closed in. Leonidas and his company sold their lives dearly and went down fighting to the end. The courage of that last stand won a name of imperishable glory ; and though the loss of the pass opened the southward road to the invader, yet the heroic example thus set by its defenders did much to stiffen the resolution of their countrymen. When a Persian detachment made its way to Delphi and was repulsed by the determination of the mountaineer inhabitants who rolled boulders down the hillside on the invaders' heads, it seemed almost as though the gods of Greece had at length begun to assert themselves to some purpose.

To the Peloponnesian Greeks Thermopylae threw a new and critical importance on the defence of the Isthmus ; and they redoubled their efforts to complete its fortification. But for the unfortunate Athenians, upon whose country the invader was rapidly descending, there was small comfort in such measures. Yet they did not lose heart, and the desperate policy they now adopted was a measure of their indomitable spirit. Shipping away their womenfolk and children to places of safety on the neighbouring shores, they abandoned the city, and manning every trireme that was fit to take the water stood by in the Straits of Salamis to await the Persian fleet. Some few of them, indeed, more superstitious or more obstinate than the rest, refused to quit the city, and pinning their faith upon the Delphic oracle's advice to rely on their ' wooden wall ', barricaded themselves as best they might in the Acropolis. Their defence was stubborn and unexpectedly prolonged ; but the end was certain, and the Athenian sailors in the neighbouring straits saw first the buildings of the town itself, and then of the sacred citadel above it, go up in flame and smoke. This was a trying moment, and doubly so since the Peloponnesian allies now favoured the abandonment of Salamis. The Spartan Eurybiades, who commanded the whole fleet, was urged by the Corinthian admiral to transfer its station to the isthmus where, as at Thermopylae, it might co-operate with allied forces on land. This, however, would have led to an engagement against superior numbers in an open sea ; and Themistocles rightly divined that a battle in the narrows alone offered any sure prospect of success. He carried the day against the Corinthian's policy by a threat to withdraw his ships from the alliance

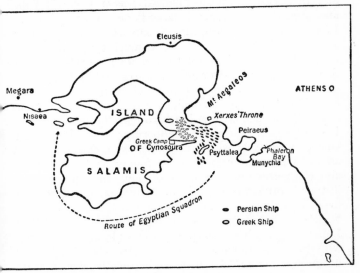

MAP TO ILLUSTRATE BATTLE OF SALAMIS

and sail them off in search of a new home elsewhere ; being anxious, however, to make doubly certain, he dispatched a secret message to King Xerxes, posing as a well-wisher and warning him that the Greeks intended flight and that to catch them would demand immediate action. The Persian took the bait. He at once sent off an Egyptian squadron to double round Salamis and block the further exit from the narrows whereby lay the Greeks' retreat towards Corinth. Meanwhile, as night closed in, he deployed the rest of his fleet between Phaleron and the island, thus blocking the eastern exit as he had blocked the western ; and on the rock of Psyttalea, which lies midway in the channel, he posted a contingent of his infantry. Day dawned, and the Greeks had barely pushed their ships out from the foreshore and were rounding the long promontory of Cynossura, or the Dog's Tail, when they saw the great Armada come streaming up the strait. By a feigned retreat they lured the Persians in still further and then closed. What followed was a pell-mell fight, and from the first it was long odds on the Greek galleys. In those narrow waters the Persian numbers never told, and their cumbersome vessels, answering a slower helm, fell swiftly to the rams of their more nimble opponents. Soon the sea was strewn with hulks. Ship fell foul of ship in the endeavour to escape, or to manœuvre ; and the King, seated on an eminence overlooking the whole channel, watched with rising horror as the disaster grew. His ships, indeed, fought stubbornly ; even the Ionian Greeks, who might well have chosen the moment to desert an alien service, seem to have fought as hard as any ; and Herodotus relates with an obvious, though somewhat ill-timed, pride the exploits of Artemisia, the Queen of his own birthplace. In eluding the pursuit of an Athenian vessel she ran down of set design the ship of a fellow-Ionian ; by which stratagem she deceived both her pursuer, who desisted, and equally King Xerxes, who, delighted at her prowess, cried, ' My men are become women, and my women men'. The struggle lasted all day ; but by sun-down all was over. As the enemy struggled to break clear of the narrows, an Aeginetan squadron fought round upon their course and took heavy toll of the fugitives. Then, as a finishing touch, when the fighting died down, a party of Greek hoplites rowed across to Psyttalea and slaughtered its garrison to a man. It is more than probable that Aeschylus, the poet, was himself of the party ; for in his play ' The Persians ' he describes the butchery in a bloodthirsty detail peculiarly vivid.

Xerxes grasped at once the full meaning of the disaster. Not merely did the loss of his fleet forbid further advance to his army; but the news of it was only too likely to shake the allegiance of Ionia behind him. He took no risks of being cut off in Europe, but set off at once for the Hellespont and Asia, leaving Mardonius—for he still had hopes of conquest—in command of the land forces.

That Salamis had saved the Peloponnese is certain; for except by a fleet the Isthmus line could never have been turned. Over Northern Greece, however, there still hung a menace. Mardonius wintered in Thessaly, and when with spring he returned into Boeotia, it was clearly his intention to secure a Persian satrapy over the lands he held. With the Athenians, indeed, he first tried what diplomacy could do, making a specious offer of independence and alliance. When they still held firm in their refusal, he descended once again upon the city and once again its inhabitants were forced to flee. Urgent appeals for help went south to Sparta; and rather than lose the invaluable support of the Athenian navy, the unwilling Spartans at last marched. Five thousand hoplites and a helot force of many times that number went up behind Pausanias into Attica. Contingents from Athens and the other allied states swelled the host to near a hundred thousand; and when the enemy retired over the ridge of Mount Cithaeron and dropped into the Boeotian plain, all followed on his tracks. They found him strongly posted under the foothills near Plataea, some ten miles or so distant from his base at Thebes (479 B.C.).

Once again, as at Marathon, the chief danger to be reckoned with lay in the formidable efficiency of the Persian cavalry. Very wisely, therefore, the Greeks took up their station on the foothills of Cithaeron and refused to be drawn into the plain. The Persian generalissimo, indeed, sent up a picked force of his cavalry to attack them there, with the result that it was roughly handled and its commander killed. This success seems to have emboldened the Greeks, who were naturally anxious for a swift decision, to take the offensive at last. They moved down towards the plain, intending doubtless to precipitate a battle on ground which would still favour

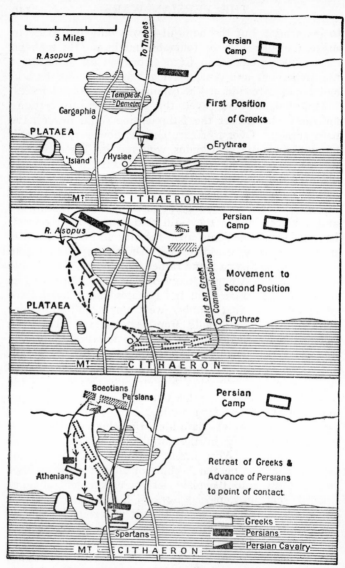

First Position of Greeks

Movement to Second Position

Retreat of Greeks & Advance of Persians to point of contact.

PLAN TO ILLUSTRATE BATTLE OF PLATAEA

the superiority of their foot. For between them and the
Asopus, beyond which lay the Persian camp, there stood
a scatter of low hills over which the dreaded horsemen of
Mardonius could scarcely manœuvre without great difficulty. They advanced accordingly to a position behind
these hills, their left flank resting on the Asopus river-bed,
and their line extending towards the Cithaeron foothills,
within easy striking distance of the enemy. But it was now
the Persians' turn to refuse engagement. A stalemate
followed, and for some while—Herodotus says ten days,
but probably exaggerates—the two armies lay confronted.
Nevertheless the Greeks' situation was anything but
comfortable. Their watering parties—and it was partly
to get water that they had descended to the plain—were
harried from the Asopus by the Persian horsemen. Their
supply-trains, while crossing the mountain pass behind
them, were cut in upon by raiders. Thirst and privation
demanded either advance or retreat ; and Pausanias chose
retreat. A withdrawal towards the foothills of Cithaeron
was planned to take place under cover of night. It was
a hazardous manœuvre, but it seems more than likely
that it was also intended to lure the Persians forward
into a decisive engagement. A curious story is told of
a Lacedaemonian captain, by name Amompharetus, who,
deeming retreat disgraceful, refused point blank to budge,
and on Pausanias protesting, seized up a monster boulder
which he threw at his feet exclaiming, ' With this pebble'
(a word that in Greek meant also ' a vote ') ' I cast my
lot against running away from the strangers.' Now
Herodotus must have drawn this story (as he drew most
of his information) from Athenian sources, which were
in his day strongly biased against Sparta ; and behind
the malicious anecdote we can perhaps detect the truth
of Pausanias' intentions. Sparta's captains were not
normally insubordinate, nor in matters of warfare were
her commanders fools. It is at least probable that Amompharetus' detachment was deliberately left behind to
be seen by the Persians, when morning broke, in tempting
isolation. If a bait was intended, the bait was certainly

taken ; for when at dawn Amompharetus rejoined the Spartan main body, the Persian cavalry were already in hot pursuit, closely followed by the Persian infantry. Their attack was delivered on the Spartan army from which in the natural confusion of a night retirement, the other Greek bodies had got widely parted. Thus left to meet single-handed the full brunt of the enemy's attack, Pausanias' men were hard put to it and for a while things looked black enough.

From behind a barricade of wicker shields the Persians played their arrows with devastating aim ; but at length the Spartan hoplites bore them down, killing Mardonius and pursuing the remnant to their camp on the Asopus. Here indeed the Spartans, unskilled as they were in methods of siege warfare, proved at a loss ; but by now the other Greeks, who had been kept in play by a force of turn-coat Boeotians, were hurrying on the scene, and the Athenians breached the palisade. The spoil taken among the tents was rich in gold and silver, and few Persians were left alive. Thus, despite the blundering of their commanders, the Greeks by sheer superiority of arms had overthrown the host of the greatest military power then known to the ancient world, and their ordeal was at an end. They signalized their victory by erecting at Delphi a golden tripod,[1] inscribed on its base with the names of the allied states, and by punishing the treachery of pro-Persian Thebes with the execution of her leading men. Overrun as she had been by the invader, submission had been perhaps Thebes' only choice ; but her unpatriotic behaviour was never wholly forgotten, and by the Athenians least of all.

One further blow (which Greek love of coincidence assigned to the selfsame day as Plataea) served to complete the triumph. The allied fleet under the Spartan Leotychidas had since Salamis lain inactive ; and, though the Phoenicians were at Samos keeping watch upon Ionia, would adventure itself no nearer than to Delos, half-way over. The news, however, of their army's northward

---

[1] Its base is now in the Hippodrome at Constantinople.

march seems to have stirred the sailors. The Athenians'
reluctance to engage their fleet while their homes were
at the enemy's mercy, must now at least have vanished ;
and, when an appeal came from the Samians, they set
out for the island. On their approach the Persians
retired to the mainland and beached their ships under the
shelter of Cape Mycalê ; but the Greeks were nothing
daunted ; they landed, burnt the ships, assailed the camp
and butchered all they found there. Not least significant
in that day's battle was the desertion of the Ionian force
—loyal hitherto in its service of the King—to the side of
their compatriots. Mycalê was a happy presage of Ionia's
liberation. Nothing more than a helping hand was
needed to secure her release from the barbarian yoke ; and
the only question now was whose that hand should be.

CHAPTER VIII

FROM DELIAN LEAGUE TO ATHENIAN EMPIRE

I. The League

TO Sparta on the morrow of Mycalê and Plataea all eyes very naturally turned. This moment marked indeed for her the very summit of a power which for more than half a century had fast been growing. Already, it must be remembered, the Peloponnesian states were in a large degree her vassals ; and her most serious rival, Argos, had in 494 been overwhelmed and crippled for some twenty years to come. Cleomenes, her able and energetic King, to whom this victory was due, had fallen into disgrace before Marathon and, according to Herodotus, though recalled soon after the battle, went out of his wits and finally made away with himself miserably in prison. But he left his country in undisputed leadership of Hellas ; and during the Great Invasion her Kings were, as we have seen, accepted as the inevitable commanders not only on land, but by sea. Nothing, therefore, was more natural than that on the defeat of Persia the Ionian Greeks should look to Sparta to secure and maintain their independence—and Sparta failed them. True, Pausanias, the victor of Plataea, seems at first to have had some inkling of the opportunity. He sailed to Cyprus, and freed most of the island from Persian garrisons, sailed back to Byzantium and there did the same ; but, like many other Spartans, bred as they were in the cramping atmosphere of an over-disciplined drill-yard, he lacked real depth of character, and success soon turned his head. He began to give himself the airs of a despot, affected Persian dress and Oriental luxury, and outraged all the Greek states by erasing their names from the Plataean tripod and replacing them by his own. It was indeed little wonder that in 478 he was recalled by the home authorities to Sparta and relieved of his command. Soon after, however, he set out for Byzantium again as a free-lance, and regaining possession of the town, embarked on a treasonable intrigue against the liberties of Greece with the Persian satrap himself. In 471 he was once more recalled to answer for his actions, and even at home in Sparta he continued his correspondence with Persia, till his courier, suspicious of the fact that no former courier had returned alive, opened a letter and laid information with the ephors. The ephors turned eavesdroppers and caught Pausanias at his game ; and when he fled for sanctuary to a neighbouring shrine, they walled up the door and left him to his fate. When the wretched man was about to breathe his last, they grew nervous of the stigma of polluting holy ground and dragged him out to die.

No one remained in Sparta capable of conceiving an imaginative policy. Completely lacking in intellectual education and sadly hidebound by their traditional conservatism, these folk were incapable of a wide or generous outlook. The coasts of the Peloponnese bounded their political horizon. The serf-system, too, on which their whole domestic economy was based, was a source of constant weakness, and the fear of a Helot rising was never far distant from their minds. Above all, they were no true sailors. They lacked the adventurous spirit of a maritime people, and were timid of distant adventure. It will be recalled how even Cleomenes himself had rejected the Ionians' appeal when informed of the three months' journey which lay between Sardis and Susa. History was now to repeat itself, and the Ionians, being forced once again to look elsewhere for a champion, looked inevitably to Athens.

When after Plataea the Athenians came back for a second time to the task of rebuilding their homes, it was in no chastened mood. In Herodotus' time the tradition was current that on the very day after the Persians had departed, leaving the city a heap of smouldering ruins, the charred stump of Athena's sacred olive had put forth a fresh green sprout. Whether mythical or no, the story was at least a telling symbol of the spirit abroad in the town. Fresh from the memory of their tremendous sacrifice and of the triumph to which it had led them, the citizens were uplifted by the most intense and conscious pride. Salamis was to them like Crecy and Agincourt and the defeat of the Spanish Armada, all rolled into one. Years after it remained the commonplace of patriotic oratory to recall those stirring days. Simply to be an Athenian was to share in the glory of them, and to have played an active part therein was a man's proudest memory; thus on the tombstone of Aeschylus the poet —the greatest poet perhaps of the whole century—the one fact of his career thought worthy of record was not his literary eminence, but this: ' To his good soldierhood is witness borne by the long-haired Mede who felt it.' The mood of exaltation lasted long in Athens; and for the moment, at any rate, it served to carry her strongly through every obstacle and discouragement to the fulfilment of her destiny. When after Plataea Sparta jealously objected to the rebuilding of her walls, the protest was ignored; and while Themistocles went south and by his glib denials kept the credulous Spartans inactive, the citizens set to, man, woman and child, on the work of completion. Thus Athens was refortified, and more than this, a defensive wall was built, on Themistocles' suggestion, round the rock-encircled roadsteads of Peiraeus and Munychia, now coming into regular use instead of the broad sandy bay of Phaleron, which, though handy enough to beach a fishing fleet, was too exposed to risk from storms or raiders to form the permanent harbour of Athens. It remained for Pericles, just twenty years later, to secure the communications between town and port by a pair of five-mile walls,[1] thus rendering Athens impregnable as an island and putting it beyond the reach of an invader to cut her off from her trade and food supplies.

[1] A third central wall was added later, probably merely to strengthen one flank.

Such labours of reconstruction might well have been sufficient to absorb the thoughts of her citizens ; but now was to be revealed the full measure of her enterprise and energy. Where Sparta hesitated and, as we have seen, eventually withdrew, Athens threw herself whole-heartedly into the cause of Ionian liberation. She it was who, stronghold by stronghold, reduced the Persian garrisons in Thrace ; she it was who after a tedious siege recovered Sestos, the key-fortress to the Hellespont ; nor was she tamely content to see the Persians quit Ionian soil. In 478 she took the lead in forming a great confed-eracy of Aegean towns and islands for the double purpose of permanent security and, if possible, of revenge. The intention was to organize a fleet capable of liberating the remainder of the enslaved Greek cities, repelling any further Persian offensive and even, if need be, of carrying war into enemy waters. Athens herself provided most of the ships. Chios, Lesbos, Samos and one or two more of the larger islands provided squadrons too. The other members of the League (even at the start several score at least in number, but too small and too scattered for effec-tive mobilization) were well content to contribute money only. The annual total to be raised was fixed eventually, if not at first, at 460 talents ; and Aristides, famed for his integrity, was entrusted with the task of assessing what share each member was to pay. When all was in working order ' Helleno-tamiae ' or ' Stewards of Greece ' were appointed to collect the money ; and the money, when collected, was lodged for safe keeping in Apollo's shrine at Delos, already from ancient times the centre of a semi-religious Ionian league. To Delos, too, the members of the League sent delegates to confer on common policy ; but from the first the Athenian voice was pre-dominant in these councils, and still more significant, the Stewards of the League's finance were men born and chosen in Athens.[1]

[1] It is possible but not certain that this limitation was not resorted to until after the transference of the Treasury from Delos to Athens in 454.

It was indeed from start to finish the pushful and ambitious spirit of the Athenian people which conceived and directed the activities of the League. The chief authors of its being passed in due course away. Aristides died before a dozen years were out ; and by then already Themistocles had vanished from the scene. In 471 he was ostracized from Athens, where, despite his many services, the jealousy of his more aristocratic rivals seems to have dogged him to the end. In exile he took a hand in Pausanias' intrigues, was discovered, tried in absence, formally outlawed, and fled to Persia. The King received him well and appointed him governor of Magnesia ; and there Themistocles lived out his life in pitiful dependence on his ancient enemy—a tragic end to the career of one whose genius had saved Greece (after 464).

Before this, however, there had appeared another figure with whom, more than any, are to be identified the chief exploits of the confederate fleet. This was Cimon, son of Miltiades, the hero of Marathon. A man of downright but genial and very popular character, trained on the old-fashioned methods of music and gymnastic rather than of Periclean intellectualism, and affecting a simplicity of life and dress more Dorian than Athenian, he was as much a friend and admirer of the Spartans as he was Persia's implacable foe ; and their defection from the great crusade must at the outset of his career have caused him keen disappointment. But that defection did not daunt him. We find him in Thrace during 476 besieging the Persian garrison of Eion. Later he is attacking a nest of common pirates in the rocky island of Scyros ; and in 466 [1] came his greatest achievement, the campaign and battle of Eurymedon. There seems little doubt (though our evidence is scanty) that the Phoenician navy was once again mobilizing for an attack on the Aegean. Cimon met it nearly half-way. Cruising along the south coast of Asia Minor and liberating as he went the Greek cities of Caria, he encountered the new armada at the mouth of the Eurymedon river. When the enemy retired

[1] The date is conjectural. It may have been earlier.

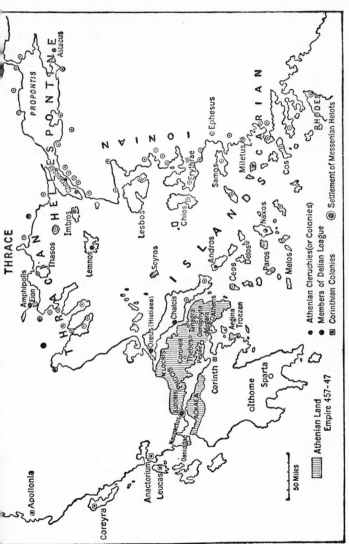

MAP TO ILLUSTRATE ATHENIAN EMPIRE

Legend:
- Athenian Cleruchies (or Colonies)
- Members of Delian League
- Corinthian Colonies
- Settlement of Messenian Helots

Athenian Land Empire 457-47

50 Miles

THRACE

PROPONTIS

Apollonia

Corcyra

Amphipolis
Eion

Anactorium
Leucas

Oeniadae
Naupactus

olothme

Sparta

Corinth

Aegina
Troezen

Megara
Oenophyta
Plataea
Tanagra
Thebes
Coronea
N LOCRIS
PHOCIS
ACHAEA

Oreus (Histiaea)
Chalcis
Athens

Scyros

Lemnos
Imbros

Thasos

HELLESPONT

Astacus

THRACIAN

Lesbos

Chios

Erythrae

Ephesus

IONIAN

Samos

Miletus

Cos

RHODES

CARIAN

ISLANDS

Ceos
Andros
Delos
Paros
Naxos
Melos

into the estuary, he followed, defeated them, and finally disembarking, won an equally conclusive victory over a Persian army on land. The treasure which fell into his hands, and which he spent on improving the walls of the Acropolis, is proof of the magnitude of the Persian undertaking.

Cimon's services were ill requited. It was a time of wars and turmoil among the nations of Greece proper, of which more shall be said in the next chapter. For the moment suffice it to say that there was no love lost between Sparta and Athens, and that, Cimon's pro-Spartan tendencies having brought him into evil odour at home, he was ostracized in 461. His policy nevertheless survived his fall. For Pericles now rose to the leadership of Athens ; and he, if no friend of Sparta, was no friend of Persia either. Now soon after Cimon's banishment it so happened that a certain Egyptian prince, named Inaros, a vassal to the Persians, rebelled against his masters and appealed for help to Athens. Egyptian trade was important, not least for the corn needed by her growing population, and Athens under Pericles' direction diverted thither 200 ships that were cruising round Cyprus. This was carrying war into enemy waters with a vengeance ; and at first the stroke promised well. The fleet arrived to find Inaros victorious in the Delta ; and, sailing up the Nile, they helped to blockade the Persian garrison in the citadel of Memphis. But there their luck ended. Three years later, in 456, they were still blockading it when a strong Persian reinforcement raised the siege and for eighteen months blockaded the Greeks in their turn on an island of the Delta. As a fleet, they were lost, and on the enemy draining the channel, they burnt their vessels and after a miserable march along the desert coast found their way to Cyrene, whence a few took ship for home. The loss of such a squadron was serious enough, but it was not all. A fresh force of fifty galleys, arriving in ignorance on the morrow of the disaster, sailed right into the jaws of the Phoenician fleet and very few ever got home. The Persians happily did not follow up this victory, but the loss of the best part of the Aegean fleet was in itself a staggering blow, and it must have been a nervous moment, perhaps critical, for Greece. Yet, as though to prove the Athenians' indomitable spirit, a similar adventure was undertaken shortly after. Cimon, who by now had been recalled from his exile, led a force to rescue Cyprus (also valuable as a corn-market) from the remaining garrisons of Persian occupation. He, too, sent a portion of his fleet to Egypt to support a new rebellion and himself settled down in Cyprus to the siege of Cition. There he died, but not before he had planned an operation which resulted in a double victory by sea and land (449).

In spite of this the Greeks were growing weary of the prolonged and somewhat fruitless operations. With Cimon's death the chief protagonist of ruthless war had disappeared, and in 448 the long chapter of the Persian Wars was closed. Though the so-called Peace of Callias seems to have involved no formal compact, yet the Great King probably undertook to move neither ships nor troops into the regions of the Aegean basin ; and Persia and Greece for nearly forty years desisted from meddling in each other's affairs. It is not till near the close of the Peloponnesian War that the great Empire of the East is once again to cast its baleful shadow across the path of Hellenic history.

II. ATHENS AND EMPIRE

While the external achievements of the Delian Confederacy had thus sufficiently fulfilled the intention of its founders, the story of its internal development presents another picture. For by the time of Callias' Peace Athens from being a predominant partner had become its mistress ; and the League had become an Empire. As in the growth of many empires, this result had been due, in the initial stages at least, more to force of circumstances than to premeditated policy. The tendency towards disunion, so strong among all Greeks, was strongest of all perhaps among the Aegean cities and islands. It had needed a strong lead from Athens to draw them together at all ; and to keep them together, as it proved, there was needed something more. The rot began with Naxos, and that in

the very year before Eurymedon was fought. What was
the cause of Naxos' disaffection we have no means of telling,
but in any case the confederate navy descended on the island
and reduced it promptly to enforced submission. Eurymedon followed ; and that decisive triumph over the
renewed threat of aggression seemed in the eyes of many
allied states to mean the end of the Persian danger, and
therefore too the end of the League's utility. They began
to grudge the payment of the annual tax ; and inevitably
there were attempts to break away. But Persia was
still Persia, and we may well believe that general opinion
was at first strongly opposed to any dissolution of the
League. At any rate there was no concerted action
among the malcontents, and Athens was able to bring
overwhelming force to bear upon the isolated offenders.
Thus Thasos, we know, revolted in 465. She had gold-
mines on the Thracian mainland which Athens coveted,
and almost certainly she had a fleet. But after a long
blockade she was reduced by Cimon, losing both mines
and fleet and, what is more significant, her independence.
She was henceforth a vassal of Athens, and what happened
to Thasos happened in due course, though not necessarily
with violence, to all or nearly all her sister-states. By
the middle of the century the three large islands Lesbos,
Chios and Samos alone retained their fleets and a nominal
autonomy (and of these Samos revolted and was reduced
in 439, while Lesbos suffered a similar fate in the opening
years of the Peloponnesian War). The rest were all
tributary members, and theirs was now no longer a voluntary payment. They, too, were firmly under Athens'
heel. Already she had ceased to convene the Delian
parliament, and in 454 she took a step which was even
more decisive. It was a moment, we must remember,
when things looked critical. Two hundred ships and
more had just been lost in Egypt, and none could tell what
Persian blow might fall. Athens, representing it perhaps
as a legitimate precaution, removed the League treasury
from Delos to the Acropolis at Athens. That stroke of
policy was a final disclosure of her hand. There could be

no further pretence now. The League was a league no longer, but an empire nakedly revealed.

That the imperialist policy on which Athens had thus embarked was due in the main to Pericles, we can hardly doubt. He first appears on the political stage as a critic of Cimon's handling of the campaign against Thasos. From that time on he goes from strength to strength at Athens, and his principle is always a firm, if judicious, handling of the allied states. A man of large enlightened vision he seems to have entertained the grand conception of a Hellas drawn together in a bond of common culture under the leadership of Athens. What is pretty certain is that by deliberate policy many members of the League were now bound each to Athens by separate and formal treaties. The terms of such treaties are known to have varied ; for some have been recently unearthed. But all aimed in one way or another at drawing the subject cities under the influence of Athenian institutions. In every case it seems certain that a democratic constitution was enforced. At Erythrae, in Ionia (a city which, like many others unrecorded, joined late under compulsion from Athens[1]), there was to be a Council chosen by lot from the senior citizens. The governor and garrison also imposed on Erythrae were clearly an exceptional measure ; for the subject states were normally left free to manage their own internal affairs—but with certain limitations. Thus, though commercial lawsuits between allies and Athenians were tried, as a rule, in the defendant's native city, those involving sums above a certain limit were often enforcedly transferred to Athens. Criminal cases on a capital charge were likewise brought there ; and the aim clearly was that so far as possible the judicial institutions of the League should be modelled on those of Athens, who in this respect most certainly was well in advance of her neighbours. No small assistance to the popularization of her methods came from one other provision in the treaties. When once in every four years the great Pana-

[1] The Carian and Lycian cities were brought into the League by Cimon after his victory at Eurymedon.

thenaic Festival was held at the metropolis, it was required of her allies to send each a deputation with sacrificial offerings. In the pageantry of that ritual these men saw the city at the height of her magnificence. They would carry to their homes the tale of what they had seen and heard ; and there was at this time in Athens such wealth of intellectual activity and such prolific output of artistic genius that they might well feel proud of their connexion with so glorious a centre of culture. It was not for nothing that Pericles boasted of his city that she was ' an education to Greece '.

This, if any, was the justification of the Periclean policy and of the selfish use (for it can be called no other) to which he put the Confederate Fund transferred from Delos. For after that transference no sort of pretence was made but that the fund belonged to Athens. True, much of it was spent upon her navy, which still served to police the seas. Much, too, was allowed to accumulate and was one day to finance her in the long-drawn war with Sparta ; but a considerable sum—eight thousand talents more or less—was spent without apology on the beautification of the imperial city. Out of this sum was built the Parthenon, Athena's new temple on the Acropolis, and the great Portico which was raised at the entrance to the hill ; out of it, too, came the gold and ivory statue of the goddess which stood within the shrine. Such a use of the allies' money may seem inexcusable to us ; but the ethics of imperialism are never very easy to define. If Pericles honestly believed that Athens had a mission to spread artistic culture by such means, other empire builders too have believed in their own mission and not always in a mission upon so lofty a plane. Greece, as a whole, was certainly the gainer by Pericles' idealism, and it is by no means sure that the allies themselves were unconscious of the benefits received. Their trade flourished, facilitated by the widespread adoption of Athenian currency. Piracy was suppressed ; and instead of the usual futile bickerings between state and state, peace reigned in the Aegean. Unity was never achieved upon so grand a scale, until imposed more than a century later by the Macedonian conqueror. Nor was there any marked sign of disaffection in the years which followed the transformation of league into empire. Even when Sparta at the opening of hostilities in 431 proclaimed it her mission to put down the tyrant city, there was strangely little response. Lesbos revolted, and, with a Spartan on the spot, some cities of the Chalcidic peninsula. But, although the Athenian fleet was much occupied in home waters, the rest of the subject cities did not stir ; the naval contingent of Chios remained loyal until after the Sicilian disaster nearly twenty years later ; and Athens was even able to employ from time to time during the war auxiliary troops drawn from the subject cities. Was such inaction a sign of acquiescence to an easy yoke ? or was it due—and here lies the rub—to fear ? All we know is that when Athens determined to strike, her methods were terrible. In 416 the island of Melos, simply because it had paid tribute to Sparta, though forcedly enrolled in the Athenian league, was for such disobedience attacked in cold blood : its adult males were put to death, its women and children sold into slavery. By that act alone the Athenian Empire must stand self-condemned. It was due, no doubt, to a mood of sullen bitterness in the course of her life-and-death struggle with Sparta ; yet she must thereby have forfeited whatever respect still lingered in her allies' hearts. As her fall became imminent, nearly all came out against her ; and then too late, when all was over, she conferred on the inhabitants of Samos, who had faithfully stood by her in the crisis, the grant of Athenian citizenship. Such a policy, had it but been adopted in a spirit of generous concession some forty or fifty years earlier,[1] might well have bound her subjects to her in a bond of grateful loyalty ; and the history of Greece, perhaps the history of the world, might have been completely changed.

[1] Yet, just when such a concession might have been the salvation of the Empire, the Athenians in 451 chose to narrow the limits of their own citizen franchise—confining the privilege to those whose parents were both Athenian-born—see below, page 151.

CHAPTER IX

THE ATHENIAN LAND EMPIRE

I. From Cimon to Pericles

HOW during the thirty years which followed Plataea
the supremacy of Athens became assured in the
Aegean has been told in the last chapter ; and it
is time that our attention was now turned to her relations
with her more immediate neighbours and (what was not
unconnected therewith) to the highly important change
which now occurred in her own internal development.

The right of self-government had, as we have already
shown, been assured to Athens' citizens by the reforms of
Cleisthenes. But the full effect of such reforms is seldom
instantaneous ; and just as our own Reform Bill of 1832
did little at first to change the type of parliamentary
members, so the aristocratic families, which before Cleisthenes' time had supplied the political leaders of Athens,
continued for a while to supply them still. For twenty
years after Plataea Cimon, the son of Miltiades, remained
the outstanding figure, and noble blood commanded a
respect and a following which the upstart Themistocles
appears to have lacked when the test of ostracism came.

Now Cimon, maintaining the strong tradition of the
more conservative element at Athens, was a staunch
upholder of the policy of friendship with Sparta—a friendship cemented during the critical days of common resistance to a common foe. The friendship was perhaps
somewhat one-sided. The Spartans' jealousy of Athens
had been notably displayed in their attempt to prevent
the rebuilding of her walls ; nor can that jealousy have
been lessened when they saw their rival assume the
leadership of the Aegean states which they themselves
had so timorously abandoned. Nevertheless there was,

as we shall see, some reason for Sparta's faint-hearted policy, and that even her jealousy of Athens was for the present powerless to harm, will be shown by a closer survey of her own situation.

During the years which followed the Persian War, and in which Sparta had declined the leadership of larger Greece, her power even in the Peloponnese had rapidly been losing ground. Argos, recovering by degrees from her terrible defeat of 494, was beginning to raise her head again; and some time about the year 473, when the Arcadians of Tegea had broken into revolt against the Spartan domination, she had ventured out to their support. Defeated, however, in a battle near Tegea, she had returned to the old hopeless efforts at reasserting her local supremacy and when perhaps two years later the Arcadians again rose, they received no help from Argos, and Sparta was able to crush them once and for all at the battle of Dipaea. Yet it was a sign of Sparta's increasing nervousness that she permitted the Mantineans, who had held aloof from the revolt of their fellow-Arcadians, to concentrate their small scattered villages upon a common capital. Nor were her troubles ended. For in 464 the dreaded thing happened. An earthquake laid the township of Sparta in ruins. Every house, except five, fell; and the Helots, seeing their hated taskmasters thus grievously embarrassed, rose in a body. It was a critical moment. Spartan detachments were cut off and butchered; even the capital was in danger; but the citizens rallied and eventually drove the Helots to take refuge on the great hill of Ithomê which protrudes its bulk in the middle of the flat Messenian plain. Here for ten years the rebels defied all efforts to dislodge them. Siege tactics were never a strong point with the Spartans; and they were driven at last to invite the assistance of the more scientific Athenians. Cimon was allowed his way and led a strong citizen force to Ithomê; but there he too failed (462). The Spartans, perhaps suspecting his followers of sympathy with the Helots, rounded on their ally and requested him to leave. Cimon went; and on his return to Athens the humiliation laid him open to the democrats' attack. He fell from power (462) and next year he was ostracized. There ended for good and all the policy of entente with Sparta ; and when at last in 455 the Helots on Mount Ithomê were reduced, Athens was able, as we shall see, to take a shrewd revenge for her old friend's discourtesy.

Meanwhile Cimon's fall had produced immediate and momentous effects. First it marked an epoch in the foreign relationships of Athens. Not merely did she break away from Sparta herself, but she proceeded to strike up two new alliances with Thessaly in the north, and (more important still) with Sparta's watchful neighbour and inveterate rival Argos (462). This new orientation of policy was to lead in the near future to a highly dramatic development of Athenian ambition and enterprise. But for the moment it is more important to note a second effect of Cimon's fall—an effect which served in the long run to change the whole character of Athenian government. For not merely did Cimon and his party now suffer eclipse, but with them passed away the whole conservative tradition of the past. The democracy, founded by Cleisthenes but not hitherto carried to its logical issue, now came in with full tide. The last surviving relic of the old aristocratic privilege was swept away, as we shall see, by a radical act of reform ; and henceforth the democratic mob was more and more to dominate the policy of the state. The man who helped to establish that mob in full power and who, when it was in power, was nevertheless able to control it, was the greatest statesman of Athenian and perhaps of all Greek history, the Alcmeonid Pericles. For with Cimon's failure had come Pericles' opportunity. In the following year (461) he rose to the forefront of politics, and the great reform of which we have been speaking cleared the stage for his long, unique reign of power.

Under Cleisthenes' system, as we have already seen in a preceding chapter, the old aristocratic Council of the Areopagus had lost its former supremacy and most of its powers had been transferred either to the citizen-assembly or to the new council of Five Hundred—most of its powers, but not all ; for the right which it retained of punishing officials for violation of the law gave it a veto (not less powerful because somewhat ill-defined) over progressive action and made it a bulwark of conservatism. In 461, acting with Ephialtes, a fellow-democrat, Pericles swept this right away, leaving the Areopagus by a picturesque survival as a court of homicide.[1] It is as though our own House of Peers were to be degraded to the functions of an assize judge. This done, Pericles moved swiftly and securely. In 458 the archonship was thrown open to citizens of even the lowest class ; and since a poor man could ill afford the leisure to hold office, both the Archons and the Councillors were henceforth to be paid. Of more doubtful wisdom was a similar provision of a fee for jurors. True, jurors were for the most part drawn from among the elderly and weakly—the old-age pensioners, as one might say, of Athens. But the fee encouraged in many a lounging, inquisitive habit and produced a somewhat morbid taste for hearing litigation. It marked a beginning of the decline in public spirit which reached its worst when early in the next century even attendance at the Pnyx [2] was rewarded by a fee.

With the Areopagus shorn of its powers, the citizen body was left in undisputed sovereignty, possessing the final voice whether in judicial matters through the popular jury-courts over which an archon presided, or in legislation and policy through its Assembly where a section of the Council took the chair. The Five Hundred Councillors (or at least a committee of them) sat in permanent session to transact current business, receive foreign embassies, and prepare matter for the Assembly's debates ; but, though

[1] The play of Aeschylus entitled 'The Eumenides', which was produced about this time reflects this political change. For the trial of Orestes for the murder of his mother takes place before a court of Athenians on the Areopagus.

[2] In a rude open-air enclosure on the Pnyx hill was normally held the assembly. Every effort was made to encourage attendance—and the market-place was always cleared when the Assembly was in session.

this gave them a certain power of discretionary control, the real executive did not lie with them. The will of the Assembly was carried into effect, especially in the important spheres of naval and military organization, and of food supply and finance, by the Ten Strategi or Generals chosen annually by direct popular vote. The President, or leading member of this board of ten, was the nearest approach to what we may call a Prime Minister in Athens ; and it was by virtue of almost continuous election to this high office that Pericles was able to exercise his unique control over the policy of the state in the sphere not merely of domestic but also of external affairs.

II. Periclean Democracy

The democracy which Pericles was to lead and to educate was perhaps the most astonishing phenomenon of all social and political history. For energy of action and fertility of mind it stands without a rival. But though the permanent fruit of its achievement was mainly artistic and intellectual, yet in order fully to appreciate the character of that democracy something must first be said about the economic development of Athens.

The population of Attica (as of all other states in Greece) was in the main dependent upon agriculture. Large tracts of her territory, it is true, were scrub-clad hill or mountain suited for nothing better than the grazing of goats. Even the occasional pine-forests, though serviceable for fuel, were inadequate for ship-timber, which had to be fetched from Thrace ; and the pasture, too, upon the lower mountain slopes was poor enough. On the flat plain below these, however, corn grew in fair abundance and (much more fruitfully than in most parts of Greece) the olive tree, the oil of which was not merely a staple ingredient in the Attic people's diet [1] but an export upon a very considerable scale. The soil, however, was not rich ; and the population never really throve, until the statesmanly

---

[1] Oil in ancient times served many purposes. It took the place of butter in cooking, and of soap in washing, besides being used, of course, in lamps.

vision of Solon had pointed another way. By encouraging the handicrafts, and in particular by inviting artisans from other lands to Athens, Solon had in fact produced a revolution in the economic life of the country. In a word, her manufactures had begun to rival in importance, and soon were even to outstrip, her agriculture. From 550 onwards the export of her pottery had assumed enormous dimensions ; and the Attic Red-figure ware was now everywhere in high demand, not least in the west among the cities of Magna Grecia and Etruria.[1]

Themistocles after Salamis had much busied himself over fostering this westerly trade ; and it is a curious proof of his interest that of his daughters he named one Italia and another after the Greco-Italian town of Sybaris. A more practical step was his cultivation of friendships with the folk of Epirus and Corcyra. The trade route to the west (since Greek sailors would always hug a shore when possible) passed up the Acarnanian coast and under the lee of the island of Corcyra, whence lay the shortest cross-sea passage to the heel of Italy. It was therefore good policy—and a policy in which, as we shall see, the Athenians long persisted—to maintain a friendly footing with these north-western districts. Corinth, however, partly by virtue of her advantageous situation on the Isthmus, and partly through her colonial connexions in the west, was more or less in a position to monopolize this Adriatic traffic, and even if Attic ware was exported

---

[1] The import trade of Athens may be illustrated by two quotations. The ' Old Oligarch ' (c. 425), as the writer of an anonymous treatise is called, says : ' The choice things of Sicily and Italy, of Cyprus and Egypt and Lydia, of Pontus or Peloponnese, or whatever else it be, are all swept, as it were, into one centre.' Hermippus, a comedian, writing about 429, lists the following items : ' Hides and vegetable relish from Cyrene, grain and meat from Italy, pork and cheese from Syracuse, sails and papyrus from Egypt, frankincense from Syria, cypress wood from Crete, ivory from Libya, chestnuts and almonds from Paphlagonia, dates and fine wheat-flour from Phoenicia, rugs and cushions from Carthage ; from Rhodes raisins, from Euboea pears and fine sheep, slaves from Phrygia, mercenaries from Arcadia, and from Perdiccas, king of Macedon—lies by the shipload.'

to Magna Grecia, it was probably Chalcidian ships that carried it. The Aegean, therefore, especially in the years of which we are now speaking, played the chief part in the prosperity of Athens. Her command of the sea must have made her merchant ships the leading carriers; for the Ionians, crippled by the oppression of the Persian conquest, had dropped out of the race. The silver coined from her mines at Laurium circulated, as we have seen, among her subject cities, and much of it came back in the shape of tribute to be paid to the shipwrights and sailors of the imperial city. More and more, too, foreigners were attracted thither by commercial prospects or came to settle in the home of culture. So the population grew; and, as it grew, the demand for manufactured articles grew with it. Industry throve. In the workshops of the cobblers and the potters, the armourers and weavers, fullers, dyers and the rest of them, slaves worked beside their citizen masters, and metics beside both. Of the latter many made their home in the Peiraeus, which became in due course a busy town, humming with manufacture and quayside activity, and laid out in fine straight streets unlike the winding alleys of the old-fashioned capital; and even up at Athens, when in 478 the walls came to be rebuilt, a larger circuit had been deemed advisable, so much had the population of the city grown. Now of this growth of population two main effects are to be noted. First, the home-grown corn of Attica proved wholly insufficient for new needs; and one of the chief preoccupations of her statesmen was soon, as we shall see, to provide Athens with secure supplies from overseas. To maintain those supplies, moreover, Athens was dependent on the supremacy of her fleet; and the efficiency of that fleet was in turn dependent on the prompt and regular payment of the League tribute. The Athenian democracy therefore was strongly Imperialist. It believed in a firm handling of the allies and backed Pericles loyally in the policy described in the foregoing chapter. In the second place, commercial peoples are by nature adventurous. They must of necessity take risks; and risks successfully taken invite the taking of others. So the Athenian democracy was not tamely content with what it had. It wanted more. The lure of trade beckoned ; and when the chance came to join issue with Corinth, their chief rival in westerly waters, the Athenian democrats were ready enough, as we shall see, to embark on a policy of adventurous expansion.

The most important consequence, however, of the urban concentration at Athens was cultural. Town life, as always, sharpened men's wits. Daily intercourse bred the habit of discussion. The chance of attending debates in the Ecclesia or trials in the Law Court provided a first-rate political education. The desire to succeed, whether in public life or in business, encouraged a desire for instruction ; and, as we shall see in the next chapter, the opportunity of hearing lectures or arguing with professors was eagerly seized. Besides all this, there was abundant activity in art and literature. At the dramatic festivals men could hear masterpieces of tragedy. Eminent writers, like Herodotus, were attracted to a city where their works were sure of a public. Sculptors were carving statues, and architects under Pericles' patronage were soon to raise buildings which are still the wonder of the world. Nothing, in fact, is more astonishing than the exuberant energy which the Athenian people threw simultaneously into the arts both of peace and of war. In a famous speech, recorded by Thucydides, Pericles boasted of the versatility of his countrymen ; but of that versatility no better example could anywhere have been found than in the character of the great statesman himself.

Pericles was a man of such surpassing and many-sided genius that it is difficult to find his parallel in history. He combined in his own character qualities rarely, if ever, found together. He had the practical shrewdness of a financier. He was deeply imbued with the philosophy and science of the day ; he was a keen patron of the arts. His interests were intellectual and his friends the foremost thinkers and writers of the time ; yet no demagogue ever knew better how to control a recalcitrant mob. His serene and majestic presence, together with a studied aloofness of manner and life (for he appeared but seldom in public), all served to surround his personality with a certain awe and glamour ; and when he deigned to mount the platform before the assembled populace, he spoke to them—one might almost have said preached—in terms of a lofty idealism, recorded for us with all but verbal accuracy in the pages of Thucydides. For thirty years and over he was to dominate and direct, as none did before or after him, the policy of Athens. It was during the second half of that period that Pericles won his real claim to fame as a patron of art and as a minister of peace. But peace had not always been his way ; and during the earlier years of his rule Athens embarked, as we shall soon see, on a daring policy of almost deliberate aggression. The fact was that the breach with Sparta in 462 brought to an end the temporary harmony of Greece. Cimon's victory at Eurymedon a few years earlier had removed the menace of Persian attack which had served to keep the various states together, and among those jealous neighbours war was now sooner or later inevitable. True, Sparta's hands were temporarily tied by the revolt of her Helots. But Athens had other rivals ; and, conscious of her liability to attack, she took her measures. It must have been about this time that the plans were laid for the construction of her Long Walls linking city and port, which, when completed, would render her as impregnable as an island. But the work was not finished until 457 ; and in the meanwhile a challenge of war had been offered and accepted.

III. The Land Empire

The challenge came of course from the great commercial power of Corinth. Intermediate between Corinth and Athens lay Megara, a little state also of much commercial importance, which normally leant for support on her larger neighbour of the Isthmus. In 460, however, the Megarians quarrelled with Corinth and appealed for Athenian alliance.

The appeal was welcomed, and, as a first-fruit of the alliance, Athens assisted her new friends to build between their city and their port a system of Long Walls on the model of which her own similar walls were soon now to be completed. To Athens herself the friendship of Megara offered new and attractive possibilities; for on the further side of the Isthmus her ally possessed a port at Pegae, opening on the waters of the Corinthian Gulf. Hitherto the westerly trade-route, which ran through that gulf and up the Adriatic to the cities of Sicily and Magna Grecia, had largely been Corinth's preserve. Her colonization of various points along the north-west coast of Greece (of the island of Corcyra and above all of the important town of Syracuse) had given her a line of political connexions which did much to secure to her the rich trade of the West. To Athens, whose commercial activities had largely been confined to the Aegean, the opportunity offered by the use of Pegae was not to be despised. Pericles' statesmanly eye can hardly have been blind to the tempting vision; and, when Corinth sought to punish Megara's defection, war was accepted with alacrity. Nor, as it proved, was Corinth to be the only foe. A growing fear of Athenian naval supremacy drove into her arms her traditional rival Aegina, and the two maritime states prepared to stand together. Athens, who had long coveted this neighbouring island, could have asked nothing better; and the more so since things went well with her arms. By sea at Cecryphaleia she defeated the Corinthian fleet and then laid siege to Aegina. By land her general Myronides, commanding a force composed of only ' the oldest and youngest ', beat a Corinthian army which came out to raid the Megarid. This was in 459; and since that very year saw also the dispatch of Athens' cruising squadron to the adventure on the Nile, we cannot but feel astounded at the vigour and audacity of a people who out of their strictly limited resources of man-power could dare to undertake so many simultaneous campaigns. As a telling memorial of their indomitable enterprise we may still read in an inscription, now kept in the Louvre at Paris, the following

10

proud, but simply worded epitaph : *Of the Erechtheid tribe, these are they who died in the war in Cyprus, in Egypt, in Phoenice, at Halieis, in Aegina, at Megara, in the same year.* These from one tribe alone ; but happily for Athens the sacrifice was not in vain. By 457 Aegina, deprived of Corinth's support at sea, was beaten to her knees and the terms of her submission were harsh. She was compelled to accept the status of a subject-ally and to submit to the payment of tribute unusually heavy. Thus the prosperous little island, which, full in view upon the Athenians' south-westerly horizon, had long flaunted her independence under their jealous gaze, was brought at length beneath their mastery. ' The eye-sore of the Peiraeus ' was an eye-sore no more, but a symbol of the Empire's growing strength.

Meanwhile Sparta, whose hands were well occupied with the revolt of her Helots, had been watching the struggle with anxiety, and already before Aegina's fall the manifest failure of Corinthian arms had brought her too into the war. She did not at first plan any direct blow against Attica itself, but undertook an expedition into Boeotia, ostensibly with the object of settling a border feud between Doris and Phocis, but in reality to bolster up the power of Thebes as a make-weight against Athens. The scattered cities of the Boeotian plains, normally constrained to a grudging acknowledgment of Thebes' hegemony, had welcomed the degradation which her unpatriotic action in the Persian Wars had brought upon that city and had taken the opportunity to assert their independence. The Spartan expeditionary force succeeded in restoring to Thebes her lost hegemony ; and they were preparing to march homeward past the borderland of Athens when a treacherous hint from some disgruntled aristocrats within the city, put it into their heads to attempt a surprise attack on the Long Walls then in process of completion. They had reckoned, however, without Pericles. His spies had learnt the secret ruse ; and an Athenian army, marching out across the northern frontier and meeting them near Tanagra, succeeded in putting up so tough a fight, that a truce was called and the Spartans, though technically victors, withdrew home without more ado (457). They had better not have meddled; for now the Athenians' spirit was aroused. If Sparta could bolster up the supremacy of Thebes, they could play the opposite game and seek to detach the unwilling confederates from the power of that hated city. So in the following autumn they in their turn were marching on Boeotia, where they defeated the Thebans at Oenophyta (457), and then, leaving Thebes herself in isolation, proceeded to take under their wing the other Boeotian cities, who welcomed, it would seem, the change of masters.

Here, then, was a new and startling development in Athens' policy. Ambitions, hitherto confined to the control of sea-board states easily accessible to the attentions of her fleet, were now directed towards the acquisition of a mainland power, the extent of which increased apace. The growing prestige of her name, aided perhaps by a corresponding hatred of Sparta, soon brought in fresh recruits for the new confederacy. Phocis, which lay on the far side of Boeotia, now elected to join, and Northern Locris, its next-door neighbour, was coerced and in all probability Southern Locris too. Tolmides with an Athenian fleet cruised round the Peloponnese to the Megarian port of Pegae, ravaging Sparta's chief arsenal en route, and probably now too bringing into the new League the long coastal strip of Achaea (455). Extending as it did along most of the south shore of the Corinthian Gulf, it is easy to see at what this last acquisition aimed. In form, indeed, the new Athenian league seemed merely a northern counterpart of the Peloponnesian confederacy of Sparta (a similarity confirmed by the known fact that some at least of the new allies were ready to lend contingents should Athens so demand). But its real purpose—and here we surely see the brain of Pericles at work—was undoubtedly to break the power of Corinth. The north shore of the Corinthian Gulf, from Boeotia to Locris, was now under Athens' grip; with the acquisition of Achaea the southern shore was so no less; thus over Corinth's westerly trade-route was laid a strangle-hold. And, as though this was not enough, Pericles now proceeded to a last and crowning stroke. In 455 the Helots of Mount Ithomê surrendered to Sparta, but under the terms of their capitulation they were allowed to quit the Peloponnese. This was the opportunity for the Athenians' shrewd revenge of which we spoke above. They settled these Helots at Naupactus, a harbour situated in Southern Locrian territory and commanding the very jaws of the Corinthian Gulf (455). Corinth indeed seemed doomed ; and even Sparta must have felt not a little nervous. Mistress of the Aegean already (for it was within a year that the treasury of the League was transferred to the Acropolis), Athens bade fair to dominate the Adriatic also. On land she was well on the way to challenging Sparta's supremacy ; nor can we doubt that had her military efficiency been equal to her naval, Athens would sooner or later have brought all Greece under her sway.

It was, however, to political miscalculations rather than to military weakness that Athens was to owe the loss of the Land Empire she had thus rapidly acquired. These years of exuberant and successful enterprise were followed at first by a period of quiescence. Such output of energy had perhaps exhausted Athens ; the loss of her 250 ships in Egypt required recuperation ; the drain upon her manpower which that disaster cost her must have been crippling ; and Pericles himself seems to have seen the necessity for a pause. He was content to forget old quarrels and allow Cimon to return from exile and to negotiate in 451 a Five Years' Truce with Sparta. Whether or no he equally approved of Cimon's resumption of the war on Persia is more than we can tell, but when the latter fell in Cyprus, Pericles lost no time, as we have seen, in concluding an agreement with the barbarian enemy. His attention was rightly concentrated upon dangers nearer home ; nor were these long in coming. At the time of their conquest of Boeotia the Athenians, contrary to their habitual practice, had placed the power within the various cities in the hands of certain oligarchs. These were doubtless those members of the Boeotian aristocracy who had been punished for their Medism during the Persian Wars by outlawry or dispossession ; and their natural hostility to Sparta, as the author of their punishment, made them now correspondingly favourable to Athens. But, though replaced in power as the agents of Athenian domination, they proved, it would seem, incapable of maintaining it. They had taken the usual precautions of exiling the most dangerous of their political opponents ; and these had lost no time, as was only to be expected, in plotting to turn the tables. Since such exiles now represented the patriotic cause of Boeotian independence, they were in a good position to rally the efforts of their countrymen ; and so successful were their intrigues that by 447 two of the leading Boeotian cities were already once more in their hands. The Athenian army which attempted to recover them was cut up at Coronea ; and in the twinkling of an eye the fruits of Oenophyta were lost. The whole of Boeotia passed out of her hands, and soon even Athens herself was in danger. For the patriot exiles of Boeotia had spread their net wide. Phocis had succumbed to their influence, and deserted the Athenian alliance. And now upon the news of Coronea, Megara upon one flank and Euboea on the other came out in open revolt. No sooner had Pericles crossed over to Euboea than he was recalled by the ominous message that a Spartan army was marching through the Megarid and threatening Athens itself. The danger was grave enough, but Pericles' swift return, the strength of the city-walls, and (some said) a tactful bribe paid to the Spartan King himself, induced him to withdraw and abandon the attempt without a fight. Athens was saved ; Euboea she reduced at leisure and treated to harsh terms ; but the whole of her Land Empire, acquired with such swift ease a bare ten years before, was gone past recovery ; and she was lucky indeed to save anything out of the wreck. The fact is that in the peace negotiations which followed, the Spartans let Athens off surprisingly lightly (445). Cautiously anxious perhaps that she should meddle no more in the Peloponnese, they not only agreed to recognize Athens' right to her maritime empire, but they actually allowed her to retain both Naupactus and Aegina. Though such concessions cannot have given much satisfaction to Corinth, the Athenians' abandonment of Pegae and Achaea was something to the good, and she was at any rate temporarily placated. There was a feeling of goodwill and friendship in the air, and a desire to restore some sort of unanimity to Greece. Nevertheless the jealousies between commercial states die hard. For trade touches men's pockets, and between Corinth and Athens had been sown the seeds of enmity which were one day to bear the bitter harvest of the Peloponnesian War. The Peace agreed on at Sparta was to be a Peace of Thirty Years. It did not last fifteen.

To Athens the understanding thus concluded, whereby Sparta should dominate by land and she by sea, was certainly a blessing in disguise. The inhabitants of Attica were willing enough and numerous enough to man her ships ; but there was not enough material for an efficient land army as well. The numerous problems, too, both of her Aegean Empire and of her own domestic economy, were enough to tax even the statesmanship of Pericles ; and, while peace afforded him the opportunity, he wisely set himself to consolidate his country's position and resources. Even now his strong imperialist policy met, it is true, with opposition from the conservative faction. This time they were led by Thucydides, the son of Melesias,[1] who disapproved in particular of the expenditure of money from the confederate treasury upon the adornment of the city —'like a vain woman,' he said, ' decking herself out with trinkets'. But the opposition was overborne and Thucydides himself ostracized in 443. Pericles, therefore, was free to tighten the rein upon the subject cities. These were now divided for convenience of taxation into five great districts, the Hellespont, the ' Thraceward ' region, the Islands. Ionia, and Caria. The tribute which of late had been partially relaxed, was exacted to the full. Samos, whose aristocratic government revolted (440–38) and intrigued for

---

[1] Not to be confused with the historian Thucydides. son of Olorus.

Persian help, was reduced by Pericles in person and compelled to pay a huge indemnity. Finally there was a further great extension of the policy—adopted first at Chalcis in the time of Cleisthenes—of planting ' cleruchies' or settlements of Athenian citizens at important strategic or commercial points. Already since the conclusion of the Five Years' Truce such outposts of Empire had been founded on various islands of the Aegean, Naxos and Andros among them, and also, covering the vital Black Sea trade-route, along the Thracian Chersonese (447). The policy was unpopular with the rest of Greece, since the original inhabitants were generally deprived of land for the Athenian settlers' benefit ; and it was in the new spirit of compromise, bred of the Peace settlement of 445, that when Pericles, two years later, sent out some colonists to Thurii in South Italy (the historian Herodotus among them) he invited the co-operation of other Greek states, making it a Pan-Hellenic affair. In the Aegean, however, he was less cautious. Euboea soon after her revolt and her reduction was forced to submit to a cleruchy at Histiaea (or Oreus) at the north end of the island. Of still greater importance, perhaps, was the plantation of a regular colony at Amphipolis, situated just north of the Chalcidic peninsula, and commanding both the coastal trade-road from Thrace to Macedon and also the Strymon valley up which led the inland tracks to Mount Pangaeus and its gold-mines.

Like the ' Coloniae ' of the Roman Empire, these cleruchies served a double purpose, not only as strategic garrisons, but also as a useful overflow for a surplus population. For there seems no doubt that about this time, despite the drain of war upon her man-power, Athens was suffering severely from overcrowding.

One symptom of her embarrassment was the measure above-mentioned whereby in 451 the rights of citizenship were suddenly confined to persons whose father and mother were both Athenian born. This limitation must have disfranchised many who were of Metic origin and we may well believe that it discouraged, and was intended to discourage, the too rapid influx of fresh alien immigrants.[1] None the less the fact remained that there were too many folk in Attica ; and one of Pericles' most anxious pre-occupations was the food supply. Big granaries had recently been built at the Peiraeus ; but with Attic soil so largely taken up with olive culture, it was no easy matter to fill them, and two-thirds of what was needed came probably from abroad. In the Mediterranean world the chief grain-growing districts were three—the Levant (that is, Cyprus and Egypt), Sicily, and the Black Sea littoral. Egypt was somewhat distant, and though large supplies are known to have come through, they were inevitably dependent upon the goodwill of Persia. Sicily was still to a large extent dominated by Corinth and her offshoot Syracuse. The Black Sea remained ; and hither accord-ingly, perhaps in 437, we find Pericles himself conducting an important naval mission through the Hellespont. Arrangements seem to have been concluded with the native princes of South Russia ; and the corn-route was further safeguarded by the planting of a trade-station at Nym-phaeum in the Crimea and of a cleruchy at Astacus in the Sea of Marmora. Henceforward then supplies were well assured ; and until she should have lost her command of the sea, and her control of the Hellespont along with it, Athens was to be in no serious trouble about corn. With the league cities well under control, an invincible fleet on the seas, and an enormous reserve of treasure accumulating yearly in her citadel, she could look ahead with confidence to the renewal of the conflict, which Pericles must clearly have foreseen and for which he had thus systematically prepared.

[1] There are clear signs that unemployment was a problem which Pericles had to meet. His introduction of the jury-dole and his promotion of building activity may have been deliberate remedies. The curtailment of the franchise was in this case due to a natural desire to confine the dole and other such benefits to true-born Athenians. The number of citizens who were sent overseas as cleruchs during this period (460–430) must be reckoned in the neigb-bourhood of 10,000 persons.

CHAPTER X

THE AGE OF PERICLES

I. TEMPLES AND SCULPTURE

THE historian of the fifty years which followed Salamis and with which we have been concerned in the two preceding chapters, is unhappily but very ill provided with sound contemporary evidence. Herodotus' narrative closes with the end of the Persian Wars ; and, although Thucydides gives an introductory sketch of earlier Greek history, his real business does not begin till the opening of the Peloponnesian War in 433. For the intervening period we are therefore dependent partly on the very inadequate accounts given by these two contemporary historians, but mainly upon the second-hand evidence of later writers, supplemented or corrected by inscriptions or other such records as archaeologists have unearthed. It is a cruel chance which has thus deprived us of an intimate knowledge of that period in Athenian history which was certainly the most happy, and which in output of both literary and artistic genius was almost certainly the most brilliant. By reason, however, of this same artistic and literary activity we are able in a large measure to supplement the deficiencies of actual historical record and to interpret the development of Athenian thought and taste through the medium of the statues, books, and buildings which a kinder fate has preserved for us ; and before embarking upon the long and tragic story of the conflict which was now for a quarter of a century and over to rack and well-nigh ruin the Hellenic world, it will be well for us for a while to turn our thoughts to these products of a saner and a happier age.

The Athenians of the Periclean Era were heirs to an artistic tradition of whose splendid promise something has

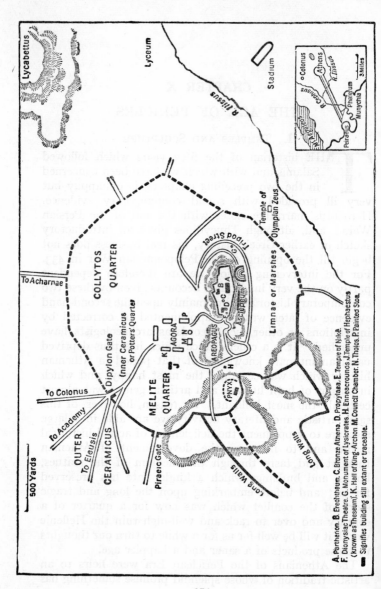

A. Parthenon. B. Erechtheum. C. Bronze Athena. D. Propylaea. E. Tempe of Niké.
F. Dionysiac Theatre. G. Monument of Lysicrates. H. Enneacrounos J. Temple of Hephaestus
(known as Theseum). K. Hall of King-Archon. M. Council Chamber. N. Tholos. P. Painted Stoa.
■■■ Signifies building still extant or traceable.

already been said and of which they in their turn were to show themselves worthy successors. Nevertheless they were a very different people from their ancestors of the preceding century. Not merely had their whole outlook upon life been changed by the experiences of that terrible ordeal through which they had so recently passed, but they had also embarked with deliberate and proud enthusiasm on the difficult task of self-government. Now democrats and aristocrats rarely think alike. Milton and Bunyan write in a very different vein from the Cavalier poets or the Restoration dramatists ; and the fact is that those who have to work to gain a livelihood do not see the world from the same angle as those who are under no such necessity. We must never forget, therefore, that for the majority of Fifth-Century Athenians life was a stern and serious business ; and their attitude towards it is naturally reflected in the work of their artists and their poets. Through all the period's literature there runs a profound questioning over the problems and mysteries of existence. Its tone, though buoyant, is full of solemn earnestness. It never strays far from the larger and deeper issues of character and fate ; and in all the pages of the historian Thucydides there is only one grim joke. Of the art, too, the same is true. The cheerful smile which plays on the lips of the earlier sculptured figures is no longer to be seen on the works of Pheidias and his contemporaries. The features of both his gods and men alike wear the air of those who have known life's passion and life's bitterness and have risen above them to the austere but serene habit of a complete self-mastery. His Zeus or Athena could never condescend to what is mean or trivial ; and even in the procession of youths and maidens which he depicted in his famous Parthenon frieze, there is no touch of levity. All is as solemn as a church-parade. In the buildings of the epoch, too, compared with what little we know of earlier architecture, we miss equally the note of gaiety. The Parthenon, one might almost say, is a temple with a frown. From this, however, it must by no means be inferred that the Athenians were a glum or puritanical folk. Nothing could be further from the truth. They abounded in vitality, making the very most of life and having plenty of fun. But at the same time they cared intensely and passionately about everything they did ; and under all their best activities there lay the solemn high seriousness of temper of which we have been speaking. Above all, it was markedly present in that circle of brilliant men who gathered round Pericles. It was not for nothing that Pericles himself was nicknamed ' the Olympian ' ; and in a man of so commanding a character it was inevitable that his earnest idealism should stamp its influence upon his personal associates. Perhaps, indeed, the influence was felt through the whole town ; and Athens was small enough for that.

It was Pericles' ambition, as we have said above, to make Athens not merely the most powerful, but also the most beautiful city in Greece ; and there could have been no more fitting site on which to begin his work than the Acropolis. This splendid rock, whose broad and level platform had been further extended and secured by Cimon's buttressing of its southern cliff, offered, in fact, an unrivalled setting for an architectural masterpiece. Since time immemorial, moreover, it had held the shrine of Athena, the city's patron goddess. This edifice, which lay close to the northern cliff of the hill and overlooking the town below it, had probably been rebuilt more than once during the successive stages of its history ; Pisistratus the tyrant had certainly restored and embellished it ; but the Persian sack left it in ruins ; and the citizens on their return from Salamis had found no better use for its dismantled remnants than to build them into the reconstructed defences of the hill (whence they have only recently been unearthed by archaeologists). A new and more magnificent temple was

---

PLATE XIV

The Acropolis seen from the west. On the left side of the rock platform is visible the Erechtheum ; across its near front the Propylaea or entrance gates, on the right of which is perched the little Temple of Niké ; behind and above emerges the Parthenon.

ACROPOLIS FROM WEST

meanwhile in contemplation, not indeed on the old site, but more centrally and upon the highest point of the great rock platform. The foundations were prepared, but whether because Themistocles was its author and fell soon into disgrace, or whatever were the reasons, the scheme was allowed to lapse ; and it remained for Pericles to carry it out upon a yet grander scale.

About 448, true to his ideal that Athens should lead Greece, he had summoned a congress of all Hellenic states to organize a general restoration of the temples destroyed by the Persians His invitation met with a cold refusal ; and Pericles set independently to work upon the task of building a worthy shrine for Athena upon the new Acropolis site. The result was the temple known as the Parthenon, or Maiden's House, among all architectural monuments of antiquity the most impressive in the grandeur of its design, and the richest in the artistic quality of its adornment. The style chosen was the Doric, in which the surrounding columns were of a simple dignity enriched only by the patterns painted on their capitals, but a style in which, however, magnificent scope was given for the display of the sculptor's art. High up in the gables east and west were set groups of statuary, representing at one end the birth of Athena from the head of Zeus, and at the other the contest of Athena and Poseidon for the land of Attica. In the space beneath the roof, and above the row of pillars which surrounded the shrine walls, ran at intervals a series of square ' metopes ' in which were set two-figure groups of Lapiths and Centaurs or other mythical heroes in conflict. Finally, high up on the shrine wall behind the pillars, ran a continuous frieze of figures in low relief, representing the procession of citizens to the goddess' temple at the Feast of the Panathenaea. The beauty of these works—many of which were brought to England by Lord Elgin in 1816, and are now in the British Museum—it is difficult to overestimate. That good sculptors were common in Athens we have already seen in the preceding period, and now under the controlling eye of Pheidias, who certainly designed most of the figures and probably gave the finishing touches to many, the best of the city's craftsmanship was concentrated upon the execution of this supreme achievement. The world has never seen its like, nor is it probable that it will see its like again. For if in the mellow ruin of decay the Parthenon still has power to move men's minds to awe and wonder, what must it not have been in the original splendour of its flashing marble,[1] in the perfect symmetry of its unmarred proportions, in the fresh strength and delicacy of its carvings as they came clean from the sculptor's tool. To the proud people who raised it, at any rate, it must have seemed no less a worthy symbol of their own new-found national greatness than a fitting habitation for the great goddess for whom it was planned. The making of the Great Statue of Athena which was to stand within the sanctuary was entrusted also to the care of Pheidias. His skill had already been displayed in a gigantic bronze image of an armed Athena which stood just within the entrance gates of the citadel. This time, however, he set to work in materials much more precious. A vast framework of wood, first shaped to form the figure, was then cunningly overlaid with gold and ivory—gold for the draperies and ivory for the flesh ; and both upon the shield she held beside her and the helmet which crowned her head all the skill of the metal-worker's

---

[1] Considerable painting in bright colours enhanced the original effect. Traces of this colouring can still be detected. But the whiteness of the marble has weathered to a mellow tone of gold.

PLATE XV

The Parthenon as it appears to one entering by the Propylaea. The centre of the temple was destroyed by the explosion of a powder magazine placed there by Turkish defenders in 1687 and exploded by the artillery of the Venetian army which was attacking it. Note the Doric style and compare the details of Plate XVI (a).

No photograph, for some reason or other, ever does justice to the grandeur of the Parthenon; nor, of course, to the rich golden hue to which its marble pillars have weathered.

PARTHENON FROM WEST

craft was lavished. Yet so cautious and far-sighted were the schemes of Pericles that the plates of precious metal were left easily detachable and ready to hand for minting, should financial needs require it.

Work upon the Parthenon was begun in 447 ; and by 438 the building was finished and the statue of Athena installed. But neither were Pericles' ideas as yet complete, nor the drafts upon the resources of the Imperial treasury exhausted. A start was immediately made upon a magnificent new Portico or Propylaea which was to guard the entrance to the hill ; and, close beside this, a little shrine, perched upon a projecting bastion of rock and already begun perhaps many years before, was brought to completion and dedicated to the goddess of Victory or Niké.[1] With this the adornment of the Acropolis might well seem to have been complete and Pericles have rested content with his handiwork ; but in one curious respect his schemes had failed to satisfy the superstitious requirements of the Athenian mind. The sanctity of Athena's cult centred, as it so happened, in a carved wooden image of unknown antiquity and with no pretence whatever to beauty, which had previously been housed in the temple sacked by the Persians. Pending the erection of a more worthy sanctuary it had presumably been given a temporary dwelling on the old traditional site ; but though Pericles doubtless intended its removal to the Parthenon, the conservative instincts of the priesthood intervened, and intervened successfully. The ancient image was not moved, and some fifteen years later, when under the leadership of Nicias the conservative faction was for the moment to the fore, it was decided to build it a home on approximately the old site (420). The new building, known to us as the Erechtheum, stood slightly nearer to the northern cliff than the pre-Persian temple. Since the cult of Athena was herein combined with the cult of Erechtheus, an ancestral deity of Attica, and possibly too that of Poseidon, the ground

---

[1] The completion of the temple by the addition of a balustrade of bas-reliefs was not, however, achieved until the last years of the century ; and possibly the temple itself dates from c. 420.

plan was unusual and irregular, including two projecting porticos, in one of which the famous Caryatid maidens play the part of pillars as support to the roof. The style was Ionic, which, unlike the Doric, is richly encrusted with the most exquisite carved mouldings, and the capitals of which resemble in outline a pair of curling ram's horns. To the severe and simple grandeur of the Parthenon beside it, the fragile delicacy of this much smaller temple provides a perfect foil. The Erechtheum could never, indeed, rival the dignity of its great neighbour ; but to it, none the less, was yearly made the pious pilgrimage of the Panathenaic procession ; and the old and hideous idol it contained still continued to receive the public homage which Pericles clearly intended should be paid to Pheidias' stately colossus of ivory and gold.

II. Religion and Poets

This clash between superstitious conservatism and progressive idealism was typical of a conflict which had been going on, one might almost say, since the days of Homer himself. The Greeks were not, like the Hebrews, a deeply religious race ; but they were at least a thinking race ; and since most of their imaginative literature bore in one

---

PLATE XVI

(a) A view of the ' Theseum ' (originally in all likelihood a Temple of Hephaestus). Note the details of the Doric style : fluted pillars with plain ' cushion ' capitals ; on the entablature above, the fluted ' triglyphs ' and the alternating slabs called ' metopes ', here uncarved and perhaps originally painted, but in most temples carved in semi-relief ; surmounting all the gable or pediment, which was normally filled with a sculptured group. Under the pillars and on the wall of the actual shrine or cella may be seen the figures of the Frieze. (b) Part of the Frieze from the east end of the Parthenon, showing three gods.

Note the extreme delicacy of the carving, both of the anatomy and the drapery. Its perfection inclines one to think that Pheidias himself may here have given the finishing touches.

THESEUM

PART OF PARTHENON FRIEZE

way or another upon the problem of the relations between God and man, it is essential that, before we proceed to discuss the poets of the Periclean Age, we should say something about the previous evolution of religious thought.

Long ago in prehistoric times we pointed out how the Homeric poems represented an advance from the primitive atmosphere of superstitious magic to a more rational and idealistic conception of the deity. In the old indigenous cults of that early age, the main motive in men's minds, so far as we can judge, was a desire to propitiate the unseen powers either of Nature or of the ghostly dead, powers habitually symbolized under the form of some animal (most often bull or snake) and worshipped with rites of a frequently cruel and sometimes bestial character, among which human sacrifice itself was not altogether unknown. But the Achaeans, entering, as we saw, from the north, brought with them a loftier creed which they proceeded to blend and merge into the old, superimposing upon the degraded indigenous cults new gods of their own—gods human in shape, human too in their attributes, their passions and desires, the gods, in fact, whom we meet in Homer and elsewhere, Zeus, Athena, Poseidon and the rest. In the great group of saga poetry which came to pass under the common name of Homer, the stamp was henceforth for ever set upon the orthodox conception of the powers above. The old boorish legends were transformed or overlaid by a purer and more intellectual mythology, containing stories of undying beauty which have been the inspiration of poets in all ages, and attributing to the gods themselves sublime and clear-cut, though somewhat over-abstract, personalities. Thus the ghastly memory of some genuine antique ritual was arrayed with solemn beauty in the famous tale of Iphigenia's sacrifice at Aulis (further to be purged of its barbarity by the version of later poets, who asserted that Artemis had rescued the maiden from the altar by the miraculous substitution of a doe). Thus, again, Athena, once the ' owl-faced ' goddess, became an embodiment of all that is lovely in life, the Maiden Deity, chaste, majestic, and serene, sprung at birth in full-grown

11

vigour from the head of her father Zeus, and destined to be the patron of the arts and labours of man. Yet the old primitive cult with which hers had been identified was even in Pericles' day not wholly forgotten ; and in the great image which Pheidias made of her, the old symbolic animal still found a place, lurking under the shelter of her golden shield in the form of a monstrous snake. So, too, though much of the early ritual had by now been cleansed of its more unseemly elements, much that was gross still remained. The festival of Dionysus was celebrated in dances and comedies of a flagrant indecency ; and even in Fifth-Century Athens the sacrifice of criminals as human scapegoats seems to have been a practice not wholly abandoned.[1] The fact is that in the new and higher conception of the deity there was still little enough to satisfy or elevate the souls of men. Zeus, Athena and their fellows were too cold, too abstract and aloof to win men's hearts ; and not unnaturally men therefore clung to the familiar customs and ideas of an immemorial tradition. That perhaps is why the hideous old idol of the Erechtheum excited a devotion which Pheidias' sublime idealization of the goddess entirely failed to command.

Now in the orthodox or official creed thus compounded of these dual elements there were two special flaws or weaknesses, each in its turn producing a reaction in Hellenic and especially in Athenian thought ; and the first of these weaknesses concerned the nature of existence after death. In Homer, and indeed in the Greek poets generally, life

---

[1] It is not indeed quite certain whether these ' scapegoats ' were actually put to death. But at the time of the Persian Wars human sacrifice was almost certainly practised by Athenians.

PLATE XVII

North porch of the Erechtheum, showing delicate forms of the Ionic style : the ' volutes ' or ' ramshorn ' capitals (now somewhat broken) ; slender columns supported on bases : entablature much less ponderous than Doric style. Much of the exquisite carving is still more or less intact. Cp. Doric style in Plate XVI.

ERECHTHEUM

beyond the grave is represented as a very miserable affair.
In the *Odyssey* the souls of dead heroes are shown to us
as tenuous, unsubstantial wraiths, gibbering like bats and
thirsting for a good strong draught of sacrificial blood.
Even in the dramatists of the Fifth Century it is with
infinite regret and horror that men and women exchange
the wholesome sunlight of the upper world for the gloomy
and joyless realm of Hades, where only exceptional saints
or exceptional sinners receive special rewards or punishments, and where for the normal individual the one luxury
remaining will be to remember the past pleasure of his
earthly life. No wonder if men craved for the assurance
of a better immortality ; and the want was supplied—
to what extent satisfied is impossible to say—by the
Mystery cults. How far back we are to date the origin
of these secret rites is more or less guess-work ; but the
cult of Dionysus, upon which they were largely based, had
probably been introduced from the north in very early
times. Even at its first coming (so legend had it) men
were shocked at the excesses of the Vine-god's devotees ;
but wild as were the midnight orgies and the hill-side
revels of the Bacchanals, it would be a mistake to suppose
that the principle underlying Dionysiac worship was simply
a craving for intemperate self-indulgence ; rather it was
a thrill of body and ecstasy of spirit responsive to that
mysterious force in Nature which is the source of all life
and growth, which brings the woods to leaf in spring-time
and sets the dead vine-shoot budding anew. At Eleusis,
in particular, the worship of Dionysus was very naturally
linked with that of Demeter the corn-goddess, and of
Persephone her daughter, who yearly went down to Hades
and yearly rose again to earth ; and from the Seventh
Century, at any rate, when Eleusis became part of Attic
territory, the joint celebration of the rites there secretly
enacted seems to have been the object of annual pilgrimage
from Athens. By the light of torches the pilgrims marched
twelve miles through the night to Eleusis, singing hymns
as they went and working their spirits to a tense excite-
ment ; and once there, no doubt, the ritual mummery

performed in the dimly-lighted hall roused in their un-
tutored souls an ecstatic sense of participation in the great
source of Life and Growth. In the Sixth Century, however,
there swept over Greece a new movement named after
the mythical seer Orpheus, and offering to men a fuller
vision into the secrets of the supernatural world. The
Orphic teachers—of whom Pythagoras (572–497), the great
mystic philosopher, was one—appealed primarily to the
more spiritual side of human nature, and they naturally
seized on the highly emotional worship of Dionysus as the
best vehicle for their message. Under their hands the
Mystery cult became almost what we ourselves should call
a ' Church ' of which the initiates alone were members,
preparing for participation in the rites by a long process
of purification, by abstinence from certain foods and in a
lesser degree by moral self-discipline. A sense of sin—
almost entirely lacking in the orthodox theology—begins
to find a place in this more mystic creed, and a sense too
of escape from sin and an assurance of rewards in the
future life. It is not strange that the mysteries became
popular ; and, if Eleusis remained a goal of pilgrims for
centuries to come, long after men had abandoned a real
belief in Zeus and his fellow-Olympians, that was the Orphic
teachers' work. They were preparing the way, it is hardly
too much to assert, for Christianity itself.

In the orthodox religion, it was said above, there were
two main flaws or weaknesses ; and of these the second lay
in precisely this lack of moral sense of which we have just
been speaking. The gods of Hellenic mythology may have
been sublime and majestic potentates, but they led shocking
lives. The multiplicity of Zeus' amours is notorious :
Hermes was the patron of crooks ; Dionysus, even during
his own festival at Athens, could be represented on the
stage as a drunken debauchee. Towards such gods man
could feel no moral responsibility ; and if obedience to their
dictates appeared to him desirable, that was because they
were powerful and not because they were good. This,
then, was the fundamental weakness of the orthodox
theology ; and in all the more earnest thinkers from the

Sixth Century onwards we begin to see a growing uneasiness and a troubled search after some deeper truth. Their message was delivered for the most part, like the message of the Hebrew prophets, in the form of poetry. The poets were, in fact, the prophets of Greece ; and each in their own way they strove to interpret, to amend, or even in the last resort, as we shall see, to destroy the old mythology. Among the earliest stands Stesichorus of Himera in Sicily, the pioneer of choric poetry, whose songs were so much a household word in Greece that not to know them was a sign of illiteracy. He gave a deep moral trend to the old barbaric legends, stressing, for example, the horror of the blood-guilt which dogged the House of Atreus, and making a truly tragic figure of Clytemnestra, who murdered her husband Agamemnon and was murdered in turn by her son. Next after Stesichorus comes the Boeotian, Pindar (522–448), more perhaps of a musician than a thinker, unrivalled in the turbulent flow of his lyric fancy, but not in any real sense profound. He seems more in sympathy with the old exuberant gaiety of the aristocratic régime than with the serious-minded intellectualism of the Fifth Century democracy ; and in his whole attitude to life he is essentially conservative. Being himself a member of the Delphic priesthood, and therefore bound to uphold the established creed, he is careful never to question the gods' morality, but rather to justify their ways to doubting man. Ingeniously enough he condones their many matrimonial blunders by glorifying Heracles and such other heroes as were born as the fruit thereof ; and the qualities too which these same heroes displayed he preaches in turn to mankind —high courage and endurance in the pursuit of honour and fame. Pindar was, in fact, a sort of Greek Malory, endowing ancient legend with an ideal of chivalry Hellenic and not mediæval ; and, even though many of his odes were written around such trivial occasions as a victory in a mule-race, he succeeds in throwing over them a glamour of romance by harking back to the theme of the lucky owner's ancestry. In other odes he more worthily celebrates the Greek triumph over the Persian invader ; but he was an aristocrat to the core, and partly because in common with other Boeotians he had advocated parley with the Persians, partly because he wrote rather for his wealthy patrons (such as the Sicilian tyrant Hieron) than for the unlettered man in the street, Pindar hardly attained the general popularity to which his genius entitled him. Books, moreover, were still a rarity ; the literature learnt by heart in the schools was largely confined to Homer and Hesiod ; and, if a poet was to wield a widespread influence over the populace, he needed some other medium of approach. At Athens, at any rate, such a medium was admirably supplied by the stage ; and it was thus no accident that the greatest Athenian poets of the Fifth Century were tragedians.

Dramatic performances, it must be remembered, took place as part of a religious celebration, the Festival of Dionysus. The whole of Athens turned out to witness them, massed in the great open-air theatre on the southern Acropolis slope. There three playwrights, officially selected, competed for the prize. Their themes were generally drawn from mythological tales, seldom from contemporary life ; and each playwright produced four plays, three of which were tragedies, more or less (as a rule) connected in plot, the fourth a tragico-comedy known as ' satyric drama '. The prize was awarded by judges, but the per-formance, though lengthy, was followed with the tensest emotion. There was never a better audience in the history of the world, and here therefore lay an unrivalled oppor-tunity for a man with a message. Many poets competed, and many even won the first prize, who are to us no more than mere names. But the works of three in particular were singled out for special excellence by the Alexandrian critics of a later age ; and to this accident we owe the preservation of some of their works. The names of this triad were Aeschylus, Sophocles and Euripides—Aeschylus, the noblest poet and profoundest thinker of the three ; Sophocles, the pious conservative and flawless artist ; Euripides, the realist and sceptic ; and of their art and thought something must now be said in greater detail.

Tradition has it that Aeschylus fought at Salamis, that

Sophocles danced among the choir-boys who celebrated the victory, and that in the selfsame year Euripides was born. Thus to the Athenian mind the elder poet became in a peculiar way associated with the great days of the Persian War. Later and more decadent generations looked back to Aeschylus (525–456) as the prophet of the city's prime and teacher of all the virtues which had made her great. Actually, however, he was ahead of his day ; and, though born at Eleusis and of a noble family, he was no unthinking champion of the orthodox creed. Rather he sought to probe behind the current theology to a deeper and more enduring truth. The plurality of gods ill satisfied his inquiring mind ; and he gropes towards Monotheism, tries to discover a directing power behind the kaleidoscope of human life and a meaning in its inexplicable tragedies. For him Zeus, ' whoever Zeus may be,' is the universal power, and that ' man must learn by suffering ' the universal law. Above all, perhaps, he was interested in the relation between the individual and Fate. He too, like Stesichorus, turned to the famous legend of the House of Atreus, tracing throughout its course, in a tremendous trilogy, entitled the *Oresteia*, the workings of an hereditary curse upon lives and characters, both innocent and guilty alike. In the first play Agamemnon, returning home in swollen pride from the sack of Troy, is slain by Clytemnestra, his unfaithful wife. In the second, his son Orestes fulfils the hideous duty of requital and takes his mother's life. In the third, avenging Furies pursue the matricide until he is acquitted of guilt before an Athenian jury on the Areopagus. This story of a doom—almost inescapable, yet by no means un-provoked by human fault—is a masterpiece of horror, perhaps unmatched in literature. The characters are cast upon a superhuman mould. Clytemnestra herself is a very fiend incarnate, beside whose remorseless purpose even Lady Macbeth, outwardly impenitent, but secretly conscience-ridden in the watches of the night, seems almost craven by comparison. Such creations plainly call for a lofty diction, and to this the turgid roll of Aeschylus' grandiloquence is admirably suited. He revels in mouth-filling, polysyllabic compounds—words, as Aristophanes humorously said, with ' shaggy crests and beetling brows '. A large portion of his plays is occupied with magnificent choric songs. For the chorus in his day was still a leading partner in the action of the drama ; and indeed since the actors themselves seem to have intoned rather than spoken their lines, the whole effect must much more closely have resembled an oratorio than a modern play.

It was one of Sophocles' chief merits (496–406) that he developed and perfected the dramatic form of tragedy, by introducing the use of scenery, by raising the number of actors simultaneously presented on the stage, from two to three, by treating each of his plays as a separate artistic unit, and above all by subordinating the rôle of the chorus to that of the actors proper. His language, compared with Aeschylus, is controlled and delicate. He understands, as his *Oedipus* and his *Antigone* well show, how to strike the note of high tragedy or pathos ; but it is done with infinite restraint. Even at the height of passion Sophocles never forgets he is an artist, a quality which makes him perhaps of all three dramatists the most typically Greek. Nor does he venture himself upon the dangerous path of religious speculation. He is always orthodox ; he played his full part in the public life of the town—serving, for instance, as steward of the Imperial Treasury in 443 and as a general against the Samian revolt in 440 ; and to the end of his lengthy years he remained invariably popular.

There could be no stronger contrast to the artistic methods or intellectual temper of Sophocles than the work of his younger contemporary Euripides (480–406). Euripides was never in his own lifetime popular (though he became a special favourite in the succeeding century). As a result, he seems to have been aloof, retiring and almost morose, spending much time at his work in a cave by the seashore. His last years were spent in embittered exile at the court of a Macedonian prince. In both thought and art—the explanation doubtless of his ill-success—he was a true revolutionary. ' I draw men ', said Sophocles, ' as they ought to be ; Euripides draws them as they are.'

In short, he was the first of the realists, and shocked men
accordingly. He took the old saga stories of a bygone age
—often the less familiar stories such as that of Jason and
Medea, which had not been staled by the handling of his
predecessors—and he tried to read into the stiff-set conventional figures they contained the actual feelings and
motives of human nature as he saw it around him. Thus,
his *Medea* is the study of a foreign woman brought as a
wife to Greece, there jilted by her husband and driven by
her passionate resentment to a diabolical revenge. Euripides had seen women so treated, and he tried to understand
and interpret through his art how they felt. Indeed for
all weak and unfortunate persons, but more especially for
women, he appears to have had a special sympathy ; but
simply because he drew them in their frailties and passions
no less than in their strength, he was termed a woman-
hater, and judged by his *Phaedra* and his *Medea* rather
than by his *Iphigeneia* or his *Alcestis*. Certainly, as is
almost inevitable in a tragedian, he was apt to look upon
the darker side of life ; and his pessimism no doubt was
even further deepened by the highly sceptical spirit in which
he seems to have approached the problems of religion.
Now it is true that in Euripides' plays the gods and
goddesses usually appear in the most correct and conventional guise ; but that is precisely what most awakens
our suspicions. At the end of a play of bitter realism,
suddenly to introduce Apollo or Athena, like a sort of
supernatural Jack-in-the-box, for the sole purpose of
winding up satisfactorily the otherwise inextricable tangle
of the plot, is scarcely the most commendable method of
enhancing the dignity of the deity. Some, indeed, have
thought with Professor Verrall that the poet was deliberately, though with great subtlety of dissimulation, poking
fun at the current theology by reducing the myths to terms
of real flesh and blood and leaving the spectator to draw
his own conclusions about the credibility of the part in
them assigned to the gods. Thus even in the most religious
of his plays, the *Bacchae*, the mysterious stranger who
impersonates Dionysus seems sometimes little more than

a mountebank revivalist, deluding his converts by stories of mock-miracles, sometimes the genuine representative of a deeply mystical creed. The poet's real meaning it seems impossible to probe. It is certain that he was no atheist, from the mere fact that he frequently prefers the use of the singular ' god ' to the plural ' gods ' ; and we may be sure that his keen mind pierced behind the hocus-pocus of Greek orthodoxy to the very roots of things. Among his own contemporaries, at any rate, Euripides was closely identified with that great intellectual upheaval which did so much to ruin (as in the ultimate issue it did so much to immortalize) Athens—the Sophist Movement ; and his attitude can best be understood from what now falls to be said of this parallel development.

III. PHILOSOPHERS AND SOPHISTS

For all this while there had been in progress throughout the Hellenic world another form of speculative inquiry, largely divorced from the problems of religion and viewing the world from a philosophic, or rather perhaps what we should call a scientific, point of view. Far away back in the Sixth Century we saw how Thales, the Ionian of Miletus (624–546), had begun to seek an explanation for natural phenomena ; and his work was taken up by other Ionians who concentrated mainly upon the fundamental question : ' What is the single all-pervading substance of which the world is made ? ' Had they been possessed of the mechanical apparatus of the modern physicists, they would perhaps have ultimately arrived at the theory of electrons. But the Greeks were no great hands at mechanical inventions ; they were not even, like the Romans, capable engineers ; and they had no idea, until much later times at any rate, of accurate tests or scientific analysis. These earlier philosophers, therefore, were quite content to rely on the evidence of their senses and the brilliant guess-work of their nimble imaginations. So their answer to this question about ultimate reality resolved itself into theories sometimes fantastic and sometimes astonishingly profound.

Heracleitus of Ephesus (c. 500), perceiving how in nature

there are everywhere continual processes of change and transmutation, how under extremes of heat solids will liquefy, liquids dissolve in their turn to vapour, and vapour under the same influence melt utterly away, declared that Fire was the ultimate reality and Change the universal law. ' All things ' he said ' are in flux ', like a river which is ever in motion, so that you can never step into the same water twice. Of such a world as Heracleitus conceived, an unresting kaleidoscope of shifting phenomena, true and permanent knowledge is clearly impossible ; for what we think to be true one moment ceases to be true the next. His theory accordingly was met with downright contradiction by Parmenides (c. 500), also an Ionian settled at Elea in South Italy, the earliest philosopher of whose writings (in verse) we have substantial remains. He roundly asserted that so far from being in flux all things are permanently the same. The river, though its waters flow everlastingly downwards, remains the same river still ; and so in like manner the changeful phenomena which we perceive are mere appearances or illusions behind which a permanent reality resides. Now a modern philosopher might, on the one hand, admit with Heracleitus that the impressions of the outer world which we receive through our senses do indeed undergo perpetual change, and that the appearance of any object is never twice precisely identical owing to variations, infinitesimal perhaps, but occurring every moment—variations, e.g., in its relation to the eye, to the sun's light, or to other objects innumerable. Yet equally might he assert with Parmenides that, despite this mutability of sense-impressions, there exists nevertheless a permanent and absolute Truth in which the Mind of men compels them to believe and which it is the constant effort of their Mind to discover. To a true realization of the part played by Mind in the problem, these early philosophers, however, never reached. Anaxagoras, of Clazomene in Asia Minor (500–428), seemed indeed upon the verge of the discovery. He explained all substances as being composed of ' seeds ' or (as we might call them) atoms, infinite in number and combined in varying ways ;

and inquiring further by what principle or force these seeds are brought together now in this way to form one substance, now in that to form another, he shrewdly assumed it to be Mind. Yet here on the very threshold, as it were, of the great discovery, he displays his limitations, for the ' Mind ' of Anaxagoras turns out to be itself a substance, infinitely rare and tenuous indeed, but corporeal like the rest. The fact is that, first and last, these men were thinking still as Thales thought, in terms of physics rather than of true philosophy. How elementary were their ideas even of physics may be seen from Anaxagoras' own declaration that the sun was a molten stone ' as large as the Peloponnese '. Even the doctrines of Pythagoras (572–497), though moving upon larger and more idealistic lines, ended equally in failure, though failure of a different sort. Exiled from Samos, he had collected in South Italy a brotherhood or school of disciples, pledged first to a strictly ascetic life according to the Orphic rules of purity, and second to the contemplation of philosophy. The mind of this singular mystic was chiefly devoted to the investigation of music and mathematics. He discovered the intervals of the octave, many rules of arithmetic, and amongst other things the spherical shape of the earth. But, when he sought, like other Ionians, to explain the composition of matter, he characteristically fell back on Number as the fundamental principle, and then went on to invent fantastic theories about the special significance of various units— assigning the number Four to Justice, Five to Marriage, Seven to Opportunity, and so forth. Thus rational thought was abandoned and forgotten in a maze of visionary symbolism. It was clear enough that these speculators, though they played their part, and no unimportant part, in the evolution of philosophy, were not to arrive within real touch of a solution. Strangely enough, the solution was to come from a far more practical line of inquiry— the search for an efficient educational method, and to this we must now turn.

As concerns education in Greece we know a good deal of what went on in Athens, something of what went on in

Sparta (which indeed was not much beyond drill and athletics), and but little of what went on elsewhere. At Athens it seems to have been compulsory since Solon's day to send boys to some sort of school where they would be taught the three R's, learning to trace their letters on little tablets of wax, to count with the aid of a reckoning-board, and to read and recite chiefly from the works of Homer and Hesiod. Education, however, was not thought complete without a further training in music and athletics. All but the poorest would learn to play the lyre or the flute, and indeed it was expected of every Athenian gentleman to be able to sing a song after supper. As for letters and music, so equally for physical training there were special schools, kept by private enterprise. In these boys learnt under supervision to run, wrestle, box, practise the long jump, throw the quoit or javelin, and, above all, to dance. This education a boy was free to continue from the age of six until he reached eighteen, when the State required him to undergo a two years' course of military training, partly at Athens, and partly on the frontier forts of Attica [1]; but after fourteen it was probable that his literary training would be pretty well complete and that most of his time would be spent in the wrestling school. During the four years' interval from fourteen to eighteen his mind would therefore lie fallow, unless some further educational subjects were devised to fill the period ; and in Fifth-Century Athens, with all the stir and eagerness of a keen commercial and political rivalry, both parents and boys were only too eager to turn this blank time to account. The democratic assembly offered grand opportunities for any who could master the rhetorical arts of persuasion. In the Law Courts equally lay a similar field ; and the lively intellects of a people already eager ' to hear some new thing ' were greedy for further acquaintance with the discoveries above-mentioned in Astronomy, Geometry, Harmonics and what not.

[1] There is, however, some reason to believe that the training of these ' Ephebes ' was an institution dating from the Fourth Century.

Now it can hardly have escaped the reader's notice that, among all the philosophers of whom we have spoken, not one hailed from Athens. This urgent demand for a more advanced education had therefore to be met by the introduction of foreign professors. To attract such to Athens (as to attract foreign craftsmen and traders) was not the least of Pericles' aims, and happily they were ready to come. For just at this epoch, and for broadly the same reasons, a similar demand for more advanced education had arisen in other parts of the Hellenic world, and had produced, as was natural, the men to supply it. Almost everywhere, but especially in Magna Grecia and Asia Minor, there were individuals to be found who called themselves Sophists or teachers of wisdom and who professed to be able to give lessons in wellnigh every subject under the sun—mathematics, astronomy, natural history, geography, history, politics, ethics, drawing, painting and music, and above all rhetoric. Though many doubtless existed of whom we never hear even so much as their names, some sophists were men of considerable distinction. There was Protagoras of Abdera, in Thrace (485–410), a ' most dignified personage ' who professed to be able to teach the whole art of good citizenship. ' Young man,' we are told of him saying, ' if you associate with me, you will be better the first day, and better still the second, and so every day better and better.' His, however, was a strictly practical training, aimed at strictly practical ends ; for of absolute truth he was utterly sceptical ; and his famous saying that ' Man is the measure of all things ' reduced Right and Wrong to mere matters of human convention or human expediency. Herodotus perhaps took a leaf from his book when he describes the horror of a certain Eastern tribe, themselves accustomed to *eat* their aged parents, on learning that the Greeks *burnt* theirs. Nor is it difficult to see that Protagoras' doctrine would be likely to have dangerous results if applied to the whole ground of morality. Then again there was Prodicus (*c.* 430), a chronic invalid who hailed from the island of Ceos. He specialized in the refinements of speech, teaching a nice discrimination in the use of words apparently synonymous, and delighting in hair-splitting quibbles. Gorgias, the Sicilian of Leontini (483–376), was a master of rhetoric as Prodicus of argument, popularizing a stilted poetical style which greatly influenced many writers of the day, Thucydides the historian among them. His methods of elaborate balance and strained antithesis may be illustrated by this sentence from a funeral speech he composed : 'When therefore they died, love died not with them, but deathless in bodies which are bodies no more, it lives when they live no longer.' The style of our own Elizabethan prose-writers was curiously similar, though of course owing nothing to Gorgias. Most remarkable of all was Hippias of Elis (c. 430), Jack-of-all-trades and master of all sciences, who once appeared at the Olympic Festival ' with everything he wore or carried, made by himself—ring, oil-bottle, shoes, clothes, and a wonderful Persian girdle ', to say nothing of epic poems, tragedies, dithyrambs, and essays in prose. He was ready to answer any question about anything, taught history, archaeology, geometry, astronomy, arithmetic and grammar. He had also invented a ' wonderful system of mnemonics whereby, if he once heard a string of fifty names, he could remember them all '. No wonder men and boys alike crowded eagerly to hear such pundits of wisdom as these. In the gymnasia pupils would spend half their time tracing triangles and circles in the sand. Even the great Pericles himself, though preferring the society and the more profound thought of the philosopher Anaxagoras, was by no means above attending to sophists. He once spent a whole forenoon discussing with Protagoras an accident to a horse at the races, one laying its death at the door of the man who threw the fatal javelin, the other blaming either the weapon or the president of the games. As we have said, it was part of Pericles' policy to encourage the learned to reside in Athens or visit it ; and first and last most of them came there. For the sophists were habitual wanderers. Since they had to make their living, they went where they could get pupils ; and some at least were able to charge heavy fees for their courses. Hippias made about £600 on a tour round Sicily. Prodicus charged £2 for a particular course, though there was a cheaper edition of it which only cost 10d. It was here perhaps that the real weakness of their educational system lay. They were bound to be popular in order to attract ; and it was a natural temptation to place speedy methods of instruction before honest inquiry for truth. Their tuition, in fact, was more nearly akin to a Pelman course or a school of Journalism than to the profound speculations of the true philosopher. Nevertheless, even the faults of their theories challenged thought and contradiction ; and out of the very clash of opinion, as will be seen, some good was to come.

We have already observed that among the names of either sophists or philosophers hitherto mentioned no true Athenian born has yet appeared. One such, however, there was whose reputation even in his own lifetime was to eclipse all others, and who in the history of world thought must rank perhaps above all the thinkers of Greece. He was by trade a sculptor, though of indifferent skill, ugly to look at, with protruding stomach, bulging eyes and a snub nose ; and his name was Socrates. Born in 470, he engaged even during early manhood, so far as we can tell, in the instruction of youth, taking no pay but forming a group or school of associates. Among these was a certain unhealthy, weak-eyed student named Chaerephon ; and when Socrates was nearly forty this Chaerephon went on a visit to Delphi and inquired of the oracle whether any man was wiser than Socrates ; and the answer was ' none '. To the humble-minded teacher this seems to have come as a staggering surprise. He seems, in fact, to have undergone some tremendous spiritual conflict, for while serving on campaign at Potidaea, we are told, he remained all one night standing in a trance of abstracted thought, oblivious of his chilly surroundings and the curiosity of his companions, until at dawn he awoke from his reverie and, saluting the rising sun, went about his day's duties. Ever after this, at any rate, Socrates adopted a new method of inquiry. Declaring himself unworthy of the oracle's high estimate, he went about to the various reputed wiseacres and sought to extract from them the truth concerning the subjects they professed. On submitting their replies to a severe test of cross-examination, Socrates, who was a past master in the art of argument, discovered to his astonishment that their theories would never hold water. Thus some one being questioned on the true meaning of courage would assert that the man who fights in ignorance of warfare is actually braver than the veteran with knowledge. Socrates would then suggest the case of the man who dives into the water without being able to swim, and force the other to admit that this is mere foolhardiness and that true courage must at least imply knowledge and not ignorance of the risks to be run. And so the argument would continue, his opponent yielding position after position before Socrates' ruthless logic, and Socrates declaring all the time that he himself was wise only in so far that, unlike others, **he** was at least aware of his ignorance. Such destructive criticism, even when directed upon conventional and accepted beliefs, is a healthy foundation for a constructive philosophy ; and Socrates, though he was for ever questioning others, had also his own creed. Now the early philosophers, while concentrating upon the problems of knowledge, had ignored the problems of conduct. The Pythagoreans, on the other hand, while emphasizing the importance of conduct, had degraded knowledge into a fantastic mysticism. Socrates, combining the wisdom of both, asserted that right conduct was the outcome of knowledge, and that if men only *knew* what was good, they would inevitably do it. Socrates' contribution then to the solution of life's problems was an immense advance upon all previous theories. For, in contradiction to the doctrine of the sceptics for whom Truth and Right were merely relative, true to-day and false to-morrow, right for me and wrong for you, he assumed, on the contrary, the existence of an absolute and eternal Truth, irrespective of mankind's changing views or conventions, and at the same time he asserted it to be the duty of the individual to arrive at this Truth by a process of sheer hard thinking. What, however, is in every preacher more important even

12

than his gospel, Socrates practised what he preached. He spent all his days, to the neglect of his home and his livelihood (for he took no pay for his teaching), in an unremitting inquiry after Truth ; and according to the Truth, as he saw it, he equally endeavoured to live. In the ultimate resort he went to his death for the sake of it, refusing his friends' offer to procure his escape from prison, because, he said, the State had condemned him to die, and one of man's primary duties is to obey the powers that be. That final sacrifice in the cause of sincerity and conscience impressed Socrates' message on posterity, as no mere words could have done ; and, though it remained for Plato to interpret that message in a reasoned system of philosophy, it was the character and life of the master which formed the foundation and inspiration of the pupil's writings.

The charge which brought Socrates to his death, and which had equally been levelled against the whole sophist class, was that 'they led the youth astray' ; and there can be little doubt that from the point of view of the normal man the charge was in the main true. Every great intellectual awakening brings unsettlement in its track. The men of the Renaissance, catching afresh from old Greek writers their spirit of unfettered inquiry, began by questioning the beliefs of the Church, then threw traditional conventions to the winds and often ended by relapsing into a discreditable licence of morals. In our own day a similar reaction against the strait-laced propriety of the Victorian age has resulted from the sudden spread of education and in particular of scientific half-truths which have caused men to question the truth of the Bible and the authority of the old ethical code. In precisely the same way the Athenians, and particularly the younger Athenians, were carried off their feet by the sudden rush of new and revolutionary ideas. They heard the morality and even the divinity of the gods called in question, and they began to feel doubts. They learnt from their teachers to quibble ; and they went off to exercise their newly-won critical powers on their parents at home. Sometimes the weapon was turned back against the teacher himself. There was a certain professor of legal science, who guaranteed that he could coach up his pupils to win any lawsuit or else would claim no fee for the course, and who once found himself unpaid. ' Sue me, if you will,' said the defaulter, ' if you lose, you cannot make me pay ; and if you win the guarantee will be broken, and you cannot make me pay either '. But such special pleading apart, the sophists' influence on their followers' morals was not always for the best. Some, like Socrates' favourite pupil Alcibiades, plunged into lives of shocking debauchery. In politics the effect was disastrous. Demagogues arose playing ruthlessly for their own hand and using their rhetorical attainments to popularize political theories in which honour, decency and restraint were abandoned for a cynical concentration upon purely selfish ends. The internal history of Athens during the last thirty years of the Fifth Century cannot, in fact, be comprehended at all without reference to these new ways of thought. There was, of course, a good side to the movement as well as a bad. Without the sophists, so far as we can tell, there might well have been no Socrates ; and if no Socrates, no Plato. Nor did these men personally intend any harm ; nevertheless, their influence upon their own and the succeeding generation was much what the influence of Machiavelli's doctrines was upon Sixteenth-Century Europe. For the fact is that intellectual growth, however inevitable and however ultimately fruitful, is never an easy and is not seldom a dangerous process.

Protest, of course, was not lacking. Aristophanes (c. 450–385), the great comic poet of the age and the regular mouthpiece of conservative opinion, was for ever denouncing the men who ' made the worse appear the better cause ', who filled the hot-bath-house and emptied the wrestling school and trained up a generation of narrow-chested windbags in succession to the stout old heroes of Marathon and Salamis. In his great comedy, the *Clouds*, he humorously, though somewhat unfairly, pictures Socrates in his ' thinking shop ', studying astronomy from a basket slung high in mid-air, and from time to time pronouncing pedantic nonsense to a group of anaemic pupils below him. But, though the years of Aristophanes' criticism, as of Socrates' chief activity, fall during the period of the Peloponnesian War ; yet, even before the rot was fairly begun, there had been attempts to stay it. We have already seen how the die-hard element in politics and religion had first opposed the building of the Parthenon and then the transference of the old image of Athena thither ; and we may be pretty sure that the same influences were again at work in the direct attack which was delivered against Pericles' intellectual associates. Anaxagoras was singled out as the object of the attack, and the charge was disbelief in the gods and unorthodox views concerning the heavenly bodies. Anaxagoras was condemned and fled from Athens to continue his studies at Lampsacus (435).[1] The attack, however, was in part at least aimed at Pericles himself ; and his enemies followed up their success by arraigning him, not this time for impiety but for misappropriation of funds. Pheidias, his friend and protégé, had already been tried on a similar charge concerning his use of the gold for the Parthenon statue, and, though the plates were detached and weighed out to prove his innocence, Pheidias had been condemned and died in prison (435 ?). Pericles, too, was found guilty and heavily fined (430). But this occurred when the war against Sparta had already begun ; the great statesman was indispensable and he was restored in due course to power. The meanness and malice of the attack is self-evident, and we must not allow the bitterness of these semi-political quarrels, nor the miserable mistakes of the unhappy years that follow, to dim the picture of what Pericles stood for in the Athens of his best days. Not merely was he the common people's idol, the guardian of their interests and the guide of their policy ; he was also the moving spirit among a band of men whose collective genius has probably never been equalled in any age of

[1] There is some reason for thinking that Anaxagoras' trial took place at a much earlier date ; but nothing is proved, and Plutarch certainly associates the three trials together.

history. Many were his close friends and associates ; all were in a greater or lesser degree dependent upon his sane and large-minded encouragement ; and before we embark on the story of Athens' ordeal and downfall we may well let our thoughts rest for a moment on that wonderful company of artists and poets and thinkers—Pheidias, whose statue of Zeus at Olympia was counted in itself a religious education ; Sophocles, in whom every charm of art, character and feature combined to win all hearts ; Euripides, whom merely to meet in Hades, men have said, it would be well worth while to die ; Aristophanes, the one and only rival to Shakespeare's comedy ; Herodotus, who has been called the father of history ; and Thucydides, his still greater successor, and (perhaps the most attractive figure of them all, though outside the Periclean circle) the garrulous, earnest, warm-hearted, imperturbable Socrates ; and besides these, the host of nameless undistinguished artists who set the marbles of the Parthenon in place, who painted the pottery and carved the gravestones which are now the pride of our modern museums ; and last, but not least, let us not forget the common multitude who had the wit and taste to appreciate and honour the genius of the great men in their midst,—And Periclean Athens was a town with not a quarter the population of Manchester !

CHAPTER XI

THE PELOPONNESIAN WAR—THE FIRST PHASE

I

THE Thirty Years' Peace of 445 involved, it will be remembered, a more or less clear understanding that Sparta should dominate the mainland and leave Athens to enjoy unmolested her supremacy at sea. The compromise worked ; and it was not between these two—in the first instance at any rate—that the quarrel began which was to involve almost the whole of Greece in the most bitterly fought struggle of her history. With Sparta's chief ally Corinth, however, it was another matter. Though temporarily placated at the time of the Peace, she was ill at ease. Athens' encroachments upon her westerly trade-route remained a permanent thorn in her side ; and not much more than a dozen years were over before she found herself in direct conflict with her great commercial rival at more points than one.

The first trouble came in the West. There, as we have seen, Corinth had long ago colonized Corcyra ; and the Corcyreans in their turn had founded Epidamnus on the Illyrian coast. In 435 the oligarch and democrat factions in Epidamnus fell to quarrelling, and the democrats appealed for help first to Corcyra, where they were refused, and then to Corinth, who sent some troops. There was little love lost between Colony and Mother-state, and the Corcyreans so far resented Corinth's interference that they went to war with her, and, being themselves exceedingly strong at sea, beat her navy handsomely. Aware, however, that Corinth had set to work on building a fresh fleet and clearly intended to renew the attack, they very prudently looked round for allies and turned not unnaturally to Athens. After a long debate, in which a Corinthian delegation vehemently protested against such intervention,

MAP TO ILLUSTRATE PELOPONNESIAN WAR

the Athenians decided to accept the Corcyrean suit and concluded a *defensive* alliance with the island power. They were free no doubt to make the alliance : but the Thirty Years' Peace was clearly from that moment in jeopardy.

In 433, after two years of preparation, a new Corinthian fleet put out against Corcyra, met her ships at Sybota and were within an ace of winning a decisive victory when ten Athenian galleys, which had been watching the engagement, suddenly intervened and saved the Corcyreans from total discomfiture. Here, then, was a definite breach of the Peace (though by whose fault it is not so easy to say), and the first blow had been struck (433).

The second was not long delayed. Among the cities of the Chalcidic peninsula—all tributary members of the Athenian League—the seeds of disaffection were being fruitfully sown by the jealous intrigues of Perdiccas, King of Macedon. Their revolt seemed imminent; and one of their number, not by any means the least influential, was Potidaea, a city originally of Corinthian foundation and still governed by magistrates sent annually from Corinth. Anxious to forestall possible trouble in this quarter (and the more so since Sybota had already embroiled them with Corinth), the Athenians now peremptorily ordered the Potidaeans to expel these magistrates and raze their city walls to the ground (432). The answer of the threatened town was an urgent appeal for Corinth's protection, and a call, readily answered, for a wholesale revolt of the neighbouring cities. Before the Athenians could close in on Potidaea, a Corinthian general had entered the town; and by the time that the siege began, therefore, they found themselves once again acting in open hostility to the forces of a power which was by treaty pledged to keep the peace with them.

So the second blow had been struck; and things were clearly working up for a general conflagration. Enmity and suspicion were in the air; and, as between France and Germany on the eve of the Great European War, so between Sparta and Athens, despite their recent agreement of 445, there now existed a bitter spirit of distrust and fear. Pericles had evidently realized that sooner or later war must come; and, if it was to come, he further foresaw that Athens' naval supremacy must be asserted to the full, and that the prize of victory would be Corinth's western trade.

Hence the readiness with which he embraced the Corcyrean offer of alliance. Hence also the swift decision with which he now threw down the gauntlet by an act of almost naked aggression. Determined to brandish, as it were, in the enemy's face the tremendous potency of Athens' maritime hegemony, he chose as his victim the state of Megara, Corinth's near neighbour and now once again her friend. In the early autumn of 432 a decree was passed in the Athenian Assembly excluding Megarian produce from all the harbours of the Aegean League. Such a boycott spelt utter ruin to a state almost wholly dependent upon trade, and in the later stages of the war Aristophanes has given us a ludicrous, but genuinely pathetic picture of a Megarian farmer driven by the pinch of want into marketing his daughters disguised as little pigs. Had the unhappy victims of this stern decree thrown in their hand and joined the Athenian League, it would have been a great strategical victory for Pericles, cutting the Peloponnesians from their Boeotian allies and preventing the passage of their troops up the Isthmus into Attica. But Megara stiffened her back, and Corinth at any rate recognized well enough the nature of the challenge which this high-handed measure involved. Her own grievances still rankled ; and her next task was to persuade the Spartans to undertake concerted action. At Sparta, to which her envoys were accordingly dispatched, there was a division of opinion. But, though the inherent tendency of the Spartan character lay towards caution and delay, the war-party carried the vote ; and it now merely remained to summon a general congress of the Peloponnesian alliance, which declared formally for war. Greek states, like most other nations when about to embark upon hostilities, preferred to manœuvre for a position of moral superiority over their foes ; and there followed a somewhat undignified exchange of cheap diplomatic scores, based, as was then quite natural, on semi-religious grounds (432–1). The Spartans, raking up the memory of an ancient act of treachery committed against Cylon and his fellow-conspirators two centuries before, summoned the Athenians to expel the accursed family of the Alcmeonidae, of which of course by far the most prominent member was Pericles himself. The Athenians rejoined by alluding to the sacrilegious murder of Pausanias in the Temple of Athena of the Brazen House. With such puerilities for prelude, the two powers embarked on a struggle which it was hardly conceivable could end otherwise than in the utter ruin of Greece. For all Greece was involved. Behind Sparta stood the entire Peloponnese, except Achaea and Argos, and of the states beyond the Isthmus, Boeotia, Northern Locris, Phocis and the colonies of Corinth which lay along the north-western coasts. Behind Athens, by free alliance, Corcyra, most of Acarnania, and with spasmodic loyalty to the treaty of 461, Thessaly ; by enforced service all the members, tributary or otherwise, of the whole imperial League.[1] So the lists were set.

The Peloponnesian War, as it came to be called, though an insignificant episode in world history if size of armaments be alone considered, has nevertheless a peculiar claim on our attention for two special reasons. The first is that its record was written by Thucydides, son of Olorus, beyond question one of the greatest historians of all time. His narrative, couched in a tense, highly antithetical, and often somewhat involved diction, is in itself a masterpiece of literature, severe in its artistic austerity, restrained in its judgments, but wonderfully vivid and stirring. Had Thucydides not been an historian, he would have made a wonderful playwright : and his keen sense of the dramatic, while betraying him at times into an excessive heightening of contrasts, serves also to endow even the barest recital of fact with all the romantic significance of high tragedy. It is typical of this quality in him that the better to emphasize the trend of events and analyse the motives of his characters, he adopts the method of inserting long set speeches, more or less of his own composition, but repre-

---

[1] Achaea, at first neutral, joined Sparta later. The chief north-western dependencies of Corinth were Ambracia, Anactorium, Oeniadae and the island of Leucas. In Thessaly the aristocrats were mainly anti-Athenian.

sentative of the opinions and policies which he imagined
to have been entertained by the speakers. The genius of
his work, however, lies no less in his scientific approach to
the subject than in its mere literary skill. As befitted an
enthusiastic admirer of the Periclean circle and a keen
student of the new philosophy, he sought a rational
explanation for all he saw or heard. Where Herodotus
would have been content to interpret events by some
superstitious fable or some crude anecdote of personal
pique, Thucydides lays bare with unerring instinct the
underlying principle of individual character or national
psychology. Even in his prefatory attempt to reconstruct,
from evidence more or less mythological, the history of
primitive times, he employs methods which, though leading
him frequently to a wrong conclusion, are nevertheless a
model of scientific deduction. A sense of the value of
evidence is, in fact, Thucydides' chief claim to greatness;
and when he comes in due course to contemporary events,
he attains in dealing with these to an impartiality which
few historians, if any, have equalled. This is the more
remarkable, since he was himself no disinterested spectator,
but an actual participant in many of the events he records.
How he was engaged during the first seven years of the
war we can only guess; but in 424 he served as general in
the North Aegean; and for his alleged culpability over the
loss of Amphipolis he suffered twenty years' exile from
Athens. Against Cleon, the probable author of his disgrace, he seems indeed to exhibit definite animus (though
an admirer of Pericles could hardly be expected to approve
the intemperate ways of an upstart demagogue). Against
Athens herself he harbours no such feeling; but though
he loved his city heart and soul, he neither withholds
criticism when criticism is due, nor fails to do full justice
to her enemies. His wanderings in exile doubtless afforded
him special opportunities of learning the truth from both
sides; and without fear or favour he sets down that truth
as he saw it. Only towards the end does his spirit appear
to have failed him; for, though he returned to Athens,
when the war was over, he lacked heart, it would seem,

to tell the tragic tale of his country's downfall; and he never finished his book.[1]

The war's other claim on our attention lies in this, that it was a very early, very interesting and very clearly defined example of a type of conflict familiar enough in the later history of Europe, the duel between land-power and sea-power — 'the Elephant versus the Whale'. Sparta's army, as we have often insisted, was invincible by land. Add to it the contingents of her Peloponnesian and Boeotian allies, and it was manifestly beyond the power of any Athenian force to risk battle with any prospect of success. Athens, on the other hand, was equally invincible at sea. With vast financial resources at her disposal (and, even when the Potidaean campaign was paid for, Pericles had still 6,000 talents stored on the Acropolis), she could count on meeting to the full her naval requirements in whatever field of action. As against her highly trained fleet, manned by citizen rowers[2] and adapted to nimble manœuvre, the enemy could make no showing. The Spartans were never great sailors, Corinth's navy was scarcely big enough to beat Corcyra's (now ranged on Athens' side), and the financial outlay involved in the building of a bigger she could never hope to meet under the war-crippled condition of her trade. Indeed, till ample subsidies were forthcoming from Persia, it proved impossible for Athens' enemies to challenge her supremacy at sea. Meanwhile, to overcome her resistance by direct attack on land seemed equally impossible. Her system of fortifications defied surprise assault, and her secure communications with the Peiraeus and so with overseas supplies made siege unthinkable. Athens, in short, was unassailable as an island. Steadfastly refusing battle on land, she could wait for the enemy to exhaust

---

[1] This is Professor Murray's explanation of the History's incompleteness; but it is equally possible that Thucydides died before he could finish it, probably in 399.

[2] In the later stages of the war at any rate the Athenians fell back upon supplementing their citizen-crews by hired rowers from outside.

his patience in fruitless invasions of her soil, meanwhile employing her ubiquitous fleet on retaliatory but non-committal raids. Such, in fact, was Pericles' strategic policy. Though, by the nature of things, it could only achieve victory by a process of exhaustion, its success in that aim seemed certain, but upon two conditions : first, that it was scrupulously maintained to the letter (no easy matter in the exuberant mood of the Athenian people) ; second, that the League members remained loyal—and therein, as we shall see, lay the rub. For, if Athens' allies deserted her, she would lose at once the tribute essential to the maintenance of her all-important fleet.

II

First blood was drawn not on Attic soil itself, but in the little town of Plataea, which lay nestling under Mount Cithaeron's northern slope on the edge of the Boeotian plain. Assistance rendered at Marathon had cemented a strong friendship between Plataea and Athens, and the jealousy of her neighbours now prompted the delivery of a foul blow, before any was struck elsewhere. A small party of Thebans were treacherously admitted into the town under cover of night and surprised the citizens into momentary surrender. Their success, however, was short-lived. With the approach of day spirits revived ; and, the smallness of the invading force being realized, they were surrounded, hunted down and captured, and (despite negotiations which were opened up with Thebes) eventually slain in cold blood. ' Upon this,' says Thucydides, ' the Lacedaemonians determined to invade Attica and sent round to their Peloponnesian and other allies bidding them to equip troops and furnish all things necessary for a foreign expedition '. It was the spring of 431. When all was ready, they set forth from the Isthmus under the Spartan King Archidamus, passed up through the Megarid, dallying en route as though still in hopes of a compromise, pausing for a while to make a fruitless assault on the frontier fort of Oenoe, and then, after ravaging the neighbourhood of Eleusis, debouched

on the plain of Athens in full view of the Acropolis itself.
The inhabitants of Attica, sending their sheep and cattle
to safe keeping in Euboea, had meanwhile collected within
the fortifications of the town ; and we can well picture
with what consternation they now saw their precious farms
go up in flames and the smoke of their burning crops and
olive-trees hang over the invader's track as he crossed the
head of the plain.   There was hot clamour to go after
him ; but Pericles' eloquence was successful in resisting
the demand.   No clash occurred beyond a skirmish of
horse ; and presently the Peloponnesian army, unable to
live long upon the land when their own supplies were
exhausted, and eager perhaps to get back to their own
farming, departed by way of Boeotia.   Such was the
ordeal which Athens was called upon to face not in 431
alone, but in four at least out of the six succeeding years.
In point of fact, however, the damage was not so severe
as might be fancied.   The destruction of crops is at best
a lengthy business ; and, though the invaders at one time
passed down as far as Sunium, they never stayed longer
than six weeks in Attica, often indeed much less ; and in
spite of all, the country was too large to ravage thoroughly
in so short a stay ; and the Athenians, we are told, ' were
able to enjoy the produce of their farms '.   The real pinch
lay not in what occurred outside the city, but what occurred
within it.

There, as might be guessed, the crowding of the refugees
was terrible.   Every open space was utilized, not excluding
sacred ground.   Huts were eventually built between the
two Long Walls ; but the congestion was none the less
serious, and in a town wholly ignorant of hygiene or
sanitation, the inevitable followed.   In the late spring of
430, plague broke out.   Infection came apparently from
the east ; and Thucydides describes its symptoms.   Hoarse-
ness, bleeding at the throat and violent coughing were
followed by convulsions and internal pains.   The body
turned livid and broke out in ulcers, and the sufferers in
their fever could bear no touch of clothes, and longed
only to throw themselves into cold water.   Death followed

swiftly on the seventh or ninth day. A few, like Thucydides himself, survived the malady ; some lingered for a considerable time as did Pericles, who succumbed in 429 after the period of disgrace of which we spoke above : and none that had been stricken recovered normal health. The plague hung over Athens all that year, and well on through the next. It spread to the army encamped before Potidaea where it did great havoc among the troops. One fourth perhaps of the entire population died [1] ; and the moral effects were even more terrible. The recklessness of despair took hold upon men's spirits. Decency and generosity were lost in selfish panic and mean suspicion. The soul of Athens was seared and embittered, so that even when the war was over, she never again recovered her coolness and sanity of temper. Nor must the strain and agony of the ordeal be forgotten when we come to pass judgment upon some of her later acts.

Even upon the enemy, meanwhile, the terror of the plague had made its mark ; for in 429 they avoided Attica and turned at the Thebans' request to accomplish the reduction of Plataea. The little town had received from Athens a guarantee of succour ; but the risk of open battle proved too serious, and the promise was not kept. So it was alone against the combined forces of Thebes and Sparta that Plataea made her memorable defence. Every device of contemporary siege-craft was brought into play against her; and at every turn she countered them.[2]

[1] Thucydides' estimate is over 4,000 of the hoplite strength and an ' unascertained number ' of other classes.

[2] *Note on Siege Warfare.*—In the military history of a people so warlike as the Greeks nothing is more remarkable than their incapacity for siege operations. The Spartans were notoriously helpless against the Helots on Ithome ; and could do nothing better than sit down to a blockade. Nor were the Athenians themselves at the outset of the Peloponnesian War in any way in advance of their contemporaries. The truth probably is that the food supply of a Greek state was so readily at the mercy of a victorious invader that defeat in the field spelt inevitable starvation and so rendered superfluous any further operation against a citadel often strongly fortified by nature as well as by science, and wellnigh impregnable to an army of heavily encum-

First when a mound of earth was piled against a section of the wall to provide a passage over it, the Plataeans raised the wall. When the mound threatened to overtop it, they tunnelled underground and drew away the foundation of the mound until it sank. Frustrated of this ruse by the laying of clay and wattles in the gap, they changed their tactics and built inner defences behind the threatened section of the wall. Battering-rams were brought up and they snapped off the noses of the machines by dropping heavy beams on them from the battlements. Finally, when an attempt to fire the city, by means of lighted faggots hurled across the wall, had been providentially foiled by a heavy thunderstorm, the enemy decided to abandon direct assault and proceed to blockade. All round Plataea they built a double ring-wall, double, that is, to preclude alike either sally or relief. In the space between these walls, which were roofed for shelter's sake, a garrison, mainly Boeotian, was left to spend the winter and starve the townsfolk out. Spring saw the end no nearer, nor summer either ; but about mid-winter of the following year a number of Plataeans, despairing of help from Athens, determined on escape. A stormy, moonless night was chosen. With scaling ladders the leaders mounted the ring-wall ; seized and held a section of it against the startled garrison, while the rest of the party slipped over ;

bered hoplite soldiers. In any case it was not till the period of the Peloponnesian War that more elaborate methods of attack begin to appear in the pages of history. Thucydides pays special attention to them, as though to a novelty. They were in all likelihood borrowed through the Ionians from Persia, which in this respect at least was far ahead of the Greeks. At any rate in the course of the war a number of new devices were brought into play ; nor do the Peloponnesians, not even the Spartans themselves, appear to have lacked enterprise in this matter. Siege engines were to have been brought to bear on Pylos ; and the attack on Plataea was every whit as scientific as the Athenians' siege of Syracuse. The chief methods adopted may be summarized as follows : (1) circumvallation, (2) assault by scaling ladders, etc., (3) mining against the foundation of the walls, (4) siege-engines. For further information see Grundy. *Thucydides and the History of his Age*, on which this note is based.

then all disappeared into the darkness, first in the direction of Thebes, thus laying a false scent, and then to Athens, where two hundred or so arrived in safety. Next summer the remnant left in Plataea were forced by starvation to capitulate, and all were put to death (427). They too numbered scarcely more than two hundred ; and the capture of Plataea was no great testimony to the skill of the enemy's siege-craft.

Pericles had laid it down that there should be no pitched battles ; but if a further justification is to be sought for Athens' desertion of her ally, it can best be found in the very heavy strain which the war was imposing on the resources of her man-power. For it must not be supposed that even her land-forces had been remaining altogether unoccupied. The siege of Potidaea alone, begun in 432 and lasting continuously till 430, had drawn out first and last 8,000 citizens of hoplite rank—the philosopher Socrates among them. It had cost 2,000 talents and a large number of lives ; so that until the inhabitants at last surrendered, driven by the pinch of hunger to the point of feeding upon human flesh, Athens could ill afford to contemplate further commitments by land. Nor, as it turned out, was such a strain upon her man-power to be allowed any lengthy respite. For in 428 the revolt of another of her subject cities was to cause her considerable embarrassment. At the outset of the war the Spartans had deliberately posed as champions of the ' Liberty of Hellas ' ; and the importance of fomenting disaffection among members of the Athenian League was certainly not lost on them.[1] Lesbos, the largest of the islands of the Asiatic coast, and one which, it will be remembered, still retained an independent fleet, had long resented the constraints upon her freedom ; and in 428, with a promise of help from the Peloponnese, she came out into revolt. Four out of the five walled towns, of which the island was composed, combined in political union, and Mitylene, which was to form their capital, was very promptly blockaded and

---

[1] It was not, however, until Brasidas' campaign in Chalcidice in 424 that really active measures were taken to this end.

besieged by an Athenian fleet and army. Early next year a Spartan commander slipped somehow into the city, bringing promise of succour to come. Spirits rose and then, when no help arrived, sank correspondingly. By summer Mitylene surrendered ; and too late by a week a Peloponnesian fleet, greatly daring, arrived in the neighbourhood.[1] The fate of the Lesbian prisoners it was left to the Athenian Assembly to determine. The horror of the plague lay heavy on the minds of the citizens still, and in the maintenance of their League they saw their sole hope of salvation. Pericles was gone ; and following the cynical lead of the loud-voiced demagogue Cleon, they determined to make of Lesbos a terrible example. A trireme was dispatched with the order to kill all adult males and sell women and children into slavery. On the morrow of this decision, a revulsion of feeling swept over Athens. A fresh meeting of the Assembly was called ; and after long debate the sentence was revoked and a second trireme sent after the first. To overhaul the lead of some four and twenty hours was no easy business ; the rowers were fed at the oar and slept and rowed in relays. Even so the first galley got to Lesbos ahead of them ; and only in the very nick of time did the message of reprieve prevent the massacre. It is an index of the swift degradation of political honour at Athens that barely a dozen years later a similar sentence was passed upon Melos for a far less offence, and this time there were no second thoughts.

In what we have hitherto said of Athenian strategy, we have dealt mainly with its defensive side ; but it would be a mistake to suppose that she never struck back. Pericles, as we have said, was wisely chary of risking his land forces outside Athens ; though, when the Peloponnesian army was safely out of the way, he indulged in an expedition of reprisals against the Megarid—a useful safety-valve to the pent feelings of the populace, who much resented

---

[1] Thucydides tells how the Aegean islanders came down to the shore to meet the Peloponnesian fleet, making sure that it must be Athenian. Their astonishment to find the contrary was profound.

their enforced inaction behind the safe shelter of the city walls. The offensive use of sea-power, whether to distract the enemy's forces or to wear down their morale by sudden raids, was not, however, an opportunity to be ignored. In 431 he sent a hundred galleys ranging round the Peloponnese and up to the north-west, landing, burning and spreading terror at various points on their route. In the following year the same tactics were repeated, Pericles himself sailing in command. Shortly after this and during the period of his disgrace, an important new departure was made. A small detachment of twenty ships was sent under Phormio to the naval station of Naupactus, and given orders to blockade the Corinthian Gulf. Its activities appear to have been tolerably successful; but the inadequacy of its numbers was the more unfortunate since considerable campaigning was subsequently to take place in the hinterland of Naupactus and the command of the gulf was therefore certain to be vigorously contested. Corinthian trade interests were much concerned, as we know, with the westerly route to Sicily, and hence also with those coastal districts of North-Western Greece along which the trade route passed. All the more ready were the Peloponnesians, therefore, upon the suggestion of their Ambraciot allies, to contemplate in 429 an offensive against pro-Athenian Acarnania. Eluding Phormio, their army was shipped across and marched inland upon Stratus. But it was a wild and ill campaigning country. The inhabitants, who unlike most Greeks still lived in scattered villages and had not known the civilizing effects of city life, preferred guerrilla tactics to a proper stand-up fight. To the Peloponnesian hoplites, as to others later, this proved most disconcerting; and they were forced to an ignominious retreat. Meanwhile from Corinth a naval squadron nearly fifty strong had been moving up gulf to join them, and encountered on its way the blockading force of Phormio. Undeterred by their inferiority of numbers, the Athenians closed, and it is an interesting token of their immense naval prestige that the panic-struck Corinthian vessels fell at once on the defensive, bunching together in a rosette formation to avoid attack in their rear, and allowed the nimbler adversary to circle round at will, charging in at unexpected angles, ripping up their oar-line by a side-long traverse or ramming them amidships. The Corinthians retired ; but in due course returned, this time nearly eighty strong. Phormio had received as yet no reinforcement ; and his case seemed wellnigh desperate. As however his vessels were scuttling into Naupactus, one of them swung suddenly round the stern of a moored merchantman, and rammed the leading ship of the pursuit. Seeing those behind it check in their course, the rest of the Athenians also wheeled about and soon had the enemy running in full flight. Phormio's double victory assured once and for all the Athenian supremacy in western waters ; and the way now lay open not merely for a complete blockade of the Corinthian Gulf, but also for a more ambitious policy in the hinterland.

In 426 Demosthenes appears upon the scene of operations in charge of an army. He was a soldier, rare enough even in quick-witted Athens, who had the imagination for bold initiative and adventurous departures from traditional routine ; and he now formed a project of striking up among the mountains of Aetolia and ultimately, as we shall see later, of invading Boeotia itself upon this western side. The Aetolians were a half-civilized folk, hostile to Athens, but not to all appearance a very formidable foe. But like the Spartans in Acarnania, Demosthenes had gravely misjudged the resistance here awaiting him. Among the rough mountain passes his hoplites floundered helplessly against the nimble Aetolians, who dogged their every movement with a continuous shower of missiles, and easily eluded their futile charges by taking to the hills. With serious loss Demosthenes returned to Naupactus, having learnt a lesson in Aetolia which he was to turn to good use, as we shall see later, against the Spartans marooned on Sphacteria.

Meanwhile in Northern Greece the conflict resolved itself into a struggle for the naval bases round the mouth of the Corinthian Gulf. The Spartans made a dead set at

Naupactus ; but were foiled in the nick of time by Demosthenes' energy. Then, when in league with the Ambraciots they proceeded to attack the Acarnanians at Olpae, Demosthenes again came up with them and by skilful manœuvre placed them at such disadvantage that they gave him a secret undertaking to withdraw and leave their Ambraciot allies in the lurch. The compact was kept. The Spartans stole off in ones and twos pretending to forage, we are told, for herbs and faggots ; and the miserable Ambraciots were abandoned to their fate. Many were slaughtered by the Acarnanians on the spot. A further large body of reinforcements, coming up in ignorance, were caught half-asleep at their bivouac and slain almost to a man ; and their total losses were so overwhelming that Thucydides himself refuses to state the figure—for no man, he says, would believe it. This success decided the struggle for the North-West in Athens' favour. Within two years she captured both Anactorium and Oeniadae, leaving no Corinthian base along that coast except Leucas. Meanwhile Corcyra, with her once powerful navy, had become a cipher. She had not rendered the aid which might have been expected of an ally, nor was she likely in the future to prove any obstacle to Athens' expansion. For a bitter feud had been raging in the island between oligarch and democrat factions, reaching a ferocity and bitterness which calls forth special comment from Thucydides. Massacre and counter-massacre took bloody toll ; and for the time at least Corcyra may be said to have committed suicide. More and more therefore was the way opening out for Athens to push her interests in the Adriatic. Sicily beckoned her on. Besides the wealth to be won by exploiting the trade of the island, there was much to be gained by interrupting the corn-supplies which it sent to the Peloponnese. Already in 427 B.C. a small Athenian force had been sent thither under Laches to support Leontini against the Corinthian colony Syracuse. Its activities, however, had not led to much ; and in the year after Olpae a fresh reinforcement was accordingly dispatched to its aid. It was the sailing of this expedition which led indirectly to the next great exploit of Athenian arms—the seizure of Pylos.

During all these years neither side had as yet adopted the plan of occupying a permanent post on enemy soil. When at a later stage of the war the Spartans tried it, they did more damage to Attica in a twelvemonth than in half-a-dozen brief annual invasions. For the Athenians,

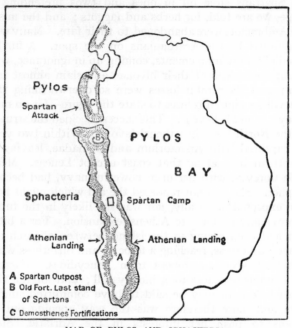

MAP OF PYLOS AND SPHACTERIA

on the other hand, the idea seemed banned by the Periclean policy of avoiding a land battle. A bold departure from this rule, due partly to accident and partly to Demosthenes' initiative, was now, however, to prove a turning-point in the war. In 425 the Athenian fleet, on its way to foster the imperial interests among the towns of Sicily, was driven by bad weather into an unused harbour on the West Messenian coast. Here lay a broad bay, crescent in shape,

across the mouth of which stretched the desert island of
Sphacteria ; while at the crescent's northern tip stood the
gaunt peninsula of Pylos, in which Demosthenes' quick eye
discerned the makings of an excellent fort. The soldiers
started building a wall ; and though not himself in command, he persuaded the others on their departure to leave
him behind with a garrison. That the Spartan army, then
in Attica, should have at once made tracks for home,
seems evidence enough how they received this news.
Demosthenes' coup had touched them indeed upon their
most tender point ; for an enemy post at Pylos was a
standing invitation for the Helots of Messenia to revolt.
So to Pylos the Spartans gathered, both army and fleet ;
and since approach from landward was wellnigh impossible,
an assault on the peninsula was planned upon the seaward
side ; but thrice over upon three successive days Demosthenes' small band beat back the landing parties from the
shore ; and before a fourth attack could be delivered, the
main Athenian fleet had itself reappeared upon the scene,
caught the Spartan ships ashore and unprepared, and,
though failing of their capture, secured the complete
command of Pylos Bay. Nor was this all ; for will it be
believed that on the adjacent island of Sphacteria the
Spartan commander, eager to prevent the Athenians from
using it and regardless of the obvious risk, had posted
420 of his choicest hoplites ; and *these were now marooned.*
To the Spartan authorities at home the lives of even so small
a number seemed a terrible stake ; and on the fate of the
island all thoughts of either side now centred. So desperate
were the Spartans that they called a truce, surrendering
their ships as pledge and suing for peace at Athens. But
the stern terms there demanded sent the envoys home
empty-handed, and the Athenians on a quibble kept the
ships. Yet such was the prestige of Spartan invincibility
that they durst not attack the island. Day after day their
patrols kept circling round it ; and the four hundred,
meagrely supplied by volunteer swimmers, tightened their
belts.

At Athens meanwhile the populace grew restive. Cleon

denounced in stirring tones the inefficiency of the generals. 'Were I of their number,' he said, 'I would soon end the business.' 'Do it then,' was the response of Nicias; and when Cleon tried to back out the Assembly, sniggering at his dilemma, egged him on till he accepted. But Cleon for all his bombast was no fool. Between him and Demosthenes there clearly existed an understanding about the way the thing could be done. He collected accordingly a large force of allied troops—not Athenian hoplites, be it noted, but slingers and bowmen from the Cleruch settlers of Aegean islands. The lesson learnt in Aetolia was about to be used. One morning when day broke as many as 12,000 troops were landed on Sphacteria; an accidental fire had burnt the undergrowth and there was little shelter on the island. The four hundred, overborne by the shower of stones and arrows, retreated to a height at the north end; but when a party of Messenians familiar with the country climbed the cliff in their rear, they saw the game was up and they surrendered.

The victory was in more ways than one a hammer-stroke. It meant, first, the retention of Pylos, useful as a refuge for Helot malcontents and as a vantage-point for future depredations—soon further to be followed by the seizure of similar posts on the Spartan island of Cythera and on the peninsula of Methana not far from Epidaurus. In the second place the haul of prisoners, though not numerically large, possessed a tragic importance for the Spartan authorities. For 120 of them belonged to the class of fully enfranchised citizens; and, since the total number of these ran to less than 3,000, the loss of their valuable persons was so severely felt that even a disadvantageous settlement did not seem too high a price for their recovery. Last, but not least, the victory of Sphacteria had a profound

---

PLATE XVIII

(a) On the right the bluff of Pylos, and beyond it the island of Sphacteria. In the further distance rise the coast-hills enclosing the waters of the bay. (b) Cape Sunium, the Land's End of Attica, surmounted by a temple.

PYLOS

CAPE SUNIUM

military effect. It shattered the legend of Spartan invincibility; and when the 300 emaciated captives were marched in their rags through the streets of jeering Athens, they appeared in very deed to be the earnest of a triumphant peace.

Peace could, in fact, have been had for the asking and on highly favourable terms; but it was far from the thoughts of those now in power at Athens. The confidence bred of the triumph of Sphacteria had swept aside the old Periclean ban on land action. A vigorous offensive was the order of the day; and in 424 Demosthenes, backed doubtless by Cleon, planned a bold and well-concerted attack on Megara and its port Nisaea. In that city, as in Corcyra, faction was rife; and a certain group within the walls, fearing the revenge of their political opponents, made a secret offer to let the Athenians in. The island of Minoa, which lay at the harbour mouth, was already in Athenian hands, and made a useful base for the operation. Thence under cover of darkness Demosthenes shipped over a force which he concealed in a clay-pit near the gate in the Long Walls between city and port. A gang of the traitor-party, who were nightly accustomed to take down a small boat to the sea on privateering excursions, jammed the gate open with the cart upon which their boat was carried. The Athenians sprang from their ambush, rushed the gate and the Long Walls were theirs. All was arranged next day to capture the city also, and here again the traitors were ready with their plan. Under pretence of a sally they were to throw open the gates, and they even took the precaution of oiling their bodies as a distinguishing token in event of a promiscuous slaughter. But the plan went agley. The opposite faction, scenting treachery, refused to open the gates; and the best that the Athenians could do was to blockade the garrison of the port, which in two days surrendered. Thus Nisaea passed into their hands, a capture which gave them henceforward a stranglehold on Megara; and encouraged by the success of this exploit, Demosthenes now proceeded to his long-cherished ambition—the invasion of Boeotia.

Here again the plan was carefully concerted and treachery

was once more to play a part in it. Demosthenes himself, with a force of allied troops, was to sail to Siphae on the Corinthian Gulf and thence to threaten Boeotia from the south-west. On the north-west a pro-Athenian party among the Boeotians were to seize the border town of Chaeronea; and meanwhile a large hoplite force from Athens was to cross the Boeotian border in the east, there to seize and fortify, after the Pylos model, the seaside sanctuary of Delium. The synchronization of these three attacks was essential to success; but the secret leaked out and all went wrong. The Boeotian democrats were afraid to rise. Demosthenes not only arrived too soon at Siphae, but found the enemy forewarned; and, though Hippocrates reached Delium and fortified and garrisoned the temple, he had not time to regain the Attic border before the levies of Thebes were upon him. The engagement which followed was the first pitched battle of the Peloponnesian War and is of particular interest in the evolution of Greek tactical formations. In a hoplite action it was the established custom for either side to form a long line eight deep, to advance the serried shield-row to the point of actual contact, and then by sheer pushing and thrusting to breach or buckle the opposing front. From this accepted formula the Thebans so far departed as to mass their right wing in a column no less than *twenty-five* deep, with the natural result that by mere weight of numbers they bore down all resistance on that flank, and then rolled up the rest of the Athenian host. Now, so long as a hoplite line retained its formation intact, the series of linked shields protected bodies well and casualties were few. Once it was broken, however, the individual hoplite's armour afforded very inadequate defence on rear or flank; and in the *sauve qui peut* he could only hope to save his skin by showing swift heels and even in the last resort by unburdening himself of his very cumbrous and now quite useless shield. As a rule, therefore, defeat meant terrible losses, and in one battle it was actually computed that the routed army lost 3,000 men as against the victors' eight. At Delium the Athenians left a thousand dead behind them, Hippocrates himself among the rest. Their fortified post was laid under siege ; and a curious mechanical fire-projector, equipped with nozzle and bellows, speedily drove the defenders from the wall and the place was captured (424). The whole campaign had been in fact a ghastly failure ; and its author's credit was severely shaken. From this point on, the fortunes of Athens, which after Pylos stood so high, began steadily to decline. Hitherto the war had gone undeniably in her favour. Attempts to reduce her by the method of annual raids had proved unavailing. Her trade, so far from suffering by the war, had benefited not merely by the complete monopoly which her naval supremacy gave her in the Aegean, but also by the hold which she had established on the Adriatic coast-line. Of Sparta's allies Corinth was hard hit and Megara starving ; and Sparta herself was ill at ease with the menace of Pylos at her very door, tempting the Helots to the thought of insurrection. If, on the other hand, her best hope of victory lay in detaching Athens' subject allies, that hope had so far miserably failed. Lesbos' fate was at once a proof of Sparta's inability to render effective assistance and a warning to all others who might wish to imitate her example. Potidaea had fared no better, and even if certain cities in Chalcidicê which had revolted with her remained still unreduced, their secession seemed no very serious threat to the stability of Athenian imperial-ism. Nevertheless, it was in Chalcidicê that the rot was now to set in. With the appearance of a Spartan in their midst the disaffection was to spread among many neigh-bouring cities ; and the spectre of a more general rebellion of the League to loom up ominously. At home in Athens de-pression set in. Depression was followed by divided coun-sels ; and the clash between the rival policies of peace-party and war-party became more and more sharply defined.

III

If we are to grasp the full significance of developments at Athens during the years which follow, it is essential that something should first be said about the condition of her internal politics. During his lifetime and with scarcely an interruption Pericles, as we have seen, had ruled the democratic assembly with almost the power of an autocrat. Nor was it the least part of the tragedy of the plague that by removing the best promise of Athenian manhood, it left none fit to assume the rôle which he had so successfully filled. There were candidates, of course, for the place ; and within a year or two of Pericles' death had arisen a man who was to fill it in a very different fashion. Cleon, the leather merchant, was a true son of the people, sadly lacking in the high principle and dignity of his aristocratic predecessor, but familiar enough, if not with the sophists themselves, at least with their sophistical catchwords that 'might is right' and 'expediency comes before morals'. His logical mind stripped Athenian imperialism of all pretences ; to him the city's policy appeared to be purely selfish, her power to rest on nothing but naked force ; and he never shrank from enforcing the appeal to bare self-interest with all the glib violence of his clap-trap rhetoric. But beyond this, Cleon was clearly possessed of considerable courage, imagination, and (as the phrase is) ' push and go '. If the war was to be conducted upon lines of brutal and unscrupulous efficiency, he beyond a doubt was the man for the job. His following in the Assembly was drawn partly from the lower strata of society, the unemployed and the ne'er-do-wells, who were easily led astray by his windy promises, and placated by such sops as the increase of the jury-dole, but more still from that very large section of the population who were interested in trade. To these latter the continuance of the war was by no means a disaster. Athens' complete command of the seas gave her a virtual monopoly of commerce, opening to her own ships the opportunities of traffic which it equally denied to her enemies. The merchants of the Peiraeus looked forward to an increased prosperity as the prize of complete victory ; and already perhaps they were beginning to cast a covetous eye upon the markets of Sicily and the West—hitherto, as we have seen, the special preserve of Corinth.

But there were other sections in Athens to whom this

view made no such appeal. First there was the small and vigorous group of aristocratic conservatives, who had been a thorn in the side of even Pericles himself. These had resigned themselves, with what grace they could, to the inevitability of the democratic régime ; but they still pinned their faith to the old Cimonian policy of friendship with Sparta. The positive treason of intrigue with the enemy which they had already committed at the time of the battle of Tanagra, and were to commit again after the Sicilian disaster of 412, may just now have been far from their minds, but they were nevertheless bitterly opposed to the war, and ready to seize any excuse for ending it. Apart from them and violently differing, in fact, from their political creed, there was a large and influential body who were nevertheless hard hit by the war and were longing for peace. These were the Agriculturists, who, till 425 at any rate, had been compelled as each spring came round, to quit their farms and leave their crops and orchards to the invaders' mercy. The voice of their complaint was now making itself heard. It rings through the *Comedies* of Aristophanes ; and it was soon to find a mouthpiece among the political leaders themselves. The accredited leader of this party of moderate democrats was Nicias, the son of Niceratus, the most trusted among the generals of the period, but totally lacking in either genius or initiative. Pious to the point of gross superstition—for he kept a private astrologer—and cautious often to the utter ruin of his plans, he nevertheless won the respect of decent folk by the gentlemanly moderation of his life and policy. As a commander, indeed, he had a record of unvarying success in minor expeditions. But his unadventurous strategy, though based on the Periclean model, did not suit the ideas of the majority in the Assembly ; and, since Cleon's victory at Pylos, his own popularity had been declining as the star of his rival rose.[1]

[1] The shifting balance between the parties can to some extent be traced by the annual election to the Board of Generals. But Nicias, as a matter of fact, seems to have retained his place through- out generally as president of the Board—the position which Pericles himself had held and to which his special power had been largely due.

The new offensive strategy, which had recently super-seded the old Periclean defensive, and which had led first to the victories of Sphacteria and Megara and then to the disaster of Delium, was only one part of Cleon's policy of 'push and go'. Under his guidance Athens was now learning to adopt towards her subject allies an attitude of naked tyranny. For Cleon believed in the strong hand; and, as we have seen him recommending the wholesale massacre of rebellious allies, so equally he did not hesitate to increase the financial burdens on the more submissive. The fact was that the drain on the imperial exchequer had been terribly severe. Over 2,000 talents had gone on the siege of Potidaea alone; and, though the Athenians themselves had done their best, and accepted in 428 the levy of a tax upon all property, this had been wholly inadequate to meet requirements; and in 425 Cleon had his way. By a stroke of the pen, as it were, he doubled and in some cases trebled the allies' tribute. The excuse no doubt was sheer necessity; but it went beyond all rights or precedents, and not unnaturally it was bitterly resented.

The first reaction against Athens' high-handed policy came in the Chalcidic peninsula. In that district Olynthus and certain other cities had broken free from the imperial yoke at the same time as Potidaea, and unlike Potidaea they had never been reduced. In 424 these cities, acting in concert with Perdiccas, King of Macedon, formed the idea of engineering a general revolt of that region and invited the Spartans to assist them. To the Spartans the idea was not a complete novelty. In 426 they had founded a post at Heraclea not far from Thermopylae, partly, it would seem, as a stepping-stone to action further north. In any case they now accepted the invitation from Chal-cidicê and the man they sent was Brasidas, a commander who had already greatly distinguished himself at Pylos and elsewhere. Brasidas for a Spartan was strangely adven-turous, and, as he also possessed considerable gifts of oratory and diplomatic skill, no better choice could have been made. With a force of volunteers and helots he marched up through Thessaly, and on arriving in Chalcidicê persuaded even some of the less willing cities to join in the revolt. His next move was a dash against Amphipolis, the key-position, as was shown above, upon the coastal road connecting Chalcidicê and Thrace (424). Its small Athenian garrison sent off in haste to summon the naval squadron which lay near-by at Thasos under the command of the historian Thucydides himself. Meanwhile Brasidas had seized the Strymon bridgehead and by tempting overtures persuaded the inhabitants of Amphipolis to throw in their lot with him ; Thucydides arrived upon the scene too late, and the town was lost. The sentence of banishment which was passed upon his negligence was a token of the consternation felt by the Athenians at home. Access to the mines of Mount Pangaeus was threatened if not lost to them. Brasidas appeared to have Thrace at his feet and beyond Thrace lay the Hellespont, whence sailed their precious corn-ships. No wonder they were perturbed. Happily, however, the Spartan Government was characteristically jealous of their commander's success, refusing to send him more troops, and Brasidas' own ideas were centred upon Chalcidicê, where partly by diplomacy and partly by swift movements of surprise he won town after town to his side. The effect at Athens was to incline men's minds more and more towards peace. Cleon— unlike Pericles, who could command both parties—was master of the extreme, but not of the moderate democrats ; and under the lead of Nicias the latter now insisted upon overtures to Sparta. In the spring of 423 a one year's armistice was concluded as the preliminary basis to a more enduring peace.

But while Nicias was busy over these negotiations, the last had not by any means been heard of either Brasidas or Cleon. In Chalcidicê the war went on, and one city at least came over to the Spartan side. In Athens Cleon argued vigorously that the future of the Empire was at stake and no truce could be recognized with rebellious allies. By the next spring he had the game once more in his hands ; and on the expiration of the armistice he proceeded to take the field himself for the recovery of Amphipolis. With a force of Athenian cavalry and hoplites and sundry allied forces he disembarked at the Strymon mouth, and presently moved up the eastern bank of the river to reconnoitre the town. Inside Amphipolis Brasidas and his garrison were determined upon action at the first opportunity ; and news reached Cleon that underneath the closed gates of the city the feet of men and horses could be seen moving about, upon which he ordered instant retreat. It was an order which no experienced soldier would have given. The Greek hoplite, of course, carried his shield on his left arm ; and thus in repassing the gates of the town the Athenians were bound to expose their right and unshielded flank to the enemy's sally. When that sally came, it threw them into confusion. Cleon, taking to his heels with the rest, was shot down from behind ; but in the hour of his victory Brasidas too fell mortally wounded and was carried dying into the town.

With the simultaneous death of these two men—the ' pestle and mortar ' of war, as Aristophanes called them— the efforts of the peace-party both in Sparta and Athens were redoubled. Nicias on the one side and King Pleistoanax on the other forwarded the negotiations, and in the spring of 421—just ten years from the beginning of the war—peace was concluded. The general principle of the settlement was the surrender of whatever each belligerent had captured in the course of the war. Thus Athens undertook to send back home the precious Spartan prisoners. She gave up Methana. She gave up Cythera ; and, incidentally, upon condition of their preserving strict neutrality, she conceded their liberty to Olynthus and a few other Chalcidian cities. On the other hand, though promised Amphipolis, she failed to recover it, and as a tit-for-tat, she refused to evacuate Pylos. So the two most important captures of the war were not given back, and indeed the Treaty as a whole was more honoured in the breach than the observance. For most remarkable of all was the complete failure to extend its provisions to the principal allies of Sparta. Its terms made no mention of the north-west dependencies which Corinth had lost; none of the Megarian port Nisaea. What is more, the Boeotians, having profited as much by the war as these others had lost by it, and being still in the bellicose mood lately bred by their victory at Delium, now felt themselves cheated of expected rewards and sullenly refused to surrender Panactum, an Attic frontier fort which they had recently captured. The truth is that, in her haste to come to terms with Athens, Sparta had selfishly ignored the legitimate claims and grievances of her allies; and the treaty was to all intents and purposes nothing better than a private compact between the two war-weary protagonists. It solved none of the real problems which lay at the root of the conflict; and, as we shall see, it did not even lead to peace. Cleon at least would have been more logical. He would never have compromised with the enemy any more than he would have compromised with the rebels of Chalcidicê. The well-meaning Nicias had done both; but whether his short views were the hope or the ruin of his country, no two persons, I suppose, would ever agree.

CHAPTER XII

AN INTERLUDE AND SICILY

I. ALCIBIADES AND MANTINEA

IF Sparta in her haste to come to terms with Athens in 421 had outraged her allies by the conclusion of a treaty in which their individual interests were almost wholly ignored, their annoyance was soon turned to utter bewilderment by the immediate sequel to the signing of the peace. For the policy of the Spartan Government was now to enter upon a new and startling phase. The truce which thirty years earlier they had arranged with Argos was due at this moment to lapse, and the fear loomed large lest their old rival and enemy of the Peloponnese should seize the opportunity to strike up an alliance with Athens. Rather than that this should happen, the Spartans conceived the astonishing expedient of making alliance with Athens themselves. The proposal was made. The Athenians, harking back to the old tradition of Cimonian policy, accepted it ; and thus the sixth or seventh week from the termination of the war witnessed the extraordinary spectacle of the two chief belligerents exchanging solemn oaths of lasting amity as though they were the best friends in the world. This move, as might be guessed, was enough to cause a pretty flutter of alarm amongst the Governments of other states ; and by a natural instinct of self-preservation they began at once to draw together. Dissatisfaction was rife among more than half of Sparta's allies. Elis and Mantinea, impatient of her detested hegemony, were for throwing in their lot with the Argives. Corinth, sore at her losses by the Peace, was ready to do the same, and would have drawn Boeotia and Megara along with her, had it not been for their incurable suspicions at Argive democracy. Even without their adhesion, the four-power coalition of Argos, Corinth, Elis and Mantinea was a serious menace to Sparta ; and, indeed, her whole League seemed well on the way to imminent disruption. Little wonder, therefore, that she was badly scared, or that, when the new ephors for 420 entered office, the sense of peril was so strong that a break with Athens was secretly envisaged. But Pylos had first to be got back, and to get it one thing was essential. Boeotia must be persuaded on her part to surrender Panactum, the Attic border fort which her soldiers had captured. To Boeotia, accordingly, the ephors addressed themselves, and all went wrong. First they were required to renew their alliance with Boeotia—a deadly affront to Athens their existing ally, to whom Boeotia was of course anathema. Then, when at their request Panactum was to be surrendered, its holders with deliberate malice first razed it to the ground. Athens was furious ; and there was every chance that, instead of surrendering Pylos, she would now break openly with Sparta and (what Sparta dreaded most) join the Argive coalition. Two counsels, however, prevailed. Nicias was for ignoring the undisguised hostility of Boeotia and maintaining the Spartan entente. The policy of open rupture found its champion in Nicias' new rival, now first emerging on the political stage, but destined to prove for many a year to come the evil genius of his country—Pericles' young nephew, Alcibiades.

In all Greek history there is perhaps no figure which so intrigues the mind as this wayward but fascinating adventurer. Alcibiades was one of Fortune's favourites. He had every advantage of birth and breeding. His exceptionally handsome looks were the talk of the town. The charm of his manner and the brilliance of his wit captivated even the solid old Socrates. He was the idol of the young Athenian dandies, setting the fashion in all things from the lisp in his speech to the swagger with which he trailed his cloak as he walked. Educated in the individualistic notions of the sophist movement, he acknowledged no restraints of convention or morality ; and his private life, if even a quarter of the ugly tales are true, can have been little better than one prolonged debauch. Yet, reckless, vain, extravagant and unscrupulous as he was, Alcibiades' genius appealed strongly to his countrymen, and especially to that section of them which had formerly followed Cleon. His infectious bravado easily outdistanced the coarser arts of the new demagogue Hyperbolus; and not once nor twice his versatile and exceptionally nimble brain was to prove more than a match for the slow-paced deliberations of Nicias.

And so it was now when in 420 there arrived almost simultaneously in Athens the ambassadors of both Argos and Sparta: the one eagerly competing for Athenian co-operation, the other playing for time till Pylos were recovered. The Spartans, in particular, made a shrewd bid for success by disclaiming all hostile intent for their new Boeotian alliance and offering to settle all outstanding differences on the spot, and as a further guarantee of good faith they assured the preliminary Council that they came with full powers to treat. Seeing that this would go far towards convincing his countrymen, Alcibiades determined upon a characteristically unscrupulous stroke. He offered the Spartans his full support for their plea, provided that they upon their part would disclaim in the subsequent Assembly what they had previously said in the Council about their own powers. The simple-minded fellows took the bait; but no sooner had they made the disclaimer than up jumped Alcibiades and roundly denounced them for playing fast and loose (as they were). Though the meeting was broken up by a shock of earthquake, the impression made on the Assembly was lasting; and, almost at once, Athens threw over Sparta and concluded an alliance with Argos. Thus mainland Greece was now divided into two roughly equal and hostile camps, based upon the natural alignment of political sympathies—on one side the four-power democratic coalition of Argos, Athens, Mantinea and Elis; on the other, oligarchical Sparta with Boeotia and Tegea in tow, and, after a brief period of wavering, Corinth.

Under such a condition of affairs the risks of a clash

were obvious ; but in Athens, at any rate, the public was weary of war, and the desire for peace ran so strong that in 418 Alcibiades failed of re-election to the Board of Generals. Sparta, relying perhaps on the pacific Nicias to keep his countrymen quiet, determined to seize the opportunity for a blow at her old rival and enemy. King Agis ' with the finest Greek army on record ' marched into the Argive plain, outmanœuvring its defenders so successfully that their overthrow seemed certain and the fall of Argos hourly imminent. Then, before a blow had been struck, he came to some secret understanding with the anti-democratic faction in the city, granted a truce and withdrew. But that was not all ; for the calculations of Athenian inactivity had meanwhile been falsified by Alcibiades' restless energy. Though no longer a general, he had worked the Assembly round and got himself sent as plenipotentiary to Argos, together with a contingent though by no means the largest available, of the citizen army. Once arrived, he persuaded the Argives to ignore their new-made truce with Agis, and embark upon an adventure of singular audacity. Taking the Athenian and other allied forces with them, they marched up into the centre of the Peloponnese, entered Arcadia, and there prepared to challenge the Spartan army to the test of pitched battle. Since the beginning of the war no such test had been accepted, much less sought against that onetime invincible army ; and nothing could have given a more manifest proof of the low pitch to which its morale and prestige had been brought by the humiliation of Sphacteria.

Arcadia, nestling high and remote among bleak tracts of barren mountains, includes two small plains. In the northern of these the Argive-Athenian force took up its stand before the allied town of Mantinea. In the southern plain, meanwhile, having hurried up from Sparta to the protection of Tegea, King Agis was marshalling his troops. The two armies met at the junction of the plains ; and, if in their present state of demoralization it still seemed incredible that the Spartans should be beaten, the incredible

nearly happened. It was a commonplace of Greek hoplite
engagements that the last shield-man on the extreme right
wing, nervous of enemy impact upon his unshielded arm,
should edge out sideways to avoid it, and, since his next-
door neighbours were bound to keep contact with his
movement, *the right wing came inevitably to outflank the
opposing left.* So it was at Mantinea ; and King Agis,
finding his left wing threatened with encirclement, first
ordered it to make a lateral movement leftwards, and then,
since this opened a hole in his centre, called on his right-
wing captains to slip round and fill the gap. The captains
thought they knew better and failed him ; the gap yawned ;
and the Argives rushed for it. All would have been up
with Agis, had not the aforesaid captains, albeit negligent
of orders, at any rate fulfilled a right wing's function, first
rolling up the Athenian force opposed to them, and then
turning from the rout to the timely succour of their
hard-pressed left. The battle was thus won ; and it was a
signal triumph for Sparta. She had wiped out the stigma
of Sphacteria ; she recovered the allegiance of Mantinea
and Elis ; and, though the Argives after a brief submission
were presently to reassert their independence, she was
beyond question supreme in the Peloponnese once more.
Thus Athens' second attempt at a land league had failed.
Alcibiades would have been wiser to have learnt the lesson
of his uncle's unhappy experiment in the same direction.

The reaction of this failure upon the internal politics
of Athens was singular. Nerves were badly frayed, and
party feeling ran high. The conservatives blamed it on
Alcibiades that a force had been sent south at all ; the
democrats blamed it on Nicias that the force actually sent
was no larger ; and it was decided to have resort to the
test of ostracism. The result was a nine days' jest in
Athens—so much so that the institution henceforward fell
altogether into disuse—for the victim of the ' potsherd '
vote turned out to be neither Alcibiades nor Nicias, but
the blatant and pernicious demagogue Hyperbolus. The
fact was that before instructing their partisans how to vote,
the two rival leaders had come to a secret understanding :

and the next few years were to witness the curious spectacle of a combination—in office, if not in policy—between the most strait-laced champion of orthodoxy and the most notorious young rake of the town. Each, of course, pursued his own bent ; and while Nicias was busy, as we may fairly guess, building the new Erechtheum temple on the Acropolis, Alcibiades was equally increasing his popularity by winning chariot races at the Olympic games. On one point, however, both were agreed, that a strong line should be taken with the subject allies. We find Nicias planning to sail north (though he was actually prevented) for the recovery of Amphipolis, which had not been restored at the Peace. Alcibiades kept pace meanwhile by planning his infamous attack on the little island of Melos. Though Melos had never, in fact, been a member of the Delian Confederacy, it had been attacked by Nicias in 426, and Cleon, claiming it as a conquest when he reassessed the tribute in the following year, had included its name on the lists. Not merely, however, had the Melians never paid up, but they had contributed to the exchequer of Sparta. As a Dorian settlement, they were in this following a natural allegiance ; but they were to pay for it dearly. Without further provocation the Athenians attacked them, captured their town after a six months' siege, then slaughtered their males, and sold their women and children as slaves. This horrible act proclaimed to Hellas—as doubtless it was intended to proclaim —that Athens regarded the sea as her perquisite and that her empire would brook no evasions. So the reins were tightened, the tribute, though reassessed in 421, was levied on a scale lower indeed than Cleon's emergency measure, but still far too high. The allies, forbidden to mint for themselves, were compelled to adopt Athens' imperial currency. Meanwhile, the ambition of her commercial magnates swelled ominously ; wild schemes were in the air ; there was even talk, it would seem, of conquering Carthage ; and then, in a final outburst of greedy megalomania, they plunged her into an adventure which for its sheer audacity we can hardly help but admire, but which was destined nevertheless to involve her in swift **and** irretrievable disaster and to provoke the nemesis, by no means ill-deserved, of her intemperate despotism. In 415 her great expedition sailed for Sicily.

II. Sicilian History

Before describing the events which led up to the Athenian expedition to Sicily, it will be well for us to cast a brief

MAP OF SICILY
TO ILLUSTRATE WARS WITH CARTHAGE AND SICILIAN EXPEDITION

glance at the previous history of the island, which, populated as it very largely was by cities of Greek nationality, has every claim to be considered an integral part of the Hellenic world.

As early as the Eighth Century, the colonizing enterprise of Greek states on either shore of the Aegean had begun, as we saw long ago, to encircle Sicily with a girdle of coastal settlements which developed in course of time into vigorous and thriving communities. The previous inhabitants— called Sicani and Siceli, the latter being immigrants from the Italian peninsula—were for the most part driven back into the hilltops of the interior or to the western end of the island where too the Phoenicians retained a group of trade-stations. Some natives, however, would seem to have been kept as serfs by the Greek invaders : and the aristocratic society, which the latter were thereby enabled to develop, accounts perhaps in no small measure for their rapid intellectual and political evolution. For the Greeks of the west were destined to rival even the Ionians themselves in their precocious adventures into the realms of philosophy and science ; and, as among the Ionians, so also in many of the Sicilian cities were evolved those tyrant-monarchies which were normally, as we have seen, the product of a commercial rather than of an agricultural life. Most prominent of all perhaps were the tyrants of Gela ; and the last of these, Gelon by name (491–478), succeeded in bringing under his sway not merely the powerful town of Syracuse, to which he transferred his court, but also most of the south-eastern districts ; while with his neighbour tyrant, Theron of Acragas, he allied himself by marriage. It was fortunate, indeed, for the survival of the Greek states in Sicily, normally independent of each other, and not infrequently at feud, that such bonds of strength and unity had been so timely woven. For a menace was now near at hand which might well have cut short for ever their promising civilization.

Since very early times the shores of the Western Mediterranean had been dotted with the trade stations of those great Levantine merchants, the Phoenicians ; and among such stations the town of Carthage had during the Seventh and Sixth Centuries begun to assume the proportions of an independent naval empire. Not merely had the Carthaginians gained control over the adjacent coasts of Africa and Spain, but by occupying the Phoenician stations of Motya and Panormus at its western extremity, they had won a footing in Sicily ; and with the formation of a large and efficient mercenary army they had begun by Gelon's time to meditate its complete conquest. In 480— acquainted doubtless with Xerxes' designs on Greece, and anxious to profit by the motherland's preoccupation—they launched their great attack on the island. Their primary objective was the town of Himera, whose tyrant, expelled by Theron, had appealed to them for aid ; and under its walls took place the famous battle, which Sicilian pride, not wholly without justice, compared to the simultaneous triumph of Salamis. Legend relates how, as the fortunes of the fighting swayed from early morning till the fall of night, Hamilcar stood offering victim after victim upon Baal's altar, and calling aloud on the god to grant him victory, and how in the decisive hour when he saw his prayer unanswered, he hurled himself as a final sacrifice into the midst of the consuming flames. The prowess of Gelon's and Theron's men had won the day and saved Sicily from subjugation to an Oriental and barbaric foe. Six years later was won off Cumae near Naples a similar victory, whereby Gelon's brother and successor Hieron preserved the Hellenic civilization of South Italy from another ' barbarian ' foe—the Etruscan princes of North Italy.

But, though the Sicilians could unite at a crisis, the old tendency to disunion remained. War broke out between Theron's successor, Thrasydaeus, and Hieron, the victor of Cumae, the patron of Pindar, and a prince of the greatest magnificence ; and thus weakened, both tyrant-houses came soon to an end. Indeed with the defeat of the Carthaginian menace the special need for tyrants vanished. The republics which replaced them, however, were no more inclined for union. The old racial jealousy between Dorian and Ionian sharpened the feud. Round Syracuse, the great Corinthian colony, were ranged the towns of Dorian origin ; while Leontini was the most prominent of their rivals. The latter it was who in 427 made the appeal for Athens' help, destined in the ultimate issue to bring such troubles in its train. Her plea was doubly apt, addressed as it was to the ancient champions of the Ionian cause and to Corinth's bitterest foe ; and it was further backed by the eloquence of Gorgias, the famous rhetorician, who came on this occasion as ambassador. Moved by his persuasive arguments, the Athenians dispatched the fleet, which en route was detained, as we saw above, over the singular adventure of Pylos. When it at last reached Sicily, its activities accomplished nothing better in the long run than to frighten the inhabitants once again into temporary union. Feuds were forgotten in the face of an external enemy, and at the famous Congress of Gela in 425 a national policy of ' Sicily for the Sicilians ' was for the first time enunciated by Hermocrates of Syracuse. Fair words, indeed ; but when the Athenian fleet was gone, Syracuse set upon Leontini and destroyed it utterly. The fears and suspicions of her neighbours were aroused ; feuds broke out once more ; and in 416 a fresh appeal for help reached Athens—this time from her old ally Segesta. Athens' first answer was to send ambassadors to explore the resources of the town. The Segestans fooled them finely by borrowing gold and silver vessels from the whole district and passing these off as the private property of whatever host might entertain the party. The result was that the ambassadors came home not merely with a handsome subsidy, but also with glowing tales of Sicilian luxury and wealth. Nor, dupes as they were, was their impression far wide of the mark. A prosperity, founded by the skilful statecraft of their great tyrant princes and fostered by a vigorous trade with Carthage, Italy and Greece, had produced in the Sicilian towns a degree of splendour and comfort unknown in the motherland. The finest linen, the softest of beds and couches, the most elaborate and precious of plate, were all to be found here in plenty. The temples still to be seen at Acragas vied almost with the glories of the Acropolis. Sicilian grandees rode in carriages, at a time when in Athens a saddle-mule was accounted a luxury. Syracusan cookery was a by-word among gourmets. Little wonder, then, that the imagination of the Athenians was captivated, or their appetites whetted, by the idea of uniting a group of friendly cities against the detested power of Syracuse—and so perhaps of ultimately securing the richest of prizes for themselves.

III.   The Sicilian Expedition

The enterprise was not undertaken without opposition. Nicias was against it, more from the belief that her Aegean empire was already as much as Athens could manage than from any true realization of the magnitude of the risk. The fact was that Syracuse was a pretty formidable antagonist, comparable in size to Athens herself. Alcibiades, however, set himself to belittle the Sicilians' strength, boastfully predicting his ability to win round half the island by diplomacy alone ; and he finally assured the Assembly that with the resources to be won by the conquest of Syracuse—and Carthage too perhaps—they would be able to make short work of their enemies nearer home, and so soon have the whole of Hellas at their feet. Such rattling of the sabre won the day.   The chief support came doubtless, as for Cleon's bold schemes, from the mercantile section of the populace ; and among those who voted for the expedition, many, we know, meant to accompany it as free-lance traders and get what commercial pickings they might from the venture.   The command of the actual expedition was entrusted to Nicias, Alcibiades and Lamachus conjointly.   Its size was not to be stinted ; for, hoping still to damp down the Assembly's enthusiasm, Nicias had pitched the scale of his requirements at the highest ; and, besides commissariat and other vessels, 130 triremes were voted him, together with 5,000 hoplites ; while to finance the undertaking the whole accumulation of six years of peace was earmarked for the war.   The Athenians, if anyone ever did, were putting all their eggs in one basket (415).

Three months or more elapsed in busy preparation, and the expedition was ready to sail when an event occurred which probably altered the whole course of its history. Outside almost every Athenian house or shrine there stood a large square pillar of stone, topped often with a sculptured head and sacred to Hermes, the god of bounds and ways. One morning Athens awoke to find that during the night these had nearly all been deliberately defaced.   The shock to the religious susceptibilities of the people was incalculable; it was as though the inhabitants of a Catholic country should awake to find their church altars defiled. Consternation reigned, and omen-mongers shook their heads over so inauspicious a send-off to the fleet. Who the culprits were remains an unsolved mystery. Alcibiades had riotous friends; but he could never have countenanced an act which might clearly end in compromising the whole expedition. Nicias and his party, who would have gladly seen it compromised, were far too pious to be suspect. The method of destruction appeared too well organized to be the result of a mere drunken frolic; and the probability is that it was the work of hired agents in the pay of Corinth or Syracuse. Alcibiades' opponents, however, saw their chance of implicating him, and began to rake up the old tale of a discreditable orgy in which he and his boon-companions were said to have sacrilegiously parodied the Mysteries of Eleusis. Deeming it wiser to wait until he was out of the way, they postponed any definite charge; and the fleet was permitted to sail. Thucydides describes in moving terms the splendour and the pathos of its departure—the entire population of Athens crowding down to the quays, the sad leave-takings and the bright hopes which the sight of the argosy inspired, the silence at the trumpet call and the solemn saying of a prayer after the herald's words in which all ashore or on shipboard joined their voices. ' Then the crews raised the Paean, and, when the libations were completed, put to sea. After sailing out for some distance in single file, the ships raced each other as far as Aegina.' Few of that great company of light-hearted adventurers were ever to see Athens again.

Among the three commanders of the expedition three different plans were held. Nicias was for confining their activities to a non-committal demonstration on behalf of Leontini and Segesta. Alcibiades favoured a diplomatic campaign to rally the malcontent Sicilian cities against despotic Syracuse. Lamachus, with the clear judgment of a plain soldier, was for springing a surprise before the Syracusans were properly prepared. In point of fact, none of the three plans was seriously adopted. The advantage of surprise was frittered away by a half-hearted reconnoitre of the Syracusan harbour; and before much propaganda could be done, Alcibiades received his recall. For in the interval the agitation over the Hermae had been recovering strength. An informer, named Andocides, had come forward with what was in all likelihood a bogus tale and dis-

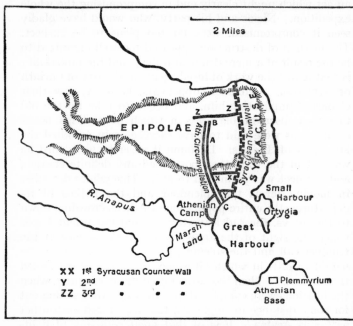

2 Miles

EPIPOLAE

Att. Circumvallation

SYRACUSE

Syracusan Town Wall

Z Z

B

A

X X

R. Anapus

Athenian Camp

C

Small Harbour

Ortygia

Great Harbour

Marsh Land

X X 1st Syracusan Counter Wall
Y 2nd . . .
Z Z 3rd . . .

☐ Plemmyrium
Athenian Base

MAP TO ILLUSTRATE SIEGE OF SYRACUSE

closed the names of various accomplices. Many were arrested and put to death. Alcibiades himself was summoned home to stand trial for alleged profanation. He preferred exile; and with an unscrupulous volatility characteristic of the man, he determined to make what capital he could out of giving advice to the enemy and made his way to Sparta. The two policies which he there advocated were each in their way ruinous to the Athenians' cause;

for he suggested first that a permanent post should be fortified and held on Attic soil ; and second, that a Spartan general should be sent to organize the defence of Syracuse. The Spartans had the good sense to obey him in both.

The year 415 was by now well advanced ; and though Nicias landed his army near Syracuse and defeated its ill-trained levies in pitched battle, he was deterred by winter's approach from following up his success, and retired to more comfortable quarters. It was not till the spring of 414, therefore, that any serious or sustained operation was begun against the city. The interval had been well used by the inhabitants. Hermocrates had been appointed general. The troops had been drilled, and the defences strengthened. While the inner keep or citadel of Syracuse was situated upon the peninsula of Ortygia, better known as the ' Island ', the town itself sprawled well across the seaward front of the broad peninsula behind. Sloping up away westwards from the town stretched the long low ridge of Epipolae, scarped at points with steep cliffs, but assailable in particular upon its northern side. Upon this side it was that while the Syracusans were still dallying over plans for its defence, the Athenians slipped ashore and rushed the ridge. Once safely ensconced thereon they set to work upon regular siege tactics. Like the Thebans at Plataea, they intended to encircle Syracuse upon its landward side with a double ring-wall running from sea to sea, within the shelter of which they would then settle down and wait until with the assistance of their fleet's blockade they should starve the city out. Accordingly they started from a point in the middle of the Epipolae ridge and pushed the northern arm of this projected ring-wall seawards. Before, however, the distance to the shore was nearly covered, they left this part of the work unfinished (an omission which later was to cost them dear), and turned to meet a new menace. For the defenders of the town were driving out a counter-wall, clean athwart the intended course of the ring-wall's southern arm and threatening to prevent that arm's construction. Waiting one day until the Syracusan garrison was taking its siesta, the Athenians launched a surprise attack, captured and demolished the obstructive wall and then proceeded to utilize its materials for the southward continuation of their own. As this advanced swiftly towards the shore of the Great Harbour, a second attempt was made to head it off, this time by a stockade across the waterside marshes. Again the Athenians attacked and carried the work ; but, Lamachus being killed in the skirmish, the dilatory Nicias was left in sole command, and though the southern arm of the ring-wall was all but completed, the northern arm was not. The error was vital ; for through that gap there now slipped into the hard-pressed city the man who was to revive the failing spirits of the garrison and very soon to turn the tables on their foe. Alcibiades' treacherous advice had done its work, and Gylippus the Spartan had arrived (414, autumn).

The second phase in the story now begins, and for the Athenians a melancholy phase it is. Nicias, no longer supported by Lamachus' downright vigour, was further handicapped by a painful disease of the kidneys, which seems to have sapped even what little initiative he had. His failure to intercept Gylippus was highly culpable and, as events were to prove, fatal. For not merely did the Spartan bring with him 3,000 men hastily got together from friendly Sicilian cities ; but, what was far more important, he inspired the Syracusans to vigorous offensive action. A third cross-wall was on his instigation begun along Epipolae ; and, though Nicias turned to carry the ring-wall northwards across the fatal gap, the Syracusans this time built quicker and succeeded in heading him off. More than this they carried their cross-wall along the whole length of the ridge and, thus gaining the advantage of superior ground, were able to keep the Athenians cooped inside the narrow space between their double ring-wall or in the unhealthy, waterlogged camping-ground at the ring-wall's harbour end. The Syracusan cavalry too, now venturing afield and unchecked by opposing horse, hovered disconcertingly behind Cape Plemmyrium, where to south-ward of the harbour mouth the Athenians had beached their fleet and pitched their commissariat base. Nicias saw his men, in fact, less besiegers now than besieged. He saw, too, reinforcements reaching Syracuse from all over Sicily ; and, if he had never believed in the campaign before, he believed in it now still less. As winter fell, he wrote home a desperate appeal for his own recall. Faced with the alternatives of either withdrawing the whole expedition, or sending another to aid it, the Athenians, with an ill-judged but magnificent bravado, chose the latter. A second armament of seventy triremes and 5,000 hoplites was put into commission ; and of its two commanders one was the hero of Pylos and the ideal man for a crisis, Demosthenes.

With 413 begins the third and penultimate phase of the campaign, and now for the first time the scene of action shifts to the sea. For during winter Hermocrates and Gylippus had been busily building up an effective fleet, already eighty triremes strong ; and so confident did they feel that with the coming of spring they delivered a combined assault by sea and land upon the Athenian naval base at Plemmyrium. The land attack so far succeeded that the whole position fell into their hands, and with it the potential command over the entrance to the harbour. The Athenian sailors, who had beaten off (though none too easily) the sea attack, were thus compelled to withdraw their base within the harbour and beach their vessels along the foreshore of the military camp. Their situation was trebly awkward ; their communications with the outer sea were threatened ; their confidence was badly shaken by their narrow margin of superiority in the recent engagement ; and, worse still, they foresaw that in the next they must inevitably be confined to narrow waters where their own skill of manœuvre would not tell. The fighting of the following weeks did not belie such fears. The Syracusans had deliberately built their vessels broad and strong in the prow, with short, but thick-set beaks[1] ; thus, though slower

[1] This device appears to have been imitated from the Corinthians who by its means had just fought a more or less successful engagement against the Athenian fleet off Naupactus. Their success was an important landmark, reversing the verdict of Phormio's earlier victories and pointing forwards to a time when Peloponnesian ships would soon prove the superiors of the Athenian.

at manœuvre, when it came in narrow waters to a test of head-on ramming, they stood the shock much better than the others' light-built boats. Things looked black indeed for the Athenians; and far blacker still would they have looked had not there arrived precisely at this juncture the long-awaited contingent of Demosthenes. Its coming seemed like a reprieve.

We are now at the fourth and final phase. Demosthenes, with his habitual quick decision, took the situation's measure; Epipolae must be retaken or they might as well go home. A moonlit night was chosen. Among the western cliffs they threaded their way up, rushed the crest, and drove in the vanguard of the rallying but startled garrison; then, when all seemed won, fell, as night-attackers will, into complete disorder. Amid mingled shouts from the victors and yells of the pursued, the rout swept back among the moonlit rocks, dashing some over the crags to headlong death and spreading sudden chaos among the reserves still waiting at the foot of the ascent. With morning it was clear to Demosthenes at least that they must quit; and Nicias, fearful of the wrath of the citizen Assembly, refused; then, swerving round, consented. On August 27th all was ready for their departure, and that night the moon was eclipsed. Soothsayers clamoured for postponement—for three days, or better still until the next full moon; and Nicias, sick, irresolute and superstitious, acquiesced. A week later the Syracusan fleet, scarcely inferior now in numbers, attacked and inflicted on them a severe defeat. The tables were now turned. Despondency reigned in the camp. Even the cheeky native fisher-boys rowed across in their boats to jeer. Omens or no omens, they must get away now. Across the mouth of the harbour the enemy had built a boom; and to break this at all costs was the only hope. As the Athenian sailors put out for the last time upon that hazardous mission, their comrades watched them from the shore in an indescribable suspense; and so long as the fortunes of the battle ebbed and flowed, they stood ' swaying their bodies now this way and now that in an agony of hope and terror'. Then, when at last they saw their vessels turn and run for shore, 'all raised', says Thucydides, 'in their intolerable anguish one universal groan.' It was certain now that they could never escape by sea (413, Sept.).

The sea thus lost them, Nicias decided on the one possible step—retreat by land. The tragedy of those closing days is best to be read in the matchless narrative of the Greek historian—the pathetic parting with the sick and wounded, abandoned despite their pitiable entreaties to certain slavery or death, the week of painful and slow dragging march, directed south-westwards but almost without aim, the suffering from thirst and sun among the hills of the interior, the unremitting persecutions of the triumphant and vindictive foe, the surrender of Demosthenes' party in an olive-grove, and then the final interception of Nicias and his men in the bed of the river Asinarus, where some were drowned in the crossing, more shot down as they huddled to lap the foul water, the rest taken alive. Of the prisoners most were kept by individual captors to serve as household slaves—a terrible fate for free Athenian citizens, but a fate they had themselves inflicted upon many. The rest, about 1,000 in number, were placed in the stone quarries of Syracuse, a ready-made prison, where they lingered horribly, chilled by night and scorched by day, unable to remove their dead and ravaged by disease, till some six months or more later the survivors were sold as slaves. Nicias himself was put to death, tradition says with torture. So died the man of whom Thucydides wrote that 'he least of any Greek of that day deserved so cruel an end, having lived his life in the practice of every virtue'. Seeing what load of misery and failure lies at his door, we at least need not contest that epitaph—a tribute to a gentleman, or is it a sneer against the limited moral code of the day?

CHAPTER XIII

THE PELOPONNESIAN WAR—THE LAST PHASE

I

NEWS travelled slow in the ancient world. None of the expeditionary force had escaped home from Sicily to tell the tale ; and one day a random stranger landing at Peiraeus, and sitting down to be shaved at a barber's shop, spoke casually of the disaster. The barber ran off with the news to the city, and no one there believed him. The stranger indeed was treated as an idle scandalmonger and clapped into irons, until by and by others arrived to corroborate his tale ; and then at last the truth broke with stunning force upon the Athenian populace. On many enough counts their case seemed wellnigh desperate—the shattering loss of men, vessels and material,[1] the enormous blow to their prestige, and the chance, now almost a certainty, that their allies would revolt. Added to all this, the Spartans had earlier in the year (413) made up their minds that the opportunity had come to strike once more. Following the advice of Alcibiades, King Agis had entered Attica, and away among the northern hills, not far from the Boeotian border, he had planted a fort at Decelea. The constant menace of this enemy post, visible to good eyes from the citadel itself, told upon the Athenians' security in many ways ; it kept their garrison upon the city walls under a constant strain of anxiety ; it rendered effective cultivation of the soil impossible ; it cut the overland communication with Euboea, the war-time repository of the Attic farmers' live-stock ; it formed an easy refuge for a growing number of runaway slaves (and 20,000 escaped, it is said) ; it meant

---

[1] Forty thousand men and 240 triremes is Isocrates' estimate.

the dismantling of their farms, which were stripped even to the roof-tiles, and, worst of all perhaps, it compelled the closing of the Laurium silver-mines and so checked the lucrative output of the mint. Realizing the full

MAP TO ILLUSTRATE LAST PHASE OF PELOPONNESIAN WAR

measure of their danger the Athenians pulled themselves together. A permanent board of ten Commissioners was appointed, as a sort of war cabinet, and these were empowered to take over many of the functions of the democratic Council, which had proved itself, as was natural, no very efficient body for the conduct of a crisis. At their instance strong measures were adopted. In the place of the unpopular Tribute was substituted a five per cent. harbour-duty on all exports and imports, levied at Peiraeus equally with other harbours of the Empire and much less objectionable in its method of collection. Sunium, the Land's End of Attica, was fortified to give protection to corn vessels rounding the Cape ; and all through the winter the shipyards worked at such pressure that within a twelvemonth 150 triremes were afloat. Nevertheless the year 413 ended amid deep forebodings as to what its successor might bring forth.

Such fears were not ill-founded. Intrigues were already on foot between Sparta and several of Athens' subject cities, among whom the news of the Sicilian disaster had aroused fresh thoughts of secession. With the almost complete destruction of the imperial fleet they saw that the whole situation was radically altered. Effective help might now be expected from the Peloponnese, and meanwhile encouragement had come from a fresh quarter. For Persia was moving. The recovery of her old coastal dependencies had never been wholly dismissed from the minds of her ministers ; and now the two satraps, Tissaphernes of Sardis and Pharnabazus of the northern Hellespontine area, were both busy preaching revolt to Athens' discontented allies. The first to raise the standard was Chios, the one autonomous island which had never yet rebelled and which in consequence still kept a fleet, hitherto a useful complement to Athens' navy and now a most valued asset to her enemies. Miletus, Lesbos, and various other states swiftly followed the lead. Sparta, playing, as ever, a cynically selfish hand, agreed to recognize the Great King's claim upon his former subjects, provided that the pay of the fleet they were proposing to send over, should be financed in part by Persian gold. This condition meant much ; for, not being themselves either a numerous or a sea-going people, the Spartans were compelled to hire the rowers who should man their ships ; and to find adequate funds for this was wholly beyond the resources of their limited exchequer. By the arrangement with Persia they were therefore provided with the one thing supremely needful, but hitherto lacking, for the commissioning of a permanent and serviceable fleet. It altered the whole complexion of the war, which was henceforth to be fought to a decision not upon the plains or off the promontories of mainland Greece, but among the creeks and islands of the Eastern Aegean.

Athens met this new and very terrible turn of events with promptness and fortitude. Though part of the Peloponnesian navy, reinforced by a squadron from Sicily, got safely across to Ionia, she cut off and detained in home waters a considerable contingent from Corinth. She recovered Lesbos, blockaded Chios, and maintained her empire in the Hellespontine regions intact. But for all her efforts disaffection spread rapidly among the southern districts. Rhodes came out against her in 411 ; and in the general landslide Samos alone of her more important Ionian subjects stood loyal. The better to preserve the Samians' allegiance she restored the island's autonomy and ensured the support of its democratic leaders by a systematic persecution of the contrary faction. Thus secured to Athens' cause, Samos became henceforward her chief naval base in trans-Aegean waters and the head-quarters of her fleet. On that fleet all her hopes now rested, for it contained the best that remained to her of her citizen mariners ; and despite all the havoc of Sicily, they were still a sturdy lot, destined not merely to uphold their country's name at sea, but also, as we shall soon show, to play a highly important part in the new and critical situation already developing at the home capital.

II

Between the ancients' political life and our own there was at least one striking difference ; for, whereas Greek democracies made far-reaching experiments in methods of representative election, they never arrived at what we should call a true party-system. Alternations of policy there, of course, were, as this or that leader succeeded to power ; and we have already seen how Cleon, when elected general, could reverse the tack which Nicias had previously followed. But the true opposition to the policies of both Cleon and Nicias came from a party in the state which never rose to power at all. For in Athens, as in almost every democratic city, there was still a faction of irreconcilable Conservatives, whose one ambition was to reform the constitution upon the old oligarchical lines ; and for these the only hope of carrying their aims into effect lay in the arbitrary methods of a *coup d'état*. To these Conservatives the crowning proof of democracy's futility came with the failure of the Sicilian expedition ; and in the general disillusionment which followed on that failure they perceived a golden opportunity of achieving their own ends. For it was bound, as they saw, to predispose other citizens also towards the idea of reform. Now, in Athens, we must remember, besides the main body of red-hot democrats, there was also a large number of moderate-minded folk, good democrats also, but detesting the aggressive imperialism of the demagogue leaders. These it was who, being chiefly men of property, most felt the disastrous effects of Decelea on agriculture, on their mining interests and even on their own household slaves ; and naturally enough they now began to ask themselves whether something should not be done to put the country's house in order and stem the reckless progress towards what to them seemed certain ruin. Accordingly it became the immediate object of the small oligarchical group to win round this growing body of moderate opinion not perhaps to their own extreme views, but to something more in sympathy with them. In any case, as the gloomy days of 412 began to draw towards winter, we may be sure that there was much laying of heads together in Athens. Secret political clubs had already been formed by the oligarchs ; and definite programmes were shaping. There was certainly talk of modifying the basis of the existent democracy and of confining the franchise to the more well-to-do classes who, bearing as they did the burden of taxation, might fairly claim the right to say how the taxes should be spent. In certain quarters there were even dark whispers of something more sweeping yet.

Upon such a situation of affairs was now to be introduced once more the sinister influence of Alcibiades. That adventurer had been compelled to leave his friends the Spartans in a hurry, being detected in a low intrigue with the King's wife. He then went to Asia Minor, and found his way to the court of Tissaphernes, where his fertile brain was soon set to work concocting schemes for his recall to Athens. Confident as usual of his own powers of persuasion, he conceived the suggestion that, if once more restored to the head of his country's affairs, he would easily be able to prevail on the Persian satrap to withdraw his financial support from Sparta and transfer it to Athens instead. Suspecting, however, that under a democratic régime no welcome would be forthcoming for one who had deserved so ill of his country, he craftily represented it as one of Tissaphernes' preliminary conditions that Athens should turn oligarchy forthwith. For any abstract choice between the one constitution or the other Alcibiades of course cared no more than did the Persian satrap himself—a tyranny would have been perhaps more to his mind ; but, posing as a would-be oligarch, he nosed out among the Athenian fleet at Samos a group of senior officers of the same way of thinking, and persuaded them to send home Pisander, one of their number, to lay these proposals before the Assembly. In the atmosphere of political discontent already prevailing at the capital, Pisander's task was easy ; and he was soon making the return journey to Samos with authority to negotiate along the lines suggested. When it came to the point, however, all Alcibiades' fine schemes crumbled away. Tissaphernes' sole concern in reality was to play off one belligerent against the other until both were worn out. This policy he had in the first instance adopted on Alcibiades' advice and, unhappily for the latter, it was very soon apparent that for the present the satrap had every intention of continuing his favours to Sparta and none whatever of transferring them to her rival. So in that quarter at least it appeared as though the affair was at an end; and Alcibiades might whistle in vain for the wind which would blow him home to Athens.

In Athens, however, the affair was by no means ended. There, the impetus towards oligarchy once given, it was proving not so easy to call halt. Hopes had been raised, and the political wire-pullers, not lightly to be baulked, went on with their work. Of these the two specially to be remarked were Theramenes and Antiphon. Theramenes was the chief leader of the moderates, and his political ideal was a return to the 'ancestral constitution' —a term which to him apparently signified a government by limited franchise as opposed to the universal suffrage of the Cleisthenic constitution. His enemies, deriding him for a trimmer, nicknamed him 'the Buskin', a boot which would go equally well on right or left leg. Antiphon was a far more interesting figure, a 'speech-writer', or, as we should say, barrister, a man of very high accomplishments, but in politics an out-and-out oligarch and a born intriguer. He never appeared on the platform or in any overt activity, but moved mysteriously behind the scenes, spinning schemes, dropping hints, and so cloaking his designs that even Theramenes himself seems to have been hoodwinked as to the precise goal at which they were aiming. Plans were very secretly laid. No one, in fact, knew for certain who was in the know and who was not. Meanwhile opposition was cowed by an organized gang of young 'bloods', who masqueraded on dark nights and murdered at least one prominent democrat in cold blood. So it was that when Pisander returned to Athens in spring to promote the oligarchical movement, he found it already well under way; and towards the end of April the plot was launched.

The schemes of the oligarchs were skilfully laid. The approval of the ten Commissioners had been secured; and all was to be done in order under constitutional guise.[1] Accordingly an Assembly was held and a motion was passed that a programme of reform should be drafted and submitted in due course to the popular vote. On the 14th of the month Thargelion (411) another Assembly was summoned, not, be it noted, on the customary Pnyx, safe within the town walls, but at Colonus, a mile or so distant outside the north-west gate. The intention was obvious—with the Spartans uncomfortably close at Decelea, and some of them possibly nearer, the unarmed lower-class mob, who held extreme democrat views, would not be likely to venture so far out of shelter ; and only the better-class moderates who served in the hoplite ranks, and so could go with spear and shield, would dare to appear at the rendezvous. A sympathetic audience being thus assured, all went smoothly with the conspirators' programme. On Pisander's motion it was carried that a new council of Four Hundred should be set up (the number itself is a significant return to the pre-Cleisthenic unit). A list of names, part oligarch and part moderate, had been carefully rigged in advance ; the machinery for their election was at once put into motion, and so the Four Hundred were constituted. Naked oligarchy, however, could hardly be expected to go down with an assembly still mainly composed of mere moderates. The oligarch plotters therefore represented their aim as a democracy of modified franchise ; and to lend colour to the idea arrangements were made for the future enrolment of Five Thousand citizens with whom should ultimately lie the sovereign power in the state and to whom the Four Hundred should in their turn be responsible. So far as can be seen, it was a pure blind. The names of the Five Thousand were never disclosed, and it was probably never intended that they should be. But it was enough that the moderates were for the moment placated ; and now came the next step. The provisional government being thus formed, it remained for them to take over the reins of power. That evening after the

---

[1] The account which follows is in the main based on Thucydides' narrative, but it is supplemented by information given by Fourth Century writers.

Colonus Assembly had broken up, the Four Hundred gathered in the market-place, loitered about unostentatiously till the day's business was over, and then, accompanied by a gang of young swashbucklers with short swords under their cloaks, they marched into the Council Chamber and showed the Five Hundred councillors the door. With this stroke the Revolution was complete, and Athens in the oligarchs' hands.

But there was one factor in the situation with which the conspirators had not properly reckoned. The rank and file of the Athenian fleet at Samos, drawn as they were from the lower strata of the population, were strong democrats almost to a man. Indeed, it was largely their absence from home which had smoothed the path for the success of the oligarchical coup, and they now refused point blank to recognize the authority of the new constitution. Assuming the powers relinquished by the democracy at home, they deposed their commanders, set up Thrasybulus and Thrasyllus instead, and actually proposed to sail back to Athens and unseat the Four Hundred for themselves. From this act of madness, which would have meant the certain loss of Ionia and the Hellespont, they were restrained by Alcibiades. Having left Tissaphernes' court, on the news that his exile was cancelled, he had come down to Samos, and there he persuaded the sailors to remain at their post and send home a demand for the immediate and unequivocal establishment of the promised Five Thousand. This statesmanlike act probably saved the situation not only at Samos, but at Athens. For there it strengthened the hand of Theramenes and other moderate members among the Four Hundred who had never intended a genuine oligarchy and whose doubts and suspicions were beginning to be aroused. It was indeed high time. Antiphon and his associates, having accomplished their first aim and secured themselves in power, were ready to proceed to their second, and they now threw off the mask. With cynical deliberation and hoping by such means to perpetuate their own power, they prepared to betray Athens to the enemy. Overtures for peace had already been officially instituted, only to meet with rejection ; but during the interval of delay the oligarchs set to work to construct at Eëtionea by the Peiraeus entrance a fort, ostensibly aimed against attack from the democrat fleet, but in reality designed for a far different end. For their real intent was nothing less than by dominating the harbour to hold up the supplies of the city, to threaten the populace with starvation, and then, when the proper time came, to let in the Spartan fleet. Even Theramenes' eyes were at length opened.

Events now moved rapidly. One day, just outside the Council Chamber door and when the market-place was thronged with people, Phrynichus, a prominent oligarch, was struck dead by an assassin. This gave the signal for a general movement against the Four Hundred. The men engaged on the construction of the Peiraeus fort suddenly turned on their supervising officer and imprisoned him in a house. Theramenes, pretending annoyance, rushed down to the port. Indescribable tumult followed. In an instant willing hands were demolishing the fort ; and a call was issued to all moderate men to rally round against the oligarchs. Nor was the stand made a moment too soon. For a day or two later the Spartan fleet itself appeared in the offing. The walls were manned, ships launched and all prepared to beat back an attack. But the Spartans thought better of it, and sheering off disappeared from sight in the direction of Euboea. The Athenians breathed again, and dispatched the home squadron in pursuit. But the crisis was not yet passed. The home squadron was defeated off Eretria ; Euboea rose in revolt (the most serious blow perhaps that Athens had yet sustained, for the island grew much of her corn) ; and only the Spartans' incredible failure to follow up their success availed to save Athens from almost certain disaster. One good thing resulted. For the panic rang the death-knell of the oligarchy. An assembly was held, this time in due fashion on the Pnyx ; the Four Hundred were deposed, and the sovereign power was

entrusted to a body of moderate citizens, nominally entitled
the Five Thousand, but interpreted to include all persons
in possession of arms. Pisander and most of the oligarchs
escaped to Decelea—a significant comment on their relations with Sparta. As for Antiphon he suffered the death
penalty. So Theramenes, honest dupe that he had been,
came at last into his own. His ' ancestral constitution '
was now in being, a somewhat complicated machinery
of government judiciously blending the rule of the Few
and the Many—' the best administration ', so Thucydides
says, that Athens ever enjoyed (411, autumn).

III

The plight of Athens at the fall of the Four Hundred
could not well have been worse. Her harbour almost
defenceless, her treasury exhausted, her fields and orchards
at the enemy's mercy, her best source of supplies lost
with Euboea, half her Empire in revolt, and her very fleet
sullen, if not disaffected—it scarcely seemed possible that
anything could save her. Yet within a year she had
recovered her command of the sea and was in the position
to make, if not an advantageous, at least an honourable
peace. And, astonishing as it may appear, all this was
largely the work of Alcibiades. Among the first motions
put through the assembly which met to depose the Four
Hundred was a vote for his recall. Instead, however, of
proceeding straight to Athens, Alcibiades remained with
the fleet ; for he rightly saw that it was in the waters
of the Aegean, if anywhere, that the decision was to be
reached. There the scene of action was now to be shifted
from the southern to the northern area of the Asiatic
coast. The Spartans had never ventured upon a trial
of strength against the Athenians at Samos, and by the
autumn of 411 Mindarus their admiral grew weary of the
weather-cock tactics of Tissaphernes, on the payment of
whose subsidies no reliance could be put. Anticipating
more dependable help from Pharnabazus in the north,
he accordingly sailed for the Hellespont. To the Athenians,
wholly dependent as they were on their Pontic corn ships,

this was an uncomfortable menace. True, they had a small squadron there blockading Byzantium, which had recently come out in revolt ; but this could have made little showing had not Thrasybulus in the nick of time brought up the main fleet from Samos. Together they brought the Spartans to battle off Cape Cynossema, or the Dog's Cairn. It was the first engagement between the two main fleets fought since the commencement of the war ; and, as might have been expected, Mindarus was defeated. But he was not put out of action, and on the approach of spring 410 he ventured out again into the open. The Athenians caught him napping off Cyzicus ; and, as the issue of the battle hung, they were suddenly reinforced by a new squadron under Alcibiades. This arrival clinched the day. The enemy turned tail and hurriedly ran their ships on shore, where after a brief tussle they abandoned them to capture. With laconic brevity the dispatch they sent home to Sparta tells its tale : ' The ships are lost. Mindarus is dead. The men starve. We know not what to do.' Thus at one blow Athens had recovered once again her command of the water. It seemed almost that she had eluded her fate.

But what neither the might of her enemies, nor the insurrection of her Empire, nor the distractions of civil tumult could effect against her, was to be accomplished by the folly of her own citizens and the vices of a democracy run mad. For now the political pendulum was to swing back again. The sailors of the fleet, becoming with Cyzicus the heroes of the hour, could no longer be expected to submit to the loss of vote imposed upon them by Theramenes' ' hoplite franchise '. So now (if not indeed earlier) Democracy was restored in all its completeness. The Assembly resumed its old powers. Unhappily it also resumed its old methods. Flooded once more with the riff-raff of the populace, it fell quickly under the spell of a new demagogue, Cleophon the lyre-maker. A man of far less ability, if more honesty, than his prototype, he followed close in the steps of Cleon. Like Cleon, being a tradesman, he was also a financier ; and by the institution of a pauper dole known as the ' Two Obol ', he further undermined the self-respect of his clients the populace. Like Cleon too (and this mattered far more), he was a violent imperialist. By his ruinous influence he inspired Athens with a feverish hope of recovering her shaken supremacy and launched her on a course of ruthless desperation in which all restraints of decency and common sense were forgotten. Talk of peace was set resolutely aside ; and indeed the terms which the Spartans put forward were clearly impossible—for they involved the permanent surrender of all Athens had lost in the war, including not merely the rebel states of the Asiatic coast, but also Euboea itself. To this there could be only one answer, and under Cleophon's guidance frantic energy was thrown into the continuance of the struggle ; but, though the new war mood was admirable in its heroism, it was warped and embittered by the recrudescence of mean suspicions, recriminations and distrust. The brief reign of the oligarchs had not merely imported into political life methods of violence and intrigue unknown to Periclean Athens, but also aroused among the lower orders a desire for retaliation and revenge. A new and vile type of ' Sycophants ' or informers arose who nosed out the past history of men of wealth or standing and haled them into the courts on obsolete or fabricated charges. In an atmosphere which reminds one of the Republican Terror in France, no one was safe from the persecution of these jackals ; and some men like Euripides preferred to leave Athens for a more congenial exile. Worst of all, accusations of negligence or treason were freely and thoughtlessly flung at responsible officials ; and such base ingratitude, as we shall presently see, robbed Athens more than once of the very servants who might have saved her at her hour of need.

Among the first to suffer was Alcibiades. After Cyzicus he had assumed the command of the fleet, and with notable success. In 408 he recovered Byzantium, and thus secured the Black Sea corn-route from risk of interference. With the new year he was welcomed back to Athens with all the honours of a conquering hero. His past misdeeds were forgotten and he made spectacular amends by leading out under military escort the annual Mystery Procession to Eleusis, which since the Spartan occupation of Decelea had been enforcedly abandoned. In the autumn of 407 he was made commander-in-chief and set out with a new fleet of over 100 sail for the Ionian coast which it still remained to recover. All winter he waited for a favourable chance to bring the enemy to battle. Then with spring of 406 he went off on a brief land-operation ; and during his absence and in blank disobedience of orders his lieutenant was drawn into an engagement and suffered a severe repulse at Notium. At once the suppressed jealousy and hatred of his political opponents at home leapt out against Alcibiades. Success alone had rendered him proof against their malice ; and now, for an error which was not his, he was relieved of his command, never to be re-elected. He presently withdrew to a private castle in the Hellespont, where he remained an idle spectator during the remainder of the war. Thus the services of a genius, which for statecraft at least none of his contemporaries could equal, were forfeited to Athens through the very fickleness of temper of which he himself had long since set so disastrous a model.

Their defeat at Notium was ominous for the Athenians in more ways than one. It stands out in the history of the war as the first main action of the fleets in open water in which the enemy had come off victorious ; and the Spartans' success was due in a large measure to the appearance of a new and striking figure at the head of their naval command. On this man, Lysander, the fortunes of the war henceforward turned. With Brasidas and Gylippus he stands out as possessed of an enterprise and independence highly unusual in the Spartan character ; but he was beyond a doubt the greatest of the three. Cold, sinister, forbidding, yet, what was strangest of all, scrupulously honest about money, he had as keen an eye for policy as for strategy ; and when appointed admiral he had at once realized that the real key to victory lay in

16

the financial support of Persia. Now it so happened that just at this moment King Darius had begun to weary of the slow progress of events, and rightly ascribing it to the lack of co-operation between his two jealous satraps, he had sent down his younger son Cyrus to replace Tissaphernes at Sardis and take command of all the Persian forces in the west of Asia Minor. On Cyrus accordingly Lysander at once fastened, and by frank diplomacy persuaded him to give the Spartan cause his whole-hearted backing. Thus assured of adequate funds, he was able to hire mercenary oarsmen in increasing numbers and to build up a fleet not merely of greater strength but also of far greater efficiency than ever in the past. That this fleet was a real menace to the Athenians, the battle of Notium gave clear proof ; and it was therefore the more fortunate for them that when next they came to meet it Lysander was no longer in command. The home government at Sparta, nervous of any potential rival to her power, forbade the prolongation of their admirals' tenure beyond a single year ; and Lysander, falling a victim to this amazing rule, was replaced by the far less experienced Callicratidas.

At first the new commander carried all before him ; he beat Conon, Alcibiades' successor, off the island of Lesbos, and blockaded him with the whole Athenian fleet in Mitylene. The situation was critical. If Conon was to be saved, a huge effort was needed ; and the Athenians rose superbly to the occasion. Work was pushed on in the shipyards with feverish haste. Hulks on the slips were completed ; vessels under repair were patched up. Slaves were promised their freedom and pressed into service at the oar ; and, more astonishing still, young aristocrats of the ' cavalry ' class took their seat on the thwarts beside them. When the fleet set forth, no less than eight generals sailed on board ; but so insecure did they feel of their crews' inexperience, that when they met Callicratidas off the Arginusae Islands, they avoided their customary tactics of manœuvre and adopted the close formation hitherto peculiar to the enemy. None the less they inflicted on him a severe defeat. The Spartan admiral himself fell overboard in the shock of a collision and was seen no more. Seventy of his ships were sunk or captured. The rest fled. So once again the heroism of her sailors had saved the day for Athens; and once again the folly of the Athenian populace was to mar the splendour of their triumph. . . . In the course of the battle there had sprung up a stiff breeze from the north. The waters had grown choppy, and the raw crews had doubtless been thrown somewhat out of gear. Thus embarrassed, the victorious commanders bungled their plans. Their choice lay between following up their success or remaining to salve the crews of their own disabled vessels; and they had done neither. The sinking hulks went down with all hands; the loss of life was considerable and at home it was bitterly resented (406). Demagogues clamoured for a scapegoat; and there was a loud demand for the trial of the responsible persons. Two of the eight generals fled into exile; the rest returned pluckily to face the music. Unhappily for them their arraignment coincided with the festival of the Apaturia, a special occasion of family celebrations, and the sight of the dead sailors' relatives draped in their black brought home to the populace only too vividly the cruel toll of their commanders' negligence. Next day no sooner was the Assembly met than a motion was brought forward that they should dispense with further hearing of the evidence and proceed to a vote forthwith and the penalty be death for all the eight culprits. The proposition was wholly illegal; for the death sentence could only be constitutionally passed on each man singly. Cries of protest were raised. Socrates, the philosopher, who happened to be the councillor presiding for the day, refused his consent to the procedure. All was useless; the vindictive temper of the hour triumphed. The vote was taken and the generals condemned to instant execution. Among them was Pericles' son. So ill did Athens on the eve of her fall recall the days of her greatness.

If ever a people went down through their own folly it

was now. Peace could have been had for the raising of a finger. Sparta put forward the old terms, offering to evacuate Decelea, and otherwise stay each as they were. But this for Athens would have meant the abandonment of all claim on her revolted allies ; and Cleophon, swaggering into the Assembly drunk and with full armour on, defeated the proposal. As a financier alone he ought to have known better ; for the enormity of the blunder was revealed not least by the growing exhaustion of the treasury. Already the government had been issuing a sham currency of gilded copper. The gold and silver offerings from the Acropolis had gone into the melting pot ; and now, when it came to hiring mercenary rowers for their fleet, the Athenians found themselves outbid by the enemy's Persian gold. In the fury of their despair they proclaimed that whoever was captured in the Spartans' service should have his right hand cut off ; and some prisoners they actually butchered.[1] But do what they might, they found the enemy's efficiency increasing, as their own meanwhile declined. For now, by Cyrus' special request, Lysander had once again been sent out, not indeed as high admiral, but with the virtual power of such (for, though the Spartan authorities in deference to their rule gave him a superior, the man chosen was a nonentity) and the two were working hand in glove together for the final effort which should bring Athens to her knees.

With a shrewd eye for strategy, Lysander eluded Conon, now the Athenian generalissimo, and made for the key position of the Hellespont (405). There hoping to cut the corn-route by the occupation of the Straits, he besieged and captured Lampsacus. Conon, gathering every vessel he could muster, soon appeared upon the scene ; and sailing up the strait till they were almost abreast of Lampsacus, the Athenians moored off an open beach of the Gallipoli peninsula opposite, near the mouth of Aegospotami or

---

[1] As a matter of fact, at the very outset of the war in 430, the Spartans had begun these barbarous practices, having commonly slaughtered the crews of captured merchantmen—not merely of Athens or her allies, but even of neutrals too.

the Goat's River. No position could have been worse; and Alcibiades, scenting disaster, came down from his castle to warn them—only to be snubbed for his pains. For four successive days they rowed across the strait and offered battle, and for four days the enemy refused. On the fifth, just as they had returned to their anchorage, and the crews were going ashore for their evening meal, an enemy boat which had followed them gave the signal. A shield flashed, and in a twinkling Lysander was out on them. There was no possibility of resistance; Conon with a few ships that were still manned escaped south into the open. The rest, some 170 in all, were taken where they lay. The prisoners, three or four thousand in number, were massacred next day in cold blood; it was a merited reprisal for similar acts of their own. One evening not many days later the tidings reached Athens, travelling up the Long Walls towards the city to the sound of loud lament. ' That night ', says Xenophon, ' none slept; nor was it so much of their dead that they were thinking as of all that they had done to the Melians and many another Greek—and how they must now themselves endure a similar fate.'

Fleet lost, corn-supply cut, every ally now, excepting Samos,[1] in revolt, a Spartan army at her gates, a Spartan fleet outside Peiraeus, the situation was hopeless. Athens was down. The Thebans clamoured for her complete destruction. The Spartans were more merciful, jealously afraid perhaps lest Thebes should occupy her harbours. Their preliminary demand—a guarantee of her future impotence—was the Long Walls' destruction; and the incredible Cleophon refused. Theramenes obtained leave to go and treat with Lysander; and once there he waited for his countrymen to come to their senses. Three months and more passed—bitter months of starvation, death and despair. Then the tide swept back. Cleophon was charged with evasion of military service and con-

---

[1] The Samian democrats held out, fearing the revenge of the oligarch faction. They were rewarded by the grant of Athenian citizenship mentioned in a foregoing chapter.

demned to death ; and Theramenes was commissioned
to go to Sparta and procure what terms he could. These
proved to be the destruction of the Long Walls and
the Peiraeus fortifications, forfeiture of all ships but twelve,
the loss of all foreign possessions, and the status of subject
ally to Sparta (404, April). The terms were ratified and
the victors did not long delay their execution. ' Lysander
sailed into Peiraeus ; and with much enthusiasm, to the
music of flute girls, they began to demolish the Long
Walls, thinking that day to be the beginning of freedom
for Greece '—a strange illusion !

PART II

CHAPTER XIV

THE NEW ERA

I. The City-state at its Zenith

SO Athens went down ; and 'the Spring was gone out of the year'. Greek History is never quite the same again. True, there still remain issues of hardly less interest and perhaps even greater importance—Sparta's blundering misuse of her second great opportunity of leadership, Thebes' brief flutter into prominence, the stealthy but continuous advance of Macedonian Philip from his usurpation of a tottering throne to the undisputed hegemony of Greece, and then, in the final climax, his son Alexander's world-shaking conquests and the spread of Hellenic culture over the lands of the Levant. But never again shall we discover in all this the glory of the Athens we have known ; for more than the passage of a few short years divides the flourishing commercial town of the Fourth Century from the proud imperial city of the Fifth. The spring is for her indeed gone by, and summer too ; and autumn is come. A faded glamour still hangs about her walls. Glints of the old beauty linger even in the slow melancholy of her decline ; and the final harvest of her intellectual genius remains yet to be reaped. But something is passed away ; there has come a change of spirit, a transition, as it were, from the full-blooded, self-forgetful exuberance of youth to the cynical, introspective disillusionment of middle age. Nor is this the end ; for after autumn must follow winter ; and Athens, no longer free, will become at last a mere cold husk of what she had once been, a home of sterile philosophies, a talking-shop, a tourist centre, the favourite academy of the gilded youth of Rome.

247

The fact is that the Fourth Century was to witness the decline and downfall of what we call the City-State. The ' Polis '—that form of political community so peculiarly characteristic of the Greeks—was an almost unique phenomenon in history [1] ; and we must never think of it in terms of our own modern countries. The picture which the City-State should call to mind must be rather of an area not much larger than a small English county, confined, as a rule, to one level plain or valley, encircled by desolate and barren mountain and containing at its centre the town and its citadel. On this town the whole political life of the City-State will centre : for of that town every freeborn man will be a citizen, whether he dwells afield or no. Hither he will come to celebrate the national festivities. Here he will answer the roll-call for service in the citizen host. Here, above all, if the state be a democracy, he will take his part in the shaping of its policy and in the framing of its laws. Nowadays our own active share in political life is normally confined to the casting of a vote at Parliamentary elections, once, it may be, in four or five years ; and the influence of political decisions upon our daily lives is apt to seem remote and indirect. But for an Athenian it was otherwise. He might any day of his life be called upon to make for himself a decision of the most urgent and immediate importance to his very existence—a decision maybe which would send him off in a state galley to die on some foreign shore ; which might bring an enemy over the passes to cut down his olives and ravage his farm ; or which might, if the luck ran otherwise and the state mines showed a surplus, even bring him a windfall of money. Under such circumstances attendance at the Assembly must have seemed a vital matter ; and, if business claims would spare him, he would go. Nor was this all ; for there was always a chance, and not too small a chance either, that the cast of a lot might single him out for service in the Council Chamber where

---

[1] Rome in early days was of course another example ; and the mediæval cities of North and Central Italy were not very different in type.

for one day in the year his turn would come to act as President and hold in his personal keeping the Citadel keys. Other offices besides were open to him, whatever his station ; Archon he might be, or ambassador to foreign states, or judge at a dramatic festival ; to say nothing of the many functions to be performed in his own local ' deme ' or parish. Little wonder, then, that the Athenian took eagerly to political life, or that he felt for his state an enthusiasm more intense than we ourselves can readily picture.

Privilege begets obligation ; and if he took a pride in his status, the Athenian took no less a pride in the performance of his duties. Service in war he regarded as a natural concomitant of citizenship, whether, as a poor man, he pulled an oar in a galley, or whether, as possessed of some means, he shouldered a shield among the hoplites. But for the rich, at any rate, peace-time equally brought opportunities of service. Direct taxation, it is true, was unpopular, and accepted only under the direst necessities of war (normal outgoings upon the payment of officials and such-like being met by harbour dues, law-court fines and the profits of state mining). Where, however, some piece of public service could suitably be undertaken by a single individual, there was no lack of volunteers. Thus, the staging of a drama at the Dionysiac or other festivals, the training of a choir for some musical contest, the organization of public games, athletic competitions and regattas, these were all financed by wealthy individuals, taken in turn from a rota. Above all, in time of war, the annual upkeep of a state galley was similarly furnished out of some man's private means ; and, whatever might be the form of such state-services or ' liturgies ', there was always a strong spirit of emulation and personal pride in their performance. Each ' trierarch ' wished to make his galley somewhat better than his neighbour's ; each ' choregus ' wished to see his drama win the prize. The number and munificence of their ' liturgies ' was often quoted by parties in a lawsuit as a proof of their good record in the past. The trophy won by his choir would often be erected by the proud ' choregus ' in some public place of the town. ' The Street of Tripods ' was so named from the dedications of such prize-winners ; and the architectural base of one of these monuments is still surviving to this day.[1]

Such admirable spirit of public service shows democratic Athens at her best. Unlike the modern Socialist, her citizens had no belief in state-run enterprise. They detested red-tape and officialdom. Rules and regulations were reduced to a minimum. Their finance was of the sketchiest. Even their police-force was composed of foreign slaves, so distasteful would the task have been to free-born citizens. Above all, they were genuinely distrustful of the professional or specialist, preferring the independence and free initiative of the untrained amateur ; and so far did they carry this preference that they were willing, as we have seen, to entrust a tradesman like Cleon with a perilous military enterprise, or appoint a poet like Sophocles as commissioner of finance. Such officials, too, were in a very real sense the servants of the citizen-body, not its masters, responsible at every turn to the Council and Assembly, and answerable at the end of their term for the conduct of their stewardship. Freedom for the Athenians was a living creed. Yet at the same time (and in this contrast lay the real secret of their political greatness) no people ever gave themselves up with more whole-hearted devotion to the service of the state. Body and soul they were its willing slaves, utterly forgetful of self and proud in their sacrifice. Athens was no place for the shirker. The man who lost his shield in battle was the butt of the boys in the street. Even to hold aloof from the normal social and political life of the town was considered the mark of sour and misanthropic character. A recluse like Euripides was bound to be unpopular ; for no man was expected to live for himself alone. If in one phrase we were to attempt to define the aim of the Greek City-State, it was the maximum

---

[1] The Monument of Lysicrates, standing below the south-east cliff of the Acropolis.

development of the individual's power—physical and intellectual alike—for the good of the whole community. He would train his body to fitness that he might serve his country in war. He would cultivate his intellect that he might play his full part in her culture. Without her he is nothing. She is the all in all of his existence. Exclusion from her privileges is the most dreaded of punishments ; exile from her confines the supreme calamity in life.

To praise the Greeks for their patriotism is no compliment. It was a second nature to them ; and Pericles was using no cant phrase when he said of his countrymen that they had ' fallen in love with their city ' as though with a mistress. This remarkable saying occurs in his famous Funeral Speech, recorded for us by Thucydides. The style of the speech, it is true, is the style of the historian, for there were no shorthand writers in Athens. But, for all that, there rings through the periods an exalted idealism which we cannot but believe to have been the authentic message of the great statesman himself ; and we seem even to hear echo upon echo of the very words he used. And, since no other words can sum up half so well the aim and achievement of Athens, it is well worth our while to quote here some portions of that speech. It was delivered at the close of the first year of the war against Sparta, in memory of those citizens who had lost their lives in the city's service. But Pericles went far beyond the immediate intention of that sad occasion ; and, as he warmed to his work, he launched forth upon an inspired and triumphant panegyric of his own people's greatness.

' Our constitution ' he says ' is named a democracy, because it is in the hands not of the few, but of the many. But our laws secure equal justice for all in their private disputes, and our public opinion welcomes and honours talent in every branch of achievement. . . . And as we give free play to all in our public life, so we carry the same spirit into our daily relations with one another. We have no black looks nor angry words for our neighbour if he enjoys himself in his own way, and we abstain from little acts of churlishness which, though they leave no mark, yet cause annoyance to whoso notes them. Open and friendly in our private intercourse, in our public acts we keep strictly within the control of law. We acknowledge the restraint of reverence ; we are obedient to whosoever is set in authority, and to the laws, more especially to those which offer protection to the oppressed, and to those unwritten ordinances whose transgression brings admitted shame. Yet ours is no workaday city only. No other provides so many recreations of the spirit —contests and sacrifices all the year round, and beauty in our public buildings to cheer the heart and delight the eye day by day. . . . We are lovers of beauty without extravagance, and lovers of wisdom without unmanliness. Wealth to us is not a mere material for vainglory, but an opportunity for achievement. . . . Our citizens attend both to public and private duties, and do not allow absorption in their own affairs to interfere with their knowledge of the city's. We differ from other states in regarding the man who holds aloof from public life not as " quiet " but as " useless " ; we decide and debate, carefully and in person, all matters of policy, holding not that words and deeds go ill together but that acts are foredoomed to failure when undertaken undiscussed. For we are noted for being at once most adventurous in action and most reflective beforehand. . . . In doing good, too, we are the exact opposite of the rest of mankind. We secure friends not by accepting favours, but by doing them. . . . In a word, I claim that our city as a whole is an education to Greece, and that her members yield to none, man by man, for independence of spirit, manysidedness of attainment, and complete self-reliance in limbs and brain. That this is no vainglorious phrase but actual fact the supremacy which our manners have won for us itself bears testimony. No other city of the present day goes out to her ordeal greater than ever men dreamed ; no other is so powerful that the invader feels no bitterness when he suffers at her hands, and her subjects no shame at the indignity of their dependence. Great, indeed, are the symbols and

witnesses of our supremacy, at which posterity, as all
mankind to-day, will be astonished. We need no Homer
or other man of words to praise us ; for such give pleasure
for a moment, but the truth will put to shame their imagin-
ings of our deeds. For our pioneers have forced a way
into every sea and every land, establishing among mankind,
in punishment or beneficence, eternal memorials of their
settlement.' [1]

The picture which Pericles or (if you will) Thucydides
has painted for us is no mere figment of the imagination.
The spirit here described has more than adequate witness
in the many works of literature and art which have come
down to us, and the words ring true. Athens in the Fifth
Century was, despite all her troubles, a supremely happy
place ; and these were days in which it was good to be
alive. ' The Athenian Community during the Periclean
time ' says Mr. Zimmern ' must be regarded as the most
successful example of social organization known to history.'
It may well be so ; but with the close of the Fifth Century,
if not before, those times had passed. The speech which
Pericles delivered beside the tomb of her fallen sons was
in a far deeper sense the epitaph of Athens too. Thucydides, composing it as he perhaps did in the days after
Aegospotami, must have already recognized it for such,
and realized that the war had proved in very deed the
grave of Athens' best self. What she will be in the succeeding century, we must now turn to describe ; it is a
less enthralling story ; but it is perhaps one of the most
interesting periods of psychological evolution which history
contains.

II. Symptoms of Decline in the City-State

That an era of decadence had set in the best Athenians
of the Fourth Century were well aware. Demosthenes
was continually harping upon the theme. His countrymen, he complains, would not drill ; they preferred to
pay hirelings to fight for them. They thought of themselves first and of the state second. Whereas their

[1] Translation by Zimmern.

fathers had built for the glory of Athens, they built for their personal comfort or pride, and compared with the humble homes of the great men of the past their private houses were palaces of pretentious luxury. Public duties were neglected ; and to obtain even a quorum at the Assembly it had proved necessary to introduce a payment for attendance. Public men lacked the self-effacing dignity of their predecessors. Self-advertisement was all too common. The bad manners of the demagogues were proverbial, ever since Cleon had set the fashion with his vulgar ways, slapping his thigh like a low tapster, keeping the Assembly waiting at his will and then dismissing it because he was busy. Even Demosthenes and his political opponents bandy the crudest of personal gibes. There were still, of course, plenty of staunch and steady-going patriots in this as in any other age, and many of them reacted against its demoralizing tendencies by modelling their lives on the severer ideal of Sparta. But, for all that, the good old days were gone by and men knew it. The very music of the time—always a telling symptom— shocked the conservative ears of Aristophanes ; and he bitterly complains of the new-fangled tunes with their trills and tremolos and discords, the rag-time of antiquity.

The causes of the decline were, in part of course, economic.[1] The Plague had sapped Athens' vitality ; the

---

[1] It has very plausibly been suggested that the decline of the Greeks in the Fourth Century may have been attributable in part to the spread of malaria. Of such a disease there seems little or no trace before the last quarter of the Fifth Century. Hesiod, though enumerating most of the troubles which beset the farmer of swampy Boeotia, gives no hint of it. But it may well be that the felling of the forests (due to ship-building, etc.) led to a decrease of rainfall, a drying up of rivers, and so to an increase of stagnant, mosquito-breeding pools. At any rate the word ' fever ' begins to occur with some frequency in the works of Aristophanes, Xenophon and other authors ; and evidence drawn from Hippocratic treatises suggests that by the year 400 Athens was familiar with intermittent and remittent fevers. It has even been conjectured that the introduction of the cult of Asclepius (the god of medicine) in 420 B.C. was due to the outbreak of this new and obscure disease with which the ordinary doctors were unable to cope.

Spartan occupation of Decelea had impoverished her countryside. Many areas of Greece had similarly suffered from the prolonged hostilities. Unemployment was rife ; and cheap slave-labour tended to oust the free worker from his job.

Perhaps one indirect result, too, of the Peloponnesian War was the rise of new centres of manufacture such as Syracuse, Tarentum, and various towns in Asia Minor, and consequent decline of the old Greek industries of the past. So more and more men cut adrift from their home-country, and sought occupation where it best might be found. Travelling teachers and itinerant doctors are now numerous ; and above all, as we shall see, soldiers of fortune become a feature of the age. Arcadians and Achaeans march with Cyrus into Persia ; and Athens hires mercenaries to fight against Philip. In other words, the City-State, with her exclusive claims and her exclusive privileges, no longer suffices to the individual's need. She is no longer all in all to her citizens ; each must shift for himself.

But in another and a deeper sense the City-State is no longer all-sufficient ; and the second cause of the decline is psychological. During the final quarter of the foregoing century the Sophists' teaching had begun to take deep root. Traces of its influence we have already seen in the words and policies of Athens' leading men. Naked appeal to self-interest is the invariable argument which Thucydides puts into the mouths of Cleon, Alcibiades and the rest. It is tacitly assumed that no more exalted motive could conceivably influence a state. But what then, it might be asked, of its individual members ? Such doctrines were scarcely calculated to make good citizens, and self-interest might well prove a double-edged weapon. Young men who had been taught, as Socrates' pupils were, to call everything in question and accept no tradition or convention at mere second-hand, were likely to end in accepting none at all ; and, though Socrates himself maintained in its highest sense an unswerving loyalty to the state, his disciples did not. Once encouraged to think for themselves, they came soon to rate their own judgment above the accepted standards of morality and religion ; and it was the same, we may be sure, with the disciples of less sterling teachers. The younger generation made light of civic obligations ; they derided *esprit de corps* ; they became, in a word, thoroughgoing Individualists. So the old bonds which had held the community together began to part ; and in this way, too, the State ceased to be the all-sufficient interest in men's lives.

But, if a decline of political and social life had set in, it would be a mistake to suppose that the vitality of men's intellects was necessarily impaired. It is true that the Fourth Century produced no poetic masterpieces, no historian who could rival Thucydides ; but the general level of intelligence had almost certainly improved since the days of the Persian War. Aristophanes complains of the hundreds of young dilettanti who were writing fifth-rate tragedies ; and abundant evidence exists of the lively wit and powers of appreciation of the normal Athenian. In his own great comedy *The Frogs*, the point of which largely turned upon a comparison between the styles of Aeschylus and Euripides, Aristophanes was able to rely upon his listeners' recognition of innumerable quotations ; and many prisoners of the Sicilian Expedition were spared, because they could recite a whole chorus from Euripides. Few London playgoers could pass a similar test on the works of Shakespeare or Sheridan ; and we may well accept the verdict of a modern writer who asserts that ' the average ability of the Athenian race was on the lowest estimate very nearly two grades higher than our own, that is about as much as our race is above that of the African negro '. What happened in the Fourth Century was that all these powers of thought, wit and imagination were diverted into new channels. Minds which hitherto had turned spontaneously outwards to spend themselves upon the communal activities of city life were now either turned inward upon themselves and devoted to philosophic speculation, or else were directed upon some specialized profession. Men became, in short, for the first time, fully conscious of their own separate individualities. Youths forsook athletics for the pleasures of intellectual conversation. They talked about their souls and analysed their emotions. Culture became a deliberate ideal ; and philosophy took the place of religion. Above all, the scope of men's activities was narrowed down. The Fifth Century Athenian, as Pericles had said, took a pride in being able to turn his amateur hand to whatever came along. The poet could turn financier ; the tradesman lead an army ; and the average man could handle a pike, appreciate a tragedy, wrestle in the gymnasium, sing a song and play an instrument, dance in a chorus, make a speech in a law-court and, if need were, turn politician. The Fourth Century, on the other hand, was an Age of Specialization ; and most of these functions pass more and more into the hands of the expert. We find professional soldiers, professional athletes, professional lawyers, professional financiers and professional artists. To our own civilization, tending as it does towards a similar specialization of function, this development is of particular interest. There was gain, no doubt, as well as loss in the process. Mankind is bound to grow up ; but it does not follow that the self-conscious age is necessarily the most pleasant. Certainly it would be hard to maintain that the city of Demosthenes and Plato was as happy or successful a place as the city of Pericles and his fellowship.

Individualism and specialization are, then, the twin key-notes of the age which now falls to be described ; and it is worth our while before embarking on its story to trace the working of this dual influence upon various spheres of social and artistic activity. We will begin with Literature ; and in this the first and characteristic note is a failure of inspiration. The mood of poetic exaltation had passed : there were no great dramatists, no second Pindar. It was essentially an age of Prose. For the most part, too, the Fourth-Century prose-writers were specialists. Thucydides, we may feel pretty sure, would have preferred success as a general, which was not granted him, to the literary success which was. But Plato and Aristotle,

17

the two great philosophers, were nothing if not students. They were far more independent of their environment than Socrates, whom we can hardly imagine apart from the sociable background of Athenian street-corners. They would have continued their work had no Athens existed ; and both in point of fact spent much time abroad. Plato, though he did most of his teaching and writing in Athens, visited the court of Dionysius, the tyrant of Syracuse. Aristotle was a native of Stagirus in Macedon and served for a period of three years as tutor to Alexander the Great. As philosophers they must always rank among the most profound thinkers of history. But the strange thing is that they seem to have remained unaware of the changes which were coming over the Hellenic world. Both, it is true, were deeply interested in politics. Aristotle collected the details of 150 different constitutions. The greatest of Plato's works, the *Republic*, is devoted to the search, in dialogue form, for the ideal system of government. Nevertheless neither philosopher conceived of any possible development beyond the narrow limits of the traditional City-State. Plato, in fact, remained to the end a magnificent but unpractical dreamer, just as Aristotle, with his more scientific and critical bent, remained what we should call a don.

The other great group of prose-writers were ' lawyers '— that is to say, they wrote speeches for parties at law to deliver in court ; for by the rule of Athenian law both defendant and plaintiff were bound to speak for themselves. Lysias, the metic from Sicily, was amongst the earliest and most successful of these ' lawyers '; he had a nice knack of suiting the style of the speech to the character of his client. The defence he concocted for a cripple in danger of losing his dole is a masterpiece of sympathetic realism. To read Lysias is inevitably to be convinced. Demosthenes, too, was a lawyer ; and though it is as a politician that we know him best, there was always something of the advocate about him. He was violent in attack and violent in defence. His speeches have blackened the character of Philip of Macedon, one might almost say, for all time, and when his burning rhetoric is turned against his political opponents—who were probably no worse than most men of the time—it is to denounce them as traitors in enemy pay. Everything for Demosthenes is either pure black or pure white ; but for tense, downright, passionate expression of his hatreds and his enthusiasms, no orator can touch him—not even Cicero or Burke. Isocrates, his contemporary, though also a speech-writer, was less of a practising lawyer than a political pamphleteer. More than any man of his day, perhaps, he realized the failure of the City-State, and he had the courage to advocate, in opposition to Demosthenes' view, the acceptance of Philip of Macedon as champion of a united Greece. We have travelled far indeed from the Periclean ideal. The historians of the period were for the most part of little importance. Ephorus, a follower of Isocrates, wrote a universal chronicle from the Dorian Invasion to the year 340 ; but though a careful stylist, he did little more in reality than dish up afresh the material provided him by previous writers. Theopompus of Chios and Timaeus of Sicily, too, were more litterateurs than first-rate historians, ignorant of real warfare and concerned to produce an interesting narrative rather than to give an accurate account of events. There is, however, one exception. Xenophon the Athenian was no arm-chair critic. His very style betrays the man. For, as compared even with Thucydides', it is plain, blunt and business-like, going straight to the point. He was essentially a practical man, deeply interested in political questions (though at Athens he took the losing side) and above all he played a prominent part in that stirring adventure whose story he wrote—the March of the ten thousand Greek mercenaries into the heart of Persia and back. But apart from this and his other historical writings, Xenophon's work has a peculiar significance, as containing the germ of biography. He wrote a memoir of Socrates, his master ; and compiled a monograph on Agesilaus, the Spartan King under whom he actually served. His story of the upbringing of Cyrus the Great contains, it is true, more moralization and romance than historical fact. Nevertheless the interest in the Individual, so characteristic of Fourth-Century thought, begins here to reveal itself. And in the sphere of Drama the same tendency is observable. Aristophanes found indeed no worthy successor. The so-called 'Middle Comedy', extending over two-thirds of the century, produced nothing worthy of special remark ; but in the 'New Comedy' of Menander a fresh note is struck. Instead of the old Aristophanic burlesque, we begin to get a less humorous but more genuine picture of everyday life. The characters are real men and women, not parodies ; and, above all, a love interest, hitherto scarcely touched by the drama, makes its tardy appearance. The romance between mistress and gallant, chequered by the obstruction of relatives and by startling transformations of fortune, kidnapping, elopements and stealthy intrigues, now started a fashion which has never died out. It is not too much to say that the Modern Novel is a direct descendant of the wit and imagination and understanding of mankind which we find in the Athenian New Comedy.

When we turn to Art, there is here, too, a similar evidence of a failing inspiration, similarly counterbalanced, as we shall presently see, by a new interest in the Individual. The craft of the potter—Athens' great speciality—is now in decline. The Sicilian disaster had ruined her trade in the West and the Italians were now manufacturing for themselves. The standard of her workmanship, too, is degraded by commercialism, and the painted figures on the vases or cups become coarse, hurried and stereotyped.[1]

[1] During the Fifth Century a new type of vase, specially used for funeral offerings, had been evolved. In this a white ground was used, and figures were drawn in particularly graceful flowing lines, filled in with brilliant colours, red, yellow, green and so forth.

PLATE XIX

The famous bronze statue of a boy, now in Florence, known as the Idolino. Though modern critics place its date during the end of the Fifth Century, the delicate mouldings of the limbs and subtle grace of the body's curve is typical of the tendencies of Fourth-Century sculpture. Cp. Plate XXIII and Plate XX.

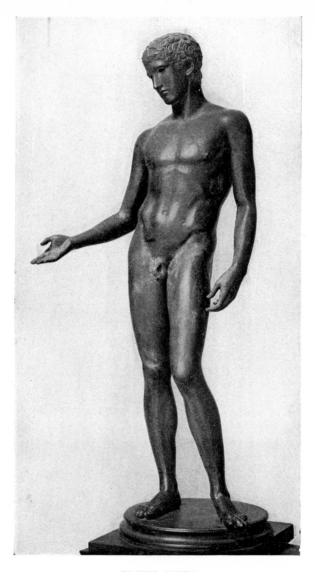

BRONZE YOUTH

In Architecture there is nothing to equal the supreme achievements of the Parthenon or the Erechtheum. But outside Athens some impressive monuments were erected ; and the introduction of the new Corinthian style, with its heavily foliaged capitals, lends a certain air of sumptuous magnificence to some of these. Less attention, however, was paid to the qualities of restraint and exquisite finish which marked the best work of the preceding century. Sculpture is perhaps the one field in which the Fourth Century really excelled. But here again the same tendency is noticeable. During the preceding epoch Pheidias, the great Athenian sculptor, and Polycleitus, his younger Argive contemporary, had both adhered to a style of severe restraint. They had condescended to no tricks to enhance the beauty of their figures. Dignity of poise and proportion was their chief aim ; and Polycleitus in particular worked out in his Doryphorus, or Spear-bearer, what were considered by antiquity to be the perfect proportions of the human figure. But with the Fourth Century a change begins. Praxiteles, one of the greatest sculptors of all time, could model the human form with unrivalled skill ; but he loses perhaps more than he gains by introducing certain tricks or affectations of style. Thus he gave to his figures a languid curve of posture which lent a graceful sinuosity to their contours, but which missed the virile energy of Pheidias' heroes or Polycleitus' athletes. One cannot but feel a doubt whether his dreamy Hermes at Olympia could stay a long cross-country run. There is more force and energy about the works of Scopas and Lysippus ; but it is typical of the period that they should have aimed at energy of mind and character rather than of mere muscle and brawn. There is a look of strained intensity about the faces of their figures—an attempt to express through the medium of marble the personality that lies within. Here again, then, we strike the same tendency towards Individualism which we have already observed in literature ; and it found expression in various ways. For one thing there is far greater realism in the reproduction of the model ; and whereas in the Fifth Century the sculptor was apt to suppress the distinctive peculiarities of an individual face or body, aiming at a traditional and general type, the Fourth-Century artist was ready to seize with special interest on such details as a wrinkle, a high cheek-bone or a swollen vein. The popularity of portraiture is another sign of the times. In the Fifth Century it had been rare ; and the famous bust of Pericles gives a highly idealized picture of a type combining calm dignity with lofty vision—the statesman in the abstract. The Fourth Century preferred a literal likeness ; and the exquisite modelling of Alexander's features or the harsh lines of Aristotle's frown are as distinctive and familiar to us as the faces of Wellington or Pitt. The gods are still idealized, but in place of a serene, impassive dignity, we now find them touched, as it were, with the perplexities and emotions of humankind, and the goddesses, like Praxiteles' famous Aphrodite, are susceptible to the feelings of female modesty. Studies of worn and wrinkled age are given with lifelike fidelity ; and children, who had hitherto been made to look more like puppets than human beings, are treated with a genuine sympathy and delight. Of the spirit of this age, in short, as perhaps of most ages, its Art is an accurate and faithful mirror.

One form of portraiture especially favoured was the figure of the victorious athlete, and athletics played so prominent a part in this as in the foregoing period of Greek history that something must be said on the subject. No people—not even the English—was ever more persistently addicted to the practice of physical exercise than the early Greeks. In Fifth-Century Athens men of every age and station repaired regularly to the gymnasium for daily recreation ; in the education of youths the palestra,

---

PLATE XX

Head of youth known as the Westmacott Athlete, dating from Fifth Century. The severely dignified but tender grace of the pose and expression is free from the touch of sentimentality which often mars the sculpture of the Fourth Century. Cp. Plate XXIII.

FIFTH-CENTURY HEAD OF YOUTH

or wrestling school, took a prominent place. At Sparta physical training was still more essential to the development of the citizen soldier. Sport in our modern sense was not the main object of such recreation; team-games, if not unknown, were rare. Physical fitness and moral hardihood were what the Greeks aimed at; and the very conditions under which they ran or wrestled were severe. In all weathers under an open sky they stripped naked; and everything was planned to test endurance. Running was practised on a deeply sanded track which gave small aid to swiftness. Races were frequently run in full armour. In boxing leather thongs were worn over the fist, but merely to save knuckles from fracture, not by any means to soften the blow. The throwing of quoit or spear was less exacting; but the wrestling, most popular perhaps of sports, was no soft option; for in its favourite form, the ' pancration ', a fall did not end the contest, but the struggle continued on the ground till one or other of the competitors surrendered. Striking, kicking, and in fact any other form of violent pressure was legitimate. Biting was forbidden, and gouging the eye, but strangling was allowed and fatal results were not unknown. To these various forms of sport an immense impetus had been given by the great Panhellenic contests of which the Olympic Festival was the most renowned. By origin such celebrations were in part at least religious; but during the Sixth Century their popularity had already developed into an international craze. Spectators assembled from all over Greece and Olympia became for a fortnight a sort of World's Fair. Men of every class competed; and one celebrated victor was a fishmonger. Though the only prize at Olympia was a crown of wild olive, the victorious athlete was welcomed home to his native city with extravagant honour and great material rewards. The whole population would turn out to greet him. Songs were composed in his honour; large sums of money might be voted him, or the right to free meals at the Town Hall for life. There is even record of one Olympic victor who was worshipped after death as a hero. But the effect of such keen competition is, as we ourselves know, double-edged. Athletics ceased to be a pure recreation, and specialization set in. During the course of the Fifth Century the professional began to make his appearance. By the time of the Peloponnesian War the Athenians were no longer a nation of athletes. The rich youths turned to horse-racing or gambling; some to intellectual conversation with sophists, and though the popularity of the games continued, the very name of 'athlete' came to betoken the professional. So in the Fourth Century we must note here again another form of the specialist, a man devoting his life to an elaborate system of training, over-gorged on a diet of meat (which the normal Greek detested) and over-developed in muscle so that the stumpy top-heavy type thus produced was far removed from the graceful proportions of his amateur predecessor. In particular this new type, muscle-bound and unevenly developed, was considered useless for military purposes. Sparta, always intent on producing the soldier, forbade such specialized training, and her citizens, once predominant among the Olympic victors, accordingly ceased to compete.

This brings us to another feature of the Age—and, indeed, one might well say, its chief curse—the professional soldier.[1] For now tactical innovations and the necessity for a more elaborate training demanded something more than an occasional appearance on the drill-yard. Long-term enlistment became the fashion, and ambitious adventurers like Jason of Pherae or Philip of Macedon depended for their success on the possession of a permanent

---

[1] Arcadia was specially productive of mercenaries, being debarred by her geographical position from the outlet of colonization.

PLATE XXI

Bust of Pericles, probably by Cresilas. Note the dreamy expression of the eyes and the composed dignity of the features. Personal traits are in the main suppressed; and the portrait is less individual than the accompanying portrait of Alexander (now in the Louvre) which clearly gives a fairly accurate presentation of the Macedonian's features.

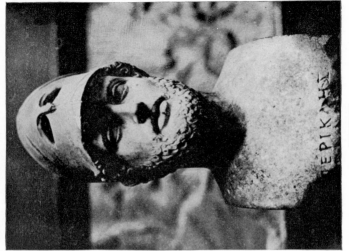

PERICLES

ALEXANDER

army. The existence of such armies was largely responsible for the endless prolongation of wars. The mercenary's
trade was a demoralizing one, for he often had to live by
rapine. Estimates of his character differ. Some say
he was drawn from the dregs of society. Xenophon,
however, found good stuff among those with whom he
himself served, for they were mostly veterans of the
Peloponnesian War. Comic drama represents the mercenary as a swashbuckling braggart ; and many, we
may be sure, were loose-livers. When disbanded they
must have been a great source of embarrassment, and
it is not easy to picture the feelings of the peaceful Greek
city by the shores of the Euxine on whom there suddenly
descended out of the blue six thousand travel-sore and
discontented veterans marching home from their campaign
in the heart of the East. If we except the citizens of
Sparta, the professional soldier had hitherto been a com-
parative rarity, though some we know found their way out
into the service of Nebuchadnezzar. For a race of fighters
the Greeks were, in fact, singularly amateurish, their
instincts being opposed to the political dangers of a standing
army. Nevertheless the military developments of the
Peloponnesian War began to set things in motion. The
stereotyped tradition of hoplite tactics was more than
once found wanting. Light-armed troops played a new
rôle, and we find Rhodian slingers and Cretan bowmen
employed at a price. Methods of training men in swift
and well co-ordinated movement were learnt. Drill grew
more exacting. Warfare was, in fact, on the way to
becoming a science ; and, though hoplites continued to
form the core of every army, the Fourth Century was to
bring with it many new tactical changes which made
increasing demand on the skill of the ordinary soldier. In
any case, provided the money was forthcoming, it needed
no great perspicacity to see that a permanent and disciplined body of mercenaries was a clear gain to efficiency ;
and of these, as we have already observed, there was by
this time no lack. The economic dislocations of the long
war. and more still perhaps the numerous evictions due

to the struggle of political factions, had thrown many a man on the world who was only too glad to fight under any master that would hire him. Runaway slaves were also good material. The result was that large numbers of Greek mercenaries went out, some to fight for Carthage, some for Persia; there were 10,000 of them at least in the army of Darius which opposed Alexander at Issus. And nearer home, too, there were to come opportunities of employment. The commercially-minded Athenians fought their wars against Philip, in the main, with hired troops; and the sacrilegious Phocian leaders who usurped the treasures of Delphi were thereby enabled to maintain such an army that it took Philip himself to destroy them. More spectacular and more interesting perhaps than any of these examples was the part played by Greek mercenaries in Cyrus' famous march into Persia. Itself a mere side-show to Greek History proper, it has nevertheless a very considerable importance, firstly because it revealed in an unexpected manner the inherent weaknesses of the Great King's régime, and secondly because its story, as related by Xenophon, is certainly a masterpiece of Greek historical literature. For both reasons, therefore, it is worth while to touch on it here.

The young prince Cyrus, as his dealings with Lysander have already shown, was a man of decision and enterprise highly unusual to find in the now decadent royal house of Persia. On the death of his father, Darius, and his elder brother's accession in 404, he at once resolved in his mind to make a bid for the throne; and his first-hand experience of the quality of Greek troops told him that in them lay ready to hand a weapon which was wellnigh invincible. Employing a Spartan named Clearchus as

PLATE XXII

(a) A figure of Socrates now in the British Museum. Note the snub nose and earnest bulging eyes for which the philosopher was famous. (b) A portrait statue of Demosthenes, dating probably from the Third Century, but vividly portraying the somewhat harsh features and angular pose of the great orator.

XXII

DEMOSTHENES

SOCRATES

agent,[1] he collected a force of nearly 11,000 Greek hoplites besides a few light-armed troops; almost every quarter of the Hellenic world was represented, Sicily and Italy, the Thracian coast, Boeotia, Acarnania and above all the Peloponnese. From Athens came a mere handful, but among them was Xenophon himself, serving as a volunteer private. These, then, were to form a stiffening to the hundred thousand Asiatic troops under Cyrus' com-

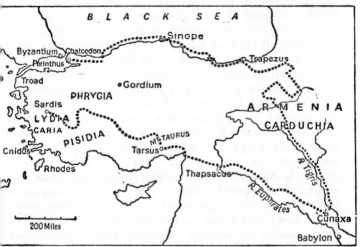

MAP TO ILLUSTRATE MARCH OF THE TEN THOUSAND

mand; and in 401 the eastward march began. It was represented at the outset as a punitive expedition against some rebellious tribes of Pisidia; and Clearchus alone knew the truth. But soon Pisidia was left behind on the flank. Mount Taurus was reached and its passes were sold by the disloyalty of the Cilician Governor. So to Tarsus; and there at length the true objective of the expedition began to dawn on the Greeks. A three months' march into the heart of Asia was not in their bargain; and they refused to go further. But, true to Greek type,

[1] The pay offered was half a daric per month—4½d. a day. or about half the wage of an unskilled labourer.

they were still open to argument. Clearchus, abandoning
the standpoint of discipline, pleaded with them for cool
deliberation ; he swore, come what might, to stand by
them ; he actually wept. Cyrus offered to double their
wages ; and they agreed to proceed. Another cowardly
governor gave them a free opening through the passes
into Syria, and soon they had said farewell to the sea.
Cyrus now openly admitted that Babylon was his goal,
and promised a bonus at the campaign's termination.
So they entered the desert—' smooth as a sea, treeless,
only wormwood and scented shrubs for vegetation, but
alive with all kinds of beasts strange to Greek eyes, wild
asses, and ostriches, antelopes and bustards'. Nevertheless the army made good going. The commissariat of
wagon convoys was efficient ; and from Thapsacus to
the confines of Babylon, a distance of over 400 miles,
was covered in thirty-five days. Some way in front of
Babylon Artaxerxes had constructed a defensive fosse
forty miles long ; but while he awaited further reinforcements to his already unwieldy host (400,000
strong, it was said) Cyrus' army reached the fosse and
crossed it unopposed. Such a menace to Babylon compelled immediate engagement. The battle took place
at Cunaxa ; and Cyrus played his cards well enough to
have ensured his success. Knowing that if Artaxerxes
were himself once routed, the remainder of his Oriental
host would melt away, the prince determined to push
home his attack in the centre where he understood his
brother to be. With this intent he ordered the Greeks,
whom he had placed on his right, to shift further inwards.
But here things began to go wrong. Clearchus, with a
Greek's habitual fear of having his right outflanked,
refused the change of plan, and leading his Ten Thousand
to a forthright charge, swept the Persian left out of existence. Victory seemed certain, as Cyrus himself now
led the assault upon the centre, and broke clean through
the Great King's bodyguard. But his own impetuosity
ruined all. Catching sight of his brother, whom he cor-
dially hated, Cyrus yielded to an impulse of passion and

spurred his horse in pursuit. Caught in the thick of the mêlée, he received a wound in the eye, fell to the ground and was dispatched on the instant. At the tidings of their commander's death, his Asiatic troops fled. Their camp was pillaged ; and when the victorious Ten Thousand returned from the pursuit, it was to find themselves isolated, without leader or purpose, in the heart of an enemy country, some 1,000 miles from Greek soil. If their adventure hitherto had been remarkable, its sequel reads more like a miracle.

Contrary to expectation, the Greeks had no thought of surrender. Their known prowess saved them from attack, and an offer of safe conduct was accepted from that crooked knave Tissaphernes. The route to be taken lay northward up the Tigris towards the Greek colonial cities of the Black Sea littoral ; but they had not gone far before Tissaphernes showed his true colours. He summoned the five Greek captains to a parley in his tent ; all five, including Clearchus, had the temerity to go ; and all five were kidnapped and sent to the Persian Court for execution. Thus deprived of all leadership, many armies would have collapsed ; but this did nothing of the sort. With an independence and an instinct for self-government characteristic of their race, the Ten Thousand held a mass-meeting, elected new commanders (of whom Xenophon himself proved the most vigorous) and under the direction of these set out northward again. The march was a terrible ordeal, and it has been described in the pages of Xenophon with much vivid and picturesque detail—of the strange tribes they encountered, not least the tattooed Mossynoeci, who counted plumpness a beauty and paraded with pride little boys like stuffed pigs, of the strange foods they ate on the way, the date-wine which gave them the headache, the honey which made them all drunk, and the barley-brew which they sipped native-fashion through straws. Food was, indeed, a crucial problem ; for they had to live on the land ; but this was not their only trouble. For some distance Tissaphernes' troops hung on their rear ; and when they reached the mountains of Kurdistan or Carduchia the wild hill-tribes began to attack them. At any turn of the road huge boulders would come hurtling down on their heads, propelled by an unseen foe. There was fighting at the passes ; and at one river crossing they were compelled to fight their way in the teeth of the Armenian satrap's forces. December found them among the Armenian mountains, and for days they struggled on through driving snow often over their waists in the drifts and suffering terribly from snow-blindness and frost-bite. Xenophon had his work cut out to keep them going at all. Then at length came the climax. The van topped a crest and catching sight of the sea raised a shout. ' Xenophon and the rearguard imagined fresh enemies must be attacking in front ; for folk were after them out of the countryside which was all in flame behind, and some the rearguard had killed, and others they had caught alive in an ambush, capturing some score of wicker-shields covered with raw cattle-hides. But the shouting grew louder and nearer, as new-comers ran up to join the shouters. Louder and louder it swelled with each fresh arrival, till Xenophon guessed that bigger game was up. So he leapt to horse and taking Lycius and the troopers, galloped to the scene of action. Then on an instant came the sound of soldiers shouting and passing down the word " The Sea ! The Sea ! " Up they all came then, and rearguard to boot, driving the pack-beasts and horses. And reaching the crest, they fell on one another's necks, Generals, Captains and all ; and they wept. The next moment someone gave the suggestion and the soldiers collected stones and built a huge cairn, and hung on it several raw cowhides and staves and the wicker shields they had captured.'

They were saved ; but there remained still a weary time ahead of them. Danger had kept them together ; but now discipline relaxed and they broke up into parties. Partly by land and partly on ship they made their way from Trapezus to Chalcedon. Thence they were conveyed over by a Spartan admiral to Byzantium, where they came within an ace of sacking the city. Most then took service under a Thracian chieftain called Seuthes, who cheated them of their pay. Finally in 399 they joined the great Spartan crusade against Persia. Xenophon himself served on Agesilaus' staff, and then, since his friendship for Sparta forbade return to his own native city, he was given an estate near Olympia where he spent twenty years of his life in hunting and writing. Ultimately he died at Corinth in 354. But his work outlived him. The Romans took him for a model. Many soldiers have studied him—our own General Wolfe among the rest. He has become the schoolboy's classic. But did the lessons of his great journal—with its startling revelation of Persian military weakness, of the Great King's incompetence and of his satraps' disloyalty—influence a mind greater yet ? Did Alexander read it ? For the story it tells first pointed the eastward road to conquest which the prince of all conquerors was seventy years later to take.

Before we conclude this section, it will be well to say something about one side of Athenian life, which in the Fourth Century assumed a growing importance—the Courts of Law. Ever since the inauguration of the famous jury system, the methods of Athenian justice had been the admiration of Greece ; and during the Periclean era there had been a considerable increase in the scope and volume of litigation. The subject cities of the Empire were compelled, as we have shown, to send their major suits to Athens. The institution of the attendance fee proves a growing demand for jurors ; and during the Peloponnesian War, when it was increased by Cleon to three obols or half a day's wage, this must have proved a boon indeed to those who were out of work as well as to those who were past it. With the closing years of the long-drawn struggle the bitterness of political strife had already served to multiply the number of trials ; and in the Fourth Century the more scientific management of commercial enterprise and banking businesses produced a growing crop of disputes about loans and mortgages and bottomry. The litigious habits of the Athenian became, in fact, one of his most pronounced characteristics. The Law Court, moreover, as Solon had intended that it should be, was a highly democratic institution. A magistrate indeed presided, but he in no way controlled the trial nor did he influence the verdict as does an English judge. All was left to the jury. Then again there was no such thing as what we call a crown prosecution ; all suits, criminal and civil alike, were brought by private individuals. This system may have avoided some dangers of bureaucratic tyranny or official mismanagement ; but it had one deplorable consequence. For, as we have pointed out above, there grew up an unpleasant type of man who spent his time in bringing suits against persons with whom he was in no way directly concerned. Such ' sycophants ' played, in fact, the part of the modern detective and crown-prosecutor rolled into one, but, since their primary object was to blackmail their victims, they were extremely unpopular ; and, as a deterrent to ill-founded prosecution, a law was made imposing on any accuser, who failed to win one-fifth of the votes, a fine of 1,000 drachmae or, in a civil case, of one-sixth of the sum in dispute. Juries were particularly down upon such tactics, and an accuser was usually careful to explain that his motive in bringing the charge was no casual impulse, but a long-standing quarrel with the person accused. Not every suit came up as a matter of course before a jury. Homicide was tried before the Areopagus. Property suits commonly went to an arbitrator. But the bulk of litigation was decided by the citizen courts, and from these there was no further appeal. Juries were large, numbering 201 or 401, or sometimes as much as 6,000. In the face of such numbers, and with the total uncertainty as to who would be cast for a particular jury, bribery or intimidation was almost impossible.

A process began with the summons, which the aggrieved party delivered in person and in the presence of witnesses. Both parties thereafter appeared before the appropriate magistrate, who duly filed the suit. Next a preliminary hearing took place before the same magistrate. Evidence was then heard and taken down by a clerk. Cross-examination there was practically none; but oaths might be required of witnesses, and the testimony of slaves was taken only under torture.[1] The written notes of the evidence, together with extracts from laws and other relevant matter, was then sealed up in a box and there kept to be read at the trial. The trial proper took place in an open-air court; and the jury were selected by lot every morning. Each party, as has already been said, must conduct his own case; and the line usually taken was to our way of thinking extremely diffuse. Only one day was allowed for each trial and the period allowed to each speaker was controlled by a water-clock; yet the speaker was apt to digress upon all sorts of side issues, blackening his opponent's character, retailing wholly irrelevant scandal, and above all expatiating on his own past career to prove what a capital fellow he was. The fact is that the juries, undirected as they were by a judge, had the vaguest ideas of the law. There was no consistency between verdicts, no observance of precedents; and an appeal to the emotions was naturally the most telling of arguments. A speaker would often parade a row of snivelling children in rags and plead for mercy as a family man. If he possessed none of his own, it was not unknown for him to borrow or hire them. Public men might be asked to intervene with evidence of character. Political issues were openly canvassed in court. Yet, take it for all in all, the system probably worked pretty fairly. Athenian jurors were no respecters of persons; and, so far as we can judge, there was real equality of rich and poor before the law. The shrewd sense of some hundreds of his fellow-citizens was likely to distinguish the honest man from the knave; and the value set on sentiment has at least a rough parallel in the methods of the French

---

[1] The underlying idea of this cruel custom was presumably that no slave would tell the truth against his master, unless constrained by pains more violent than were likely to be inflicted by the master himself when the trial was over. In point of fact, challenges to offer slaves for such examination seem rarely to have been accepted.

courts to-day. The voting was secret, and when the verdict had been given, there followed, if it stood for conviction, a fresh vote on the penalty. Either party made his own proposition : it remained for the jury to decide for one or other alternative. Execution of the sentence lay with officials of the state. Commissioners of police, known as the Eleven, dealt with sentences of death or imprisonment. Banishment worked automatically ; for a returned exile was liable to abrupt execution. Fines were paid, as a rule, to the public exchequer ; and disfranchisement was the penalty of default.

Having thus sketched the legal procedure of the Athenian courts, it will perhaps be best for us here to describe in some detail the course of a *cause célèbre* which occurred about this time—the trial of the philosopher Socrates. It took place in 399, after the overthrow of the thirty Pro-Spartan Governors and the restoration of the full democracy. Bitterness and discontent were in the air. Men were utterly disheartened by the ruin of their country and were ready to fix the blame of disaster upon any scapegoat they could find. It was under such circumstances that Socrates was arraigned. Not altogether without some show of justice, many felt that teaching such as his had helped to bring the city to her present pass. Among his favourite pupils had been Alcibiades and, even more unpopular in men's memories at the moment, a leading member of the Thirty named Critias. There was a general feeling that the prevalent atheism and immorality had been the result of too much thinking ; and perhaps Socrates' own tiresome habit of button-holing chance-comers in full-market and cross-examining them about their souls and their ideals had produced after thirty years or so a not unnatural irritation. The prosecution was led by one Anytus, a man of recognized piety and patriotism, who had helped Thrasybulus in 403 to restore to Athens her democracy and freedom. The charge consisted of two counts : first, of disbelief in the orthodox religious creed of the city and the introduction of strange new divinities : and, second, of having 'corrupted the youth'. The trial took place before 501 jurors under the presidency of the King Archon or high priest. Socrates, warned by a mysterious inner voice or 'sign', which frequently visited him, refused to prepare a defence. What he actually said we can only infer from Plato's *Apology*, a free composition based no doubt in some sense on careful recollection. He seems to have given an account of his 'call' and his methods, denied the charge of atheism, asserted that he had only striven to improve rather than to corrupt his young associates, and declared himself to have a mission from God to stir his countrymen from their intellectual laziness like 'a gadfly that settles on a sluggish horse'. It was not a very adroit defence; and there is little wonder that the verdict went against him by a majority of 61 votes. When it came to assessing the penalty, his second effort was, if anything, worse. Anytus and his associate Meletus proposed the death-sentence. Socrates, on his part, actually began by a joking suggestion that as a benefactor of the city he should be rewarded by free meals at the Town Hall for life. He ended by offering on the bond of Plato and others to pay a substantial fine. The verdict was death by an even larger majority.

So Socrates passed into the hands of the Eleven; but his execution was delayed. It was a rule in Athens that while the state galley was absent on a sacred mission to Delos, no man might be put to death. Thus Socrates was kept waiting a month. Friends urged his escape and would have provided the means; but Socrates, true to his principles of civic obedience, refused. He was too old a man, he said, to change the ways of a lifetime. On the morning of the fatal day his friends gathered earlier than usual at the prison and, if Plato's dialogue, the *Phaedo*, is an accurate account of what happened, the day was spent in a discussion on the Immortality of the Soul. Towards evening the jailer came into the room to warn Socrates that he must die that night. What followed shall be told in Plato's own touching narrative [1]—

[1] Translation by Jowett.

and he never wrote a better. ' " Fare you well," said the man, " and try to bear lightly what needs must be— you know my errand." Then bursting into tears he turned away and went out. Socrates looked at him and said, " I return your good wishes and will do as you bid." Then turning to us, he said, " How charming the man is ; since I have been in prison he has always been coming to see me, and at times he would talk to me and was as good to me as could be, and now see how generously he sorrows on my account. We must do as he says, Crito : and therefore let the cup be brought, if the poison is pre- pared : if not, let the attendant prepare some." " Yet," said Crito, " the sun is still upon the hill-tops, and I know that many a one has taken the draught late and after the announcement has been made to him, he has eaten and drunk and enjoyed the society of his beloved ; do not hurry—there is time enough." Socrates said : " Yes, Crito, and they of whom you speak are right in so acting, for they think they will be gainers by the delay ; but I am right in not following their example, for I do not think that I should gain anything by drinking the poison a little later ; I should only be ridiculous in my own eyes for sparing and saving a life which is already forfeit. Please then to do as I say, and not to refuse me."

' Crito made a sign to the servant who was standing by ; and he went out and having been absent for some time returned with the jailer carrying the cup of poison. Socrates said : " You, my good friend, who are experienced in these matters, shall give me directions how I am to proceed." The man answered : " You have only to walk about until your legs are heavy, and then to lie down, and the poison will act." At the same time he handed the cup to Socrates, who in the easiest and gentlest manner, without the least fear or change of colour or feature, looking at the man with all his eyes, as his manner was, took the cup and said : " What do you say about making a libation out of this cup to any god ? May I, or not ? " The man answered : " We only prepare, Socrates, just so much as we deem enough." " I understand," said he.

" but I may and must ask the gods to prosper my journey from this to the other world—even so—and so be it according to my prayer." Then raising the cup to his lips, quite readily and cheerfully he drank off the poison. And hitherto most of us had been able to control our sorrow, but now when we saw him drinking, and saw too that he had finished the draught, we could no longer forbear, and in spite of myself my own tears were flowing fast ; so that I covered my face and wept, not for him, but at the thought of my own calamity in having to part with such a friend. Nor was I the first ; for Crito, when he found himself unable to restrain his tears, had got up and I followed ; and at that moment, Apollodorus, who had been weeping all the time, broke out in a loud and passionate cry which made cowards of us all. Socrates alone retained his calmness. " What is this strange outcry ? " he said. " I sent away the women mainly in order that they might not misbehave in this way, for I have been told that a man should die in peace. Be quiet, then, and have patience." When we heard his words, we were ashamed and refrained our tears ; and he walked about until, as he said, his legs began to fail, and then he lay on his back according to the directions, and the man who gave him the poison, now and then looked at his feet and legs ; and after a while he pressed his foot hard and asked him if he could feel ; and he said " No " ; and then his leg and so upwards and upwards, and showed us that he was cold and stiff. And he felt them himself and said : " When the poison reaches the heart, that will be the end." He was beginning to grow cold about the groin, when he uncovered his face, for he had covered himself up, and said—they were his last words—he said : " Crito, I owe a cock to Asclepius ; will you remember to pay the debt ? " " The debt shall be paid," said Crito ; " is there anything else ? " There was no answer to this question ; but in a minute or two a movement was heard, and the attendants uncovered him ; his eyes were set, and Crito closed his eyes and mouth. . . ." ' It was a custom with the ancients, when stricken by some malady, to vow a cock or other offering to the Healing God Asclepius and to make due payment of their sick-bed vow upon recovery. So Socrates desired to pay his debt ; for he had recovered from the long malady of life.

Few better men than Socrates have ever lived. The clear and lovable sincerity of his character, the intense desire to help those about him to see the light as he himself conceived of it, the utter disregard of self whether in life or in death, these qualities all serve to set him high among the category of those whom we can only truly call saints. In an age of unsettlement and cynicism and shallow doubt, he at least stood firm, holding to the end the faith which was in him, that man must seek first to know what is right and then to do it, and that by truth alone is he saved. On the basis of such a creed, Plato was to build up a philosophy which more than any other has implanted in men's minds the conviction that Truth and Goodness are no relative or transitory notions, but the most permanent realities known to mankind. Both master and pupil, recognizing the insufficiency of mere Individualism, saw that behind the ebb and flow of man's human aspirations and opinions stands immutably the universal and eternal Law.

III. The Individualist as Despot

After all that has been said of the Individualist tendency of the Age, it can no longer be difficult to foresee wherein lay the inevitable solution for the troubles of Greece. Notwithstanding the strain and exhaustion of the Peloponnesian War, her peoples persisted for the next two generations in an endless round of suicidal conflicts ; and, as in Italy during the last years of the Roman Republic, the one hope of salvation seemed to lie in the emergence of some Individual who could impose a permanent unity upon this scene of distracted chaos. As in Italy, too, so in Greece man after man arose in whose pre-eminence there seemed to lie real hope of such a consummation. First comes Lysander with his amazing control of men, but purely egotistical ambitions ; then Agesilaus with his policy of crusade against Persia, less personally ambitious, but solely intent, as the unhappy issue proved, on the selfish aggrandisement of Sparta; finally, Epaminondas, the military genius of Thebes, far more enlightened and with a more generous vision of what a Greek should owe to Greeks. All failed; yet many men had begun to realize that the suicidal conflict must cease, and that Monarchy alone could weld together in the bond of unity and peace the jealous and warring City-States. Isocrates, perhaps the most far-sighted thinker of the age, saw in Philip of Macedon the man who might assume the great rôle. Even Plato, though he planned his ideal Commonwealth on the lines of the old City-State, pinned nevertheless great hopes on the rule of a Philosopher King. During all these years, too, and near enough at hand to reinforce or discredit by its example such men's aspirations, there flourished a monarchy of extraordinary brilliance and strength—the despotism of Dionysius of Syracuse. Perhaps, in point of fact, the character of that despotism was one reason why the Greeks were so reluctant to accept Isocrates' remedy.

The story of Dionysius' career may well be told in this chapter; for, though on occasion he intervened in the politics of mainland Greece, yet his reign was, on the whole, a spectacle viewed from afar rather than an integral factor in the Motherland's history.

Unlike the tyrants of an earlier epoch, his rise to power originated not so much from political championship of the downtrodden classes against an overbearing aristocracy as in the sterner exigencies of a life-and-death struggle against a foreign enemy. For Carthage was once again upon the war-path. At the conclusion of the Sicilian Expedition, the exhaustion of Athens and Syracuse, the two strongest naval powers of the Greek world, had reawakened in her those hopes of conquest, which eighty years before had been foiled at the battle of Himera. So in 409, on an appeal from Segesta, one Hannibal had been sent over to attack the town of Selinus. In an enormous fleet, said to number 1,500 transports, he brought with him 100,000 foot and 40,000 cavalry. Before the assault of such a host Selinus went down amid scenes of indescribable horror. The Carthaginians, with the savage fury of the Semitic, spared neither man, woman nor child. Himera shortly after suffered the same fate, and on the spot where Hamilcar had once leapt into the flames, 3,000 prisoners, as an offering to his ghost, were put to death with torture. The town itself ceased to exist. A lull of three years followed during which the Syracusan Hermocrates, now an exile from his own city, gathered some Sicilian volunteers and recovered Selinus. But he was killed in an attempt to force his way back into Syracuse, and the best hope of a united resistance to Carthage seemed destined to perish with him. In 406 Hannibal returned to the attack. This time Acragas was to be his victim ; but this time, too, the Sicilians who had made no more than a feeble show of succouring Selinus, were aroused to vigorous action by the horror of their impending fate. Even so, after an eight months' siege, which incidentally cost Hannibal his life, Acragas also fell, the Sicilian allies having cravenly deserted her, and the inhabitants stealing away under cover of night rather than await the awful doom which they foresaw. At this point it was that Dionysius appeared upon the scene. Though a mere man of the people (it is said he was a Government clerk) he understood none the less the arts of the demagogue and seized on the occasion to work upon the feelings of the Syracusan populace. Since its success in repelling the Athenian attack, the city had declined into the follies of extreme democracy, and when Dionysius proceeded to denounce the military commanders for their recent desertion of Acragas, he found a ready audience. The people appointed him first general, then dictator, and finally by an ominous subterfuge he procured the vote of a body-guard—the invariable prelude to a tyranny.

The fact was that Dionysius had all along intended to make Syracuse his ; and he shrank from no act of deceit, cruelty or oppression which would enable him to tighten or maintain his hold. Even the salvation of Sicily from the Carthaginian menace was merely a stepping-stone to the advancement of his own ambitions. For he was a true son of the Individualistic age, recognizing no authority of law which clashed with his own advantage, scorning religious scruples and ready to ransack even the temples of the gods for the enrichment of his palace. In private life he was not morally vicious, and in matters of culture not without enlightenment. His worst acts of savagery were done simply from motives of policy, not from any natural brutality or mere lust for revenge. But from first to last he was a pure egoist ; and, to give him his due, he played his lone hand with extraordinary skill.

His first step was to buy off the Carthaginians. When Gela and Camarina were attacked, he made a mere show of defence and persuaded the inhabitants, in imitation of Acragas, to abandon their walls and abscond. This done, he came to a bargain with Himilco, the successor of Hannibal, relinquishing the whole south and west of Sicily into enemy hands, and ensuring by a further and perhaps secret clause in the treaty that ' the Syracusans should be subject to himself '. It was merely a breathing-space, and Dionysius himself had intended no more. But very successfully did he use it. He walled round the heights of Epipolae and on Ortygia, the island citadel of Syracuse, he built himself an impregnable fortress. Sixty thousand workmen were employed on the construction of the walls, and five successive gateways were arranged to bar the entrance, to which none might gain admission without the tyrant's leave. Here he could safely defy (as he did more than once) any mutinous attempt to dethrone him ; and meanwhile he made preparations on the same magnificent scale for the defeat of the enemy. He constructed a navy of over 300 warships, many of a new type, equipped not as usual with three banks of oars, but with five. He maintained and trained the finest standing army which Hellas had ever known, 80,000 men strong and composed in part of mercenaries from native Italian tribes. His engineers invented (it was a real revolution in military science) a type of siege-engine or catapult capable of hurling a stone of three hundredweight to a distance of three hundred yards. Thus equipped, he ventured once more in 398 to cross swords with Carthage. For five years the tide of warfare ebbed and flowed. At one time Dionysius besieged the island fortress of Motya, and by constructing a mole through the water and employing great siege-towers of timber, he actually took it. But next year Himilco, carrying all before him, was thundering at the gates of Syracuse itself. Plague in their camp embarrassed the besiegers; a well-planned sortie put them to utter rout; and Dionysius, had he chosen, might have left none alive. But they were allowed to depart; for, knowing well enough that the longer the peril from Carthage lasted, the longer would last also his own power at home, the tyrant preferred to leave the enemy scotched rather than killed. Nor were three hundred talents, received as a bribe from Himilco, altogether to be despised. By 392, when a peace treaty was signed, he had recovered the greater part of the island, leaving only the western extremity in enemy hands. So things remained for some while, until in 383, and again in 369, the last year of his life, the old struggle was renewed; and although Dionysius made heroic efforts to capture the Carthaginian stronghold of Lilybaeum, he failed of his purpose, and on the balance lost more than he won.

Meanwhile, however, the ambitions of the tyrant were by no means confined to the recovery of Greek Sicily. As soon as his first bout of war with Carthage was over, he had begun to cast an envious eye on the Italian peninsula, where some of the cities had intervened in the late struggle against him. In co-operation with the barbarians of Lucania (whose help he did not scruple to use against his own kin) he gained control over all the Greek colonies from the Straits of Messana to the town of Croton. He treated their inhabitants, at some times with arbitrary brutality, at others with an indulgence hardly less arbitrary. After one of his victories, he set free nearly all of his prisoners; but, as a rule, we find him either selling them in the slave market or transporting them wholesale to his own capital. To infuse new and often non-Hellenic blood into the ranks of his Sicilian subjects seems indeed to have been a part of his deliberate policy. For in Dionysius there was none of the normal Greek's exclusive distrust of the foreigner. At Syracuse he had already created a new class of citizen by enfranchising slaves. His Greek neighbours of Naxos he dispossessed of their territory and gave it to native Sicels to dwell in. At Catana he similarly established a body of mercenaries drawn from Campania, thus forming a military settlement strangely analogous to the veteran ' coloniae' of Rome. Meanwhile he was spreading his tentacles yet further afield. Trade was the essential foundation of Syracusan prosperity ; and commercial and naval stations were now established in every direction. Corsica became a base for his ships. Elba was occupied, probably for the sake of its iron mines. The Adriatic he aspired to make a ' Syracusan lake ', settling colonists at Ancona half-way up the coast of Italy and at Adria near the Po mouth. The Molossi of Epirus became his allies, and he took care to maintain friendly relations with Sparta. There can be, in fact, no question that the Empire of Dionysius (for it is not too much to call it so) was the strongest military and naval power in the Europe of his day.

In the management of Syracuse he displayed the same combination of subtle tact and ruthless ferocity which marked his dealings abroad. The machinery of democratic government he normally allowed to continue. Assemblies met. Magistrates were elected ; and Dionysius himself was careful to forgo any but constitutional titles. True, taxation was grinding, for he had his mercenaries to remunerate ; and it is said that the citizens were annually mulcted of one-fifth of their capital. Nevertheless he gave the city security and a place in the eyes of the world. He built with the magnificence of a Pericles. He kept splendid court ; and Plato and Aristippus, the philosophers, were attracted thither by his patronage of the arts. For this extraordinary man was no boor, but an enthusiastic student of letters. The writing of poetry was the passion of his life. Again and again he entered his tragedies for the dramatic competitions at Athens, and, when finally he won the first prize, he is said to have celebrated the occasion by drinking so deep that it killed him. Yet for all the pomp and glamour of his rule Dionysius was never popular either at home or abroad. The curse of the tyrant hung over him, like the famous sword, held by a hair, which, as concrete parable of his own situation, he had privily suspended at the banquet-table just over his friend Damocles' head. Fear of mutiny and revolution was never far from his mind. He was always closely protected by a picked body-guard; and, since it was safer to trust foreigners than his own countrymen, he used barbarians of set choice for the purpose. He kept spies in every quarter of the city; and, though he suppressed whatever attempts were made upon his life, it was only by a policy of most brutal severity. He would exile and confiscate without trial, torture and crucify with all the ferocity of an Oriental despot, and, if policy so dictated, he would slaughter with as much whimsical indifference as he sometimes showed unexpected compassion. Such utter disregard of all decent self-restraint and of the opinion of the world about him was what more than anything else repelled his contemporaries. He was utterly un-Greek. We have seen already how he showed a most unconventional appreciation of the vitality and toughness of his barbarian subjects and mercenaries, and even in his anxiety to emulate the culture of his more artistic and intellectual contemporaries, he was apt to ruin all by his own tactless exuberance. He behaved in fact like some upstart millionaire of to-day, liking to have men of culture about him, but through underbred impatience or touchiness, failing to hit it off with them when they came. Thus Plato, who visited his court, he is said to have sold as a slave. A poet who was unwise enough to criticize his writings, he sent to the quarries; and the sequel to this outrage is no less instructive than amusing. Being released from his prison to attend at another recital, and hearing what was in store for him, the poet turned round to his guard and said simply, 'Take me back to the quarries.' The calm impudence of that saying was typical of the Greeks at their best. With them whoever assumed the right to treat his equals as chattels, placed himself automatically beyond the pale; and so it was that, despite his unquestionable genius, his high qualities of imagination and initiative, and his astonishing command over men, Dionysius never attained to one part of that prestige to which his achievements entitled him. The man who had saved Sicily from the horrors of the barbarian invasion was ranked at Athens on a par with the Great King of Persia. It was even suggested that he should be excluded from competing in the horse-race at Olympia. His reputation, in short, so far from recommending the advantages of monarchical government served merely to deepen the Greeks' innate hatred of tyranny. He died unregretted.

His son, Dionysius II, turned out a weakling; but he fell under the influence of his father's chief minister Dion, a man of lofty character and a dreamer, who entertained the somewhat fantastic notion of remodelling the city's constitution upon the ideal lines of Plato's Utopia. At his instance the philosopher was brought over from Athens. The court was set to work studying circles and parallelograms, and the young Dionysius listened to much good advice. Of this, however, he presently wearied. Plato went home, and Dion falling into disgrace was banished. In 357 he returned, having collected a small force, and, during the tyrant's absence, slipped into Syracuse, where he was welcomed by the mob as a deliverer. But the mob's favour soon veered. Once again Dion retired and once again was recalled, to save the city from an Italian swashbuckler named Nypsius. This time he came for good. Dionysius, who had held on to his castle at Ortygia, gave up the game and left the field clear for the Platonic reformer. But the Platonic reformer had learnt by experience, and in what remained to him of life, Dion assumed the powers of an autocrat. After his murder in 354 Dionysius' sway was resumed, and throughout nearly all of the Sicilian cities tyranny again became the order of the day. In 344, however, in response to an appeal from the people of Syracuse, Corinth sent over a soldier named Timoleon. Starting with a small body of mercenaries and rallying the Sicilians to a campaign of liberation, Timoleon ousted the tyrants—Dionysius II among them—and in 339 defeated a fresh Carthaginian invasion on the banks of the river Cremisus. This victory, however, he did not follow up, and having completed the suppression of the tyrants, he laid down his power and retired. For twenty years the democracies he had established held their own ; but in 316 Agathocles, the son of a potter, seized the reins of power at Syracuse. Like Dionysius I he, too, fought a fierce war against Carthage, even carrying the campaign to the African coast. Now recognized as overlord of the island, he cemented his power by alliance with Alexander's successor in Macedon ; and had not death cut short his plans in 289, he would very likely have succeeded in freeing Sicily once and for all from the age-long menace of barbarian rule.

Thus it was a singular fate, but characteristic, as we have said, of the epoch, that, while the old states of the Greek Motherland were wasting their strength in fratricidal conflict and slowly sinking into a condition of degenerate impotence, Hellenism was more and more to find its champions in individual autocrats, springing up outside the confines wherein hitherto had lain the main pivot of Greek history and employing political methods which would have filled men of an earlier age with loathing and disgust. It remained for the greatest of such autocrats, Alexander of Macedon, not merely to arrest the decline of Greece from a fatal sterility, but to carry it with him on his march of conquest into the East and there to plant it in lands where it would presently develop a new, and more universal, if a less splendid, growth. So was it that the very Individualism which exercised, as we have seen, so disruptive an influence upon the political institutions of the City-State, was also, indirectly at least, to be the means of preserving and enlarging that civilization which was the City-State's chief gift to mankind.

CHAPTER XV

SPARTA'S OPPORTUNITY

I. LYSANDER

AFTER the decisive overthrow of her fleet at Aegospotami and even before the final surrender of her city walls, Athens had found herself left alone to her fate. All her subject-allies except Samos (and Samos was soon reduced) went over to the victors, and so for a second time in her history Sparta was confronted with an opportunity and a responsibility which from almost every point of view it seemed beyond her power to embrace. The Aegean lay at her feet ; yet she was neither by instinct nor habit a maritime power. For the imperial position which seemed wellnigh thrust upon her, she possessed, despite her Peloponnesian experience, little aptitude. She had never shown much skill for tactful government, and, what was now even more serious, she lacked the man-power sufficient to exert a rule of sheer force. For the truth is that Sparta, more decisively perhaps than any other Greek State, was on the brink of a swift decline ; and this for various reasons. The number of her fully enfranchised citizens had never been great. Exclusive of the subject Perioeci and the Helot serfs, the population of Spartans amounted to something over twenty thousand [1]; but of these only two thousand now enjoyed the franchise as full citizens or peers (the qualification for which privilege was ability to make due contribution at the communal messes). And the striking fact is that by the end of the Fourth Century that number was to be halved. Much of the wastage was of course due to

[1] The population of Spartan territory is reckoned roughly at 300,000 Helots, 75,000 Perioeci, 25,000 Spartans, 2,000 of which possessed full Spartiate franchise.

the ravages of war. For, though disfranchised citizens, Perioeci and even Helots were all employed in Sparta's

MAP TO ILLUSTRATE THE WARS OF THE FOURTH CENTURY

army, it was the peers who invariably formed its kernel and who could least of all afford to shirk risks. But there was now another and more subtle influence at work to undermine the strength of the peerage. The spoils of foreign conquest and the inflow of allied tribute brought into the Vale of Lacedaemon a factor which by the Lycurgan constitution was rigidly excluded—money. The traditional iron currency was still nominally preserved ; and only the state was legally allowed to handle gold and silver. Nevertheless individuals were known to be amassing bullion on the sly, and under the roof-tiles of Gylippus' house was concealed, so his servant reported to the ephors, ' a nest of Attic owls ' (the slang phrase for Athenian drachma pieces). Now, when a Spartan grew rich, the danger envisaged by the constitution was speedily revealed. He lost his habitual self-control. He took in private to a luxurious diet. Even his womenfolk affected extravagance in dress. The result was that a new and higher standard of living became the vogue ; and of the poorer peers many bartered away their lands, and so, unable to pay their requisite mess-contribution, lost their claim to the franchise. Owing, too, to the peculiar Spartan laws of inheritance, a large number of estates passed into women's hands, until towards the end of the century two-fifths of Spartan soil were said to be in female ownership. Thus, in one way or another, the number of the true citizens shrank. And all the while not merely did the discontent of the ' Inferiors ' grow, manifesting itself in at least one formidable plot ; but the Perioeci, and more particularly the Helots, remained a perpetual and undiminished menace. More than ever, in fact, were the Spartans living on the edge of a volcano. That they were well aware of their danger is proved by their ruthless measures of suppression ; and Thucydides tells how two thousand of the more high-spirited Helots, having distinguished themselves in the course of the war, were fêted and begarlanded and paraded round the temples as though in anticipation of receiving their freedom ; but not long after they were all put out of the way and ' no man knew how each came by his end '. Such a policy, however, was a confession of weakness ; and it can never have been easy for the Government to rid their minds of fear. Overseas

19

adventure, involving as it must an inevitable depletion of the home garrison, must have caused them many a qualm ; and it is an immense tribute to the hard fibre of the race and to the bracing influence of its iron discipline that the Spartans maintained their ascendancy at all ; for maintain it they did, over mainland Greece at any rate, for a generation to come.

Yet such qualities alone would scarcely have been enough, when it came, as it now did, to undertaking the command of the Aegean. The initiative thereby demanded was not likely to be found among the hide-bound conservatives who held the reins of government and controlled the policies of state by the banks of the Eurotas. And, if we ask by what hand was this great enterprise directed, the only answer can be that it was the hand of Lysander.

Lysander was probably the nearest approach to a genius that Sparta ever produced. What we have already seen of him in naval warfare has shown him to be a bold and imaginative strategist, an organizer of exceptional gifts and a natural commander of men. But more than all this he possessed also some curious power of personal fascination. Cyrus clearly took to him and trusted him, pouring out subsidies of gold (out of which, since he died poor, Lysander cannot have turned a penny to his personal use), and once, when called away on temporary business to Persia, committing the care of his own satrapy into the Spartan's hands. So commanding, in fact, was the force of Lysander's personality, that men seemed to admire him, even while they feared ; poets wrote extravagant panegyrics in his honour, and in some cities altars were erected to him as to a god. All this is the more remarkable since Lysander's character was anything but pleasant. He had a curt sardonic habit of speech : his temper was sullen and morose, and tinged towards the end of his life with a growing melancholy. Above all, he was a complete egoist, recognizing no rule of conduct but self-interest, breaking his promises, when it suited him, with a cynical brutality (' dice to cheat boys ', he said, ' oaths to cheat men '), and subordinating every other consideration in life to a consuming passion for power. Greece, said a contemporary, could not bear two Lysanders, and during the years which immediately followed Aegospotami, he indeed ruled the Aegean like a despot.

Lysander's imperialism was modelled in a sense upon the Athenians' system. But whereas they had controlled the Aegean towns and islands by maintaining the democratic faction everywhere uppermost, he reversed the process and placed the oligarchies everywhere in power, often by methods of wholesale massacre. Ten men were, as a rule, chosen in each city to govern in the Spartan interest ; and over these so-called ' Decarchies ', or rather in close co-operation with them, was set a Spartan Governor or ' harmost ', with a mercenary garrison to back him. This dual control was brutal and oppressive. The Decarchies seized their opportunity for rapine upon their political opponents. The harmosts, who were mostly Lysander's friends or tools, behaved with all the arbitrary licence characteristic of the Spartan when temporarily freed from the shackles of home discipline. One Callibius, who commanded the Spartan garrison in Athens, was foolish enough to threaten a citizen with his staff. The man, as it so happened, was a champion wrestler, and promptly landed his assailant on the ground—a good object lesson, as Lysander pointed out, in the dangers of misgoverning free men. Whether the master was often so critical of the insolence of his subordinates is doubtful ; but, however that may be, the whole system of oppression stank in the nostrils of a freedom-loving folk. The promised liberty which was to have replaced the tyranny of Athens had turned out in the issue to be nothing better than a hollow sham, and the unhappy subject cities feeling Lysander's heavy hand must have often looked back to Pericles' rule, or even perhaps to Cleon's, with something very like regret.

Resistance first came to a head, as might have been expected, in Athens. By accepting among the stern conditions of the peace treaty, the status of a subject ally to Sparta, she, too, of course, had suffered like the rest. A garrison under the Callibius above mentioned was installed on the citadel.[1] The Council of Five Hundred was packed with men of strong oligarchical views; and a supreme body of governors was set up, consisting of thirty pro-Spartans. Among these thirty were included many who, in the Revolution of 411, had already done their best to play into the enemy's hands, and who, in the last bungling dispositions which led to the *débâcle* of Aegospotami, were suspected of the blackest treachery; and now, at any rate, if not before, these men were to show themselves the real foes of their countrymen. The Thirty Tyrants was the name men gave to them; and very richly they deserved it. The leading spirit among them was one Critias, a young aristocrat of strong, energetic character and cultured, philosophic tastes. He had once been a pupil of Socrates himself, but he exhibited in its most unpleasant light the results of the New Thought. By his side was Theramenes, adroit as ever, still swimming with the tide, but never in wholehearted sympathy with his colleagues' more violent ways. The brief rule of the Thirty was from the first a Reign of Terror. The chief democrats were swiftly either put to death or banished. Then followed a series of judicial murders, the true motive of which was more plunder than revenge. Rich citizens and, even more, rich metics (against whom no political charge could with honesty be levelled), were summarily arrested and as summarily put to death. Amongst other victims was the brother of Lysias, the lawyer, who kept an armour factory; and Lysias himself only saved his life by flight. To facilitate this blood-letting a body of Eleven Police officials was set up; but with the intention of implicating as many persons as possible in the guilt of this business, the duty of making arrests was frequently imposed on private citizens; and among the last brave deeds of the philosopher Socrates was his refusal to obey one such order. But

[1] There is some question, however, at what point the Spartan garrison was installed, whether immediately, or later at the instance of the Thirty. Accounts differ.

others, more compliant or less squeamish, accepted the harsh necessity ; and first and last it is computed that the Thirty Tyrants accounted for 1,500 lives.

Such doings could scarcely pass without a protest ; and, whatever else may be said of him, it stands to Theramenes' lasting credit that he tried to rally an opposition among the more moderate of his colleagues. He had begun by insisting in the opening months of their rule upon a more constitutional attitude ; and harking back to his old scheme for a limited franchise he procured the nomination of Three Thousand citizens, licensed to bear arms about their person and guaranteed against arbitrary treatment by a right to fair trial, but otherwise possessing no political powers. When, however, he began to protest against the growing violence of the régime, Theramenes found that he was measuring his strength against a stronger than him. For Critias would stand no weakening, and he determined to stamp down opposition by force. His coup was well staged. Young oligarchs whom he could trust were armed with long dirks and introduced in the course of a session behind the bar of the Council House. Then in a bitter harangue—for he was no mean orator— Critias denounced the tergiversations of his rival. Theramenes answered by an appeal so moving and so eloquent that it clearly stirred the sympathy of every listener. Critias grew desperate. Raking up an old grievance, he charged Theramenes with having played a double part in the previous Revolution of the Four Hundred, and striking his name off the list of the Three Thousand he there and then declared him liable to execution without trial. Theramenes, terror-struck, leapt to the altar, appealing in his agony for mercy and justice. The armed youths at the barrier fingered their dirks. Not a man dared move. The Eleven Police officials entered and tore the wretched man from his sanctuary. He was carried shrieking across the market square, hurried to the prison, and compelled without more ado to drink the fatal hemlock. In those days it was a favourite game with diners at Athens, when the wine-cups had been drained, to flick the dregs at a mark, calling each, as he did so, on the name of his loved one. A few drops remained at the bottom of the hemlock cup ; and before Theramenes laid it aside, he tipped it back in grim mockery of the game and flung the dregs against the wall of his prison, crying, ' This to my lovely Critias '. That dying speech was long remembered in Athens ; and indeed by his death Theramenes did more perhaps than in his life to save the town from the tyranny of his colleagues. For it brought to a culminating crisis the bitter antagonism between the Few and the Many.

The Thirty, driven frantic by their fears of a counter-revolution, now redoubled their violence ; and, as the toll of their victims grew, so also grew the number of the democrats who made good their escape over the frontier. In Megara and Thebes these exiles were gathering, and presently their blow fell. Thrasybulus, with a small but resolute band, came out of Boeotia and seized the border fort of Phylê among the North Attic hills. The Thirty and their minions went out to dislodge him. There was a fight in a snowstorm and they were forced to retreat. With spring they returned to the attack, but were surprised near Acharnae and again driven home. Meanwhile more groups of exiles were filtering up to Phylê ; and, when Thrasybulus, watching his chance from his eyrie in the mountains, descended suddenly into the plain, he came with a thousand men at least at his back. The Peiraeus, always a stronghold of the democratic cause, was soon in his hands ; and so cleverly did he dispose his men in tiers up a hill-side that the shower of their missiles shattered the charge of the enemy forces. Critias was killed, and his death seriously crippled the oligarchs. But, though repulsed from the Peiraeus, they were still in command of the capital. They reorganized their government and asked for Spartan assistance. Lysander would have backed them ; but his star was on the wane. King Pausanias, glad enough to reverse the policy of this much-dreaded rival, arrived as a peace-maker. A general amnesty was proclaimed, from which, since Pausanias perceived that they were not genuine pro-Spartans so much as men upon the make, the Thirty and their worst agents were excepted. Then the Spartan garrison was withdrawn ; and, after some talk of a limited franchise, the old democracy in its full strength was restored. The experience of the last eighteen months had indeed cured Athens of all oligarchical leanings for ever.

Such doings were not meanwhile without their influence upon the Greek world at large. The overthrow of the Athenian oligarchies was a signal for many of the subject states to depose their decarchies. This the Spartan Government does not seem to have opposed. Experience perhaps was teaching them that intervention would be both costly and unwise. Nor were they sorry, either, to put a spoke in the wheel of Lysander's policy. His swollen ambition had awoken fears, never far distant from the Kings' and Ephors' minds, that some victorious upstart might supplant their own authority. So in 402 the great admiral was recalled, relieved of his command, and allowed to depart in peace upon his travels. We shall hear of him again. For the fears of the Government were not ill-founded ; and he had indeed his designs upon the Spartan throne. But meanwhile his work still stood. For nearly a decade Sparta remained, what he had already made her, the mistress of the Aegean. The Ionian coast-line indeed, though not the Hellespont, she relinquished to Persia, in accordance with the discreditable bargain made during the last years of the Peloponnesian War. Most of what had been the Athenian Empire, she other-wise retained, exacting a yearly tribute of a thousand talents, and employing the money for the payments of her mercenaries and the maintenance of her own authority. Presently, as we shall see, she began to turn it to more honourable purpose and to attempt the liberation of the Ionian states from the servitude into which she had sold them.

II. AGESILAUS AND PERSIA

During the second half of the Fifth Century the Persian Empire, save for purposes of trade, had practically disappeared out of Greek history. The menace of military conquest had passed ; and Greeks upon either side of the Aegean basin were left free to develop their culture and pursue their quarrels in complete isolation from the wider world. The great power which ruled the Orient had become to them during this period little more than a purveyor of delicious luxuries or a butt for stock jokes in a play. Then in the last stages of the Peloponnesian War all was changed. At the cost of their unholy compact the Spartans had paved their way to victory with subsidies out of a satrap's treasury, and Persia became once more a factor of growing importance in the politics of Greece. Henceforward relations of one sort or another are continuously maintained between East and West. Commanders learn to hobnob on familiar terms with men whom they had once regarded as their bitterest foes. Private soldiers engage themselves to march and fight side by side with the despised barbarians. Politicians accept bribes and crave alliances from the underlings of the Great King. All eyes, in short, are turned eastwards, and thus, for better or for worse, Hellas emerges from her isolation into contact with the wider world once more.

But such contact had its dangers. We have seen with what effects the influx of Persian gold now threatened Sparta. The habits of Oriental luxury were infectious. Many a Greek who grew familiar with their attractions succumbed to the lure ; and there was a real risk, as the later history of Rome proved, that the East might prove more insidious as a friend than as an enemy. As an enemy, indeed, Persia was no longer much to be feared. At the time of the Great Invasion she had been a rising power, her folk were then a highly intelligent and lively people. Her soldiers, though no equal to the Greeks as infantry, had fought with real courage. Above all. her monarchs had been men of character and organizers of extraordinary skill. But it had presently become apparent how important a part in Persian history Darius and Xerxes had played, and how much a strong hand was needed to hold the unwieldy empire together. For when with the accession of Artaxerxes I in 464 the best qualities of the royal blood began to fail, an inevitable decline set in. A series of weaklings filled the throne. Satraps, always ready enough to assert their independence, quickly got out of hand. Many were by now disaffected, some even ripe for revolt ; and it only needed a severe strain to demonstrate the rottenness of the whole imperial structure. Such a demonstration was given, and given in a most spectacular fashion, by Cyrus' expedition in 401. The story of that famous march—the unresisted progress to the very gates of Babylon, the dramatic defeat of the King's vast army by the Ten Thousand Greeks, the still more dramatic reversal of fate which followed Cyrus' death in the battle—all this has already been told. The consequences, however, it still remains for us to trace, and they were momentous enough. Indeed, it is not too much to say that they changed the course of history. For Cyrus' exploit had opened men's eyes. It had made them see in Persia not merely a useful source of financial subsidies or an opening for commercial enterprise, but a possible field for military conquest, and conquest of which the prize would be lands almost without limit and treasure beyond the dreams of human avarice.

How low Persia's military prestige immediately sank in the eyes of the Greeks is shown by the fact that in 400 B.C. the Spartans abandoned their recent policy of conciliation, and embarked upon a war of almost deliberate aggression. The original intention was, it is true, of a defensive character. Tissaphernes, who on Cyrus' death had been restored to his former satrapy, had soon found his hold loosening over the Ionian cities so recently ceded to Persia ; and active measures on his part provoked an appeal to Sparta to save them. The appeal was answered. Thibron was sent over with a force into which he enlisted large numbers of the famous Ten Thousand ; and with these he was not merely content to perform his original mission, but pressing up into the hinterland carried war into the enemy's country. Strange to say, the Ephors approved the aggression, and in 399 Dercyllidas, who took over command, improved the success by sweeping the Troad. The campaign of liberation seemed to show good promise ; but by this last attack the northern satrap Pharnabazus was aroused ; in co-operation with Tissaphernes he brought the Greeks to a standstill, and the news that he was organizing a powerful naval armament awakened the Ephors to the need for more resolute measures. It was clear even to them that some leader of higher qualities was wanted, and to an impartial observer it must have been equally clear that Lysander was the man. This, however, was not to be ; and, as we shall see, the most that the ex-admiral could procure was that his own nominee should be entrusted with the command.

The story of Lysander's final intrigue for power and final failure reads more like a fairy tale than sober fact, and it may serve to remind us how deeply rooted even now in the Hellenic character was the hold of religious superstition. When after his humilation in 402 he was allowed to go off on his travels, it was not in Lysander's character to relinquish all ambition. On the contrary he at once began scheming not merely how to recover his lost authority, but how to perpetuate it beyond all possibility of interference *by securing for himself the crown.* The Kingship at Sparta was not, it is true, a more than nominal sovereignty. The royal power was subordinate to the Ephors, and even in the conduct of campaigns, its proper sphere, liable to their close and hampering supervision. But permanent at least it was, and in the hands of a genius of Lysander's quality it might well have become a despotism. Across his path to the throne, however, there lay one barrier, almost insuperable in a state rigidly observant of constitutional precedent. The office was hereditary, and confined with jealous scruple to the line of two ancient families. To upset so well established a tradition Lysander had but one device—and that by our modern standards the most extraordinary—to enlist on his behalf the authoritative pronouncement of some oracle. With this end in view, he set out to visit a famous sanctuary of Zeus in Libya, with what result we know not. But among the Delphic priests, at any rate, he found some backing, and mysterious tales began to be put round that a son of Apollo was about to make his appearance on earth and reveal the god's wishes. What those wishes would have been we can readily guess. But some hitch seems to have occurred. The promised revelation hung fire ; and when King Agis died in 398, Lysander, instead of entering himself as a candidate for the throne, was forced to be content with backing another. This was Agesilaus, a stepson of Agis, but preferred in the event to his half-brother whose legitimate birth was disputed. Agesilaus' accession reawakened all Lysander's hopes of achieving his old ambitions. He had found what appeared to him the perfect tool. The new King was a modest, middle-aged fellow, lame of one leg, short of stature, almost insignificant ; and, when he was sent over to take up the command in Asia Minor, Lysander, who accompanied him, must have thought that the game was as good as won, and that the command of the Aegean would soon once more be his.

It at once became evident, however, that Agesilaus took himself seriously, and that he meant to conduct the campaign his own way. There was a curious vein of romance as well of strength in his character. He seems to have viewed himself in the rôle of a new Agamemnon, and before embarking for Asia he actually visited the harbour of Aulis, whence in mythological times the Achaean host had set forth for Troy. So high ran his hopes that he even had dreams of being ' able to capture the Great King himself ' ; and, once arrived at the front, he asserted himself to some purpose. He snubbed Lysander by appointing him carver at table, and eventually succeeded in getting quit of his most unwelcome presence. In the campaigns that followed Agesilaus showed, too, that he could fight. There were no half-measures with this enthusiastic crusader. To him the Persian was the hereditary foe of Hellas, whose recent services to Sparta were best forgotten and whom it was a positive pleasure to attack. He had the true Spartan contempt for Oriental luxury, and when he found himself master of the satrap's pleasure-park he ravaged it without mercy. As a tactician he had (for a Spartan) unusual originality. Realizing how dangerous a weapon the Persians possessed in their cavalry, he made shift to meet it with cavalry of his own. The Greeks had never been strong in this department of warfare. Thessaly alone bred horses fit to mount a really efficient troop ; but Agesilaus' innovation was so successful that not merely did it enable him to defeat on their own ground the Persians' combined cavalry and foot (a feat which hitherto no Greek had ever achieved) but it paved the way for a new form of tactics which Alexander was subsequently to develop and in which hoplites and horsemen acted in close co-operation. Thanks largely to this tactical ingenuity Agesilaus was able to achieve a conquest of considerable dimensions, though of no lasting permanence. Possessing as he did the command of the seaboard, and withal a keen eye for strategy, he was able to strike or feint in north or south at will, and thus kept Pharnabazus and Tissaphernes from effective combination. In 396 we find him pushing boldly into Phrygia, and in 395 he marched almost to the gates of Sardis itself. The extent of Agesilaus' successes caused the disgrace and death of Tissaphernes ; and when Tithraustes, the new satrap, bought off a renewal of the southern offensive, Agesilaus turned his attentions once again to Pharnabazus and the north. This time he penetrated as far as Gordium, over three hundred miles up country ; and he even began to dream of wresting Asia Minor from the Persian rule. But, brilliant and spectacular as were these raids, they secured him no effective hold upon the wide expanse of country so rapidly overrun ; and events were imminent which were to undermine his whole position. For now the nemesis of Sparta's sins was close at hand. Not even Agesilaus' championship of Ionian liberty could atone for his country's ten years' misrule of the Aegean ; and among the homeland states no less there was a growing discontent at the monstrous selfishness of Spartan leadership.

The fact was that Thebes, Corinth, Argos, and above

all Athens, were only too eager to shake off the galling bonds of an enforced alliance, and now further to work upon their latent disloyalty there came over, as an emissary from the satrap Tithraustes, a certain Greek named Timocrates. The object of his mission was to check Agesilaus' dangerous activities in Asia by stirring up trouble in Greece ; and as an aid to his anti-Spartan propaganda Timocrates brought with him the most telling of arguments—gold. For the satrap had put at his disposal the sum of fifty talents ; and by the discreet disposal of the money among leading politicians in the malcontent states, he soon produced the desired result. Thebes headed the revolt, and in 395 scored an initial success by routing the force which the Spartans sent into Boeotia and killing Lysander, who led it. With Argos, Corinth and Athens behind her, she was able to release Northern Greece from the hated supremacy, and in 394 the Confederates even made bold to risk a trial of strength in the Peloponnese. Though severely repulsed near Nemea, they at least had the doubtful satisfaction of knowing that they had fulfilled the original purpose of Timocrates' mission. For already Agesilaus was on his way home. The edict for his recall had gone forth ; and reluctantly abandoning his dreams of Asiatic conquest, the King had marched back his army by way of the Thracian coast and down through Thessaly.[1] In Boeotia he brought the Confederates to battle near Coronea, and though beating them in the field, thought it prudent to make home for the Peloponnese. Henceforward operations centred mainly round the Isthmus.

For years the tide of dreary conflict ebbed and flowed around Corinth. At one time she lost both her Long Walls and her harbours ; and the city itself was laid under blockade. Athenian reinforcements, however, did something to relieve the pressure. One captain, named Iphicrates, was particularly active with a mercenary band of light-armed

---

[1] It is noteworthy that Agesilaus' cavalry, trained in Asia Minor, were here able to meet the crack Thessalian riders on at least equal terms.

and highly trained peltasts ; and these in one memorable engagement achieved a striking triumph. A Spartan *mora*, or battalion of six hundred hoplites, was marching in rash proximity right under the gates of Corinth, when Iphicrates and his men came out upon them. It was the story of Sphacteria over again, but on this occasion the tactics of the light-armed troops were even more scientific. In vain the Spartans charged, each time to be eluded by the more nimble adversary ; in vain they attempted to shake free from the galling pressure. At length they were borne down by the repeated assaults which never even came within their spear-length, and they perished almost to a man. The Athenian victory, though in no way decisive, possessed a twofold importance. Its tactical lesson went home. It encouraged experimental departure from the hard-and-fast method of fighting, a more systematic training of light-armed soldiery, and the combined use of other arms alongside the traditional hoplite formation. To the losing side it was a real catastrophe. With their dwindling man-power the Spartans could ill afford to lose even six hundred lives—one battalion out of the six of which their army was composed ; and still less could they relish yet another disproof of their reputed invincibility. The greatness of Sparta was, in fact, visibly on the wane. Taken on the balance, the results of the ' Corinthian War ' had hit her severely. She had lost her hold on Northern Greece. She had abandoned her offensive in Asia, and now was even hard put to it in maintaining her prestige in the Peloponnese. Nevertheless it was by sea rather than by land that the worst blow befel her ; for in the meanwhile Persian naval activity had robbed her of the command of the Aegean.

In the earlier stages of the war between Sparta and Persia, and just before Agesilaus himself was sent to the Asiatic front, it will be remembered that Pharnabazus the satrap had set about preparing a fleet. He had procured Greek rowers to man it, and not less important, a Greek admiral to take charge. This was Conon the Athenian, who, after his escape from Aegospotami, had gone off as a freelance to Cyprus, and who now embraced with joy this golden opportunity of avenging his previous defeat. Not much was achieved for a year or two ; but in 394 Pisander, whom Agesilaus on returning to Greece had left behind in command, gave battle at Cnidus, off the south-east extremity of Asia Minor, and was there utterly routed by Conon's Greco-Persian squadron. The victory of Cnidus made history. Its first and immediate consequence was that the Aegean passed under the control of Persia, and that the subject cities seized eagerly upon the chance to throw off the Spartan yoke and expel the garrisons which Agesilaus on Lysander's model had reimposed upon them. The second and indirect consequence of Cnidus was the revival of Athens. For Conon had not forgotten his countrymen, and, when his master Pharnabazus had finished with his services, he obtained leave to sail a part of his squadron to Athens. There he assisted, no doubt with Persian money, in the rebuilding of the Long Walls to the Peiraeus, which after Aegospotami had been razed to the ground. With her impregnable fortifications thus restored, Athens was enabled once more to raise her head in the world. The Aegean states, now set free from the Spartan control, began to look towards her for leadership. With Rhodes, Eretria, and other island cities, she contracted some form of alliance ; over Lemnos, Imbros and Scyros she resumed actual possession ; and presently Thrasybulus, the hero of the democratic restoration, sailed to the Hellespont, enlisted the friendship of Byzantium and recovered the free use of the important Pontic corn-route. Such activities upon the part of Athens' fleet began to make the Persians fear lest the whole Aegean might pass again into her hands and the fruits of the victory of Cnidus be lost to them.

This fear it was that gave Sparta her chance. At the present low ebb of her fortunes she had but one resource left--the recovery of Persian support. Hitherto, indeed, her overtures for a renewed entente had fallen on deaf ears ; but now the growing menace of a revived Athenian League produced a far more favourable atmosphere at

Susa. So, when in 388 the Ephors sent their agent Antalcidas to approach the Great King, his appeal met with an
excellent reception. A Persian squadron was lent him.
Dionysius of Syracuse contributed another ; and with
these, in addition to Sparta's own contingent, Antalcidas
was swiftly able to win back the command of the Hellespont and so bring Athens to her knees. Hitherto the
most bellicose spirit among the war-weary ranks of the
Confederates, she now became the most eager for peace.
In 387 a congress of Greek states was summoned to Sardis ;
and there the assembled delegates—unconscious, it would
seem, of a humiliation enough to have made their fore-
fathers turn in their graves—listened while the satrap
Tiribazus announced the Great King's terms. That a
foreigner's dictation should have been accepted as a
settlement of the Greeks' own domestic feuds was bad
enough, but the conditions of the settlement made it
infinitely worse. ' King Artaxerxes deems it right that
the cities of Asia, with the islands of Clazomenae and
Cyprus, should belong to himself. The remaining Hellenic
cities, small and great, he wishes to leave independent,
with the exception of Lemnos, Imbros and Scyros, which
should be Athenian as formerly. Should any of the
parties concerned not accept this peace, I, Artaxerxes,
together with those who share my views, will war against
him or them by land and sea, with ships and money.'
So the treaty ran ; and thus, by as vile a bargain as
ever was struck, the Asiatic cities were abandoned once
again to the barbarian yoke. So much was obvious ;
but what did not at the moment appear upon the
surface, was the true effect of the settlement upon the
homeland states. Athens was intended, of course, to
forgo her aspirations to a new Aegean League ; Thebes
to relinquish whatever claim she had to dominate her
sister cities of Boeotia. Corinth and Argos, closely linked
by the war, were to separate their connexion. But what
then of Sparta ? Was she to gain or to lose ? No hint
indeed gave warning ; but, as events were soon to prove,
her rôle under the settlement was to enforce in her own

interest or to override at her own discretion the unpopular terms of the Treaty. Persia was behind her. The unity of her late enemies had been broken up ; and her way lay clear to recover step by step the supremacy which had slowly been slipping from her grasp. Sparta used her opportunity with the same brutal effrontery that she had shown in Lysander's day ; and it is little wonder that her neighbours were soon bitterly regretting the bad bargain they had made, or that the memory of the King's Peace, as men called it, came to stink in the nostrils of the entire Hellenic world. For it brought not peace, but a sword.

III. SPARTA'S ABUSE OF THE KING'S PEACE

It was not, we may be sure, from purely disinterested motives that both now and on many subsequent occasions the Great King intervened to settle the domestic feuds of European Greece. It is true that the traditional policy of Susa, initiated in the final stages of the Peloponnesian War, had now done its work, and that by judicious use of subsidy and intrigue the Greek States had been encouraged to wear one another down to the point of temporary exhaustion. But there can be little doubt that besides the advantages of a settlement which gave him the Greek ' cities of Asia ', the King had another end in view. About this time revolt among his dependencies was seriously exercising his mind. Evagoras, the Greek prince who now ruled in Cyprus, had rebelled in 389, and Egypt, which had established its independence as early as 404, was assisting the secession. A big effort to crush the dangerous tendency was essential ; and not less essential to the success of that effort was the enlistment of Greek mercenaries whom all men recognized since Cyrus' expedition to be the best fighting material in the world. Now such mercenaries would naturally not hire themselves abroad, so long as employment could be found at home. The pacification of Greece was the preliminary step to raising a corps fit to crush the revolt ; and in point of fact we find Evagoras fought to a standstill in 381 by

20

forces raised from the Ionian seaboard. Six years later as many as 12,000 Greeks under Iphicrates, the Athenian, accompanied a great Persian expedition which attempted, though without success, the recovery of Egypt. The mercenary weapon was, however, double-edged; and others besides the Great King could, as it proved, employ recruiting sergeants. In 366 when all the satraps of Asia Minor rose in revolt, Ariobarzanes of Phrygia made special efforts to raise forces from Greece, and overtures from Egypt induced the aged Agesilaus to lead a hired contingent of Spartans to the banks of the Nile. The revolt was indeed suppressed, but its lesson was ominous. The instability of the Persian realm was once again proclaimed and no skilful manipulation of Greek politics could avail to save it in the coming days from the conquering army of one who could offer better prospects of pay and plunder than any satrap.

Meanwhile in Greece itself, to which we must turn back, the effects of the King's Peace were, as has been hinted, very widely different from men's anticipations. It is true that it brought to the Greek towns of Asia Minor material advantages which to some extent counterbalanced their political degradation. The reopening of the trade routes with the East restored to Ephesus much of its old wealth and importance, and gave to such islands as Chios and Rhodes a new lease of prosperity. But in European Greece it was a different story; and her condition in the years immediately following the Peace was perhaps more deplorable than at any other period of her history. The fever of bitter hatreds and mean cupidities, which had involved her states in nearly half a century of uninterrupted strife, was not even now allayed. The mischief was merely driven inwards and continued to perform its devastating work in a more unwholesome and insidious form. For the temporary lull of inter-state hostilities produced a hideous recrudescence of domestic faction. Wits and energies till recently employed against external enemies were now to find less honourable occupation in a struggle for political power or personal revenge. Party groups intrigued without regard for the public interest, ruthlessly exiling opponents when victorious, or, when exiled themselves, weaving plots in neighbouring cities for the recovery of their lost power. The decencies of public life were forgotten. Persian gold had already spread the habit of corruption ; and there was no meanness or treachery to which men would not stoop in the selfish pursuit of their interests. Such a miserable condition of affairs—further complicated by the presence of large numbers of mercenaries on land, and of piratical freebooters at sea—Sparta, at any rate, made no attempt whatever to control. On the contrary, she was prepared, when occasion might offer, to exploit it for the purpose of extending her own supremacy. There were scoundrels to be found in nearly every city, eager to feather their own nest by playing into her hands ; and it was not like Sparta to refuse such opportunities. So by act after act of violence during the next few years she showed that the Peace Settlement which she had been foremost in prompting was in reality a mere stalking-horse for her own sinister designs. Agesilaus, it would seem, was the leading spirit in this aggressive policy, and, as in his previous dealings with the Aegean cities, so now among the states of European Greece he aimed at establishing, wherever possible, a governing body of pro-Spartan views.

The first to suffer were the Arcadians of Mantinea. In 385 their city was attacked without any decent justification. Its fortifications were breached by the diversion of a flooded river against the unstable masonry : and, the town being captured, its inhabitants were compelled to break up into scattered villages and to accept an oligarchical régime. On the invitation of some political exiles, a similar coup was effected at Phlius, and a similar constitution set up. Such measures cowed the Peloponnese, and meanwhile Sparta had gone forward to tackle Northern Greece. There Thebes had already been humbled ; for under the terms of the Peace her confederate cities of Boeotia had received their autonomy. In the further north, however, there existed round about the Chalcidic

Peninsula a similar confederation of cities, which under Olynthus' leadership was now rapidly extending the circle of its authority. Two neighbouring towns, resentful of this growing interference, appealed in 382 for Sparta's help. An expedition was sent north, and after a two years' siege Olynthus was captured, and the Confederation dissolved.

With such high-handed dealings Sparta, it might be thought, should have rested satisfied ; but it was in the very course of this campaign against Chalcidicê that she committed the most notorious and most unscrupulous of her crimes. In 382 Phoebidas, one of her commanders, was passing close to Thebes, when he received from a magistrate, named Leontiades, a secret offer to betray the town. Jealousy of a political rival was the traitor's motive ; but Phoebidas had no excuse beyond the desire to gain credit at home. The Thebans were at peace with Sparta, and utterly unsuspicious. Their women-folk were due, as it happened, to celebrate a yearly festival, during which the Cadmeia, or citadel, was cleared of all its guards to make way for the enactment of the secret rites. At the height of the summer noon, when all the males were indoors for their siesta, Phoebidas and his troops descended suddenly upon the gates. The traitor Leontiades admitted them. They rushed the hill ; and before any in the town were well aware of it, Thebes was in Spartan hands. The whole of Greece was horror-struck at so appalling a breach of international morality. But Agesilaus backed up the act of his subordinate ; and, Sparta officially approving the capture, a permanent garrison was installed on the Cadmeia. It seemed, indeed, as though the Spartan hegemony was now to be riveted more tightly than ever before upon the lands of Northern Greece. In all the Boeotian cities narrow oligarchies were installed ; and at one, if not more, a Spartan garrison was posted. The strictest precautions were taken against counter-revolution. But all proved in vain. By the sheer monstrosity of her behaviour Sparta had overreached herself ; and in the very city which she had so cruelly victimized, she ended by awakening a spirit of national pride and energy destined to be in the near future a serious menace to her actual existence.

Three years passed. The Spartan garrison, over a thousand strong, still occupied the Cadmeia. Leontiades, having rid himself by banishment or execution of his political opponents, was still in enjoyment of the power he had so treacherously won. All seemed secure. But during these three years a band of Theban exiles, chief among whom were Pelopidas and Melon, had been laying their schemes in Athens for a counter-blow. By December 379, their arrangements were complete. Within Thebes itself they had a useful accomplice in the secretary of the ruling magistrates ; and by him a small band of seven conspirators, disguised in peasants' clothes, were smuggled inside the gates. A day or two later a wine party was held at which the chief supporters of Leontiades were guests. In the course of the evening a letter was brought in, addressed to one of the leading magistrates. It contained a disclosure of the impending plot, ' Business to-morrow ', said the recipient carelessly, and put it under his pillow unopened. Supper was over and the guests were drinking deep, when seven women were introduced, heavily veiled but possessing, so the wily secretary declared, no ordinary charms. Once inside the room, it was the work of a moment for the conspirators to doff their mummery, draw daggers and dispatch the sodden and unarmed banqueters. Leontiades they caught at his own house, as he was retiring to rest, and killed in his bedroom. Then on to the jail, where they released and armed a large body of political prisoners. Meanwhile a mob of citizens was surging into the streets. The captain of the Spartan garrison, scared by the wild doings of the winter night, lost nerve and made no move. By dawn it was too late. Reinforced by returning exiles, volunteers from Athens and from Boeotian towns, the citizens besieged the hill and all but carried it. The garrison surrendered and was allowed to march off home, and the Spartans' subsequent effort at recapture proved a miserable fiasco ; and not merely did it fail, but it resulted indirectly in a fresh blundering act of madness which made recovery impossible. A small garrison had been left behind to winter in Boeotia under the charge of an officer named Sphodrias ; and it occurred to this man that a surprise such as had succeeded against Thebes might equally succeed if tried on Athens. One evening, accordingly, he set out to cross the range of Cithaeron, to march under cover of night into Attic territory and descend on the Peiraeus, over thirty miles away, in the misty hours of dawn. So badly, however, did he miscalculate his distance that sunrise found him still ten miles from his objective. As quickly as he could he slunk back home ; but the tale of the night's doings was out. Athens was furious, as well she might be ; and when Sphodrias' attempt was condoned by the Spartan Government, she lost no time in ranging herself at the side of Thebes. From that day onward, Sparta's fortunes underwent one long decline. Year after year Agesilaus crossed the Isthmus and ravaged the Theban plain ; but he could not provoke a pitched battle, and eventually the attempt was abandoned. Thebes was left at liberty to recover her ascendancy over the other Boeotian towns ; and she rapidly did so. Her success, considering all that she had undergone, was striking enough in itself ; and it proved to be the prelude of yet more remarkable achievements. But meanwhile it was more than rivalled by the maritime activities of her newly made Athenian allies.

Not even the conditions of the King's Peace, declaring though these did the incorporation of the Asiatic Greeks with Persia and the political autonomy of the rest, had quite availed to destroy the growing influence of Athens in the Aegean. With Byzantium, Chios, Mitylene, and Rhodes she had already resumed close relations ; and now no sooner had Sphodrias' raid brought her once more into the conflict than she issued an appeal to the Hellenic world at large to form a defensive league against the common menace of Spartan aggression. The response from the mainland states was naturally disappointing, for to them the Athenian fleet could offer little safeguard ; and Thebes alone enlisted. But among the maritime communities there was more enthusiasm. Besides the cities above mentioned, many islands became members of the League ; and, fearful of repeating the errors of her old supremacy, Athens was scrupulous in avoiding all possible offence to their susceptibilities. The tax to be levied on the new League-members she·no longer called ' tribute ', but simply ' contribution '. The constitution she proposed was equally unobjectionable. Side by side with the authority of her own Assembly there was to be a congress composed of allied delegates ; and, to avoid suspicion of reviving the once unpopular system of ' cleruch ' settlements, it was forbidden for Athenian citizens to hold any property on allied soil. The guiding hand in the early years of the Confederacy was Callistratus, a statesman and orator of no small breadth of vision ; but the hero of its militant activities was Chabrias, a professional soldier who had led mercenaries in Egypt and there studied the art of trench-digging and field works. As a sailor, too, he seems to have been equally at home ; for he was put in command of the Athenian naval squadron ; and, when in despair of reconquering Boeotia, Sparta turned her attention to the sea and sent out her fleet to embarrass the new Confederacy, Chabrias succeeded in catching it off Naxos and practically destroying it. Had he not paused from the pursuit to assist some sinking vessels of his own, not a Spartan ship would have escaped. As it was, the victory gave him complete command of the Aegean, enabling him to recover amongst others the island of Delos and induce Olynthus and the Chalcidic League to enter the Confederacy.

Such successes notwithstanding, the war put a severe strain on the Athenian treasury, which, even though supplemented by a home levy upon property, was now seriously depleted. Peace parleys were begun and a treaty actually concluded when Sparta unexpectedly revived the war. She had been receiving advances from Dionysius of Syracuse, and now proceeded with his aid to attack the island of Corcyra. Foiled once again by the arrival of an Athenian squadron, the Spartans thought better of their renewed aggression and turned their thoughts towards peace. Antalcidas for a second time went up to Persia, and on his representations the Great King dispatched an envoy to assist negotiations. In 371 a General Conference of states was convened at Sparta. Callistratus and his colleague Callias came as delegates from Athens. Epaminondas, a friend of Pelopidas, represented Thebes. The outcome was the framing of a comprehensive treaty which, while recognizing Athens' right to retain her new Confederacy, guaranteed the independence of Hellenic states in general, and recommended that, if any were the victim of aggression, others at their own option might rally to its defence. Here at last then was a basis for a genuine pacification on terms of mutual tolerance, and, if need were, of mutual support. Greece appeared to have learnt after these many years the bitter lesson of her long-drawn conflict. Lofty sentiments which men seemed almost to have forgotten, now once again found utterance. Delegates spoke generously of the ties of common interest and of common blood ; and it was with high hopes of the future that, when the drafting of its conditions was complete, they came to set the names of their various states to the historic document. The oaths were duly taken, the names were signed and the business done. All looked well. And then on the very morrow—totally unexpected, seemingly at variance with the whole spirit of the Conference, and by whose fault it is even now not easy to determine—there came a rift. Epaminondas, it would seem, when signing for Thebes had assumed that thereby he was signing for Boeotia also ; assumed, in fact, that the Congress recognized the right of Thebes to dominate her neighbour cities. This on the following day was vehemently challenged by Sparta. There was a hot dispute. Epaminondas deliberately altered the document in the sense he desired. Agesilaus lost his temper and struck the alteration through. A deadlock resulted ; and upon this disputed issue the whole work of the Conference was wrecked. Within a month the Peace of Callias, as men called it, had become a ' mere scrap of paper '.

CHAPTER XVI

THE ASCENDANCY OF THEBES

I. From Leuctra to Mantinea

HITHERTO in the history of the Hellenic world the inhabitants of Boeotia had played upon the whole an inconspicuous and at times even a discreditable part. The Thebans' tame submission to the overwhelming odds of the Persian Invasion had left a slur on their good name which their more heroic, though less sorely tried, compatriots had long remembered ; and even during the succeeding century they had so far subordinated their policy to Sparta's lead that they had earned the bitter detestation of Athens, more especially since in the final phase of the Decelean occupation they had been chiefly responsible for the wholesale spoliation of the outlying Attic farms and villages. Nor did the national character of the Boeotians do much to endear them to their neighbours. They were of a somewhat boorish agricultural type, full-blooded and boisterous, proud of their muscles and athletic prowess, but producing no great art and few men of real intellect or culture ; so that the quick-witted Athenians invariably regarded them as fools. As soldiers, however, they were by no means to be despised. We have already seen them defeating the Athenians in fair field at Delium ; and the history of the next few years was now to prove that, united under the leadership of a really able commander, they were capable of greater things yet. Hitherto such unity had been largely lacking in the history of Boeotia. The inhabitants of those wide and fertile plains had never coalesced in the bond of a common citizenship as had the inhabitants of Attica or Corinth ; and the Confederate League in which Orcho- menus, Thespiae, Coronea and their other townships gathered, acknowledged only with a grudging and precarious loyalty the leadership of Thebes. Nevertheless, by virtue of her greater size and of her central position among the cities of the League, Thebes had not merely remained its centre and the place where its delegates met, but had succeeded also in exercising a preponderant voice in the formulation of its policies. But her constant efforts to extend or tighten her control had not unnaturally excited the jealous resentment of her fellow-cities ; and whenever Sparta found herself at enmity with Thebes, she had always done her best to foster and aggravate such jealousy and to weaken the position of her potential rival by under-mining the unity of the League. With this intention it was that, when at the close of the great Peace Conference of 371 Epaminondas claimed under the Theban signa-ture to include the whole of Boeotia, Agesilaus raised his objection. That objection was perhaps scarcely valid ; for, as Epaminondas pointed out, Sparta herself had signed for her subject cities and no protest had been made. The probability is, however, that the King, of whose personal animosity to Thebes there is no question, had intended from the first to pick a quarrel upon whatever pretext, and, when once he had succeeded in detaching her allies under the plea of a general peace settlement, to fall swiftly upon his victim and crush her in isolation. At any rate the blow, when struck, came with a startling suddenness. Without even waiting to consult their Peloponnesian allies, the Spartans ordered King Cleom-brotus into Boeotia ; and there in the neighbourhood of Leuctra he encountered the massed levies of the Federal League.

During former invasions it had been the Thebans' policy to refuse all open battle and retire behind walls. This time, however, a very different counsel had prevailed. Epaminondas and Pelopidas, the two most influential of their leaders, were intent on a trial of strength ; and, as it turned out, they had good grounds for their confidence. Not merely had they by now, despite all past handicaps, a well-equipped and well-disciplined army, drawn from a population almost unequalled as fighting material ; but they also brought to the battle a profound and original conception of offensive tactics. Hitherto it had been the usual effort of Greek armies to defeat their opponent at his weakest point. Epaminondas decided otherwise, planning to deliver his main assault upon the enemy right, where under Cleombrotus himself was ranged the contingent of the Spartan invincibles. Against these he pitted his own strongest corps, the Thebans, massed—on the model so successfully used at Delium—to a depth of fifty shields, and headed by their crack regiment, the Sacred Band, in which pairs of sworn friends fought side by side. Upon the outskirts, his highly trained cavalry dispersed with ease the feeble resistance of the Spartan horse ; and, as their charge swept round the flank of Cleombrotus' contingent, the whole weight of the Theban phalanx was simultaneously thrown against its front. The shock must have been tremendous ; but, slender as was the composition of the Spartan line—twelve deep to the others' fifty—it stood firm against the blow. For some while the fight hung at a deadlock, either side straining every muscle to the tense pressure, but progressing not a foot. Then ' One step more,' Epaminondas cried ; and with the answering effort of a final heave his men bore the Spartans down. As they retired doggedly from the field, their allies, both from centre and from left, turned tail and fled without a blow. The Boeotian divisions opposed to them, which had been moving up in échelon formation [1] and delaying their assault till the Theban blow was struck, had never even the chance to grapple. Epaminondas' corps had won the day single-handed and

---

[1] These tactics had two special advantages. It was a common occurrence that battles which seemed won by the victory of one wing, were lost by the defeat of the other. By thus delaying to bring his weak right wing into action until the blow of his left had thoroughly done its work, Epaminondas obviated that risk. Again, it was very usual on Greek battlefields for the right wing to outflank its opponents (cp. the battle of Mantinea in 418) ; by making sure of defeating the Spartan right, that risk was equally discounted.

had shattered once and for all the age-long legend of Spartan invincibility. The fact is that at Leuctra a secret was disclosed. So long as Sparta was alone in maintaining what we may call a regular army, accustomed to daily drill and a lifelong habit of discipline, so long did she almost inevitably triumph over the other states which only called their fighters from workshop, farm or counter where necessity arose. But now that soldiering had become a real profession and the art of war was beginning to be scientifically studied, others were training armies as well as she, and Sparta's monopoly of victory was gone for ever. Her citizens took the blow, involving though it did most serious casualties, with remarkable sang-froid ; and Xenophon tells how the relatives of the fallen even vaunted the pride of their loss, while it was the survivors' friends who hung their heads for shame. Nevertheless, their hopes of recovering their hold on Northern Greece were wrecked at Leuctra ; and the hour of Thebes had struck.

The victors set to work with energy to reap the fruits of their triumph. Many of their neighbours were ready enough to resume an old alliance. Phocis, Locris and Aetolia joined with them. Even Euboea came in ; and within a year or two Thebes found herself at the head of a powerful Confederacy extending from the Aegean to the Adriatic. She was not, however, without a rival in her sudden and unexpected prosperity. For shortly before this, and in a quarter where it was least to be expected, there had arisen a new power in the land. Among the many scattered townships of the Thessalian plain, backward in civilization and distracted by interminable feuds, there was one which had at last produced a man of unquestionable genius. The career of Jason, the prince of Pherae, was like the flash of a meteor across the Greek political horizon. By the aid of a well-trained body of mercenary troops and a diplomacy which was certainly none too scrupulous, he had established himself at the head of a united Thessaly, and with the best cavalry in Greece to back him, aspired to extend his influence beyond his own country's borders. It is asserted on good evidence that not merely were Jason's ambitions set upon the hegemony of Greece, but that like a premature Alexander, he had dreams of marching eastward and conquering the Great King. With intelligible eagerness he had embraced the chance of allying himself to Thebes ; and at the hour of her peril he had promptly led his army south, only to arrive at Leuctra too late for the fight. He refused, however, to assist in an attack upon the Spartan camp, and when a truce was once concluded, betook himself off homewards—there to meditate what further designs it is beyond our power to tell. He was scheming, we know, to preside over the Pythian Games at Delphi. Some say that he intended to make a grand appeal for a general Greek co-operation in his Persian plans ; others that he had his eye upon Apollo's treasure-house. But, be his purposes what they may, treason soon cut them short. He was one day holding a review of his Thessalian cavalry when a party of young men in hot dispute approached him, and making as though to invite his arbitration in their quarrel, they suddenly drew swords and cut him down.

Jason's death not merely removed a dangerous rival from the path of Thebes, but it opened to her the opportunity of extending her power northwards. In the years which followed, Pelopidas made several expeditions against Jason's nephew, Alexander of Pherae ; and, though in 364 he threw away his life in the rash pursuit of the defeated foe, his successes led to the temporary subjection of the whole of Thessaly. In the meantime, however, the growth of the Theban supremacy owed less to Pelopidas than to his still greater companion-in-arms. With the exception of Philip and Alexander of Macedon, to whose military education his example contributed much, Epaminondas stands out as the most brilliant commander that Hellas produced. At a moment when tactical science was undergoing rapid developments, he seized not merely upon new methods of equipment and training, but on new methods of fighting a battle ; and his victory at Leuctra has shown

us already what those methods could do. But Epaminondas was something more than a general. He was also
a great patriot, utterly free from those narrow and selfish
ambitions which involved so many of his contemporaries
in shameless intrigues, capable of the staunchest friendship towards a fellow-commander, whom most Greeks
in his place would have marked down as a dangerous rival,
and—most singular of all—humane enough to ignore the
harsh rule of his countrymen which punished political
exiles, when captured, with death. Something of his lofty
outlook he must have owed to his education ; for he was
a man of genuine culture, a musician of merit and a student
of Pythagorean philosophy. In those very arts which
his countrymen so notoriously lacked he specially excelled.
He could sway an audience by his powers of rhetoric,
and win a bloodless triumph by the shrewd strokes of
his diplomacy. He must have possessed, too, something
of that personal magnetism which is the gift of great
commanders. His very presence was of itself enough to
inspire confidence not only in the men of his own command,
but among the ranks of his allies ; and had it not been
for his premature death on the battle-field he might even
have ended by uniting Greece as she had never been united
before. It is improbable, however, that Epaminondas
himself thought in terms of Pan-Hellenic union. It was
for Thebes, not for Greece, that he worked, and in that
cause he took as the main object of his life the isolation
and the overthrow of Sparta. For the first time in their
history the old masters of the Peloponnese were now made
to tremble not merely for such authority as they still
exercised over their more immediate neighbours, but for
the actual security of their homes. And had the Theban
Government's policy been less spasmodic, or had Epaminondas himself been given a freer hand, then complete and
lasting victory must almost inevitably have been theirs.
For the conditions were favourable and the time was ripe.

The news of Leuctra, dealing as it did the final blow to
Sparta's military prestige, had thrown the Peloponnesian
States into a ferment. Everywhere her influence was

sorely shaken. And the oligarchies which she had supported in the various cities were now bitterly assailed. At Argos there was bloody revolution, the mob beating many of the upper class to death with cudgels. In Arcadia the inhabitants of Mantinea, whom Sparta had forcibly dispersed among scattered villages, resumed their capital, building a new ring-wall, the foundation-stones of which it is still possible to see to-day. Tegea, to the south of them, raised openly the anti-Spartan standard, and formed an Arcadian Federation with a permanent force of five thousand regulars recruited in the main from mercenary veterans. Sparta's embarrassment was Thebes' opportunity; and finding Argos and Elis prepared also to stand with her, she had swiftly determined to strike. In the year after Leuctra Epaminondas was sent south. Much time was wasted in coercing some lukewarm cities, and winter was upon him before he could turn his steps towards Sparta. Nevertheless, the attempt seemed still worth making, and rallying to their side many discontented Helots, the Theban army marched south into the Vale of the Eurotas. It was an enterprise unique in the annals of Greece. Never before had Sparta witnessed the camp fires of an enemy, and even her stoical women-folk were beside themselves with terror. The long straggling town —little better than a village—was without ramparts, without even a ditch; and throwing hasty barricades across the entrance to the streets, Agesilaus prepared his small but resolute army (reinforced at the last moment by some allies and loyal Helots) to resist the expected assault. But the assault never came. Unable to draw out the enemy into pitched battle, Epaminondas shrank from the terrible losses which the Spartans at bay might inflict. Fording the Eurotas, now swollen by snow-water spate, he circled round the outskirts of the town, and content with that demonstration turned away to sweep the southern districts of the valley. Then, leaving behind him a trail of burning farms and villages, he departed as he had come. But Sparta's troubles were not yet over. Both among her Helots and her subject Perioeci defection had seriously begun. In the westerly plain of Messenia, secured from the immediate menace of reprisals by the snow-clad range of Mount Taygetus, the malcontents could safely venture to defy their Spartan overlords; and here it was that Epaminondas now proposed to construct for them an effective rallying-point. The gaunt hill of Ithomê, which had formed the Helot stronghold in the great insurrection of a century before, was selected as the most advantageous site. Thither were gathered the best masons that Greece could furnish, and soon a magnificent line of embattled walls, planned on the newest models of the fortifier's art, arose around its slopes. The Spartans, with their dwindling man-power and notorious inaptitude for siege-craft, made no attempt to take it; and the loss of Messenia, depriving them as it did of nearly half their territory and half their serfs, must have hit them very hard.

So successful, in fact, was this experiment that next year Epaminondas reappeared in the Peloponnese and repeated it. In Western Arcadia he founded a second fortress similar to Ithomê, but on even a larger scale. Megalopolis, or ' the Great City ', was to be its name, and within its ample walls was provided accommodation not merely for the inhabitants of neighbouring villages, but for the Federal Parliament and standing army of the whole Arcadian League. Thus on a fresh flank Sparta found herself faced by another and even more powerful antagonist. Indeed, the pretensions of the new Arcadian nationalism were mounting rapidly; and Thebes herself began to realize that in her desire to provide a counterpoise to Sparta's influence in the Peloponnese she had raised up a formidable rival to her own.

This disturbing fact was further thrown into prominence during the peace negotiations which presently followed. In 367 the various belligerents resumed the recent practice of sending delegates to Susa and soliciting the arbitration of the Persian King; and Pelopidas, the Theban envoy, there succeeded in extracting a form of settlement highly favourable to his own state. But at the subsequent Conference which was convened in Greece, it was the Arcadians who roundly refused to accept the suggested terms or to bow to the dictation of Thebes. The whole plan was thus ruined ; and the folk who had ruined it followed up this assertion of their right to an independent policy by entering into alliance with Thebes' watchful enemy, Athens. The truth is that the Arcadians were growing too big for their boots, and even beginning to view themselves as the future masters of the Peloponnese. In a high-handed manner they seized the sanctuary of Olympia from Elis, helped themselves to its treasury, and assumed armed control of its historic Festival. Peace was eventually patched up and Olympia restored to its owners. But at the winding up of negotiations, the Theban representative made a treacherous attempt to arrest the anti-Theban members among the Arcadian dele-gation ; and by the monstrous blunder of this coup he forfeited for his country whatever right she still possessed of controlling her former protégés. Tegea and Megalopolis stood loyal, it is true. But Mantinea and all Northern Arcadia went over bodily to the Spartan camp. Athens and Elis joined them ; and it was abundantly clear that, if Thebes was now to recover her hold over the Peloponnese, it could no longer be by diplomacy.

In such circumstances it was that Epaminondas for the last time was dispatched south across the Isthmus, and at the head of a large array, drawn from the forces of the Theban Confederacy and the Thessalian cavalry, struck down in the direction of the central plains. Near Tegea he joined hands with that city's contingent, but instead of pursuing the immediate object of his mission and turning north to reduce Mantinea, he suddenly deter-mined to spring a surprise attack upon Sparta. Luck at first seemed to favour the stroke, for, as Epaminondas raced southward, Agesilaus, by a directly opposite but more circuitous route, was simultaneously hurrying north to the support of Mantinea. Sparta was thus left depleted of troops, and it seemed as though nothing could save her. But already, had Epaminondas but known it, the

21

game was up. A deserter from his camp, a certain long-distance runner of Crete, was on the way to warn the King of his peril, and when the invaders arrived upon

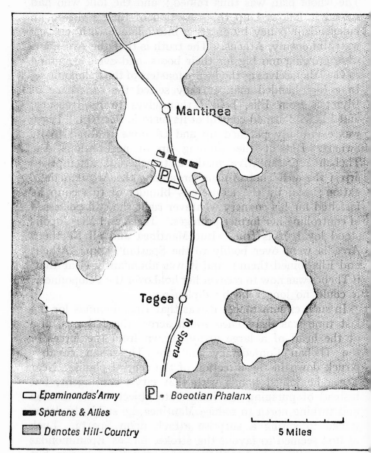

Epaminondas' Army   P = Boeotian Phalanx

Spartans & Allies

Denotes Hill-Country   5 Miles

BATTLE OF MANTINEA

the outskirts of the town, it was to find Agesilaus' men back at their posts. Thus once again foiled of his hopes, Epaminondas turned swiftly on his tracks and attempted by another quick movement to surprise Mantinea before its allies could arrive. As his advance guard of troopers swept up into the plain, the citizens were engaged in hastily salving their harvest, and they would have fallen an easy prey had not some Athenian cavalry, who had that moment arrived, beaten off the attack. This second reverse seems to have decided Epaminondas to await a pitched battle ; and, as soon as the Spartans and Athenians were marshalled in strength before Mantinea, he quitted his base at Tegea and moved northwards to force a decision. To this the final and crowning triumph of his military career the great commander brought not merely an army of highly disciplined northerners, trained on the model of the Theban phalanx which had won the day at Leuctra, but also an ingenuity of tactical manœuvre as far surpassing his own previous methods as he himself surpassed all other generals of his time. As at Leuctra, he threw forward, well in front of the rest, his deeply massed left wing of Thebans and Boeotians, holding back his other corps in echelon formation, but posting an advance guard on some rising ground to prevent any outflanking of his right. As his great forward column moved to the attack, he swung it unexpectedly leftwards and close under the mountain slopes which hedge the west side of the plain. There he halted it, and, still more surprising, gave the order to ground arms. The day was by now far advanced, and the enemy, rashly assuming that he did not mean to fight, made a movement to retire. No sooner was their battle-order broken than Epaminondas charged. His left went crashing through the Mantinean and Spartan fronts opposed to it, and the whole enemy line was dissolving in utter confusion when Epaminondas himself went down, mortally wounded in the breast. It was a singular tribute to his commanding influence that no sooner did the news of his fall become known to his followers than the impetus of their attack at once flagged and collapsed. Without him they seemed helpless. The pursuit was called off ; and as though he had himself taken full measure of the situation, Epaminondas' last instructions, before the spear-shaft was drawn from his side and the life-blood allowed to flow out, were to make a swift peace with the enemy (362).

The dead man's parting advice was followed. Thebes made peace ; and indeed she could scarcely do otherwise. For with his passing the mainspring of her vigour was gone ; and after her brief period of greatness she sank swiftly again to the rank of a second-rate power. That fate was deserved. Her Government had never made proper use of Epaminondas' great genius, and more than once by their wilful futility they had actually undone his good work. In 366 he had enlarged the Theban Confederacy by rounding the Corinthian Gulf to Achaea and securing the adhesion of the cities of that long coastal strip. Next year, however, the edict had gone forth that these cities should depose their oligarchies, and by the foolish endeavour to enforce this constitutional change Thebes soon lost her new allies. Again, in 364, on Epaminondas' initiative a bold bid had been made to undermine the Athenian naval supremacy, and for the first time in her history Thebes had built a large squadron of warships, which under Epaminondas himself had sailed into the Hellespont and there succeeded in winning Byzantium over. With that, however, the new maritime activity ended. The financial strain of its maintenance was too severe, and nothing more was done with the fleet. Such faulty co-ordination of external policy can scarcely be laid at Epaminondas' door. Still less is it fair to condemn him because he failed to consolidate within Boeotia herself the new spirit of national greatness or to endow her with such a permanent form of constitutional machinery as might have enabled that greatness to survive his own death. Epaminondas was not blind to political issues. Some effort he almost certainly made to unify the scattered townships of the plain by making their inhabitants citizens of Thebes, as the Attic folk had long ago been made citizens of Athens. To do more than this, however, would in all likelihood have involved him in the personal assumption of autocratic powers. He might, in fact, have made Boeotia greater, had he chosen to become a Dionysius or a Jason. But such a line of action was utterly foreign to Epaminondas' character. Soldier-like, he believed in submission to authority, and at times he carried it to remarkable lengths. At the end of his first and most successful Peloponnesian campaign he was impeached for having exceeded his commission ; and he stood his trial without apparent demur. A little later, having failed of re-election to the high command, he served in Pelopidas' army as a common private of the ranks. Such a spirit of patriotism was rare in Fourth-Century Greece ; but Epaminondas was something greater even than a patriot ; and if he put country before self, he also put honour before country. We are told that he actually refused to join in the famous coup which relieved Thebes of Spartan occupation, from no other motive than that it involved treachery. That spirit has been rare in all ages ; and we cannot but feel that the man who steered his course through times so difficult on such high principles was deserving of a better country and of a nobler cause.

II. THE ATHENIAN REVIVAL

The settlement which was concluded after the Battle of Mantinea was a more genuine pacification than the Greek States had yet achieved. Guarantees were given not merely to abstain from aggression, but also, if aggression occurred, to combine for the defence of its victim. Exhaustion had indeed done its work ; and Greece fell into a temporary condition of torpor. Thebes, as if crippled by Epaminondas' death, drew in her horns. Sparta, though eager to recover Messenia, lacked funds for the campaign, and so low did she stoop to acquire them that she hired out a contingent to a rebel prince in Egypt where the veteran Agesilaus at the age of eighty-four met his death in the desert. Arcadia, which well might have stepped into Sparta's place in the Peloponnese, went to pieces through disunion. Megalopolis, designed to be its common capital, lapsed into insignificance, and the ' Great City ', as some wit expressed it, became in the

end a ' great wilderness '. Athens alone among the late
belligerents retained something of her old vitality and
ambition. So much indeed did her policy in the Aegean
seem to smack of her former Imperialism that she began
to get herself into bad odour with her confederate allies.
The moving spirit in her aggressive policy was Timotheus,
the son of Conon. He succeeded not merely in capturing
Samos in 365, but also in recovering a hold in Chalcidicê,
where Potidaea, Pydna, Methone and several other cities
passed again into the possession of Athens. Their seizure
and the planting of a cleruchy at Samos—an act in complete
contravention of the Confederacy's charter—brought many
of the leading members into open revolt. Timotheus fell
into disgrace ; and some rebel states were permitted to
retire from the League. Her new Chalcidic acquisitions
Athens kept (and a highly important part they were to play
in her subsequent dealings with Macedon) ; but for all that
her star was on the wane. The financial strain of the war
had told heavily on her resources, so that she welcomed a
respite. It was clear that the temper of her remaining allies
would brook no real revival of her old Periclean supremacy ; and bit by bit the unity of the League declined.

Nevertheless for Athens herself these were times of
considerable prosperity. Though the commerce of the
West had by now passed definitely into the hands of
Syracuse, there were better prospects than ever in the
eastern field. These it was for the dominant sea power
to exploit ; and Athens did so with manifest advantage.
To a greater degree than even in Periclean days her port
became the commercial centre of the Aegean. The Crimean
corn trade, in particular, was largely conducted by her
merchant-ships which acted as carriers for other countries
besides their own.[1] Commerce became, in fact, the staple
means of livelihood for citizens as well as for metics, so
that many Attic farmers sold their land and migrated
to Athens. Business was planned on a more elaborate and
more scientific scale. Bankers, like the celebrated Pasion,

---

[1] Law, however, compelled them to bring all corn first to Athens ;
about a third being used for re-exportation.

were ready to advance loans on the security of freights or vessels. Money was plentiful, thanks partly to the influx of gold from Asia and partly to the renewed working of the Laurium silver-mines ; and large private fortunes were undoubtedly made. It was inevitable perhaps under an advanced democracy that this growing capitalism should be subjected to rigorous taxation ; and we have already seen how a property-tax was imposed to meet the naval requirements of the new Confederacy. But this was not all ; for more and more it had become the accepted principle that the rich should pay not merely for the regular state services, but also for the maintenance and even for the amusements of the poor. Some time since —by 389, if not before—the fee for attendance at the Ecclesia had been introduced ; and somewhat later there was revived a system—first employed perhaps by Pericles in the Fifth Century—whereby an annual distribution of money was made among the poorer citizens to assist them in paying for their seats at the Dionysiac and other public festivals. To make due provision for such distributions a special ' Theoric Fund ' had been inaugurated ; and when this ran a risk of deplenishment through the heavy strain of naval expenditure, a certain Eubulus won great popularity by setting it again on its feet. A more scientific handling of public finance was typical of the times, and whereas in the preceding century State liabilities had been met in a curiously hand-to-mouth fashion, budgets were now drawn up with intelligent foresight. The result was that Eubulus, though devoting the entire surplus of State revenue to the Theoric Fund, was yet able, by careful economy at home and a policy of peace abroad, to improve the public services in various ways —strengthening the navy, organizing the water-supply, and bettering the roads. No important public buildings, however, were erected during this epoch ; and it was not until after Chaeronea that the eminent financier Lycurgus gave a permanent stone structure to the Theatre and to the Stadium or Race-course. Here we may once again discern the tendency of the times.

It is evident, in short, that the revived Athens of the Fourth Century was a more practical, more comfortable, and more pleasure-loving town than that which Pericles or even Alcibiades knew. Her old idealism had been replaced by a more materialistic outlook. Yet something, too, she still possessed of the ancestral spirit, of its vices and its virtues alike. Her jealous democracy was still ready to visit disgrace or death on the failure of its appointed commanders ; even Timotheus, despite his many services, was at one point condemned to pay a crushing fine, and Callistratus, after receiving sentence of exile, risked return and met his death. Demagogues still declaimed and still denounced one another. Party spirit could run high at a crisis ; and for all its waning interest in political problems even the Ecclesia could become the scene of memorable debate. How much still remained of the old traditional passion for freedom was an issue now soon to be tested. In the coming years, when the danger of absorption by Macedon was threatening all Greece, the Athenians alone could be looked to for a bold, decisive lead. Nor was there wanting a voice—the voice of Demosthenes—to rekindle in them the old fires of a smouldering patriotism and to summon the descendants of those who had beaten back the Persian at Marathon and Salamis, to stand forth once more as the champions of Hellenic liberty. It may be true that Demosthenes' ideals were narrow and shortsighted. It is certainly true that the response to his call was tardy and, as the event proved, ineffectual. But Athens would have been Athens no longer, had that call fallen altogether on deaf ears ; and we can at least admire, even while we may find cause to criticize, her not wholly unworthy leadership of that last forlorn hope.

III. Fourth-Century Monarchies

Yet, while our imagination inevitably lingers over the last free and prosperous years of the Athenian State, it is impossible to deny that in some sense the vigour of the Hellenic stock had now worked itself out and was failing among those peoples who had hitherto been the very focus of its many-sided life. It was not with Athens, far less with Thebes or Sparta, that the future of Hellenism lay. Their day was over, and the youthful exuberance which had once been theirs, is more and more to be sought in those outlying states that had hitherto played but a secondary part in the history of the race. As we have observed above, the Fourth Century is remarkable for the rise of principalities which owed their foundation and their prosperity to the personal genius and enterprise of some individual statesman or adventurer. Sometimes it was a philosopher-politician like Archytas of Tarentum, more often an ambitious upstart like Dionysius of Syracuse. But the significant thing is that such men, though living on the fringes of the Hellenic world and coming therefore into closer contact with the barbarian influences outside it, were, perhaps for that very reason, tenacious upholders of its cultural tradition and admirers or patrons of its art. One such was Mausolus of Caria, whose ambitions in the Aegean, as is mentioned elsewhere, brought him into conflict with Athens. Though Caria was now strictly a province of the Persian Empire, Mausolus, whose crown descended to him from his father, Hecatomnus, ruled it to all intents and purposes as an independent prince, paying tribute to the Great King indeed, and ranking as a satrap, but otherwise left free to govern at his own discretion. He included within his realm not Caria only, but the neighbouring land of Lycia and the Greek promontory of Halicarnassus, to which he transferred his capital and where on a small island adjacent to the town he built himself a strongly fortified castle. Though a ' tyrant ' by power and position, he nevertheless refrained from interference in the political institutions of the country and, like Pisistratus at Athens, was more in practice than in theory the master of the State. Nor was this the only proof of his enlightenment, for he must clearly have appreciated what was best in the arts of Greece, and when he died in 353, his widow Artemisia, who succeeded him on the throne. built in his honour a monument so famous in antiquity that it has added the word ' Mausoleum ' to our language. Four of the foremost sculptors of Greece worked upon its statuary, the celebrated Scopas among them, and the shattered remains of their handiwork may be seen in the British Museum, a fitting memorial to a great and cultured prince.

More interesting still perhaps and certainly more romantic was the story of the dynasty which had been founded by the Greek Evagoras in Cyprus. This astonishing adventurer was the descendant of an ancient family which at one time ruled the Greek inhabitants of the island, but which, about the middle of the Fifth Century, had been ousted by the Phoenicians. In 410 Evagoras had seized the Cypriot town of Salamis, and from there had succeeded in gaining command of the island. After the fall of Athens Conon and many of his fellow-exiles had taken refuge at the prince's court, and, though he acknowledged the Great King's suzerainty and (except for one brief period of rebellion) was content to pay him tribute, Evagoras, like Mausolus, was a genuine supporter of all things Greek. When in 374 he was eventually murdered, he was succeeded by his son Nicocles, a student of philosophy and friend to Isocrates, the Athenian pamphleteer ; and one striking result of this Cypriot dynasty's influence was the growth of Hellenist tendencies in the Phoenician town of Sidon, an area hitherto uncompromisingly Oriental. The importance of Evagoras' kingdom as an outpost of Greek culture was eclipsed of course by the still wider spread of Hellenism through the East due to another and a greater dynast. For of all the monarchs of the type we are describing, by far the most notable example is to be found in the persons of the Macedonian Kings. A backward country, considered by its neighbours almost outside the pale of Hellenic civilization, Macedon still possessed all the rude and youthful vigour which those more sophisticated neighbours now so noticeably lacked. Yet it was precisely because in her two kings Philip and Alexander she discovered men who, besides an outstanding military genius, possessed also a profound sympathy for Greek culture

and Greek ways, that her rise was so swift and its consequences so momentous. Thus, in the ultimate issue,
Hellenism, which was decaying slowly at the core, was to
receive a new lease of life from a source which, if not
actually foreign, was at least external to the traditional
centres of its inspiration. In the coming conflict, therefore, between the infant realm of Macedon and the older
states of the South the real interest centres in this strange
anomaly that from the very power which by most men
was regarded as the deadliest enemy of Hellenic culture,
was to spring the man whom it is no exaggeration to call
its second founder.

CHAPTER XVII

PHILIP OF MACEDON

I

THE bankruptcy of the Greek political system (though nobody perhaps beyond one or two clear-sighted thinkers was even dimly aware of the process) had long been tending towards its inevitable end. The ideal of the City-State, self-contained, self-supporting and proudly self-sufficient, had been weighed in the balance and found wanting. The selfsame energy of mind and character which had impelled the Hellenic race along the precocious lines of its political development had also bred in them the insatiable craving for aggrandizement which forbade their various states to live at peace. Both within and without, in domestic faction and in war of state with state, the fevered animosities of more than half a century had reached a pitch which compelled the search for some solution other than a continuation of the suicidal conflict ; nor were signs altogether wanting that the lesson had gone home and that the genius of this people was feeling at length its faltering way along more hopeful paths. Experiments in combination of one sort or another had of late years multiplied apace. Federalism was in the air. Arcadia had tried it, though with short-lived results. Olynthus had tried it and far more successfully. Corinth and Argos in the course of their struggle with Sparta had effected a political amalgamation astonishingly complete ; and Athens' new League, in striking contrast to her old, was based on a genuine recognition of its participants' autonomy. Yet these had been at best but local efforts. No bond had been discovered whereby to knit together in one amicable whole the entire Hellenic race ; and all hope of that solution was perhaps finally destroyed by the breakdown which followed hard upon the conclusion of Callias' Convention. A last alternative remained. Among all the leading states which had each in turn essayed by force of arms to impose on Greece an imperial unity, not one had even for a brief period succeeded ; but, where they failed, success was now awaiting a small and untried people, hitherto insignificant and universally despised, Greek only by a doubtful title of half-breed origin,[1] barbaric in manners and in form of government, yet tough of fibre, and fit, under proper leadership, to make incomparable soldiers—the wild northern tribesmen of the Kings of Macedon.

II

A narrow strip of plainland between the mountains and the sea formed the true home and cradle of the Macedonian folk. But though access to the coastline was denied them by the interposition of Olynthus and other Greek towns, they had spread their conquest widely over the ranges of the hinterland, and imposed some sort of suzerainty over its savage mountaineers. The mountains indeed claimed a large part of the Macedonians' interest and attention. There they did much pasturing of sheep and goats, though the farming of their native plain was by no means unproductive. There, too, since they were mighty hunters, they spent much of their time in pursuit of the lion and the boar. With such a manner of life their habits harmonized. They dwelt in scattered groups of ill-made huts, dressed in coarse homespun or in wild beasts' skins, and indulged in scandalously deep potations, for which they became in fact a by-word throughout Greece. Unlike their more civilized neighbours, they habitually went armed. Murder and blood-feuds were of constant occurrence, and till he had killed his man, whether of his own folk or the enemy, the Macedonian wore a

---

[1] Opinions are divided whether the Macedonians were Greeks akin to the Thessalians, and intermarried with some non-Hellenic strain, or whether they were an Aryan people who borrowed largely in their speech from the Thessalian vocabulary.

cord around his waist. It is the more remarkable that their Kings, who enjoyed the unlimited power of absolute despots, made a constant endeavour to introduce more cultured ways. Archelaus, who reigned at the end of the Fifth Century, had been an ardent builder, had constructed roads, and above all had gathered to his court at Pella Greek artists and craftsmen and poets, the tragedian Euripides among the rest. Amyntas, who after a period of chaos succeeded to the throne, was for a while hard put to it in maintaining his kingdom. At one time he was driven from his capital by the Illyrian tribesmen ; at another he was closely pressed by the Chalcidic League. But thanks partly to Sparta's suppression of Olynthus, he eventually succeeded in re-establishing his supremacy, and when he died in 369 he left Macedonia no mean power. He had three sons, Alexander, Perdiccas. and Philip. The first was murdered—no infrequent fate among Macedonian Kings. In 359 came a fresh Illyrian inroad, and Perdiccas was mortally wounded in battle. His son was a minor ; and the only man left fit to hold the realm was the third of the three brothers, Philip. Thus, at a moment more critical perhaps than any in Macedonia's previous history, did the regency pass into the hands of the man who was destined to raise her to an unimagined pinnacle of greatness.

In character Philip was like his Macedonian subjects, a compound of widely different elements. All their fierce, hot-blooded energy and their powers of physical endurance he inherited to the full. He loved the wine-cup, and his drunken orgy upon the night of Chaeronea sullied the brilliance of that crowning triumph. Alongside of his men, who loved him for it, he would endure the keenest of privations, the bitterest of cold and the worst hazards of the fight ; and in the pursuit of his ambition ' he counted it as naught '—they are his arch-enemy Demosthenes' own words—' to have an eye put out, a shoulder broken, an arm and a leg rotted away '. In the pursuit of his ambition, too, he would stick at nothing. Deceit was ingrained in his character ; and his path to power was strewn with broken promises, hypocritical professions. and acts of the blackest treachery. It is little wonder that his opponents regarded him as the deadliest enemy of all things Greek. But there they were wrong. For deeply imbedded in the nature of this extraordinary man was a most ardent respect and admiration for the culture of his Hellenic neighbours. To be recognized as one of them was the most cherished ambition of his life. To conciliate their sympathy he was even willing to forgo more rough-and-ready methods of bending them to his will. And, when Athens at last lay at his feet, he spared her for no other motive that we are able to discern than a genuine reverence for her intellectual greatness.[1] There was one excellent reason why Philip should thus have appreciated Hellas. As a boy of fifteen, when Pelopidas' campaigns had swept beyond Thessaly into the borders of his country, the young Macedonian prince had been singled out as a hostage and carried off to three years' exile in the Boeotian capital. But at Thebes he had learnt more than simply to admire Greek culture. Epaminondas was then in the hey-day of his military career, and the brilliant lessons of his strategic science had not been lost upon the boy. When he returned to Macedon and came at the age of twenty-three to take possession of the throne, he was destined to put into practice the principles thus imbibed, proving himself a master of organization, leadership and strategy second to none in the ancient Greek world—with the single exception of his son.

The moment of Philip's accession to power was, as we have said, critical enough ; and he met the situation with a characteristic combination of will and energy. The various pretenders to the throne he either killed or banished. The Paeonian mountaineers who had swooped down on him from the north, he bought off with bribes. The Illyrians he defeated in battle and reduced to a condition of complete subjection. And all this while, as the instrument of victory in this as in many a subsequent campaign, he had been busily organizing a really efficient army

[1] It is possible, however, that Philip counted on Athens' *naval* assistance in his projected campaign against Persia.

from the mixed material of his native Macedonians and mercenary soldiers. A highly serviceable cavalry he already possessed in the crack corps of aristocratic riders known as the ' Companions '. But the infantry, as he found them, were ill-organized and worthless. He made them the best in the world. For Philip's innovations marked a real revolution in military history. Taking the heavy-armed Greek phalanx as his model, he transformed it from a mere pushing machine into a weapon of offence infinitely more mobile and elastic. First he adopted a much less compact formation, spacing his men at maybe a full yard's interval between each shield. Secondly he equipped them with a far longer spear, the famous Macedonian pike or *sarissa*, the extra size of which not merely gave to his front rank a longer reach than their opponents, but also enabled his second and even perhaps his third ranks to bring their points into play from behind.[1] To handle such a weapon and to manœuvre in such formation demanded the highest degree of both skill and discipline ; and Philip was tireless in the drilling of his troops. Since, too, rapidity of movement is the essence of strategical success, he accustomed them to long marches —thirty or even thirty-five miles in the day, with a month's provision of flour and full baggage on back. Though all this took time, it was clear that, when Philip came to measure his strength against his Greek neighbours, he would prove, to say the least of it, a formidable antagonist. Two further elements there were, however, which went to ensure his future success. First he aimed at making his force not merely a professional but a national army. He was not even afraid to draft into its ranks recruits from the mountain tribes he had subjected ; but so successful was he in inspiring them with a spirit of enthusiastic loyalty that they became good subjects no less than good soldiers ; and community of service proved a sure foundation for Macedonia's political union. Philip, in

[1] In later developments of the Macedonian phalanx a pike of 24 feet long was apparently known. And the points of no less than five successive ranks projected out in front of the first line.

short, was making a nation as well as an army ; and a nation of fighters was something new in the annals of Greece. For not even the Spartans, when we remember the doubtful loyalty of their serf-population, can be said to have achieved that.

The second requirement in the building of his army was money to maintain it, and to meet this need Philip had early laid his plans. North-east of Macedonia lay the rich gold-mines of Mount Pangaeus, the approach to which was guarded by the coast town of Amphipolis. Long since lost to the Athenians in their war against the Spartans, this town had hitherto eluded their efforts at recapture ; and now Philip went cleverly to work by flattering their hopes of its recovery. In the second year of his reign he besieged and took Amphipolis, and when the Athenians protested, promised to exchange it for Pydna—a seaport of theirs which he himself much coveted as an outlet to the Aegean. As soon, however, as Amphipolis was his (together with gold-mines that were soon producing him a thousand talents yearly), he forgot a promise which he never meant to keep, and proceeded in the following year to lay hands not merely on Pydna, but on Potidaea also. Having thus secured for himself both a stable source of revenue and an opening for maritime expansion, Philip could afford to snap his fingers at all expostulations. But he was careful, as ever, to cloak his real designs under a diplomatic pretence of conciliation. Olynthus' alarm he pacified by presenting her with Potidaea. Towards Athens he consistently professed the friendliest of feelings. When any of her citizens were found among his captives, he released them without ransom ; and indeed he seems to have been genuinely reluctant to provoke her hostility. Such methods were successful. Athens, though momentarily alarmed and very naturally indignant at the seizure of her dependencies, was soon lulled back into a grudging acquiescence ; and, truth to tell, she was at this moment in no position to retaliate. For her allies were again in revolt. To this in large measure they were instigated by Mausolus, the powerful satrap of Caria, who having established himself in virtual independence at Halicarnassus, was now casting a jealous eye on Athens' Aegean supremacy. With his aid Chios, Rhodes and Byzantium broke loose from the Confederacy ; and, as their example was rapidly followed by others, and as the Great King threatened to assist the rebellion, Athens had little choice but to acquiesce, and she was left with only Euboea, the Thracian Chersonese and a few northern islands in tow. Her attempts to reconquer the rebels had depleted her treasury ; and exhaustion forbade the undertaking of any fresh enterprise. So it was that the blow which in these early days might well have availed to check the aggrandizement of Macedon was never struck ; and Philip was left free to consolidate his growing kingdom and to lay his plans at leisrue for the further humiliation of Greece.

In an Athens weary to death of paying mercenaries to lose battles and more concerned over the price of fish at Peiraeus or the preparations for a new comedy than with the storm-clouds fast gathering on the political horizon, there was nevertheless one man at least who would not willingly blind himself to the omens of trouble. Demosthenes was one of those natures who look, almost by instinct, on the darker side of things. Though the son of a well-to-do Athenian manufacturer, the Scythian blood which he inherited from his maternal grandmother had perhaps infused into his veins something of the dour, melancholic spirit bred in wild dwellers of the northern steppes. The unhappy experiences of his boyhood had further embittered a disposition preternaturally morose ; he had been a weakly child, left early to the care of a widowed mother and to the mercy of three guardians who swindled him. Their fraud had helped, however, to determine his career. For on coming of age he had undertaken to prosecute ; and the experience acquired in conducting the suit proved an excellent preparation for ' the bar '. In writing speeches for clients Demosthenes soon showed his rare talent for tense style and close reasoning. For the art of oratory, however, he was less gifted. Extempore speech never came easy to him ; and at the outset he was seriously handicapped by a certain clumsiness of gesture and an imperfect utterance. To overcome these weaknesses he subjected himself to a most rigorous training, declaiming as he walked uphill, reciting poetry with pebbles in his mouth and even practising gesture in front of a mirror. The result was that, though, like Disraeli, he was laughed down on his first appearance in debate, the time came when the Assembly were compelled to hear him. By the sheer force of his rhetoric this sour-faced, ungainly prophet of disaster forced on his unwilling audience the unpalatable truth about facts they would not face, and attained at last so commanding an authority that almost despite themselves they rose to a height of heroism little to be expected in this most unheroic age. Demosthenes' triumph was the more remarkable since he had many bitter opponents on the public platform. These were days in which the populace was more than ever at the mercy of the glib professional speaker. The Assembly was managed no longer by men who were themselves members of a responsible executive. For the highly specialized development of military science required that the command of armies should now go to soldiers proper rather than to gifted amateurs like Pericles or Cleon. Politicians were, therefore, free to urge a course of action the consequences of which would not of necessity recoil upon themselves. The result was that clap-trap orators went out for catching votes, by preaching a policy along the lines of least resistance. There were prophets in plenty to cry 'peace, when there was no peace'; and even among the more responsible leaders like the financier Eubulus or the stern old-fashioned soldier Phocion, there was a growing tendency to advocate concentration on domestic prosperity and the abandonment of expensive overseas adventures. One other line of argument there was, however, which, in his attempt to rouse his countrymen against Philip, Demosthenes must have found it even more difficult to meet. Isocrates was an old man when the great duel came to be waged between the man who wished to fight Philip to the death and the men who simply wanted to ignore him. He had seen Greece torn by interminable feuds and his own state worn out in the effort to establish an unpopular hegemony. He wished Athens, therefore, to forgo all dreams of empire and unite with her sister-states under Philip's leadership for the far more worthy and more repaying task of conquering the East. Such prophetic anticipation of what Philip's son was actually to achieve seems to verge on the uncanny ; but Isocrates' programme would have involved, in part at least, the surrender of that which to the true Greek patriot was dearer than anything in the world—political freedom.[1] Demosthenes was wrong, no doubt, in imagining that the Athens of his day had power to stem the tide of Macedon's rising strength ; but beside Isocrates, the essayist and dreamer, he at any rate stands out as a man of vigorous action who was not merely convinced of the justice of his cause, but ready to go through fire to support it. It was an uphill battle ; but, if ever a man did, Demosthenes deserved his triumph, even though that triumph led to the ultimate ruin of what he most had prized.

During the first years of Philip's reign, however, not even Demosthenes' keen eye would appear to have discerned the peril threatening from this young power of the north. In his earliest speeches upon foreign policy no mention is made of Macedon ; and it seems clear that, like other Athenians, he was lulled into a sense of false security by the absence of any direct threat to Greece. For after the seizure of Pydna and Potidaea, Philip had waited, contenting himself merely with a campaign in Thrace and the capture of Methonê, the last Athenian seaport on the borders of his realm. He was an adept at waiting ; and sure enough the chance of meddling further in the affairs of Greece soon came. In 356 there had occurred north of the Isthmus an event in itself sufficiently extraordinary, but by no means out of keeping with this

---

[1] It is probable that Isocrates' views were to some extent those of Xenophon also, whose leading idea seems to have been to show that the Persian Empire was the natural enemy of Greece, and its conquest the national duty.

Iconoclastic age. The Phocians had seized the sanctuary of Apollo at Delphi. This monstrous deed of sacrilege had its origin in this wise. The Amphictyonic League —an inter-tribal union of great antiquity, but in the past of merely religious significance—had recently been revived for her own political purposes by Thebes ; and through the instrument of its authority Thebes had further proceeded to bully her neighbours the Phocians. Threatened with confiscation of land for some religious misdemeanour, they had stiffened their backs ; and one of their number, named Philomelus, had proposed as a counterblast to assert their old claim to the shrine of Apollo. The coup presented small difficulty. A fund was raised. Mercenaries were hired ; and Delphi was occupied. But once possession was achieved, the Phocians began to realize that there was only one real method of maintaining it. The god's immense treasure lay ready to their hand, and what easier than to use it ? Desperate from fear of Thebes, they began at first ostensibly to ' borrow ' ; then, dropping such pretences, to mint the gold into money ; it goes perhaps without saying that the use to which they put it was the recruitment of a formidable army of highly paid mercenaries. In due time they were attacked by Thebes, and on the slopes of Parnassus suffered a serious defeat, in the course of which Philomelus, their leader, being driven to the edge of a precipice, refused capture and hurled himself over. But Onomarchus, his colleague, stepped into his shoes, reorganized and enlarged the still formidable army, and began audaciously to terrorize the inhabitants of the surrounding districts. He soon had Locris, Doris, Orchomenus and even Thermopylae under his heel. The seizure of this valuable pass gave him access to Thessaly ; and there he proceeded to strike up an alliance with Lycophron, prince of Pherae. Thessaly was, as usual, distracted by feuds. Lycophron had his enemies in the rival princes of Larissa ; and these, seeing him reinforced by his new Phocian allies, resolved not to be outdone. Without further hesitation they invited Philip of Macedon to assist them.

Knowing as we do with what far-sighted deliberation Philip's ambitions were calculated, we can readily picture the eager satisfaction with which he hailed this chance to set his army marching down the southward road. What must have pleased him even better was to be coming in the guise of a champion to uphold the insulted cause of the Greeks' own deity against a set of sacrilegious marauders. The assumption of that rôle suited his book to perfection, and he preached the religious crusade to his men. Nevertheless his first serious contact with Greek hoplites was far from reassuring. After an initial success he was met and defeated by the superior numbers of Onomarchus' mercenary army. His own hired soldiers even threatened to desert him and he was forced to retire —but only, as he told them, 'after the manner of a ram to butt harder next time'. He was as good as his word. In 352 he descended again into Thessaly, and, in the Battle of the Crocus Fields, drove back the Phocian army to the sea, where many were drowned in an attempt to swim for safety.[1] Three thousand who were taken prisoners were slaughtered in cold blood, and the dead body of Onomarchus—slain in all probability by his own disgruntled followers—was brutally impaled. The fruits of the victory it remained for Philip to gather. He captured Pherae and the South Thessalian port of Pagasae ; and by the autumn he began to turn his steps towards Thermopylae. But the wonder of wonders had happened. The Athenians were at last aroused. The loss of Methonê had opened their eyes, and now that they saw Philip, like another Xerxes, bearing down with his host upon the confines of Greece proper, they acted like men and moved north to Thermopylae. When Philip learnt that the narrow pass—the only direct route between Thessaly and Phocis—was held by Athenian soldiers, he discreetly withdrew. Contenting himself with consolidating his gains in Thessaly, he resolved once more

[1] In this battle Philip's use of cavalry to roll up the Phocian left marked an important tactical advance. For here his horse was used for actual attack rather than for mere envelopment.

to lie low and bide his chance. So again the curtain falls, and for three years little is heard of him.

At Athens in the meantime the expected had happened. After Philip's retirement the old sense of false security had returned. The bold mood which had carried the citizen army to Thermopylae gave way to complacent inaction. The peril, in a word, was forgotten—but not by Demosthenes. In 351, while still a freelance orator and without official standing, he delivered the earliest of his tremendous orations, denouncing Philip as the common enemy of Greece and calling on his countrymen to arouse themselves and prepare while yet there might be time. In his first ' Philippic ' he struck at once the note on which he was to play with tireless reiteration throughout the succeeding years. The Athenians must rise to the occasion, shake off their comfortable habits, and be ready to fight, not with the futile make-believe of debate and diplomacy, but in real and deadly earnest, serving in the ranks themselves, not leaving all to hirelings. ' As for Philip,' he said, ' conquests already won are not enough for him. Every day the circle of his ambition widens ; and while we sit complacently with folded hands, he spins his web around us. When, O men of Athens, will you turn and do your duty ? For what is it you are waiting ? For something to compel you ? As though humiliation, as we experience it to-day, were not the most compelling force known to a free man. Or have you indeed naught better to do than to stroll around asking the news ? Athenians enslaved and Greece manipulated by a man of Macedon—is that not news ; Philip is dead, say they ? Or not yet dead, but sick ? Dead or sick, it makes little odds to you. For should an end be made of him, you would soon erect another Philip for yourselves.' On Athens' military methods he poured a withering scorn. A skilful strategist, so he declared, will direct events, not wait upon them. Watch a barbarian at his boxing. ' When struck, he fumbles to the place where the blow fell. Strike him elsewhere, there go his hands again. Face up to his opponent or parry properly he neither will nor

can. So, if the Athenians will but march, the campaign
will itself disclose the weak points in Philip's armour.
He is their mortal enemy. For years past he has put
them to scorn. What they have trusted others to do for
them has always gone amiss. What remains must depend
upon themselves alone ; and, unless they choose to fight
Philip upon some foreign field, the day may well come
when they must fight him upon Attic soil itself.'

It was not long before the chance came for the Athenians
to translate into action Demosthenes' advice. When the
curtain is again raised in 349, Philip has thrown off the
mask and attacked the Chalcidic Confederacy. Olynthus
sent frantic messages for help to Athens. Demosthenes
pleaded for the diversion of the Theoric Fund to military
purposes and for the dispatch of a citizen army to the
north. But his was merely a voice crying in the wilderness.
He held as yet no official position, and his warnings fell
once again on deaf ears. The Theoric Fund was not
touched ; and the only force sent were some mercenary
troops under Chares. The revolt of Euboea—a well-
timed diversion due to Philip's intrigues—effectually
prevented further reinforcements ; and Chares, when he
reached Chalcidice, made his presence a doubtful boon,
plundering the allies in true *condottiere* fashion to make
good arrears of pay. One by one in pitiful succession the
towns of the League succumbed. By the summer of 348
it was the Olynthians' turn. In a curt ultimatum Philip
told them that either they must quit their city or he
Macedon, and promptly laid it under siege. Too late
the Athenians took alarm at last and dispatched a force
of citizens. The winds were contrary and they never
reached their goal. Philip in the meanwhile was closing
in. He had paid agents in this as in most other cities
—did he not boast that with a mule-load of silver he could
win past any gates ?—and the traitors' dirty work was
soon done. Once in possession, he determined to make of
Olynthus a terrible example ; and the news of her fate
sent a shudder through the entire Hellenic world. The
inhabitants, ten thousand in number, were all sold as

slaves. The city itself, together with its thirty-two confederates, was laid level with the ground. Seven years later, Demosthenes assures us, no man could so much as trace their site.[1] Henceforward at any rate Greece knew clearly with what manner of foe she had to deal.

All the more does the aftermath of Olynthus' fall come upon us with something of a shock. Philip was back at home in the winter of that year and not ill content with the triumphs it had brought him, when there were presented for audience at his court in Pella a party of ten Athenian politicians. Philocrates was the author and leader of the mission : and among his colleagues were Aeschines, the ex-actor and future rival of Demosthenes, and, singularly enough, Demosthenes himself, inconsistent no doubt with his own strongly expressed principles, but a little flattered perhaps to receive official rank at last and perhaps honestly convinced that the best must now be made of a bad job. For the purpose of the ambassadors was to open negotiations. Their country was heartily sick with the unending state of war, dating, nominally at least, from the seizure of Potidaea ten years back. An attempt to rally the other states against the common menace had proved a dismal failure, though Aeschines himself had stumped the Peloponnese. Peace seemed the sole alternative ; and the instructions of the ten ambassadors were to inquire what Philip's terms might be. The series of harangues which they delivered in his presence were not a great success ; and even Demosthenes, though he had bragged of having ' a good sound cart-rope to stop Philip's mouth with ', stuttered and broke down when the time came. Nevertheless Philip was himself all courtesy. He entertained the envoys with lavish hospitality, loaded them with gifts, flattered them into an agreeable opinion of his benevolence, and then sent them home with the somewhat one-sided but not unreasonable proposition that either side should keep what it had. This

---

[1] It is probable, however, that this was a rhetorical exaggeration and that Olynthus alone was made an example, the rest merely losing their political independence.

done, he disappeared into the north; and, while the ten ambassadors, now duly authorized to undertake another mission for the final ratification of the terms, were awaiting him at Pella to administer the oath, he for his part was still busily engaged in extending his Thracian conquests towards the Hellespontine districts and adding fort after fort [1] to the already lengthy list of captures, which, the treaty once ratified, would be permanently recognized as his. Such a piece of sharp practice should at least have put the envoys on their guard. But it was not the last. In the course of the negotiations the Athenians had more than once requested Philip to include their friends the Phocians within the treaty's scope; and Philip had replied evasively. Thebes, he said, was his real enemy (welcome news to the Athenians!), and as for the Phocians, there was not the smallest need to include them in the treaty, for he meant them no harm in the world.

The hypocrisy of these professions would appear to have been wholly lost upon the envoys, as was equally the motive of his deliberate procrastination in the taking of the oath. For he would not take it at Pella; but, escorting them in his train, proceeded to march with his army down through Thessaly, and not till he was well within easy striking distance of his intended victims did he finally consent to ratify. The Athenian ambassadors departed complacently satisfied that all was well, but they had not as yet reached home when the startling news arrived that Philip had passed Thermopylae. Phalaecus, who now commanded the Phocian mercenaries, but was quarrelling with the Phocian Government, had sold the defile,[2] and the wretched people whom Philip had professed to wish so well were abandoned defenceless to their fate. Phocis was given up to fire and sword. Its

---

[1] These conquests were made at the expense of Cersobleptes, King of Thrace. But they were near enough to Athens' Hellespontine dependencies to make her feel uncomfortable.

[2] As a matter of fact, Phalaecus had little choice. His treasury was now exhausted. Athens had deserted him; and unless he had given up the defile, his mercenaries would either have melted away or sold *him* to Philip.

townships were laid in ruins; its inhabitants dispersed
among scattered villages; and their future fortunes left
in the hands of Thebes. By the enemies of Phocis Philip's
action was applauded to the skies. As a reward for his
vindication of Apollo's cause he was given the seat on
the Amphictyonic Council left vacant by the profaners
of the Delphic shrine; and—a still more signal honour
—he presided a few months later over the famous Pythian
Festival, then due to be held within its precincts. On
Athens the downfall of Phocis left a very deep and very
different impression. The citizens were bitterly conscious
of the failure of their diplomacy. Recriminations between
the duped ambassadors made fine matter for debate;
but they could not undo past history. Philip had now
succeeded in planting his foot firmly in the very heart
of Greece, and it was unlikely in the extreme that he
would soon withdraw it.

From Phocis to Athens was not more perhaps than
twenty or thirty hours' marching; and Philip could have
appeared before the gates of Athens any day he pleased.
He was now beyond all question the strongest military
power in the Greek peninsula. He had paid agents and
supporters in wellnigh every town and troops in many.
His intrigues had given him a strong footing even within
the Peloponnese. The Arcadians erected his statue in
bronze. Argos voted him a golden crown. Athens almost
alone remained recalcitrant, even surlily demurring to
sending her representatives to the celebration of the
Pythian Games. Yet so far from retaliating, Philip proceeded to woo her like a wayward mistress, sending
ambassadors and letters to expostulate against the campaign of misrepresentation and calumny with which he
was assailed, repeating his professions of friendship;
and striving by every means in his power to soothe her
fears. Whatever was his motive—and we can scarcely
doubt that it was a heartfelt homage to her intellectual
culture—he clearly wished to win Athens, if possible,
by sympathy rather than force, and he was prepared, as
usual, to wait. For his was no narrow ambition, and

other schemes were revolving in his active brain. He
was beginning even at this date to entertain dreams of
Oriental conquest, and meanwhile he was content to occupy
his energies in other fields than Greece. During 345,
and afterwards for the five succeeding years, he did not
appear, so far as we know, on the south side of Thermopylae.
He went campaigning in Epirus and perhaps reached the
Adriatic. Then he turned northward to an ambitious
scheme of conquest which kept him through bitter winter
in the wilds of Upper Thrace. Here, however, he was
treading once more upon delicate ground ; for among
the overseas possessions which Athens still most dearly
cherished was the adjacent peninsula of the Thracian
Chersonese, guarding the vital entrance to the Hellespontine trade-route. Philip, in fact, was asking for trouble.

Nor in her present mood was it in the least degree likely
that such a menace would be overlooked by Athens. The
peace of Philocrates had not allayed the suspicions of
Demosthenes. On the contrary, it led to a redoubling of
his energies and to a manifest increase of his popularity.
Disclaiming his own responsibility in the ill-starred negotiations, he rounded on the colleagues who had accompanied
him to Pella. It must have been partly his work that
Philocrates, as the author of the mission, was hounded
from the city. Against Aeschines, as Philip's chief dupe,
he proceeded with impeachment. The conduct of the trial
brought him no real credit. The charge of accepting
Macedonian money which he freely levelled, he was unable
to substantiate ; and after much mud-slinging between the
two great orators, Aeschines was acquitted. Meanwhile,
as the now recognized spokesman of the Athenian people,
Demosthenes had been moving heaven and earth to rally
opposition against the common enemy of Greece. When
an embassy of protest came from Macedon, he answered it
by delivering the second of his great ' Philippics ', a
masterpiece of invective as bitter as it was brilliant. In
342 he toured the Peloponnese in a somewhat fruitless
effort to form a Panhellenic League of resistance. Under
his influence Phocion was sent over to Euboea, where he

succeeded in expelling Philip's partisans. Under his influence, too, an envoy went up to Susa to give the Great King warning of Philip's dangerous projects. Athens, in short, was on her part also working up for trouble ; and so far from serving to conciliate her feelings Philip's patient forbearance seemed merely to embolden her. Men came actually to believe that fear, and not benevolence, was the true cause of his pacific policy ; and when finally the imagined threat to her precious Chersonese began seriously to agitate the public mind, Demosthenes was allowed to take ship to the Bosphorus, and there endeavour to persuade Byzantium into making an open stand. Recent as was her defection from the Athenian League, Byzantium was found ready to forget past differences and fall in with the proposal. Prevailing on her neighbour Perinthus to join with her, she declared for war against Macedon. Almost simultaneously the pillar which stood in Athens, engraved with the terms of Philocrates' Peace, was officially removed from its place. Philip's patience must have been strained very near to breaking-point. Nevertheless it was the cities of the Bosphorus and not Athens which were now to feel his hand.

The campaign which followed was a notable example of Macedonian siege-craft, forerunner of Alexander's still more celebrated beleaguerment of Tyre. Both Byzantium and Perinthus were strongly fortified, Perinthus in particular standing out to sea on a rocky eminence and connected with the land by only a narrow spit across which had been constructed at least two defensive lines. To starve out Perinthus was impracticable since the Persian satraps, having received instructions to make things hot for Philip, were ready enough to provision it by sea. Philip was, therefore, compelled to a direct assault, and he brought to bear upon the town's defences every imaginable weapon of engineering science. Huge wooden towers, a hundred and twenty feet high, were wheeled against the walls. Sappers and battering-rams were set to work at undermining their foundations. Catapults kept up a continuous bombardment. The two external lines of defence were thus carried, and though their rock fortress was wellnigh impregnable, the besieged were now hard put to it. Strong storming parties, attacking by day and night, kept them at constant tension; and their spirits were beginning to flag when after three months of operations Philip suddenly called off the siege and swooped upon Byzantium. But here again he was countered by a resistance no less obstinate. An Athenian squadron, commanded first by Chares and then by Phocion, routed his fleet, and, blocking the southward passage through the Bosphorus, kept it pinned in the Black Sea. Realizing his failure—the most serious rebuff perhaps of his entire career—Philip decided on retreat. He threw Phocion off the scent by causing a bogus message to fall into his hands, extricated his fleet, marched off his army and threw himself with undiminished energy into an entirely new campaign against the Scythians. He killed their King and took enormous booty of female slaves and live-stock; but in the course of his march home he had an unpleasant brush with some wild Balkan tribesmen and was wounded in the thigh. He retired to Pella to nurse a gangrened limb. It was the early spring of 339.

And now, like a bad penny, the Amphictyonic Council turn up again, quarrelling amongst themselves as usual, and ready over a trifle to give Philip his crowning chance. And so, as the curtain rises upon the final act of Greece's tragedy, it opens with something very like a farce. The quarrel began as follows. A year or two earlier the Athenians had refurbished and set up afresh at Delphi a set of shields captured long ago at Plataea in the great Invasion and engraved with the inscription ' *Taken from the Persians and Thebans when they fought together against the Greeks.*' This offensive reminder of Thebes' discreditable past was not a tactful gesture. There was little love lost between the two rival cities; and some sort of retaliation was only to be expected. At the Amphictyonic Council, held late in 340, a certain Locrian of Amphissa, acting, we may be certain, as the tool of Thebes, was to propose a fine of fifty talents upon Athens. It was a dramatic moment when Aeschines, the Athenian representative, arose to make his speech. By a brilliant twist of argument he shifted the whole ground of the debate, and turned the tables completely on Amphissa by denouncing her instead for the sacrilegious cultivation of some consecrated soil in the plain-land below Delphi. The Amphictyonic Council were transported by his eloquence, and next day they descended, with picks and mattocks in hand, to make havoc of the impious defilement. The Amphissans came out at them, and beat them off; and by this further outrage against the sacred councillors added a fresh count to their guilt. Early in 339 a second Congress was held—this time at Thermopylae. War was declared against the offending party; and, since other states held back from undertaking operations, it was subsequently decided to entrust Philip with the task.

Philip at once marched south and took up his position near the junction of the two roads, which led, one of them towards Delphi and Amphissa, and the other towards Thebes. Greece watched for his next move with breathless anxiety; and what was their consternation when Philip took not the road for Delphi but the road for Thebes. It could mean nothing else but a declaration of war; and when the news reached Athens that he had occupied Elatea, there was a scene of indescribable panic. Some ran, Demosthenes tells us, to drive the hucksters from the market, some set fire to the wicker booths which lined it, trumpeters were sent through the streets sounding the alarm, a few more practical spirits hurried to the Generals' houses to knock them up and bid them summon a meeting. At the next day's assembly, hastily summoned at dawn, Demosthenes alone dared face the crisis. Now and henceforward he was supreme in Athens. And he had his way. The Theoric Fund was at last converted to a war-chest. Troops were made ready for marching. And, above all, Demosthenes was commissioned to go himself to Thebes and there, if possible, to persuade her inveterate rival to forget the past and make common cause with Athens. He succeeded, and together the combined

Theban and Athenian armies proceeded to block the passes between Elatea and the south.

Philip, however, appeared to be in little hurry. He was taking no risks and preferred to await further reinforcements. Perhaps, too, he had some hopes that by intrigue or otherwise he might induce some change of heart in his opponents. All through the summer of 338 there was no movement. Then at last in early autumn Philip struck. By the aid of another bogus letter he threw off its guard the garrison of one pass, and, fetching a circuit through Amphissa, outflanked the main Greek force which held the other. It fell back on Chaeronea, and in the neighbourhood of that city took place the decisive battle in which the fortunes of the City-State went down for ever. Against the Athenians, who held the left Greek wing, Philip employed the stratagem of a pretended flight. Crying ' On to Macedonia ', the excited citizens rushed forward in eager pursuit only to find themselves trapped ; and Philip soon had them running in the opposite direction —Demosthenes along with the rest. On the Greek right the Thebans, against whom Alexander—now a youth of sixteen—was pitted, put up a sterner resistance. The Sacred Band went down fighting till not one was left alive. But it was only a matter of time. Philip's victory was complete. That evening he celebrated his triumph in a disgusting orgy from which, as night wore on, he reeled out drunk on to the field of battle, and there as he danced among the corpses of his enemies, he chanted over and over again in tones of bibulous mockery the words ' Demosthenes, Demosthenes, son of the Paeanian deme '. It was the opening preamble of the great orator's decrees which had served so long to baulk him of his hopes ; but, Demosthenes or no Demosthenes, Athens was at his mercy now and it remained only to be seen how he would use her.

Despite all his frustrated efforts and her continuous refusals, the charms of Athens still seemed to exercise their spell on Philip. Perhaps even now his experience at Perinthus gave him warning of what Greeks behind strong walls were capable of doing; and he stayed his hand. To the Athenians' own surprise they were given generous terms—immunity from invasion, the retention of a few Aegean islands, and freedom to trade at sea. But though the citizens still continued to conduct their own affairs and under the efficient administration of Demosthenes and Lycurgus resumed their lives of security and comfort, the true glory had departed, and never again could Athens hope proudly to raise her head or feel herself the free city she had been. For Philip was master now, albeit a lenient master; and throughout the rest of Greece he was meanwhile proceeding to impose his will.

Thebes, who had been his ally against Phocis and who he felt had played him false, paid dearly for Chaeronea. The citizens taken on the field of battle were sold as slaves. The anti-Macedonian party were exiled. A garrison was posted on the Citadel. All Northern Greece was secured by similar garrisons placed at strategic points; and in the Peloponnese, Sparta alone, though she had her country ravaged, refused to bow before the conqueror. Towards the end of 338 Philip convened at Corinth a Congress of representatives from all the cities; and by the statesmanlike machinery of federal union which he there imposed upon them, he gave to Greece at last the cohesion so long lacking. In this Pan-Hellenic League, of which Philip was of course to be the controlling head and the military commander, each state was to be allowed the management of its own affairs and was prohibited from interference with its neighbours. No tribute was to be exacted; and apart from the garrisoning of the strategic points—notably Thermopylae, Chalcis, Thebes and Corinth—no military occupation was enforced. A federal Council was to control the League's affairs, and what was still more important, at the first meeting of that Council in 337 a project was announced which might better than all else avail to weld the states together in the united service of a common cause. For now it was that Philip made public declaration of his intended campaign against Persia; and then and there by an enthusiastic vote arrangements were set on foot for the provision of ships and men to join the great adventure.

The adventure was made ; but it was not Philip who made it. He was home that year in Macedon when in the midst of his preparations for the coming campaign an ugly quarrel broke out within his family. The beautiful Olympias, mother of Alexander, was not the only woman Philip had wedded. Six or seven other wives he is known to have had, and he now proposed to take another, the niece of his general Attalus. At the celebrations which followed the wedding he sneeringly remarked over his wine that he hoped his new consort would present him with a ' legitimate heir '. Stung by the ill-founded insult, Alexander flung a goblet which struck Attalus in the face. Philip started up sword in hand and made for his son, then reeled and fell—for he had been drinking heavily— and it was now Alexander's turn to sneer at the man who ' talked of crossing from Europe to Asia, and yet could not even steer his way from couch to couch '. After this incident the feeling between father and son was so bitter that Alexander left the court ; and Olympias, who accompanied him, set herself to study revenge. Next summer (336) on the eve of his departure for the East, Philip was celebrating another wedding between his daughter Cleopatra and an Epirot prince. It was an occasion of great pomp. Philip's statue, surrounded by images of the twelve chief gods of Greece, was carried in procession to the theatre. The King himself, to advertise his confidence in the populace, was walking somewhat ahead of his bodyguard, when suddenly a man rushed forward and plunged a dagger into his side. The assassin was caught and killed without confession ; but there is little doubt that he was an agent of Olympias. Thus by the mother's bloody vengeance the son, who was indirectly the cause of the tragedy, succeeded to the dead father's throne ; and at the age of twenty, Alexander, the most ambitious perhaps of all the world's great conquerors, inherited both the power and the opportunity to translate his ambition into fact.

But he inherited something more than a mere instrument of conquest, for to Philip, above all, he owed it that he was accepted by the Greeks as a Greek, and that he was thus enabled to carry with him and transplant into the East the vital spark and inspiration of Hellenic culture. To such a consummation nothing but the long years of patient, undiscouraged effort which we have traced above could possibly have brought a King of Macedon. When we recall what manner of kingdom Philip had inherited —the gross, uncultured habits of its people, the complete absence of any honourable tradition, the contempt in which it was held by its Greek neighbours—we cannot but feel astounded at the extraordinary genius of the man. By nature headstrong, impulsive, prone to notorious vices, and shrinking from no risk when adventure thrilled his blood, Philip yet knew how to curb and discipline his feelings, so that by the slow and subtle patience of his diplomatic opportunism he achieved what no forthright exertion of physical force could ever have won for him. Above all, beneath the more unlovely aspects of his character, the treachery, the lies, the often brutal treatment of his enemies, we can discern a vein of true idealism ; and in the ultimate issue the idealism triumphed in his life. Philip's real aims were doubtless bred of personal ambition, but it was an ambition which demanded a persistent effort to raise both himself and his cause on to a higher and nobler plane. In the midst of his drunken orgy on the field of Chaeronea a disgusted Greek observer had remarked to him that the man who was cast for Agamemnon's rôle should not play the part of the buffoon Thersites ; and Philip, taking the hint, broke off his riot. The story goes far to show that his ambition was not a self-indulgent, but an exacting one. It demanded not merely that he should conquer Greeks, but that he should be worthy to be their leader. Now, though to be Greek was not by any means to be good ; yet, in the world as Philip knew it, Hellenism unquestionably represented the highest standard of what a man should be ; and it must stand to his lasting credit that he not merely acknowledged that standard as his life's ideal, but strove by life-long persistence to achieve it. If posterity owes much to Philip's son, it owes also a debt—and no small debt—to the father who bequeathed to Alexander an ideal so high, who set him his task and who equipped him with both the power and the training to accomplish what is perhaps (if we except Rome) the greatest cultural conquest in the world's history.

CHAPTER XVIII

ALEXANDER AND GREECE

ALEXANDER was twenty years old when he ascended the throne of Macedon and inherited the task, which now inevitably accompanied it, of invading the East. At an age when many English boys have barely left school he felt himself fully equal to the double burden thus imposed on him; and indeed, though Alexander never suffered from modesty, he had good grounds for his confidence. Nature had endowed him liberally, and more than liberally, with almost every quality which makes for success in life. He was extraordinarily handsome. His smooth, fair skin, generously modelled features, large fiery liquid eyes, full chin and sensuous mouth were so admired by antiquity that generations of sculptors assimilated their type to his model. He had the physique of an athlete; but, though his father would have entered him for the Olympic foot-race, he himself cared little for field-sports. Hunting was his chief pastime; and he early made a name for daring horsemanship by breaking Bucephalus, the unmanageable Thessalian steed. In character he was of a passionate, emotional temperament, given like his father to banquet and carouse; but, like his father too, he was normally able to hold his impulses under an iron control, so that by the ancients he was taken as the pattern of an almost ascetic purity of life. Everything, in fact, throughout Alexander's career was strictly subordinated to the end he had in view. For the flame of his idealism burnt strong. He was passionately addicted to reading poetry, and kept a copy of the *Iliad* always beneath his pillow; and so steeped was he in Homeric mythology that he had come to view himself as a sort of superman or hero, made, like

357

his favourite character Achilles, of finer stuff than ordinary folk. So, since early boyhood he was conscious of a mission in the world, and his mother had done her best to encourage the belief. His natural abilities were extreme, and under the guidance of the great Aristotle, who for three years became his tutor, these were developed to the full. From such training he acquired not merely a strong bent for systematic organization, but a real love of knowledge for its own sake. With boyish precocity he had been impatient to probe the deepest mysteries of philosophy, before he had well mastered its elements ; and throughout his life he continued to take a keen interest in botany, zoology and other sciences. Adventure, whether in the field of intellectual study or amongst the limitless deserts of the East, was, in fact, the mainspring of Alexander's whole personality ; and such was his natural capacity for leadership that he imparted his zeal to others and could inspire his soldiers with the same unbounded belief in his star that he himself possessed. Greek mercenaries, whose fathers had grumbled at Cyrus when he proposed to lead them beyond the bounds of Asia Minor, were found ready to follow Alexander past the ranges of the Hindu Kush or through the wilds of Turkestan. His men loved with a sort of awed wonder this headstrong, high-spirited, imperious youth who moved among them as at once their darling and their dreaded commander, now handling them with the skill of a veteran strategist, now striding foot to foot with them in a forced march or riding at their head in some impetuous charge, but always exacting from them the same full measure of courage and exertion that he himself invariably displayed.

To the Greek people, when they came at length to know more of him, the personality of Alexander could hardly fail to make its appeal. He had all the qualities they most admired—physical perfection, intellectual ardour and the spirit of enterprise. Nevertheless his early relations with his Hellenic subjects were none too happy. Philip's death had been the signal for a simultaneous rising of all his subject provinces. Thrace, Illyria and Thessaly were up in a moment, and in Greece there was a rush to arms. Thebes attempted to expel its garrison. Demosthenes passed a decree in honour of Philip's murderer. Within a few weeks Alexander had shown, by a quick grasp and handling of the situation which not even his father could equal, that he would stand no trifling. Greece he knew must at all cost be salved ; for it was as her representative and champion that he meant to march into the East. He struck down with lightning rapidity. The Thessalians had occupied Tempê ; but he forced an entirely new route along the coast, where his engineers cut a rock-path on the steep cliff of Mount Ossa, and appeared in the plain at their rear. Thessaly, lying thus at his mercy, capitulated. Another lightning march and he was at Thermopylae, where the Amphictyonic Council tendered its submission. Athens was by now sending an embassy for peace, and the Pan-Hellenic Congress, welcoming him with apparent enthusiasm, elected him as their country's leader against the Persian foe.

Greece being thus secured, Alexander turned north to Thrace—a region which he could ill afford to leave disaffected in his rear when he should come to enter Asia. The campaign was remarkable both for the characteristic audacity of his advance—in which he far surpassed the more tentative Philip—and equally for the ingenuity of his tactics. At one point his army was threatened by a regular avalanche of war chariots which the tribesmen were preparing to roll downhill upon them. Alexander told his men to go down on their knees, place shields on back, and let the cars run over them. The ruse succeeded, and not a man was killed. When he reached the river Danube, he determined to cross, but lacked vessels to transport adequate troops. He at once collected native fisherman's canoes, and with the aid of cables succeeded in passing his army over in a night. Having put a wholesome fear into the Thracians—for he attempted no actual addition to his father's conquests—he turned against the Illyrians, who by now were threatening Macedon. He was fresh from a bloody victory over these northern foes, when bad news came in from the south. A rumour had been put about in Greece that he was dead. Demosthenes actually produced a man who had seen him fall. Egged on by Athens, Thebes arose in arms. Two Macedonian officers were murdered, and the garrison on the Cadmeia besieged. Then, when the rebels least expected it, Alexander himself appeared ; and this time Thebes' punishment was terrible. The sack which followed a fierce assault accounted for six thousand lives. The remainder of the inhabitants were sold into slavery. Their land was distributed among their old enemies ; and, though with a characteristic zeal for letters, Alexander caused the house of the poet Pindar to be spared, the entire city was otherwise levelled with the dust. Cowed by the fate of Thebes, Athens grovelled to the conqueror, and once again Alexander was merciful. His original demand for the surrender of Lycurgus, Demosthenes and other agitators, he eventually withdrew ; and once again peace reigned.

The master's whip had cracked, and Greece knew now, if not before, that her true liberty had vanished. When in the following year Alexander quitted Europe, to which he was never destined to return, his undertaking was followed with mixed feelings. The military aid, which in the enthusiasm of the moment had been voted by the Congress of Corinth, did not amount to much ; and a hope still lurked that he might fail in his enterprise and perish. In 331 Sparta, irreconcilable as ever, headed a forlorn revolt of Peloponnesian States ; but it was soon crushed by Antipater, left behind as Alexander's vice-gerent in Macedon. For the rest Greece remained tranquil. Athens, prospering once again under the able administration of Lycurgus, saw the wisdom of a waiting policy, and even Demosthenes urged discretion. Meanwhile, as Alexander's conquests grew, the magic of his romantic progress began to catch Greek fancies. Men poured out by tens of thousands to share in the pickings of his triumph and to find careers in the new lands whose wealth and resources sounded almost fabulous. It was not until the last year of his life that Alexander became once more a source of direct offence to his European subjects. In 324, when his conquests were complete and the accumulation of mercenaries and other Greek adventurers was becoming a source of awkward embarrassment, he announced his intention of repatriating all political exiles. To Athens this meant the reinstatement of the Samians whom she had evicted from their homes and the exappropriation of her own citizen settlers ; and she felt a strong objection. At the very moment, too, an incident occurred which brought a sore temptation to her patience. A certain Harpalus, kinsman to Alexander and by him entrusted with the care of the chief treasure captured in the East, had decamped with a large sum of money, and now appeared off the coast of Attica, proposing to lead a revolt. The Athenians, despite their grievance against Alexander, acted charily, arresting Harpalus and depositing his treasure of seven hundred talents on the Acropolis. By and by it was discovered, however, that half of the sum was missing. Demosthenes, who had been appointed one of the custodians, was convicted of having taken twenty talents—for political purposes, no doubt ; he was imprisoned and then escaped into exile. He was destined, however, to assist in striking one last blow for Greece. In 323, when the news of Alexander's death reached Athens, she at once raised the standard of revolt. Many states joined her. Demosthenes was recalled ; and for a while affairs looked promising. The Confederate army marched into Thessaly, but after some initial success was defeated by Antipater at Crannon. From sheer disunion—that traditional curse of Greek politics—the cause then went to pieces ; and the states were severally reduced. Athens was severely treated ; for Antipater did not share Alexander's tenderness for culture. Her democracy was limited by a property franchise. A garrison was installed at Munychia ; and last, but not least, the anti-Macedonian agitators were to be given up—Demosthenes among them. The unhappy man fled to Poseidon's temple on the island of Calauria. When the soldiers sent in search of him arrived at the place, they found he had retired inside the sanctuary and there sat down to write. As he wrote he sucked his pen ; and when they entered, he staggered to his feet and fell dead upon the altar. The pen—so tradition says—was poisoned. Thus, with the final extinction of his country's liberty, perished also the man whose whole life had been devoted to its preservation. With the history of Athens and of European Greece we shall henceforward have little concern. A wider Hellas unfolds for the historian ; and wider issues will now chiefly occupy our thoughts. For during the dozen years which elapsed between the sack of Thebes in 335 and his own death in 323 Alexander conquered the East.

CHAPTER XIX

THE CITY-STATE AND ITS LEGACY

THE brief life-work of Alexander had, in relation to the Greeks, two main results. First, though he treated them on the whole with liberal sympathy, yet by his swift and terrible punishment of rebel Thebes he proved, as has been said, that all real hope of regaining their liberty was gone. There would be no true revival of their treasured independence.[1] But their Culture—and this was Alexander's second and most genuine achievement—was to be spread throughout the East and given permanent root in the lands of the Levant. Thus, as the spirit of Hellas itself decayed, it found a new life and a wider scope elsewhere, transforming the face of history and giving to the eastern half of the Mediterranean world a character which for hundreds of years was destined to distinguish it in sharp contrast from the western half. But, before we turn to tell the story of Alexander's conquests and of the civilizing influences they carried with them, we may well pause to survey for the last time the city from which in the main those influences sprang.

I. LIFE AT ATHENS

To say our farewell to Athens, we can hardly do better than mount her Citadel and, passing under the stately Portico which guards the entrance to its summit, take up our stand where the Parthenon, Erechtheum, and

---

[1] As will be seen later, the Greeks after Alexander's death were able to enjoy for considerable periods a precarious independence, but the shadow of Macedonian power always hung over them and a free foreign policy was rendered virtually impossible.

Phidias' bronze colossus of Athena still rise in silent witness of the proud days now gone by.[1] If we turn to the southward side of the Acropolis we shall find little there which will detain us long—the precinct of Asclepius, god of medicine, straggling along its slope, and, flanking this again, the rock-scooped semicircle of the Theatre from which, beyond the stage, the eye may travel over four miles of level country to the sea, where on the right jut forward the rock harbours of Peiraeus with Salamis behind, and on the left stand up the blue outlines of Aegina and the distant mountains of the Argolid. A furlong or so from the Theatre still stand the remains of the great Temple, begun by Pisistratus and never finished[2]; but there is little else. For the houses have not as yet much spread this way and it is upon the Acropolis' north side that the town proper lies. Upon our left, as we pass to this other side and look down over the cliff, sprawls out a fringe of low rock hillocks. The nearest, a spur of the Acropolis itself, is the Areopagus, where still meets for murder trials the ancient Council that in bygone days controlled the destinies of Athens. Beyond this, across the valley, stands the Pnyx hill from whose rock-hewn platform a long line of famous orators have swayed the Assembly with their rhetoric. Further away and on our right rises the gaunt cone of Lycabettus, too steep a hill for building or other practical uses and barely so much as mentioned in Attic literature. In the level ground, flanked roughly by these hills, nestles the wide semicircle of the town itself—a huddle of low, single storied houses, divided by a network of narrow, winding streets. These lead for the most part (though there is no ordered plan) to where close underneath the Acropolis' sheer descent, spreads out the Market-place—a broad and open square round which are ranged the most important buildings of the city's public life. At the near end is the circular Tholos where the Council of Five Hundred sleeps and

---

[1] The scene here depicted refers of course to the time of Alexander. The bronze colossus was transported to Constantinople.

[2] It was rebuilt later by the Emperor Hadrian.

dines, and the Council Chamber where its debates are held. Flanking the square upon the right is a line of pillared porticoes—above all the ' Painted Stoa ' adorned with famous frescoes by the painter Polygnotus, amongst them the Battle of Marathon and the Sack of Troy. Upon the left are the offices of the King Archon, still the high-priest of Athens, before which on graven tablets are set for public inspection the laws that govern the town. Of other halls and temples, of the statues that surround them, or of the stately avenues by which many are approached, there is no room here to speak ; nor is it an easy matter, from the shattered remnants that remain of some and the bare historic records that alone tell us of others, to recon-struct and call up before the eye the true artistic splendour and perfection of Athens at her prime.

In such an environment, rich in memories of the past and full of the eager stir of present business, the Athenian citizen spent his life. It was essentially an open-air life. For in a climate little subject to extremes of cold and marred only by rare bursts of stormy downpour, all public business—political assemblies, theatrical perfor-mances and even judicial trials—could safely be held under the friendly sky. So the Athenian citizen was little within doors except for sleep and meal-times. He went in all weathers clad in two simple woollen garments—a loose shirt or *chitón* hanging to the knee and a heavier cloak which, if need were, would envelop the whole person. Folk who affected a Spartan austerity of habit were often content with only one of these, and even forwent the wearing of sandals which was the common use.[1] The daily routine of a man of means and leisure was pretty well defined. Poor or rich, all Athens rose at dawn. Toilet was a brief business when clothes were so few and simple ; and hair-dressing was done at the barber's.[2] Breakfast, too, was soon over, consisting as it did of a mere sop of bread dipped in wine. Then our friend was ready, staff in hand, and with a slave or two in attendance, to take

---

[1] Hats were worn only for journeys.
[2] Shaving did not become the vogue till Alexander set the fashion.

the morning streets. If he had a call to pay, this was the hour to pay it. Otherwise he inevitably drifted towards the market-place. There the country-folk and hucksters would by now have set up their booths, and from nine to twelve it was a busy scene. In the adjacent streets were rows of shops and stalls, grouped together by trades, as in the medieval fashion. Purchases made and a slave sent home with the parcels, our citizen was free to do business, if he had any, among the bankers' tables, or to stroll around talking to friends under the shadow of the surrounding colonnades. Talking and walking were the two favourite pastimes of the Greeks ; and there was always a gossiping throng round the barber's shop or the perfumer's, or (less respectable) at the wine shop. By noon it was time to be thinking of the first solid meal of the day ; and after this luncheon or *déjeuner*, a siesta would be taken during the midday heat. Then up and to the gymnasium, where more talk, some exercise and, to conclude, a bath. There were several public bath-houses in Athens, and sometimes a bath-room in a rich man's mansion ; but bathing was no luxury as in the days of Rome—a cold-water douche, a rub-down with olive oil, and then a laborious scraping with an iron instrument to cleanse away the dirt. Towards evening came the dinner, a more elaborate meal. The diners lay prone on couches, while the slaves brought in small stools or tables on which was each guest's food. The Athenians were not great eaters, their diet consisting chiefly of fish, birds and vegetables generously cooked in oil ; but butcher's meat was seldom tasted. The poor folk were mainly vegetarians, living on soup and porridge, with sausages on gala days. The meal well over, the drinking began enhanced perhaps with a performance of dancing girls or flautists. The wine was a thick syrup and was plentifully watered ; and, though young sparks would often make a night of it, the Athenians were far from drunkards, and, compared with the mighty topers of Thrace or Macedon, their habits were positively abstemious. Indeed, the most marked feature of Athenian life was the studious void-

ance of both luxury and excess. The complex paraphernalia of comfort they left on the whole to the despised
barbarian, and their nimble wits were never employed on
the invention of practical contrivances such as the modern
world so loves to multiply for its amusement or its ease.
Athens was a place quite lacking in ' up-to-date conveni-
ences '. Many of what we should consider the necessities
of life were noticeably absent—no clocks except rude
dials, no fires beyond portable braziers, no books to speak
of, no maps, no newspapers, no drains. There was simply
no conception that such things were at all desirable.
' Greek literature, like the Gospels, is a great protest against
the modern view that the really important thing is to be
comfortable '.

The leisure and opportunity to devote his time to other
ends than grinding toil in provision of a livelihood, were
more than anything else what a Greek gentleman demanded
of life. Not that he was by any means an idler ; and in
our attempt to picture the spending of his days we must
not omit from count the deal of lively business that went
on in them—the performance of public and official duties
in peace as well as war, the commercial enterprise, the
supervision of farms and workshops, the craftsmanship
of tool and paint-brush, to say nothing of the part played
by individuals in the preparation and celebration of the
numerous state festivals. Into all these activities he
entered with ready zest ; but he would never willingly
have submitted to the drudgery of a counting-house desk
any more than he was ready to undergo what he considered
the indignity of menial labour. That neither this nor the
petty worries of domestic management were ever much
required of him, was due to the existence of two other
elements in the Athenian social order, his women-folk and
his slaves.

Of women, throughout these pages, little has been said.
For in the public life of Athens they counted not at all.
In the eyes of the law, indeed, they possessed no independent status, for, whatever her age, a female had always
to remain under the tutelage of some male. The home

was, in short, the proper sphere of the woman, and her first business in life was to get married. Girls were less numerous than boys at Athens; for parents were chary of bringing up unwanted daughters, and many a female infant was put out of the way at birth. So to remain unmated was thought a grave disgrace; and marriage, often at so early an age as fifteen years, was the habitual rule. Thereafter it became the duty of the wife to keep the home, ordering the slaves about their household duties and ministering to her husband's needs and pleasures. The seclusion of the woman's life was strict. Wife and daughters lived in a separate quarter of the house, the most distant from the street. The central cloistered court round which every rich man's house was constructed, and on to which the dining-rooms and bedrooms opened, was not denied to them. But, if they were surprised there by male visitors, they would scuttle shamefacedly for shelter; and though custom permitted them, when attended by female slaves, to walk the street, they would not stop to converse with men, nor would they ever attend a meal at which men guests were present. In fine, it was their duty to keep always in the background, and, as Pericles once put it, ' to be spoken of by men neither for good nor ill.' Nevertheless, though their lives were circumscribed and perhaps a little dull, it would be a grave mistake to suppose that the women-folk of Athens were downtrodden. The statues we possess of them show a fine, self-respecting type, befitting the mothers of lithe athletes and stalwart soldiers; and many touching epitaphs remain telling of devoted attachment between

---

PLATE XXIII

A bas-relief from Naples, generally supposed to represent Orpheus saying farewell to Eurydice while Hermes stands beside to conduct her to the nether-world. More probably it represents the farewell of a husband to a wife. Its tender pathos is typical of the gravestones of the Fourth Century. Cp. far greater restraint of Fifth-Century work, Plate XI.

XXIII

RELIEF OF MAN AND WIFE

husbands and wives.[1] Some movement, too, towards a more liberal emancipation began, towards the close of the Periclean era, to find expression. Euripides, as we have seen, felt keenly the injustice and indignity of women's status. Aristophanes, with his jesting earnest, seems, in one of his comedies, to betray the same uneasiness. Philosophers even debated the question of reform. The feminist cause, however, though women's condition probably improved during the succeeding century, never made real headway ; and the reason is not far to seek. For there existed in Athens another type of woman, who appeared all too much in public and in the company of men, and whose example it ill befitted any respectable wife to follow —the large and disreputable class of courtesans.

The very considerable number of these latter at Athens was due in a great measure to an historical reason. The time had been when women of non-Athenian birth had been freely admitted into honourable society. Cleisthenes, Miltiades, Themistocles and Cimon were all sons of such foreign mothers, and no one thought them the worse for it. In 451, however, a law was passed confining citizenship to the sons of Athenian parents on both sides ; and so the tragedy began. The foreign women inevitably sank to the position of dishonour. Some, indeed, like Aspasia, the famous mistress of Pericles, attained a considerable influence even among public men ; but the majority of such unfortunates became social outcasts, degraded by the stigma which attached to their profession and eyed askance by the legitimate wives, who in secret envied, though they dared not imitate, the larger liberty which the courtesans so openly enjoyed.

Of the slaves' position at Athens, provided we accept the system, better things can be said. By Greek opinion, at any rate, the system was accepted, just as the ' sweating '

---

[1] This, for instance : ' Atthis who didst live for me and breathe thy last toward me, source of joyfulness formerly as now of tears, holy, much lamented, how sleepest thou the mournful sleep, thou whose head was never laid away from thy husband's breast, leaving Theius alone as one who is no more ; for with thee the hopes of our life went to darkness.'—Translation by Mackail.

system of labour was accepted by our great-grandfathers ; and Aristotle himself, for all his genuine enlightenment, regarded slavery as inevitable, arguing that some men are 'servile by nature'. For, in theory at least, slaves were drawn from the 'barbarian' races. Sentiment was, on the whole, against the enslavement of Greeks, and the sale of entire populations conquered in war, as practised by the Athenians at Melos or by Philip at Olynthus, came always as something of a shock. The markets were more normally supplied from external sources, and a lively trade in kidnapping went on around the coasts of Thrace, the Black Sea, Asia Minor and the Levant. Outlandish names of slaves, such as Pardocas or Thrax, would some-times betoken their origin ; but more often they received nicknames, such as Xanthias or Pyrrhias, the 'Redhead'. At Athens the swift industrial development which followed the Persian Wars greatly enlarged the number of slave employees. By the end of the Periclean era they very nearly equalled the free population, and in the succeeding century they possibly surpassed it. Every well-to-do householder would possess perhaps a dozen, a factory-owner of course far more. His rights over them were wide ; and though death might not be inflicted, the punishment of thieves or runaways would be pretty severe —the lash, the pillory or even branding. The fact is, however, that the good sense of the Athenians told them that ill-treatment did not pay. Slaves worked better if they were kindly handled—above all, if they were given some prospect of emancipation. To accumulate some savings was clearly permitted and many bought them-selves out. Xenophon gave their liberty to five out of his thirteen slaves ; and Pasion, the famous banker, was among the number of such freedmen. The result was that the slaves at Athens were no cringing creatures. One writer tells us that they would not even make way for gentlemen in the street, and were in fact indistinguishable in dress and manner from the ordinary citizen. Nor were the tasks assigned to them by any means all degrading. Many, of course, did menial service about the house ; but a good master and mistress would treat them as one of the household and even nurse them in sickness. Others performed clerkly work, copying manuscripts or keeping accounts. Some were hired out under contract for harvesting, olive-picking or other agricultural occupations; and those engaged on trades or handicrafts used to work side by side with the free labourers. The state itself employed a few Thracians as police.

In one department of industry, however, the conditions were inhuman enough to bring condemnation on the whole system. At the beginning of the Fifth Century, when new and rich veins of ore had been discovered in the silver-mines at Laurium, there had been a rush to exploit them, and since citizens refused the uncongenial job of working underground, recourse was naturally had to slaves. Henceforward the offscourings of the market —the vicious, the unsightly or intractable—were drafted off in gangs to the mining area. There they were condemned to life-long drudgery, laboriously excavating the narrow winding galleries or sinking deep shafts in the rock, shackled, nearly naked, branded with their master's token, utterly without hope of escape. Nobody cared. Nicias, whom Thucydides describes as the paragon of virtue, is known to have owned a thousand of these wretched creatures. Other Athenians, no doubt, were sometimes sorry for slaves, but it never occurred to them to think of changing existing conditions. For they were no more critical than most men of the environment in which they lived.

Such social limitations must not be lost to sight when we come to make our final estimate of the Greek City-State. Honestly viewed in the light of this dependence on slave-labour, Athens must be regarded rather as an aristocracy of an exclusive citizen body than as a genuine democracy. In this sense, and indeed in many others, its culture will appear to have been the outcome of highly specialized circumstances. Its sheltered isolation from the outer world, for instance, was an essential condition for its very swift and precocious internal development.

It has been said, not without truth, that it was a sort of 'forcing house', like the modern English boarding-school; and indeed between the two institutions there is very much in common. In both we find communities of a privileged class set free, through the services rendered by members of a class less privileged, to devote themselves to a higher cultivation of physical and mental powers. In both the female element of society is kept rigidly in the background, and the atmosphere is masculine throughout. Under these conditions there is developed in both a very conscious concentration on certain well-defined ends. The traditions of public spirit and of public service are intensely strong and deliberately encouraged. Competitive emulation provokes the keenest enthusiasms. Athletic prowess may assume, as at Sparta or Thebes and perhaps at some public schools, an unduly prominent place in the community's life. But under the influence of some great leader or teacher an intellectual activity no less remarkable may be developed. The chief defect in both systems is perhaps the too exclusive preoccupation with their own petty internal affairs, the narrowness of outlook which tends to ignore the larger issues of the outside world and complacently to write down the members of other communities as 'barbarian' outsiders. Nevertheless, there is a virtue complementary to this defect. For in both systems the qualities of mind and character developed by the close discipline of their sheltering walls are capable also of being readapted to a larger environment and permeating by their influence a wider society. So, at least, it was with Athens. Had her career been merely an isolated episode in the evolution of mankind, we should look with no common admiration on the richness and brilliance of her intellectual and artistic achievements. But, just because they were so rich and so brilliant, they could not fail, when carried outwards, to influence the world and colour the whole history of subsequent civilizations. And before we pass on to consider the earliest phase in this expansion and dissemination of the Hellenic spirit, we may do well to ask ourselves what precisely the Hellenic spirit meant. What, in other words, is the legacy of Greece ?

II. THE GREEK SPIRIT

The most fundamental article of the Greek's creed was his intense belief in human life. He would never have even begun to understand the self-abasement and self-depreciation of the Hebrew, crying, ' I am a worm and no man.' For to him human life was a splendid, even when a tragic, affair, and human nature was the cap and summit of the universe. In Greek literature the very gods themselves compare by no means favourably with the sublime heroisms and generous loyalties of man. A complete dependence upon God and His will was not part of their religion. Still less did Greek writers expend their sympathy on lower orders of creation. Birds and beasts and even the very features of the countryside appear, if they appear at all, simply as a background to man's life and action. There was no school of landscape painters in Greece. Three-quarters of the poetry of Wordsworth, Shelley or Tennyson would have meant little or nothing to them. And even when dealing with man's life itself, the Greek writer would, as a rule, confine his attention to the main and central issues—love and hate, pride and lust, fatherland and family, disease and death. There was no searching after subtle by-paths of psychology, no sympathy with abnormalities, above all, no indulgence of sentimental moods. The Greek was not interested, like our own romantic poets, in the impression made by some act or object upon his own emotions. He strove always to see and show things objectively and as they really are. Nor did the Greek ever shrink from facing facts. His faith in human nature led him to accept it as a whole, and to follow where it would lead him. So for him there were no refusals such as so many other nations or creeds have made. He did not, like the Puritan, fear the emotions, or, because desires are dangerous, seek to ban them from his life. Nor, on the other hand did he fear the use of reason, or, because thinking may lead to dangerous issues, refuse to think. He believed, in fine, that human nature was all one, its gifts all healthy and wholesome if properly used ; and his ideal of life was the fullest possible development of all the human powers and faculties, physical and moral, emotional and intellectual.

Such then, was the creed of the Greek ; and since he believed passionately in human nature and cared passionately for human life, it followed inevitably that he acquired a higher sense of its dignity and a more profound sense of its significance than is given to most men. It has been said that Thucydides, in his history of the Peloponnesian War, magnified a series of border raids into the proportions of a great conflict ; and this in a sense is true. But he was able to enhance the interest of the episode because he saw deep down into the issues it involved, and he was able to see thus deeply because he also deeply cared. This faculty of fine perception was the secret of the Greeks' extraordinary sense of beauty. Few peoples, if any, have ever so whole-heartedly pursued the beautiful. They were never content to let things be so long as it seemed possible, by the addition of a further touch, to bring them a step nearer to perfection. So they would take—from some neighbour nation, it may be—the model of some architectural ornament, and then, by a gradual correction of its proportions or its curves, produce a miracle of perfect form. Or, again, they would take some crude old story—some gross barbarity, let us say, of human sacrifice—and from their deft manipulation would emerge the rare delicacy and pathos of Iphigenia's sacrifice. This gift you may call imagination, if you will ; but it springs in the last resort from a keen and appreciative perception which is trained to notice and remember the perfect curve of a pebble or a vine tendril, or the poignancy of a father's grief for a lost daughter. Above all, however, the Greeks knew that the essence of good art is restraint. The artist's emotion must indeed be strong, but it must never be his master, or he will cease to know what he is doing with it. So the Greeks never allowed themselves to be carried away by their emotions. They selected what was significant in it and suppressed what was irrelevant. Thus, in their drama they refused to portray violent death upon the stage, because they knew that the real tragedy of death lies in its effect upon other men's lives, not in the crash of the axe or the flowing of the blood. There were no cheap appeals to tawdry sentiment in Greek literature—no flashing, as it were, of the limelight. This combination of vital imagination with a self-imposed restraint was the twin foundation of their swift artistic progress. Instead of impetuously experimenting along new lines, they were content to limit themselves by the acceptance of the traditional formulae—a particular pose for a statue, it may be, or a particular form for a pillar. But their craving for perfection never permitted them to be satisfied with an exact reproduction of what had gone before. They were not like the Egyptians, who often for many centuries would continue to repeat the same formula of pillar or statue with slavish imitation. Each fresh artist in succession strove to add some touch of improvement, some individual contribution to the common formula. And the result was a steady and rapid evolution towards a perfected type of beauty. The same, in a sense, is true of all departments of Greek life. In politics, in philosophy, in education, things never stood still ; and it was the constant effort of each generation to go one better than its predecessor. And so it was that the Greeks, though never ashamed to borrow from external sources, were also themselves great originators, and it is perhaps their chief claim to artistic and literary pre-eminence that they developed methods of building or writing or modelling which furnished the permanent models of style to posterity. A large majority of the art-forms known to man are Greek by origin. Homer's Epics were the model for Virgil and Milton. The Attic Drama was the model for the Roman playwrights and the French Classicists. Attic speech-writers inspired Cicero, and through him other orators for a thousand years and more. Elegiac, lyric and pastoral poetry took its source among the Greeks. History and biography began with them. Their architectural forms taught the Romans how to build, and since the Renaissance their influence has been continuous. No artist who writes or builds or models can afford to ignore his debt to them. For, above all, their works not merely set a fashion, but contain also a vital germ of inspiration which is for ever blossoming forth anew and bearing fruit in fresh experiment.

Art, however, is not the only way in which the Greeks have influenced the world. For, if they believed in culti-vating the Emotions, they believed no less in cultivating the Reason also. They were great inquirers after truth, men of an insatiable curiosity. They wished to find an explanation of everything in heaven and earth ; and, what is more, they firmly believed that an explanation could be found. Some men have been content, especially in the realm of religious thought, to deny man's power to probe the deepest mysteries, and have accepted blind instinct or unreflective ecstasy as the only sure guides to truth. But that was not the Greeks' way. They believed that all existence is rational, amenable, that is to say, to the reasoning powers of man, and that by sheer hard thought all things can be made clear. So it was that not merely did their inquiry give the first impulse to all subse-quent philosophy, but their methods of rational analysis became inevitably the framework on which much of the world's thinking has been done. Thus, when the early Christians began to reason about their innermost convic-tions hitherto but vaguely formulated, and to define in set terms what precisely they believed about the relations between man and Christ and God, it was through the medium of Greek thought that they discovered their dogmas. The theology of the Catholic Church, though its spiritual inspiration was drawn from Palestine, is for the most part Greek in form.

Equally, too, in the affairs of practical life, did the Greek employ his reason. He desired, above all, a state of society in which all was decently ordered and thought out, and from this desire sprang the countless political and constitutional experiments of which we have traced the story. And when Hellenic culture came to be spread over the East, one of the main results was to encourage other peoples in forming the habit of a well-planned city life, with elected magistrates, well-defined spheres of official responsibility, administrative routine. Not that the Greeks believed in hard and fast systems, as the Romans did. Codification of laws and the elaborate mechanization of a governmental hierarchy, which was Rome's gift to the world, were not in keeping with their genius. The intense vitality of their creative impulse forbade them to pin their faith on anything static or unprogressive. The Greek was for ever improvising, meeting a problem or a danger when the problem or danger occurred, not planning in advance some infallible organization to cover all contingencies. This quality in him is perhaps one reason why his country's greatness was in a material sense so transitory, its positive achievements outside the realm of art so few. And it is also the reason why the influence of Hellenism has been so lasting. For wherever men have breathed the air of the Greek spirit and recovered in any true sense its free, untrammelled outlook upon life, its inspiration has always led them to think for themselves, to think clearly and to shake free from the shackles of blind superstition, deadening convention or dull inertia. 'Nothing moves in the world' it has been truly said 'which is not Greek in origin.'

III. PHILOSOPHY AND SCIENCE

The manifestation of the Greek Genius was not confined to one particular city or to one particular epoch; but in much that we have been saying, we have of course been thinking principally of Athens, and of Athens during the Sixth, Fifth and Fourth Centuries. What she performed in the realm of art during the Periclean era we have already seen; but for her highest achievements in the realm of thought we must turn to the Fourth Century. For then it was that, in the work of Plato and Aristotle, Attic philosophy reached its true consummation; and, though Socrates may well be considered the real founder of that philosophy, yet it must always be remembered that he committed nothing to writing, and without Plato to record and interpret his teaching, he would be little more to us than a celebrated name.

The precise relation between Plato's written work and Socrates' oral teaching is a problem which in all probability will never be completely solved. For Plato, in imitation of his master's conversational method, wrote all his treatises under the form of dialogues, in which, though Socrates is almost invariably the chief spokesman, it is impossible to tell whether the theories put into his mouth are historically his or Plato's. But, just because Socrates' teaching was entirely conversational and proceeded, as it were, at haphazard, it is only reasonable to suppose that, in the process of reducing it to fixed literary form, Plato must not merely have given it a more precise definition, but must also have developed it along the lines of his own thought ; and in fact we find a clearly marked advance from the theories put forward in his earlier dialogues to those put forward in the later. What, however, is certain enough, is that Plato owed to Socrates' original inspiration his very definite belief in the existence of an Absolute Truth. In a world in which personal morality, religious creeds, and international conventions were rapidly crumbling under the disintegrating influences of the new critical movement, Plato made an ever-memorable stand on the basis of that fundamental belief. When other men were saying, ' What may be true for you, may be false for me ', or ' What is right for you, is wrong for me ', he utterly denied that Truth, Goodness or Beauty could be relative terms at all. He held that Justice, for example, is not a matter of mere expediency, but as permanent and as invariable a reality as that two and two make four. Such realities, or ' Ideas ' as he called them, he regarded as the ultimate foundation of existence. They are fixed, eternal entities ' laid up ', as he declared, ' in Heaven ' ; and it is only in so far as a particular act partakes in some degree of the ' Ideal ' Justice, or as a particular object reflects the 'Ideal' Beauty, that either can be said to be beautiful or just. These 'Ideas', or realities, Plato would further have us believe, are in a sense summed up in the uniting reality of Goodness, which is God—whether a personal God or a supreme creative force he does not anywhere clearly define. Furthermore, since man is himself God-like, it is by the divine element in our natures—call it soul or spirit or what you will—that we are enabled to make contact with the 'Ideal' world. The vision of what is really true or good or beautiful is, in fact, the most precious part of our human inheritance. It is the only sure guide in a life chaotic with apparent contradictions and conflicting standards. And to cultivate that vision is not only the most important of man's duties, but also the highest possible exercise of his intellectual faculties. Nor is this vision to be won by a vague and emotional ecstasy, but by processes of reason and a strict discipline of the intellect. So for Plato philosophic contemplation is the surest road to happiness ; and partly because he was deeply imbued with Pythagorean theories about the mystical significance of numbers, partly because mathematical principles are more demonstrably true than any other, he came to regard the study of higher mathematics as the most fruitful form of such intellectual training. For this reason he assigns to it a very important rôle in the ideal education which he formulates. For Plato did not by any means disregard the claims of practical life. He himself travelled, as we have seen, to Syracuse, there to become the tutor of the younger Dionysius, and in the most famous of his dialogues, the *Republic*, he was at pains to sketch in considerable detail his conception of an ideal community and its educational methods.

Disgust with the fickle ways and individualistic licence of Athenian democracy caused him to turn for his model rather towards the more stable and more disciplinary constitution of Sparta. Communism, so complete that it extended even to wives and children, was to be the rule among the Guardians of his Utopia. All was to be subordinated to the object of producing a race healthy in mind and body, and above all of producing a governing class—for his state was to be a rigid aristocracy—which should be capable of ruling according to the principles of 'Ideal' truth and justice. In the concluding books of his *Republic* the education of these governors or 'guardians' is very carefully planned, leading them up through a course of music, literature and gymnastic and above all of mathematics and astronomy to the contemplative study of the sublime truths of which we have just been speaking. Once thoroughly inspired by the vision of 'Ideas' they are to return again to the workaday world and govern by the light of that vision. Whether such a scheme would work in practice, even Plato himself appears to have been a little dubious ; for at the end of all he hints that perhaps a Philosopher King would be a more practical ruler than his Philosopher Guardians. We ourselves may equally feel a doubt whether Plato's State would be particularly Utopian ; and certainly for the mass of its inhabitants it would not be a very comfortable or human place to live in.

After thus walking among the clouds with Plato, we drop to earth when we pass in turn to Aristotle ; but at any rate we feel our feet to be once again on solid ground. Aristotle was not a native Athenian, but an Ionian of the Northern Aegean. Like most of his scientifically-minded countrymen he was little given to mysticism, and, though a fervent admirer of his master, Plato, was a much more practical man. Biology was his real forte, but he turned his mind to almost every department of learning, and there is hardly a single subject on which he did not write and write with the most inimitable common sense. For Plato's theory of 'Ideas' he had little use, considering them to be too elevated and aloof to have any real bearing on actual life. He maintained that general principles or 'universals', instead of being separate and self-existent entities, are simply the result of our own processes of thought. We perceive a similarity between two things and classify them under a common head as 'beautiful' or ' ugly ', ' sweet ' or ' bitter ', and so forth. This theory may not explain, and indeed Aristotle never did explain, what is the ultimate basis of this similarity. But it is a manifest aid to clear thinking ; and Aristotle himself built up an elaborate set of formulae by which processes of right reasoning are governed. In a word, he was the founder of what is called ' formal logic ' ; and his terminology was in fact destined to provide the vehicle of philosophic thought for nearly a thousand years to come.[1] His discrimination between ' form ' and ' matter ', his analysis of the meaning of ' causation ', and his definition of psychological faculties, established principles of thought which continued to hold the field even down through the Middle Ages ; and, when he came in turn to deal in his *Ethics* with the questions of human morality, there too he characteristically enough produced a formula. Virtue consists, he said, in striking a ' mean ' between two extremes —between, for instance, extravagance on the one hand and stinginess on the other, or between the excessive rashness of the foolhardy and the excessive caution of the coward. Though he held, like Plato, that the contemplative life was the highest of human activities, he held also that men as a whole must find their happiness in association with others and by developing in some form of society their best capabilities of mind and body. He remained a firm believer in the City-State, and he even quaintly defines the size of the ideal society as such that no member shall be a complete stranger to any other. Aristotle, in short, brought to bear on every problem the power of orderly and discriminating reason so dear to the Greek mind. His instruction, which was very popular, was carried on in the gymnasium known as the ' Lyceum ', and from the 'peripatos ' or ' walking colonnade ' where his lectures were normally given, it came to be called the

---

[1] As Latin, however, came to be the recognized language of scholars, the Greek terminology was replaced by Latin equivalents. Such words as ' substance ', ' essence ' or ' entity ', though Latin in form, are an attempt to reproduce the meaning of their Greek originals.

Peripatetic school of philosophy as opposed to the Academy ' where Plato's students gathered.

There were in Athens two other famous groups of which some mention should be made, both more or less direct offshoots of Socrates' teaching. Antisthenes, the founder of the Cynic School, emphasized the sterner side of the Socratic ideal and maintained that virtue was to be obtained by complete independence of material needs and comforts ; the Cynic must be content to forgo all ties of friendship, state or family, all allurements of pleasure, everything, in short, but the barest necessities of life. One of his followers, the famous Diogenes, lived, as all know, in a tub. The Cynic tradition was subsequently taken up, though in a more sensible form, by the Stoics, who without going to these lengths believed that a man should be so master of his soul that neither pains nor pleasures could in any way affect the inner happiness derivable from virtue and virtue alone. The second offshoot of Socrates' teaching were the followers of Aristippus of Cyrene, known as the Cyrenaic School. Taking the Socratic doctrine that the Good is that which serves some useful end, they proceeded to interpret the useful as equivalent to the pleasurable, and to seek happiness through the indulgence of their desires. With them the later Epicureans, or followers of Epicurus, so far agreed that they also took Pleasure as their aim ; but they drew a more praiseworthy distinction between the lower desires which should not be gratified and the higher desires which should. Reason was to them, as to so many Greek philosophers, the only sure guide in life, the safeguard equally against the enticements of vice and also against the deceits (as they considered them) of orthodox religion. Throughout the succeeding centuries until the influence of Christianity began to make serious headway, the thinking folk of the world were divided between these two camps of Epicureans and Stoics.

No account of the thought of the Greeks would be complete without some reference to their mathematical and scientific studies ; nor is it always realized how much solid work they did in this direction and in how many ways they laid the foundation of all subsequent inquiry. In the realm of mathematics, and more particularly perhaps of astronomy, they owed something to the researches of the Babylonian and Egyptian pioneers. Thales of Miletus (624–547) is said to have brought back geometry from his travels in Egypt ; but what was there studied for the merely practical purposes of building and such like, he pursued in the pure spirit of inquiry. Amongst other Theorems he proved the equality of the angles at the base of an isosceles triangle. The next great name in the line of such mathematicians was Pythagoras (572–479). He classified numbers as odd, even, prime and so forth, and examined their properties, discovering in them, as we have seen, a mystical as well as a purely mathematical significance. In geometry his most famous discovery was that which concerns the squares on the sides of a right-angled triangle. In astronomy he was the first man to hold the view that the Earth is spherical. Of his pupils and many able successors there is no room here to speak. Plato, though much addicted to the study, was no original mathematician. Aristotle's genius moved in other lines. But slightly younger than these two there appeared the most famous of the geometricians of antiquity —Euclid of Alexandria. He wrote thirteen books of Elements of which no further description is needed ; and, though much therein contained was the work of his pre-decessors, the whole arrangement and the perfected style of the proofs were his own. More original perhaps than Euclid was Archimedes of Syracuse (c. 287–22). His invention of a water-pump is well known and so is the story of how he discovered the displacement of water when sitting down in his bath, and ran out into the streets, naked as he was, exclaiming triumphantly, ' I have found it.' His works on Hydrostatics, the Parabola, and other subjects, which included the first rudiments of Trigono-metry, marked a real epoch. About the same time Era-tosthenes of Cyrene made a similar advance in astronomy, discovering a method of measuring the Earth, estimating the size and distances of Sun and Moon and explaining eclipses. A little later Apollonius with his treatise on Conics brought Greek Geometry to its culminating point.[1] Thus, in origin at least, it will be seen that the whole mathematical science is essentially the product of this keenly inquisitive race. The very terminology still remains, as it began, Greek throughout, and, if they had been nothing else, the Greeks would have gone down to history as the inventors of mathematical method.

The other branches of inquiry in which the Greeks most excelled were medicine and biology ; and to these again the Fourth Century made a noteworthy contribution. Important medical work had been done at the end of the Fifth Century by the famous physician Hippocrates, a native of Cos, who travelled much and spent a part of his time in Athens. His observations of certain maladies were carefully noted down, and together with other similar records were later incorporated by some Alexandrian scholars in a regular treatise, which gave a detailed description of forty-two cases, including quinsy, epilepsy, tapeworm, and what seems in all probability to have been typhoid fever. Hippocrates' curative methods were founded on the philosophic theory that the body is compounded of the four elements—earth, air, fire and water —the perfect harmony of which is necessary to the restoration of perfect health. The whole science was, in fact, based on a very imperfect knowledge of physiological facts ; and it was not until the Third Century that anatomy was at all carefully studied and dissection practised. Scientific observation of the animal and vegetable kingdom made, however, great strides with Aristotle. Previous to him, the interest in such things had been purely practical and directed towards men's every-day needs. But with Aristotle the desire for knowledge became an end in itself, and he set to work with systematic thoroughness to classify and tabulate his observations—of the habits of fish, their appearance, food and migrations—of all sorts of insects, bee, bumble-bee, house-fly, hornets and moths, and of

---

[1] It remained for another Greek of Alexandria, Diophantes (c. A.D. 250) to develop the new notation of Algebra.

a thousand other phenomena. He divided animals into those with blood and those without it, air-breathing and water-breathing, wild and tame. Theophrastus, his pupil, wrote a treatise on plants and examined with real skill the processes of germination; and during the Third and Second Centuries an enormous amount of work was done at Alexandria on biology, botany, geology, scientific agriculture and other departments of learning. The tendency among Alexandrian scholars was rather towards applied science than abstract theory. We find them, in fact, treading on the verge of very remarkable inventions, and one Heron, for example, came within an ace of anticipating the steam-engine by learning to propel a ball with the aid of hot vapour. In spite, however, of their laborious and often profound observations of phenomena, the researches of these men were very severely handicapped by the weakness and poverty of their technical appliances. Without microscope or telescope, for instance, it was impossible to carry biology or astronomy beyond a certain point. And, on the whole, it remains true of Greek scientists that they were stronger on the theoretic side than on the practical, more ready in their approach to a problem to use their eyes and their brain than their fingers. Nevertheless, this defect was, in reality, their strength. For it is the inquirer after truth rather than the mechanical inventor that gives the true impulse to science. Newton and Einstein will stand out in history when Edison and Marconi are forgotten. So the more practical Romans were destined to add little to the discoveries made by the Greeks. In the Middle Ages no perceptible advance was made; and it was not till the Renaissance gave a fresh stimulus to the study of the Hippocratic and other Greek treatises that light began to dawn and science again to move forward. Thus it was upwards of two thousand years in the history of the world before the wits of mankind were able to surpass the scientific triumphs which the Greek pioneers had achieved in little more than two hundred.

25

CHAPTER XX

ALEXANDER AND THE EAST

I

IN the April of 334 Alexander prepared to cross from Europe into Asia. A *point d'appui* on the further side of the Dardanelles was already assured him ; for Philip had some time since thrown an advance guard into Phrygia, and thus a footing had there been made good. In its original conception the campaign was intended to be a joint operation of land and sea forces ; but before he finally quitted the Ionian coast and struck up into the interior of Asia Minor Alexander was, as we shall see, to change his mind and (with the exception of twenty Athenian vessels kept as a hostage for the city's good behaviour) to dismiss his entire fleet. The fact is that he had by then begun to realize that, without the whole-hearted support of the Greek maritime states, he could not afford to keep in being a navy strong enough to cope with Persia's Phoenician squadrons, and such support, as became increasingly evident, it was useless to expect. But though in thus abandoning to the enemy the command of the sea he was taking an undeniable risk, the risk was not so great as it might appear. For the army he led was to be independent of its communications. His plan was to accumulate in each district that he conquered sufficient supplies for an advance into the next. On this method the only essential conditions of security were an efficient commissariat and an unbroken continuity of success. Alexander, as it proved, could command both. His military forces were in numbers not very great—thirty thousand foot, of which half were native Macedonians, half Greeks whether mercenary or provided contingents, and five thousand horse, of which the spear-point was the

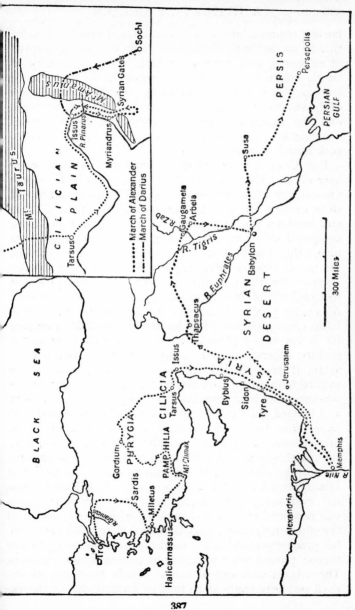

MAP TO ILLUSTRATE ALEXANDER'S MARCH—I

387

famous regiment of the aristocratic Companions.   Besides
this he carried with him a formidable siege-train, a corps
of engineers, and, by a characteristic touch, a party of
Greek scientists.   The tactical methods he intended to
employ were largely those of Philip ; but his manipulation
of the various arms was even more original than his father's,
and the ingenuity already displayed in his European
campaigns was to find plenty of scope in the still sterner
task ahead of him.

For Alexander's conquest of Persia was no mere walk-
over affair.   The armies of King Darius were on their own
ground formidable fighters.   The skilful horsemanship of
their cavalry and the long-range volleys of their slingers
and bowmen placed at a serious disadvantage any force
composed solely of slow-moving hoplites.   Cyrus, recognizing this, had backed up his Greek mercenary foot with
the use of Oriental troopers ; and Agesilaus, using against
Persians for the first time a combination of horse and
foot exclusively Greek, had taught strategists a new lesson.
Alexander profited thereby, and it was an essential factor
in his coming successes that he himself was able to support
his heavy-armed phalanx by a light-armed force and a
cavalry superior to the enemy's.   Even so the Persian
army, if properly led and organized, might well have
availed to stop him ; for besides the native infantry whose
weakness had long since been clearly proven at Marathon
and Plataea, the Great King—learning a lesson from Cyrus'
expedition—had now recruited a large body of Greek
mercenaries.   Fifty thousand is the traditional figure ; but,
though this is almost certainly too large, it was enough,
we may be sure, to turn the scale in Darius' favour, had
Darius been a man.   But he was not.   As a King he was
not even competent.   What little tradition of rulership
still remained at Susa had vanished with the extinction of
the direct royal line ; and Darius, a mere third cousin of
his predecessor and called suddenly from obscurity to the
throne, proved quite incapable of pulling things together.
The satraps were out of hand.   Whole provinces, as we
shall see, were ready at an invader's approach to welcome

him as a deliverer. The Empire, in short, was rotten to the core. Even the recovery of Egypt which had recently been effected in 343, had been due to the genius of a Rhodian adventurer Mentor and the fighting quality of the Greek mercenaries who followed him. Had Mentor lived, he might well have defeated Alexander; but no one of equal ability remained. And if cohesion of administrative policy was not to be found among the Empire's rulers, still less was cohesion of strategic plan to be looked for in its military command. Like Demosthenes' 'barbarian at his boxing', the Persian generals invariably waited for Alexander to strike his blow. They anticipated nothing. Darius himself lacked even the ordinary quality of courage; and, whenever he found himself in personal danger, as he did at Issus and Arbela, he simply ran away. Under such leadership it is little wonder that the forces of the illimitable East went down before a few thousand Europeans; but, had a commander of even moderate genius been found on the Persian side, the issue might have been very different.

Alexander's first concern, when he had crossed the straits, was to pass at once to Troy and there pay his homage to the famous site on which his thoughts so often dwelt. With a company of his friends, all naked according to the curious custom, he marched round Achilles' tomb and laid on it a garland. But other business was awaiting him. Not sixty miles away up the Hellespont lay the combined forces of the three westerly satraps. Though their numbers were unquestionably inferior, they had taken up a strong position on the further bank of the Granicus River. There close to the steep ascent of the rock-bed they massed, to meet the Macedonian charge, the flower of their cavalry, with the intention, as the issue showed, of either capturing or slaying Alexander himself. The actual fight was little better than a scramble. While his phalanx held the Persian horse in play with their long pikes, Alexander crossed over at the head of his Companions and flung himself into the fray. More than once his own life was in danger and the white plume upon his helmet was lopped off. But the enemy was broken.

Their loss was heavy, especially among the cavalry. Two of the three satraps fell and the third committed suicide. The Greek mercenaries whom he found among the captives, Alexander ordered to be slain as traitors ; but by and by he learnt a better plan and took such prisoners into his own service. The way was now clear. No organized opposition remained in Asia Minor ; and the progress of the march was easy. The Greek towns of Ionia responded readily to Alexander's proclamation of democracy for all. At Miletus he met with some resistance from Memnon, late captain of the King's Greek mercenaries at Granicus. Dislodged from Miletus, Memnon fell back on Halicarnassus. Dislodged again, he took to the sea and with the Phoenician fleet, which had somewhat tardily arrived, he threatened trouble in the Aegean. But with his death next year the danger vanished and the fleet's activity collapsed. As winter drew on, Alexander left his main body of Greeks at Ephesus under Parmenio's command, and himself with the Macedonians pushed on along the southern coast. Despite the hardships of the weather and the difficulties of the route, which at one point involved wading waist-deep round the sea-washed cliffs of Mount Climax, he reached Pamphylia in safety and with the spring of 333 struck inland towards the high central plateau of Phrygia. The general conception of Alexander's strategy, as later events will show, was to reduce the Levantine seaboard, before broaching the problem of the interior. But for this diversion into Phrygia he had a special reason. For that way ran the great high-road from Ephesus and Sardis towards the east, and the use of it was essential to the bringing up of his main troops. At Gordium, Parmenio joined him with his army reinforced by fresh drafts from Greece and Macedon. At Gordium, too, occurred the episode of the famous knotted rope, of which tradition told that whoever should untie it, was destined to win the crown of Asia. Alexander after a moment's hesitation severed it at a stroke, and, with the glamour of the omen fresh upon him, hastened forward to measure swords with Darius himself.

For with spring and the news of his enemy's approach the Great King had bestirred himself. He had not, it would seem, raised his feudatory levies, but with his standing household troops of foot, cavalry and archers, stiffened by a strong mercenary corps of Greek hoplites, he had now advanced up the banks of the Euphrates and thence struck across in the direction of the advancing foe. In the angle where the shore of Asia Minor swings sharply south toward Syria there lies the narrow coastal plain of Cilicia, a crescent strip surrounded by the encircling chains of the Taurus and Amanus Mountains. Outside that chain and in the Syrian plain south-east of it, Darius encamped at Sochi and there waited. His unhappy satrap Arsames was thus left to hold Cilicia unsupported, and very naturally he failed. Alexander swooped down upon the pass over Mount Taurus with incredible rapidity, covering sixty miles and over in a day and a night's marching; and he was soon quartering his army at Tarsus. It was the height of a hot summer; and here a fit of sharp sickness seized him, caught, as is common, in those fever-ridden plains and aggravated by a foolish plunge in an ice-cold river. Directly he recovered, he marched forward to make battle; and, thinking still to find Darius in the neighbourhood of Sochi, he took the coastal road through Issus, Myriandrus, and the Syrian Gates. What then was his surprise when he found that the enemy had quitted Sochi, marched by a devious route over Mount Amanus, and appeared in the Cilician plain across his rear. His communications with Europe cut, his sick and his rear depots in enemy hands, the decisive battle still to be fought and fought *facing homewards*—it might seem that Alexander, as he retraced his steps towards Issus, was in an ill position. But in point of fact he knew already that the enemy had made their capital mistake. In that confined and narrow battle-ground between the mountains and the sea, it was impossible for their superior numbers—how far superior we cannot really tell—to give them any advantage. They were caught indeed in a trap. As he approached the River Pinarus, behind which their lines were drawn,

Alexander made his dispositions in accordance with the method inherited from Philip. The heavy troops he massed in the centre round the Macedonian phalanx. On their left or seaward side he placed the Thessalian cavalry under Parmenio, on their right the Companions and his other native cavalry under his own command. Nor was it a mere matter of personal fancy which set Alexander himself among the horse. For at Issus, as always in Macedonian tactics, it was the cavalry's business to decide the battle, the infantry's merely to hold the enemy front engaged, while the charge on the flanks went home. The plan, however, did not here proceed too smoothly. For, as the infantry advanced to the grapple, a patch of broken ground at the river-bank somewhat disarranged their order. The enemy's Greek mercenaries confronting them took advantage of this embarrassment, and it was only by a severe effort that the Macedonian phalanx was able to hold its own. Even more unfortunate was the experience of Parmenio upon the left ; for he was called upon to meet the main thrust of the enemy's cavalry and his Thessalians were driven back. But on the right meanwhile Alexander, after a series of charges, had carried all before him, and breaking through with a rush, he turned to attack the Persian centre upon both flank and rear. King Darius was sighted, but he did not await the onslaught. Turning his chariot, he made for the mountains, got to horse, and oblivious of his army, of his camp at Issus, and of the royal harem which had been there deposited, he scarcely drew rein till he had crossed the passes and could make for safety at Thapsacus, nearly a hundred miles away. At the first news of their master's flight the Persian army wavered and broke. Huge numbers were butchered on the spot. Their camp at Issus was taken, yielding enormous booty, and even more important, since they were invaluable hostages, Darius' own mother and the queen-consort.

The victory of Issus, if swiftly followed up, might well have decided the struggle. But Alexander was in no hurry ; and to the pursuit of his fugitive enemy he apparently gave not a thought. The complete subjugation of the Levantine seaboard was still his first concern, and with the air of one who knew precisely what he wished to do and when to do it, he turned away from the direct route to Persia and led his army southward down the Syrian coast. Here a proposal of peace was presently brought to him, offering not merely enormous ransom for the captured queens, but in regular fairy-tale fashion, the hand of Darius' daughter in marriage and one-half —that is, the western and smaller half—of his kingdom. ' I should accept,' said Parmenio, ' if I were Alexander.' ' So should I,' was the answer, ' if I were Parmenio '; and the offer was indignantly rejected. The truth is that from the day of Issus onwards the character of Alexander's ambition seems to have become more and more deliberate. In the enormous wealth and paraphernalia of the royal camp there captured, he had caught a glimpse of what Oriental kingship meant. There can be little doubt that he was somewhat dazzled, and that realizing that such wealth and power were now well within his grasp, he began to assume already something of that harsh and autocratic temper that so marred his later years. The romantic dreams of chivalrous adventure faded ; and there emerged a purpose more stern, a policy more conscious, and a personality more relentless and less lovable. The man in him was hardening.

This psychological change in Alexander's character was very markedly revealed in the treatment that he now meted out to all who dared cross his path.[1] Northern Syria and the Phoenician cities of Sidon, Byblus and Aradus yielded without a blow. But Tyre refused all overtures, and a siege—among the sternest fought in all antiquity—was the result. The city stood on an island, nearly half a mile out to sea, its high walls rising abruptly from the water's edge. The presence of the Phoenician fleet, now recalled from the Aegean, forbade attack by

[1] It must of course be remembered in Alexander's favour that Orientals are most easily impressed by methods of punishment Oriental in character.

sea, and there was no alternative but to drive out a causeway against the landward side of the fortress. For some while the work made good progress, but the builders, coming presently under the range of the defenders' catapults, were unable to proceed till wooden shelters were set up to shield them. These the Tyrians promptly set alight with fire-ships and followed up their success by landing on the mole and destroying a large part of it. Against a repetition of such tactics Alexander determined, to collect a fleet, and vessels from Cyprus and Sidon, now his by right of conquest, were soon pressed into his service. Under their protection the mole again went forward and was at last abutting on the fortress walls. Engines of war were hauled out to its extremity, others floated on broad-bottomed merchant ships ; and under their combined onslaught a breach was eventually made. Alexander's men poured up. The Tyrians, now at bay, fought with the desperate ferocity of a Semitic people ; but their end was come. Eight thousand were slaughtered, as the fight ran through the streets. Two thousand prisoners, it is said, were hanged. The women and children were sold into slavery. The siege, which had occupied very nearly seven months, was perhaps the most brilliant of all Alexander's feats, but the brutality of the final sack displayed in its worst light his hardening temper. This showed again at Gaza—the only city of Palestine and Philistia to hold out at his approach ; for on its capture after a three months' siege, he caused the Governor to be tied living to his chariot-tail, and then, in imitation of Achilles' treatment of Hector, proceeded to drag him at a gallop till he died.

Late in 332 he marched on Egypt ; and Egypt, so recently re-enslaved to the yoke of the Persian King, welcomed him as her deliverer. At Memphis he entered with triumphal pomp, and left a garrison. More important still, he sailed down to the Nile mouth, and recognizing at once, as with a practised eye, the makings of an excellent harbourage, he there proceeded to trace out the ground-plan of a brand-new city—to be called like many another of his similar foundations after its founder's name. Alexandria was destined to become in later years nothing short of the metropolis of the Levant. There can be little doubt that Alexander himself meant it to fill commercially the place of Tyre ; but that he foresaw at this date its future value as a trade-link with Arabia and the Indies can hardly be credited. The choice of site was simply a lucky shot, and by no means the only one which Fate allowed him. The winter was spent in organizing Egypt ; and this he did with systematic thoroughness. For, as will later be seen, Alexander's genius was strongly developed on the constructive side. Asia Minor, soon after the Battle of Granicus, had been provided with an effective government ; and it seems clear that he was consciously building an Empire as he went along. Before quitting Egypt, however, he found time for other less practical concerns. With a small escort he made a pilgrimage through the desert to the shrine of Zeus Ammon, one of the most famous oracular seats of the ancient world ; and here, evidently to his great delight, he was slauted by one of the priests as the god's own son. The impression made on him was beyond question very deep ; and what strange surmises of a more than human destiny began now to take shape within the young Macedonian's mind, we can but dimly guess. His growing power, if it somewhat turned his head, did not at any rate impair his common sense. He had all his wits about him when, with the spring of 331, he retraced his steps through Syria and struck out into the heart of the East.

The route he took carried him far North again, avoiding the Syrian and Mesopotamian deserts, and crossing first the Euphrates, then the Tigris in the upper regions of their lengthy course. Beyond the latter and guarding, as it were, the inner threshold of his threatened realm, he found Darius, encamped near the meeting-place of the many great roads from east and west which once converged upon the historic site—long since reduced to ruins—of the Assyrian Nineveh. This time King Darius had with him a true Oriental host. For, while Alexander was wintering in Egypt, a tremendous effort had been made at Susa. All the feudatory levies had been summoned, and they had come in their strength—'Nomads of Turkestan, Pathans and hillmen from Chitral and Khond and all the range of the Hindu Kush, wild mountaineers of Southern Persis, Lars and Lurs, and Kurds and Bedawin from the Mesopotamian and Arabian wastes.' Old scythe-chariots —long the terror of the East—had been refurbished and their drivers drilled. Most embarrassing of all, since horses will not face them, elephants had been brought into the line.[1] At Gaugamela, or the Camel's House, some distance from the town of Arbela (which gave its name to the engagement), Alexander found himself confronted by this formidable host ; and, as he lay in bivouac on the last hill-ranges overlooking the morrow's battle-field and gazed out under the darkness at the innumerable watch-fires of the Persian camp or listened to the hum of that unsleeping multitude which stole up to him on the night breeze, even the victor of Issus must have realized with a qualm the magnitude of the task awaiting him. Parmenio, conscious that in an open plain the Macedonians could not fail to be outflanked by numbers so superior, advised a night-attack. 'I will steal no battles', was Alexander's answer, and he prepared his plans to meet the menace of such envelopment. The formation he adopted for his infantry was in effect a hollow square, on the front face of which stood the phalanx, and on right and left, as at Issus, were thrown out Alexander's Macedonian and Parmenio's Greek cavalry. The course of the day's action, too, is curiously reminiscent of the earlier battle. Parmenio on the left was beaten back till he was forced to send urgent appeals for assistance. The phalanx equally was broken through by a furious rush of Indians, but the superb quality of their discipline was proof against all shocks. When the scythe-chariots charged, they opened their ranks and let them pass through harmless. Though 'far outflanked, at one time almost surrounded, cut off for three parts of the day from their only support, the

[1] They were apparently not used in the battle.

entrenched camp behind them, they remained steady as on parade-ground.' And meanwhile Alexander on the right had first held the enemy, then letting loose the crowning charge of his Companions, had broken their resistance utterly. As he wheeled in upon the centre, Darius fled. No Oriental host will fight without a leader, and the news of his desertion at once discomfited the whole of his motley array. All that evening and far into the night the rout and slaughter swept onward to the River Zab. Alexander himself rode fiercely, at one moment meeting and felling in single combat the leader of some enemy horse. And not till he reached Arbela, over sixty miles away, was he willing to call off. The Persian army, as an army, had ceased to exist. Darius was a fugitive, and the crown of the East had passed to the conqueror's head.

Alexander was now free to gather at his leisure the spoils of his decisive victory. Babylon, once a jealous rival and always a fretful subject of the Persian Kings, welcomed him with festoons of flowers and hymns of triumph. Susa, the Persian capital, opened its gates and an immense hoard of royal treasure fell therewith into his hands. Steady accumulation of bullion had long been the policy of the Great King's exchequer. Fifty thousand talents were found at Susa alone. At Persepolis an even greater haul was made ; and altogether the value of the treasure taken by Alexander in the East has been reckoned at seventy or eighty millions sterling. The reduction of the hill country, which was the true home of the Persian race, formed the army's next objective. Here the satrap Ariobarzanes made a last heroic stand, holding the passes grimly for five days, and when outflanked by Alexander's discovery of a more devious route, retiring to sell his life dearly before the gates of Persepolis. The town itself was given up to fire and sword. The great palace of Xerxes was deliberately burnt, as though to give the world proof that the rule of the great Persian dynasty was over. It now only remained for Alexander to capture, if possible, the last and least worthy successor of that historic line.

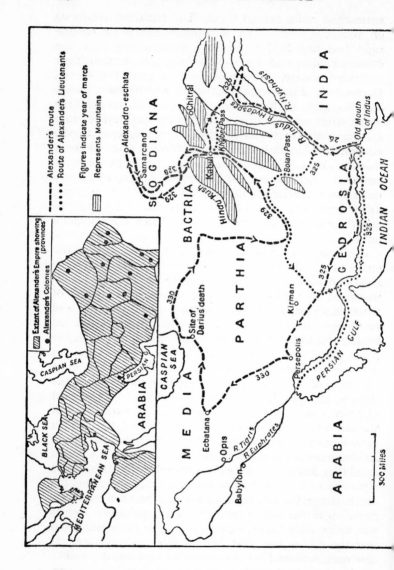

After Arbela Darius had fled to Ecbatana in Media, and at fresh news of the enemy's approach he took flight again beyond the River Oxus. But his ambitious cousin Bessus had even now been forming designs upon the tottering throne, and determined to supplant him. The wretched King was cast into chains, placed in a litter and hurried off along the road to Bactria. At this the last remnant of his army scattered. There was to be no further rally, and for the pursuit it was simply a matter of rounding up the fugitive. An exciting chase began. At the final stage the Macedonian riders were utterly exhausted ; but Alexander dismounted them and setting on their steeds the most athletic of his officers, he followed on into the night. At daybreak, after a ride of nearly fifty miles, he came up with his quarry. But he never took Darius alive. Sick of the craven spirit of the man, his followers stabbed the King, and, as he breathed his last, the pursuers found him. Alexander, strangely touched, threw his cloak over the corpse, and mindful perhaps of his boyhood's chivalry and how Achilles had surrendered Hector's body for the burial, he delivered it over unharmed into the hands of the queen-mother. So the last of the Achaemenians slept with his fathers in the royal tombs at Persepolis.

With the death of Darius the Persian Empire passed conclusively into Alexander's keeping. Of the administrative organization of his new dominions more shall be said hereafter. But of the change which now and henceforward came over the whole character of his enterprise it is important to take note. He had set out from Europe as the champion of Hellas against her hereditary foe. But after the capture of Susa and Persepolis his original purpose was achieved. The crusade was over ; and realizing this Alexander had immediately begun to adapt the basis of his fighting forces to suit the new conditions. Those Greeks who had come with him as members of the voluntary contingents furnished by the homeland states, he either disbanded and sent home to Europe or allowed to re-enlist on the same footing as the rest of his army. Henceforward, therefore, in the long campaigns ahead of him, Alexander commanded forces which, whether Greek or Macedonian, owed allegiance solely and directly to himself. To his Macedonian staff, long accustomed to regard themselves as the head of a national army, this was no welcome change. They were now virtually the bodyguard of an Oriental potentate ; and their privilege and prestige appeared to be diminishing as the self-importance of their Captain grew. For Alexander's attitude was changing. He was no longer one of them. The aloofness of the despot replaced the easy courtesy of earlier years. He adopted, for State occasions at least, the robes and insignia of the Persian royalty. Native courtiers became his favourites ; and, to cap all, since European troops alone could not suffice to hold so large an Empire, native soldiers were being trained in Macedonian tactics, and, it was understood, were eventually to be drafted into the phalanx itself. There is little wonder that there was a grievance felt and that murmuring began. Philotas, Parmenio's son, was detected in a conspiracy. Under torture he declared his father an accomplice. Whether the evidence were true or false, Alexander did not hesitate. Three swift dromedaries were at once dispatched with Parmenio's death-warrant, and, as the aged general turned to read the letter handed him, he was cut down from behind. The lesson went home. A year or so later there was an ugly brawl over the wine-cups, in which Alexander, resenting some outspoken words of criticism, attacked Cleitus, his master of horse, and ran him through with a pike. The fit of remorse, as violent as the hot temper which had caused it, can hardly have availed to allay the discontent. But Parmenio's fate was remembered and there was no more murmuring among the officers. To the rank and file, in the meanwhile, Alexander remained as much as ever a hero. The prize-money he gave was lavish ; knowing, too, the Greek passion for athletic sports, he provided them whenever possible ; above all, he still had a human touch in dealing with his men, and the tale is told how he restored a frost-bitten private by giving him a seat at his own fireside. For his future schemes of conquest, therefore, the implicit loyalty of his army could be relied upon, and Alexander used it to the full. For the subjugation of the Persian Empire alone was not enough for him. Had that been his sole objective, he would have marched straight for Susa after Issus, or after the capture of Persepolis would have turned back to secure Armenia and the north-west provinces. But there can be little doubt that his eyes were set upon a still more visionary goal and that he conceived it as his mission to carry his conquests throughout Asia. To us with our knowledge of geography the idea may seem fantastic; but Alexander did not possess that knowledge; and, as he pushed yet further eastward, the mere lust of acquisition took a stronger and stronger hold upon his mind, till he set no limit to his marching except that which Nature imposed.[1]

The first four years after Darius' death were spent in overrunning the eastern provinces of the old Persian Empire, a wild region loosely held by the King's rule and occupied, in the north especially, by powerful local chiefs. The route which Alexander chose was through Afghanistan and northward over the Hindu Kush ranges into Bactria. Bessus, who had set himself up as King of that province, was rounded up in 329; and, after his nose and ears had been cut off, was crucified—a barbarity of which Achilles himself would hardly have been guilty. In 328 Alexander pushed north to the subjugation of Sogdiana, with its famous capital of Samarcand. Here he espoused the celebrated Roxana, attracted no doubt by her unrivalled beauty, but partly hoping also by the bond of a political marriage to secure the allegiance of an unruly people. Here, too, on the extreme border to the north he founded

[1] Some critics hold, however, that Alexander's excursion into India was merely an attempt to extend his conquests over the region originally subjugated by Darius I. This view hardly explains his expedition to the mouth of the Indus, nor the elaborate preparations for fresh campaigning which were going forward when he died. The fact is that to Aristotle's notion, and presumably therefore to Alexander's as well, there was very little land beyond what he had already conquered when he finally turned back.

Alexandroeschata or Alexander's End, a final outpost on the confines of the ' Scythian ' waste. Such settlements, half military, half commercial in intent, were an important feature in the organization of his captured provinces. Sixteen Alexandrias alone are known to have existed, and there were many other such foundations, some actually in India, which passed under various names. Of their size and character little indeed is known ; but at each point it is clear that the Emperor left behind a portion of his troops and camp-followers—those least capable, no doubt, of continuing the march—to a weary and inhospitable exile in the uttermost parts of the earth. Grim as the prospect was, the posts were faithfully held ; and at was not till some years later, when the news of Alexander's death reached them, that a general exodus began and these marooned wretches trooped westward by the thousand to regain touch with civilization once more. The demands, indeed, which Alexander made upon his men seem to outrun the limits of all human endurance and fidelity ; and, as though what he had hitherto asked of them were not enough, he set out towards the end of summer in 327 to recross the snow-clad passes of the Hindu Kush.

India was little known to the men of the Fourth Century. What knowledge had filtered through from Darius' conquests of the Punjaub district had been forgotten. Herodotus, who tells something of them, was now but little read. So it was into an uncharted world that Alexander was now venturing, and he believed the Indus, till facts proved otherwise, to be somehow connected with the Upper Nile. By the Kaoshan Pass, fourteen thousand feet above sea-level, Afghanistan was entered, and there in the high plains of Kabul the lines of the campaign were laid. The main body under Hephaestion were sent forward to take the Khyber route to the River Indus ; Alexander himself struck north-east into the mountains towards Chitral and spent the winter in making war upon the wild hill-tribesmen. With spring he joined his main body on the Indus, crossed the river by a floating bridge which Hephaestion had constructed, and proceeded boldly to the conquest of the Punjaub. On the River Hydaspes his way was barred by a powerful rajah, Porus. The native host was here no undisciplined rabble, but a highly trained force of natural fighters, supported by war-chariots and elephants. In the Battle of the Hydaspes Alexander encountered perhaps the sternest task of his whole progress. But his ingenuity triumphed; and so much was he impressed by the courage and stern dignity of the enemy leader that he promptly pardoned and reinstated him. Here it was that death overtook Bucephalus, the famous Thessalian war-horse, which had followed his master's fortunes through so many campaigns; and now indeed, as though aptly to the omen, those fortunes too had nearly reached their limit. The rains had set in. As they crossed the Land of the Five Rivers, the troops were drenched with the torrential downpour and stifled by the unaccustomed heat; and when at last they approached the Hyphasis and were faced with a twelve-days' march across the Indian Desert before they could reach the Ganges, their hearts began to fail, and for the first time they mutinied. Three days Alexander waited in his tent for the men to change their mind, then gave the order for retreat. The soldiers crowded round him and wept tears of gratitude when they caught the hope that now at last they might see their homes again.

The way of the return was not to be the way of the advance, and it was even more romantic. A large number of vessels had been prepared upon the Indus and side by side with this flotilla the army made its way south towards the sea. According to the idea of Greek geographers the earth was surrounded by an encircling ocean, the western arm of which lay, as all knew well, beyond Gibraltar and the Pillars of Hercules; but the eastern arm was largely fable. To probe this mystery and know himself at the world's end was now Alexander's hope. For scientific exploration was not the least of his interests, and the discovery of a sea route to India would greatly facilitate its conquest to which he almost certainly intended to return. So down the Indus he went, meaning to follow its course to the mouth. Some three hundred miles short of that objective, he sent the main body of his troops homewards by way of the Bolan Pass ; and then with a picked force and the accompanying flotilla he himself pressed on towards the estuary. This reached, he left Nearchus, a much valued lieutenant and his boyhood's friend, to continue the homeward voyage up the coasts of the Persian Gulf ; and with a view to preparing advance depots for the fleet's provisioning and watering, himself plunged into the arid wastes of the Gedrosian Desert. It was a hideous march—mile after mile of drifting sand into which feet sank as into mud, not a living soul to be seen beyond a few half-human Ichthyophagi (who used pounded fish for flour), water only at rare intervals and then often undrinkable. Hundreds sickened and died in agonies ; and it was a very sorry and exhausted remnant that Alexander eventually brought into camp near Kirman, where he joined hands with his main body. News of Nearchus and the fleet was still to seek ; and when at length a party of those who had made the voyage came in, no one at first could recognize their sea-bleached and weather-worn faces. They, too, had strange tales to tell —of high monsoons that had held them weather-bound, of ferocious savages who had attacked them from the shore, and, stranger still, of certain spouting monsters, which, when charged by a daring captain, had dived and come up again beyond the ship. Nearchus was ordered to continue his voyage to the head of the Persian Gulf ; but already he had proved what Alexander wanted—the existence of a sea passage to India, opening the way to commerce in the future and in the immediate issue beckoning the conqueror on to fresh efforts in the East.

So the next two years were spent on busy preparations for another expedition—this time by way of Ocean and Arabia. Ships from Phoenicia were sent overland in sections to Thapsacus and floated down the Euphrates. Military arrangements upon a vast scale were undertaken and no expense was spared. Meanwhile Alexander was busy over a thorough reorganization of his empire and his army. During his absence in India things had not unnaturally got a little out of hand. Harpalus, his treasurer, had been guilty, as we have seen, of embezzling the funds and had fled at his approach. Many of his governors had equally been guilty of oppression. These he severely punished, some with death. Such disciplinary measures were, however, of small moment compared with Alexander's more constructive schemes; and it was during these months that he bent his mind most seriously to the task of empire-building. One problem in particular seems to have been uppermost in his thoughts. For he had begun to realize that, if he was to weld his miscellaneous subjects into one united whole, he must take some steps towards a racial fusion. He and his officers, to set a good example, proceeded to marry native wives. Rewards were offered to any among the ranks who would do the same; and it is said that as many as ten thousand complied. This process of fusion Alexander proposed yet further to extend by transporting large numbers of Asiatics into Europe and large numbers of Greeks and Macedonians into the East. But for the time being the policy was most effectually forwarded by his thorough-going reorganization of the army. We have already seen that after Arbela he had begun to train Orientals in Macedonian fashion. A large corps of these were now ready for use, and he proposed to incorporate them wholesale in his regular formations. Henceforth only the more important posts and battle-stations of the phalanx were to be held by Macedonians; and the bulk of the fighting force was to be composed of light-armed native archers and spearmen.[1] To make room for these new recruits was the next step, and those of his veterans whom he thought to be past service, Alexander now proposed to send back home, imagining, as

---

[1] It is to be supposed that the duty of these light-armed troops was to skirmish out ahead of the phalanx and then, when the battle came to close quarters, to take shelter among the heavy-armed ranks. Alexander was, in fact, creating a formation which had all the solidity of hoplite bodies, combined with the mobility of peltasts —a combination which the Roman legion notably displayed and which enabled it to beat the phalanx.

was natural, that they would welcome their discharge. To his surprise they did nothing of the sort. A regular mutiny broke out at the suggestion and they flatly refused to go. None the less, by announcing that he would form a purely Persian army, he had his way in the main. Ten thousand veterans went home, very liberally rewarded. The rest stayed. It now remained to put the finishing touches to the preparations for the great expedition and then to set forth once more upon the march of conquest.

Alexander had reached the pinnacle of his greatness. He saw himself, there can be little doubt, as potentially at least the master of the world. Already he had begun to claim, what has so much scandalized posterity, some sort of divine honours. To ourselves this must inevitably appear either monstrous or ridiculous. But two things are to be remembered. In the first place, the deification of human beings was no uncommon practice in the ancient world. Even the pupils of the Academy erected an altar to the memory of their master Plato ; and after his death Alexander was unquestionably worshipped in Egypt as well as in Macedon.[1] In the second place it is by no means certain what precisely were the powers he claimed. He assuredly did not himself believe that he was God. He even joked at the idea in private. In all probability his imagination placed him among the ranks of the heroes of divine descent, and perhaps, as fitted well with Persian notions, as God's vicegerent on earth. What, however, is pretty certain is that he desired to impress his Oriental subjects by posing as the god of his own countrymen ; and perhaps too he hoped, as did the Roman emperors at a later date, to unite his whole dominion by the bond of this common cult. At any rate we may be sure that it was for political ends that Alexander requested the Greek cities in 324 to accept him as a god. No great objection was raised. In every way his imperial schemes seemed to be prospering ; and, as he was on his way to Babylon in the spring of 323, there came an even more significant

[1] The acceptance of his deification by Orientals (other than Egyptian) would, however, have been precluded by their creed.

tribute to his growing prestige. For he was met upon the road by an embassy from the nations of the West. Ethiopia and Carthage, chieftains of Spain and Gaul, and (though Rome was unrepresented) many tribes of Central and Southern Italy—all these had sent to make him overtures of friendship. So far already had the magic and terror of his name now penetrated ; and with this crowning demonstration of his widespread influence what vistas of world-dominion did not seem to open out ! With a high heart then, as we may fancy, Alexander moved on to Babylon—now elevated, in place of the less central Susa, to be the capital of his realm.

There the great expedition was preparing which should carry him a step further to the fulfilment of his ambition. The conquest of Arabia was to be its prime objective, and therewith the further opening up of the ocean route to India. It was summer now. Babylon was full of notables of every race, gathered to speed the young conqueror upon his way. Many farewell banquets were held, and after a succession of late nights Alexander awoke one morning in a high fever. The expedition was due to start in three days' time, and he put it off one further. But his strength did not rally ; delirium set in and wild rumours flooded the camp. His veterans, torn by suspense, demanded to see him, but, when they were admitted to file through his chamber, Alexander had only strength to touch their hands and give them a meaning look. Towards sundown on the next day he died. Then suddenly men realized that all was changed and the world was without a master. ' A great terror seized upon the stoutest hearts. While the body of the great King lay alone, and deserted by the amazed household, stray shouts broke the anxious silence of the city. Men hurried to and fro in the night without lights and muffled in disguise ; seeking in tumultuous council or in random inquiry, to forecast what would happen on the morrow. There were confused sounds of mourning and woe, not round about the bier of the great King, but for the disasters which each awaited in his home.' In Greece the news was received with blank incredulity. ' It cannot be true,' one said, ' for if it were, the whole world would assuredly stink of his corpse.'

II. CHARACTER AND WORK

It has been the commonplace of historical criticism to say that in the last few years of his life the character of Alexander deteriorated, becoming impatient, petulant and even a little unbalanced. That he was impatient is true enough. For to the very end of his days he remained the sanguine, impetuous, dare-devil boy that he had always been. During his last campaign in India he was watching with growing irritation the slow progress of an assault upon a fort. Presently seizing a ladder he mounted the wall himself, and, being the first over, leapt headlong into the midst of the enemy whom he kept at bay single-handed until seriously wounded in the lung he was rescued by his squires—incredible folly in a commander-in-chief, but typical of the man ; and if he went forward to conquer when he should have stayed behind to organize, it was due to the same defect in his qualities. If, again, it is said that his temper was at times uncertain, then there is little wonder in that, seeing under what strain of ceaseless brainwork and heavy responsibility he lived during those last years—a strain so overwhelming that he is said upon occasion to have collapsed into deep sleep for thirty-six hours at a stretch. But that his powers had suffered any real deterioration there is indeed no sign. His strategical dispositions remained as skilful as they had ever been, his touch upon the battle-field as sure. To compare him with other great commanders is not easy ; for in a sense perhaps he never encountered an enemy truly worthy of his steel. But the fact remains that during ten years or more of fighting, frequently against heavy numerical odds, in circumstances often totally unexpected and always unfamiliar, he was never beaten ; and of how many can that be said ? The character of his leadership, too, was in a sense unique. Napoleon's men fought for France, as well as for Napoleon ; and most of the world's great armies have served a cause as well as a leader. But after

Arbela, at any rate, the men who followed Alexander were fighting his battles and his alone. Mere love of gain or adventure, seeing how great was to many the cost, will hardly explain such fidelity. There must have been in him some magic of personal magnetism, inspiring his company with the sense that they were assisting in the execution of some great idea. Indeed, the whole secret of Alexander's greatness seems to reside in the fact that along with an untiring capacity for action he combined a rare quality of vision too ; and, as time passed, that vision became not dimmer, but more clear and well-defined. He began his conquests as the champion of Greece against her traditional foe. He ended by envisaging a universal empire in which nationalities would be merged in one allegiance and barriers of race forgotten. Nor was this ideal a mere idle dream towards which no steps were taken. The constructive quality of Alexander's genius stands beyond question. During the short space of life allowed him, and in years which were mostly spent upon the march, he yet found time so well to organize his new-won empire that even during his long absence in far-distant lands it somehow held together. But he did more than this. For the consequences of his work, brief as it was, transformed the East, giving it intellectually and morally an entirely new outlook upon life. There stands Alexander's true claim to greatness. As a conqueror he was perhaps unrivalled in antiquity ; and the genius of his military exploits so impressed themselves on Asia that the romance of his career became a fairy tale in the folk-lore of a score of languages, and two thousand years later, when Napoleon appeared in Syria, the Bedouins told one another that it was ' Iskander ' come again. But the influence of his constructive statesmanship went deeper still, producing in the history of civilization consequences which he himself for all his powers of vision could never dimly have foreseen.

Detailed information about Alexander's constructive schemes of Empire is unfortunately scanty. We can tell moderately well what was done in Asia Minor and Egypt

—the first to be settled and already to a large extent imbued by civilizing influences. Of other provinces, which were less fruitful soil, correspondingly less is known ; and it is not always easy to be seen how far his successors carried out Alexander's policy or how far they departed from it. One thing, however, is clear, that in general Alexander's methods were conservative, and that he adopted, wherever possible, the machinery of organization which he found ready to hand. Thus, in Asia Minor he restored to their old autonomous status the Greek cities that welcomed his coming, and granted them the democratic privileges which they so highly prized. In the rest of the old Persian Empire he accepted the satrapy system, often confirming the appointment of existing Asiatic governors. The finance of the Empire, however, he concentrated in the hands of his own nominees. Harpalus, as we have seen, was entrusted with the exchequer of the central provinces. A Greek, named Cleomenes, exercised a similar function in Egypt. Apart from the accumulated treasure which fell to him by capture, Alexander also drew a large revenue from the old royal estates, which he kept in his own hands. These were worked by a serf population which, like the villeinage of Anglo-Saxon England, paid to him as their overlord an annual tithe of the produce. Unfortunately the opportunities for extortion were great, and the predatory instincts of the European controllers were not curbed by any sense of official responsibility. In fact, the general outcome of Alexander's conquests was undoubtedly to lay the East at the mercy of the exploitation of the West ; and it was a rich harvest.

Nevertheless Alexander's own ideal was clearly very different. With him conquest did not find a natural sequel in oppression, and he aimed ultimately, as we have said, at amalgamating his scattered and heterogeneous empire into one harmonious whole. Not that he endeavoured to impose any hard and fast system. Thus, although he desired to be a god to the Greeks, he never made that demand on the Persians, to whose religious conceptions such an idea would have been altogether alien. Again, while he restored democracy in Ionia, it is very doubtful whether he allowed it in any of the cities that he personally founded. In other words, he suited his policy to the character of his subjects, and in dealing with peoples so diverse in blood and creed and custom no other plan was really practicable. Two leading ideas, however, he seems to have had for achieving some unification. On the first of these we have already touched—fusion of races. That principle he applied in various ways, but in every case it proved a failure. Thus in the administration of his captured provinces he clearly wished to employ Asiatics and Europeans side by side. But out of eighteen native satraps whom he reappointed, few proved worthy of the trust. Ten were deposed ; some died ; and only three were still in office at the time of his own death. Again, we have seen how in the army he was engaged in drafting Oriental soldiery into the ranks of the Macedonian phalanx. The policy brought nothing but discontent, and after his death it was almost immediately abandoned. Nor was his project of wholesale transportations ever destined to come to fruition. Such a measure was not, of course, unknown in antiquity. The Kings of Assyria and Babylon practised it, and the deportation of the Hebrew peoples is a sufficiently well-known example. Nevertheless Alexander made no attempt to move Asiatics to Europe, and though many Greeks, as we shall see, came voluntarily to Asia, the real need, if any genuine fusion of race was to be achieved, was for Greek women. The intermarriage of a few thousand Macedonians with Oriental wives was not enough, and the half-breed population resulting from such unions must speedily have relapsed into barbarism. For it is the mother who sets the tone of the home. The fact is that Alexander was faced by the same problem which modern European nations have encountered in their occupation of backward countries. We ourselves have not attempted in India, for example, to promote a racial or even a social fusion between our settlers and the natives. The obstacles for Alexander were not indeed so great ; for between Greeks and Persians the difference of blood is comparatively far less than between British and Indians. Nevertheless, even had he lived, it is unlikely that he would have made much real progress. East is East and West is West; and how to bring them together is a problem that still defies the powers of human statesmanship.

A more promising line of policy was to leaven the East with the methods and ideas of the West. In other words, the Levant might be Hellenized as India has, in part at least, been Anglicized, or as Gaul and Britain in early days were taught the ways of Rome. And to this end Alexander's second great idea was clearly aimed. Town life, as has often been said, was the very essence of Greek civilization. That town life, too, is the most effective civilizing influence among backward peoples, history has repeatedly proved. It was the Roman borough or colony planted in Britain or Gaul which formed the true foundation of those countries' cultural development. So Alexander, it is clear, was displaying real insight when he deliberately planted, at almost every stage of his advance, a township planned on Greek models and populated for the most part by Greeks. Over seventy of such foundations are known to have existed. Twenty-five can be identified. Some, like Alexandria, became great and flourishing cities. Others, planted in regions as inaccessible as Baluchistan itself, rapidly dwindled and were lost, though Merv and Kandahar, refounded by his successors, retained no small importance. The general purpose and character of these colonies appear to have been twofold. In the first place, each received a nucleus of discharged veterans, who might serve, if need be, as a garrison and outpost of Empire. Secondly, inducements were offered to emigrants from Greece. A motley horde of hangers-on followed, we know, in the wake of Alexander's camp, craftsmen, physicians and seers, money-changers and traders, musicians, athletes, jesters, clerks and even women. Many of these were ready enough to settle; and to a people whose instincts were essentially commercial and who adapted themselves easily to new surroundings, the opportunity was irresistible. So a further host of settlers began to flow out East, and to people the new cities which Alexander had organized upon congenial lines. For in these mushroom towns the very planning of the streets and buildings was on a strictly Hellenic pattern: a central market-square round which were grouped colonnades of public offices and temples. The code of laws under which the new city should be governed was equally modelled upon the traditional Greek lines. Magistrates were elected to control the streets and market, and no doubt to hear disputes. Whether in some cases a Council and Assembly was permitted is uncertain; but in any case the supreme authority was vested, as a rule, in a governor appointed by Alexander himself. Nevertheless the settlers enjoyed a highly privileged position. They alone constituted the citizen body; and though, in Alexandria at any rate, the population became exceedingly mixed, the Greeks were inclined to be very exclusive and to keep themselves aloof from the natives. The tendency was, in fact, as we remarked above, to treat the Oriental merely as an object for commercial exploitation. No true national feeling emerged. The influence of the Hellenic institutions and culture thus planted in the 'barbarian' East was very slow to extend beyond the walls of the towns. They remained more or less like civilized islands in the midst of an uncivilized sea.

Nevertheless within these limits the effect on the intellectual thought and moral outlook of the East was, as we have said, profound. For one thing the Greek language took firm and permanent root round the shores of the Levant. The Jews of Alexandria adopted it for the famous Septuagint version of their Scriptures. Palestine itself became bilingual. Meleager, one of the most famous of Greek epigrammatists, was a native of Gadara. We can be almost certain that Christ Himself frequently talked Greek, as His disciples habitually wrote what was by then a somewhat debased and colloquial form of it. Where language penetrated, it was inevitable that Greek methods of thought would follow, and, rigidly antagonistic though it was to external influences, even Judaism was deeply affected. The free and liberal outlook resulting from an acquaintance with Greek literature produced a party of Hellenizing Jews not only among the scattered groups of the Dispersion, but also in Jerusalem itself. The main object of such Hellenizers was to rationalize the Law of Moses, to dispense with much of its more exacting ritual, and by breaking down the narrowly exclusive limitations of Jehovah worship, to adapt it more readily to the needs of mankind. Among the followers of this movement Christianity was to find many converts, Stephen the Martyr being one of the first ; and indeed, it was largely because the Greek language had provided a common vehicle of thought and expression that St. Paul and the other early missionaries were able to spread their message so freely in Asia Minor and elsewhere. In short, the influences which sprang directly or indirectly from Alexander's colonization gave a wholly new tone to the eastern half of the Mediterranean world, and a tone moreover which was by no means obliterated by incorporation in the Roman Empire. On the contrary, the Hellenized eastern provinces of that Empire, surviving the chaos and disruption of the West, maintained for centuries a culture distinctively their own. The civilization of the Byzantine Emperors, stereotyped and degenerate though it was, owed more to Alexander than it owed to Rome ; and Constantinople, their capital, remained the home and centre of Greek scholarship until in the Fifteenth Century A.D. the city passed into the hands of the conquering Turk.[1]

But, if by the introduction of Hellenic culture Alexander's policy transformed the East, the process involved, as it was bound to do, some transformation of that culture also. Yet, if the change meant some deterioration, it meant gain as well ; for though the transplanted Hellenism lost its old creative impulse and something of its pristine purity, it acquired in compensation a broader basis and a more universal outlook. Greece, as Alexander found

[1] Yet it should be added that the Arabian civilization, territorially almost coextensive with Alexander's empire, retained much of Hellenistic culture. Its science, medicine and mathematics thus lingered in Samarcand and found their way to Cairo and Cordova.

her, was wedded to an ideal infinitely narrow, exclusive, almost parochial, unable to conceive of any better social system than the *Polis* in which a strictly limited citizen body enjoyed exceptional privileges at the expense of its unprivileged slaves ; unable equally to compose the age-long differences between petty state and petty state, even when the futility of their interminable conflicts was long since manifest to every eye ; unable, above all, to imagine a world in which Hellene and barbarian would stand on an equal footing and races of different origin or tradition might be bound together in the ties of a common allegiance. Such a unity, in a political sense at least, Alexander manifestly failed to impose ; and the inhabitants of his Empire never came to recognize themselves as one nation. But in a wider sense he succeeded beyond all that he himself could ever have dreamed. For by breaking through the crusted shell of narrow prejudice which for so long had cribbed and confined it, he set the Greek genius free to spread its wings abroad in unrestricted flight and find a lodgment wherever men were prepared to receive it. If he did not create a new national spirit, Alexander created something which at the time was perhaps even more needed : a cosmopolitan or international spirit, a spirit in which a community of intellectual ideas and cultural standards was to transcend the boundaries of country or of continent, a spirit which enabled Zeno the Stoic (himself a Semite of Citium in Cyprus) to boast himself ' a citizen of the world ' and a believer in the brotherhood of mankind, and which more than three centuries later made it possible for St. Paul to preach a state of society wherein there should be ' neither Greek nor Jew, Barbarian or Scythian, bond or free.'

CHAPTER XXI

THE HELLENISTIC AGE AND AFTER

I. ALEXANDER'S SUCCESSORS

ALEXANDER left no heir. A son was born to him by Roxana after his death ; but the boy never came into his heritage and met eventually with a violent end. The Empire, lacking a supreme controller, and falling a prey to the ambitious rivalry of Alexander's generals, went rapidly to pieces, and out of the pieces these generals carved for themselves considerable kingdoms. Antigonus, who was perhaps the ablest among them and who at any rate aimed at holding the Empire together, was overthrown in 301 and committed suicide. The rest divided the spoils. Cassander, son of Antipater, who had been Alexander's viceroy in Europe, retained Macedon and Greece. Ptolemy, long since its governor, held Egypt. The Eastern provinces went to Seleucus, and into his hands presently fell Asia Minor also, which at first had been Lysimachus' portion. These three kingdoms, ruled by a succession of powerful monarchs, remained in being till the Romans appeared on the scene. The Seleucid realm, indeed, suffered a gradual diminution, its more distant eastern dependencies falling away,[1] and Asia Minor being in part overrun by a horde of invading Celts who settled in Galatia, in part split up into the independent monarchies of Pergamum and Pontus. The Macedonian kingdom, which passed into the hands of

[1] In Bactria, however, a Greek dynasty survived till the end of the Second Century B.C., a centre of civilization which much affected both India and China. At the end of the Third Century, Antiochus III reconquered the other eastern territories of his Seleucid predecessors. Alexander's policy of city-building was notably continued by the Seleucids, and their power only really crumbled before the progress of Roman armies early in the First Century B.C.

Antigonus Gonatas, remained virile and compact, and though Greece was able for a time to recover something of her old liberty, she was never genuinely free from the menace of intervention from the North. Most prosperous and most brilliant, however, of the three dominions was the Egypt of Ptolemy and his successors. She enjoyed, thanks to Tyre's destruction, a complete command of the eastern waters of the Mediterranean. Trade flowed in to her from India and Arabia; and her merchants even competed with Carthage in the west. Her government was conducted on the old lines of native administration rather than on Greek or Macedonian models; and Ptolemy was content to assimilate his power to the dynastic tradition of the Pharaohs.[1] But he was none the less a man of more than ordinary culture and enlightenment, and he soon made Alexandria an intellectual centre second to none. The 'Museum' or University of Scholars, which he founded, became the scene of scientific research and literary labour unrivalled in antiquity. Here Euclid worked and Eratosthenes and many another of the brilliant thinkers of whom we spoke above. Side by side with the Museum, Ptolemy founded his famous library. In it all the literature and learning of the world was gathered, and hosts of copyists were kept busy in adding to its treasures. Trained critics were engaged in editing the more famous of the classics, dividing up their contents into chapters, books and volumes, to suit at once the convenience of the reader and also the limited proportions of the flimsy papyrus rolls on which the works were copied.[2]

[1] Nevertheless, the scientific bureaucracy instituted by the Ptolemies was a successful method of government and was largely adopted by the Roman Emperors after their annexation of Egypt. It involved, to a large degree, the exploitation of native labour, and the heritage of this tradition became a more or less permanent feature of Egyptian history.

[2] Alexandria did a lively trade in book production, in which the Ptolemies obtained for their country a virtual monopoly by forbidding the export of papyrus. As this was unobtainable elsewhere, the scribes of Pergamum, also a great centre of culture, were forced to write on parchment—a word which is itself derived from the city's name.

Grammarians and commentators wrote learned treatises on the rules of syntax, compiled dictionaries, and expounded or criticized the masterpieces of earlier days. Among the Alexandrian scholars pedantry was, in fact, to take the place of genuine creative work, or even, since they were no great philosophers, of adventurous speculation. Much solid and even brilliant work was done in the scientific sphere ; but, so far as concerned literature and art, a decline had set in. The old spirit of Hellas was dead and the period of the decadence is known, by way of distinction from the true Hellenic, as the ' Hellenistic Age '.

The weaknesses of Hellenistic writers were due, however, not to any lack of fidelity to the past, but to an excess of it. Had they been willing to submit themselves to the foreign influences by which they were surrounded—the Persian, the Egyptian, or above all, perhaps, the Hebrew —the result could scarcely have been other than a discovery of new ideas and an outburst of original invention. For the fact was that the genius of Greece was stale, and badly needed the infusion of fresh blood. But unfortunately the Alexandrians were too jealously conservative of their heritage and, determining at all costs to preserve its purity from the contamination of such ' barbarian ' influences, they continued to look for their inspiration to the models set by the masterpieces of earlier days. Thus the source of originality was dried up and the place of imagination taken by a sterile and academic ingenuity. The Alexandrians became for the most part mere imitators, selecting as the model of their style now this author, now that, and attempting to combine the best qualities of Hellenic literature in an extremely erudite but over-laborious eclecticism. Such virtues as they possessed lay in a perfection of polish and refinement rather than in fertility of ideas. Callimachus, one of the first keepers of the Ptolemaic library, the compiler of a literary catalogue and himself the author of books which filled eight hundred rolls, was justly celebrated for the exquisite finish of his elegiac epigrams ; and among them is the famous epitaph best known to English readers through Cory's translation :

> They told me, Heraclitus, they told me you were dead ;
> They brought me bitter news to hear and bitter tears to shed.
> I wept as I remembered how often you and I
> Had tired the sun with talking and sent him down the sky.
> And now that thou art lying, my dear old Carian guest,
> A handful of grey ashes, long, long ago at rest,
> Still are thy pleasant voices, thy nightingales awake :
> For Death, he taketh all away, but them he cannot take.

Another writer who eventually retired to Rhodes was Apollonius, the author of an epic entitled the *Argonautica* —a work which, though little applauded by his contemporaries, exercised a great influence on Virgil in the composition of his *Aeneid*. But by far the greatest of the Alexandrian poets was Theocritus, a strange figure writing in the sophisticated atmosphere of the cosmopolitan city about the love-making and pastoral pleasures of idealized peasants in an idealized Arcadia. In style he harked back to the model of the Homeric hexameter, but by his exquisite gift of language and an unusual combination of wistful humour and tender pathos he succeeded in creating a world of extraordinary freshness and delicate beauty— a success which doubtless owed much of its inspiration to the poet's own longing to escape from the over-civilized environment in which his lot was cast. His work set the pattern for pastoral poets of many succeeding ages, Virgil among the rest, and in his own epoch he was followed by Bion and Moschus, both careful stylists, but lacking the fire and passion of genuine emotion.

While poetry was thus flourishing in Alexandria and while the rival art of sculpture was carried on, with similar success, and similar defects, at Pergamum,[1] Athens remained the true home of philosophical inquiry. Of the foundation of the Stoic school by Zeno we have already spoken ; and neither of this nor of its rival school, the

---

[1] The Pergamene school of sculpture produced such works of art as the ' Dying Gaul ', now in the Capitoline Museum at Rome, and the ' Laocoön ' group, also at Rome.

Epicurean, need more at this point be said. But it is important to remember how long the intellectual supremacy of the Athenian people outlived their city's political and economic decay. As the commercial focus of the Mediterranean shifted and the Aegean trade passed more and more into the hands of Rhodes, the Athenians devoted themselves with even greater ardour to the business of speculation and debate. Their highly sceptical and inquisitive temper is well reflected in the experience of the Apostle Paul, who found on the Areopagus an abundance of listeners, but very few to believe. For during the years of her decline Athens had become as sterile in her way as Alexandria itself. Lectures were delivered, and young students gathered from all parts of the world to hear them. But the true Hellenic spirit could not survive in an atmosphere where political life had become a dead issue, and minds, once so active in the application of ideas to practical ends, were now compelled to feed upon theories alone. For, though Athens was still free to manage her own affairs, the shadow of Macedon loomed large on the northern horizon, and she knew that her only hope of security lay in a dull impassivity. Except for two brief attempts at regaining a free hand, once in 301 and again with Sparta's aid in 266, the days of her bold, adventurous policy were gone for ever; and she could only cherish in pathetic impotence the memory of a time when, as a leader among Greeks, she had truckled to no man and knew herself, morally, socially and intellectually, to be the superior of the whole human race.

Among the other states of the Greek peninsula a similar condition of precarious independence prevailed; and, though liable on occasion to feel the strong hand of some Macedonian monarch more ambitious than the rest, they were permitted to enjoy for considerable periods a completely free hand in self-government. The Pan-Hellenic Union, inaugurated by Philip, had indeed soon broken down, but the example of its federal institutions proved infectious, and the cities of mainland Greece (with the exception of Sparta and Athens) had now the good sense to combine in two fairly comprehensive and fairly stable groups. The vigour which served to set such movements on foot came from two people hitherto inconspicuous, and now perhaps the more virile, because slow to develop. First, as the Fourth Century had drawn to its close, the peasant population of Aetolia had instituted a league which came to embrace not merely the majority of northern states, but also, south of the Isthmus, a part of Arcadia, and Elis. The policy of the league was restless and predatory, befitting the leadership of a people only partially civilized and more interested in plunder than politics. The constitution of its federation, while leaving the ultimate sovereignty to the votes of the entire citizen bodies and the conduct of ordinary business to a Council which those bodies elected, nevertheless placed the supreme executive power in the hands of a single official ; and he, as seems characteristic of the League's militarist tendency, was the army's commander-in-chief. The other Federation, which sprang from the revival of an ancient league among the cities of Achaea, came somewhat later into being, and about the middle of the Third Century B.C. embraced Corinth, Megalopolis, Sicyon, Argos and other neighbouring communities. Though its constitution was similar to that of its Aetolian rival, it was more pacific in policy. Its chief founder, Aratus, was no soldier, and though for a while it maintained itself against Macedonian encroachment, its military strength was not great, and in 224 fear of Spartan aggression drove the League into subservient dependence on Antigonus Doson, who aimed at re-establishing under his own suzerainty the policy of Pan-Hellenic reunion. After his death, the Achaean League recovered its independent status, and under the patriot soldier Philopoemen began to exert a more stalwart and more salutary influence, aiming at a genuine reunion of Hellas, on the basis of its own democratic institutions, and advocating a conciliatory policy of international equity But such efforts were frustrated, now as so often throughout the history of the race, by the quarrelsome and selfish attitude of neighbouring cities. Greece, under whatever leadership, would not combine; and her lack of combination paved the way for her approaching and, as it proved to be, her permanent subjection to a new enemy. For the turn of Rome had now come.

During the years when Alexander's successors had been squabbling over the division of his Empire, Rome was completing her conquest of the Italian peninsula. By 282 Tarentum, alone among the chief cities of the South, stood out against her growing supremacy, and its inhabitants, picking an unnecessary quarrel, proceeded to summon from across the Adriatic the formidable military assistance of Pyrrhus, King of Epirus. Though Pyrrhus' well-trained phalanx and highly skilful generalship inflicted severe reverses on the Roman arms, the instability of the Italian Greeks, in whose interest he had come, served largely to counterbalance his successes, and after the withdrawal of his forces Tarentum was speedily reduced. Rome's attention was next directed towards Sicily. There a more or less continuous and uphill conflict had been waged, as of old, against the aggression of Carthage. After Timoleon's death Syracuse had fallen once again under a tyrant, Agathocles by name, who, by uniting the Greek cities under his armed hegemony and by enlisting the friendship of Macedon and other Hellenistic monarchies, held out for a while good promise of achieving the expulsion of Sicily's hereditary foe. But his death in 289 had put an end to such aspirations; and it remained for Rome in her first Punic War (264-241) to accomplish at once the liberation of the island from the age-long menace and its permanent subjugation to her own imperial yoke.[1] In the second Punic War, by her successful resistance to Hannibal's invasion and by her crowning triumph at Zama on Carthaginian soil, she reduced to impotence her one formidable rival in the West; and it was obvious that a trial of strength could not now be long delayed with the still powerful and warlike realm of Macedon. King Philip, who occupied

[1] At first Hieron II, King of Syracuse, who had been allied to Rome in the war, was permitted to rule the eastern part of the island under Roman protection.

its throne, had during the Punic War allied himself to Hannibal, and, though the actual assistance which he gave had amounted to very little, it had been sufficient to awaken the hostility of Rome. In the first Macedonian War (200–196) the consul Flaminius inflicted a decisive defeat on Philip's army at Cynoscephalae, but after declaring the Greek cities free from Macedonian interference and placing them under the nominal protectorship of Rome, he then withdrew. The next thirty years were occupied in answering the challenge of the Seleucid Empire by the conquest of its remaining dependencies in Asia Minor and in completing the task, which Flaminius had begun, of reducing Macedon. The turn of the Greeks came next. In most of their cities a pro-Roman faction had now sprung up, and the futile bickerings of these petty states was soon to hasten the inevitable end. In 146 a rising in Macedon had decided the Romans to convert that turbulent protectorate into a subject province, and the extension of this policy to Greece itself was prompted by the chaotic condition of that distracted country. Sparta and the Achaean League were once more at loggerheads ; and, when the Roman commissioners gave their verdict in Sparta's favour, they were hissed by the Corinth mob. War followed. Little resistance was offered, except at Corinth ; and after a siege that city was captured by the consul Mummius. Hitherto the Roman policy had on the whole been sympathetic to the Greeks. But the revenge now taken on Corinth for her mob's discourtesy was quite needlessly barbarous. The city was practically destroyed and the victorious consul, himself a man of neither breeding, taste nor culture, amused himself by sending off in ship-loads, for the glorification of his coming ' triumph,' scores upon scores of the priceless artistic treasures of which the town was full. It was a tardy act of grace that in the subsequent organization of the conquered country Athens and Sparta were allowed to retain the status of autonomous allied cities, exempt from the galling burden of imperial tribute.

II. Greek Influences on Rome

It is a commonplace of history that the conquered country ' took its captor captive ', and that the influence of Greek culture wrought a complete transformation of the whole intellectual and moral outlook of the Roman people. It must not be supposed, however, that the operation of those influences was delayed till the actual consummation of Mummius' conquest or that their sources were by any means confined to the states of the Greek peninsula itself. Rome's first serious contact with Hellenism had begun with her capture of Tarentum. The effect upon her literature was direct and immediate ; for Livius Andronicus, the dramatist, was brought back to the capital among the prisoners of that city. Nor is it surprising to find that Naevius and Ennius, the most prominent among her earliest poets, were both natives of the South and so born in close proximity to cities of Greek origin. During the half-century which elapsed between the Battle of Zama and the siege of Corinth, Hellenism attained an extraordinary vogue among a certain section of Roman society. The younger Scipio was an ardent admirer of Greek manners, Greek literature ; and so equally was Aemilius Paulus, the conqueror of Macedon. A growing intercourse between the two peninsulas brought about in the Republic a natural sense of sympathy towards a kindred people enjoying institutions very similar to her own and a civilization which she could not pretend to rival. Above all, the demand for administrative ability, which increased as the confines of the Empire grew, compelled the unintellectual Romans to embrace with ready zeal the educational methods of a people long accustomed to the discipline of style and thought. Even so hardened a conservative as Cato learnt Greek in his old age   Parents hired Greek tutors for the instruction of their sons ; and the study of Greek rhetoric became the staple training of young aspirants to political or forensic eminence, such as the brothers Gracchus. In the last century of the Republic it became increasingly common for well-to-do parents to send their sons to the University of Athens, where they would learn to declaim and to argue. Philosophical discussion ranged the more thoughtful of the educated class into the opposing camps of Stoic and Epicurean doctrine ; and Greek ideas had by now permeated through and through the whole temper of Roman society. To talk Greek was becoming as common an accomplishment as to talk French with us, and Greek words slip as constantly into the private correspondence of Cicero as will a Gallicism into the columns of *The Times*. Above all, as every one knows, Latin literature was developed almost entirely on Greek lines. The satire alone was a form of composition indigenous to Italy ; and in every other genre the model was taken from Hellenic sources. The plays of Plautus and Terence were largely transcripts from the New Attic Comedy. Cicero's style was moulded by close study in the twin schools of Attic and Rhodian oratory, the one terse and restrained, the other, as was characteristic of Asiatic culture, more flowery and diffuse. Horace borrowed his lyrical prosody from metres originally invented by such poets as Sappho or Alcaeus, based his thought on the doctrines of Epicurus, and even affected in his syntax a frequent imitation of Greek idiom. Virgil himself, the Laureate of Roman Imperialism, began in his *Eclogues* with a close copy of Theocritus the Alexandrian and ended in his *Aeneid* by drawing largely from the model set by Apollonius of Rhodes.

From what has been already said, it will at once be seen that the main influences under which these Roman writers fell were Hellenistic rather than Hellenic. This was but natural, seeing how close and how continuous had become the intercourse between Italy and the chief cultural centres of the eastern Mediterranean. For the Empire had been growing. By the time of Augustus, Asia Minor, Syria and Egypt had one by one been brought within its compass ; and thus of all the peoples now subject to its sway one-half at least, and that by far the more important and more educated half, was deeply imbued with the ideas and speech of Greece. It is often insufficiently realized how large a part this Hellenistic civilization played in the history of the Roman world, and how profound too was its influence upon the Roman character. From the first the effects of contact with Greek thought and manners had been, as was inevitable, a rude unsettlement of the old Republican conservatism. Men trained, as the old-fashioned Romans were, to an almost Spartan austerity and self-restraint, could not fail to be profoundly affected by those sceptical and individualistic doctrines which we saw long since to have so seriously undermined the morale of Fifth-Century Greece. And the results were the same. Time-honoured traditions were questioned or discarded. New luxuries and vices, unknown to the Rome of Papirius and the Decii, were brought back to the capital by provincial governors or capitalistic merchants. A cynical pursuit of self-interest and self-indulgence was ominously displayed in the decadent tendencies and fierce internecine conflicts which heralded the fall of the Republic ; and with the coming of the Empire things grew not better, but much worse. The saner Romans, indeed, strove to uphold a dignity of life traditional to their breed, and in their heart of hearts despised the moral lightness of the Greek. But the sheer need for sharp wits and trained intelligence in the administration of affairs made it almost impossible to do without him. Greek slaves were habitually employed to keep accounts. They were used as scribes and secretaries and tutors. Above all, we now find freedmen of Greek origin occupying important places in the Imperial Civil Service ; and the worst Emperors, such as Nero, allowed men of this type to rise to positions of close familiarity and trust. For better or for worse, in fact, the civilization of Italy, and through Italy the civilization of her subject provinces in Spain, Gaul, Great Britain, the Balkans and North Africa became by the time of the Empire fundamentally Greek. Throughout these provinces fine cities such as Timgad on the fringe of the Sahara, were constructed largely on Greek patterns and in a style of architecture predominantly Greek. Even in the sphere of law, so characteristically Roman, the leading ideas of systematization were in a great degree derived from Hellenistic sources. The debt Rome owed to Greece was immeasurable, but the price she paid was high. For meanwhile the Imperial city itself was losing its native character, and to the disgust of old-fashioned moralists like Juvenal, the opportunities which it offered were attracting in ever increasing numbers a sharp-witted, shallow and acquisitive horde of Hellenized provincials. The 'hungry Greekling', who could turn his skill to everything from dancing on the tight-rope to surgery or surveying, had become, in fact, as much a curse to Rome as the negro has become to the United States. And the trouble was that he was still apt to be a more intelligent man than his masters.

But for all that it must not be supposed that the influence of Hellenism was altogether vicious or that the better side of the Greek spirit was altogether dead. Not merely did it bear good fruit in the minds of cultured Romans, who consoled themselves for the loss of the old traditional religion or morality by the study and practice of philosophic doctrines, but in the realm of Greek literature itself there was still sound work to be done. Towards the end of the First Century A.D. Plutarch was compiling his famous *Biographies*. The great cultural revival under Marcus Aurelius produced the witty and satirical Lucian, and the greatest of all ancient physicians, the Alexandrian Galen. Pausanias, the great antiquarian and traveller, flourished a little later, and in A.D. 204 was born Plotinus, the Neo-Platonist and the noblest of the latter-day philosophers. But all this time there had been growing, in spite of vigorous official opposition, a movement which, while in no sense independent of Hellenic thought, was essentially antagonistic to its pagan creeds—the Christian Church itself. In A.D. 323 (a date which by an odd coincidence repeats the figure of Alexander's death) the Imperial power passed into the hands of the great Constantine who, by declaring Christianity the religion of the State, struck a death-blow to the old order. And, though forty years later Paganism enjoyed a brief revival under Julian the

Apostate, yet his despairing confession of failure proclaimed once and for all the triumph of ' the pale Galilean ' and the final passing of the gods and ideals of Greece.

III. HELLENISM AND CHRISTIANITY

Born as it was into an environment already deeply tinged with Hellenistic culture, the relations of Christianity to Greek thought could hardly fail to be of great and even vital import to its early development. It is true that the character of Christ's own message was such that it would probably have been almost incomprehensible to a Socrates or an Aristotle, and that in the first instance Hebrews alone were capable of fully appreciating and accepting it. Yet, once it had found its Jewish adherents, it was essential to the wider propagation of the Gospel that these should employ some vehicle of expression common to men of every race and every class ; and they found it, of course, in the debased colloquial Greek, at that time almost universally current in the eastern half of the Mediterranean world. But it was not merely as a vehicle of missionary propaganda that Greek proved so useful to the early Christians. For in the evolution of their actual faith it was equally to play an all-important part as a medium of ordered thought and systematic formulation of belief. Dean Inge has said that between Palestine and Christian dogma ' there is very little connexion ' ; and a profound truth lies behind this apparent paradox. So long as men's personal memory of Christ was vivid and all-absorbing, and their hope of His imminent return still strong, there was little room for speculation or reflective questioning. But when both the memory and the hope began to fade, the more thoughtful among believers were almost of necessity compelled to ask themselves what precisely it was that they believed. Was Christ God, or was He man ? If He now reigned in Heaven, what was His relation to the Supreme Deity and what His relation to His followers on earth ? Now, in seeking a solution to such questions, it was equally inevitable that men should turn increasingly to the one method of probing and expressing truth then recognized by the ancient world—the Philosophy of the Greeks. Thus even in so early a theologian as the writer of the Fourth Gospel we find much that displays a close affinity to the theories of both Platonists and Stoics ; and when he declares that ' the *Word* became flesh and dwelt among us,' he is employing the actual terminology of the contemporary pagan schools. Still more were the writings of the Early Fathers saturated with the thought of Greek logicians and metaphysicians. Neo-Platonism, in particular, though itself a rival and eventually an antagonist of the Christian Faith, exercised a profound influence upon such a man as Origen. The Gnostic heresy was an attempt to capture the new theology in the interests of Greco-Oriental thought. The very Creeds themselves were the Church's answer to problems raised and formulated in terms of current philosophy ; and the more complex of them can never be understood in their full significance without intimate acquaintance with the intellectual background on which their phraseology was based. In short, if Hellenism was primarily the means of enabling Christianity to spread beyond the narrow limits of a small Jewish sect, it was equally the means whereby the Faith was raised above the level of a merely emotional mysticism and securely grounded on the essentially Greek belief that Truth is knowable and that even the deepest of religious mysteries can be apprehended by the mind of man.

But, though intellectually the debt of Christianity to Hellenism is great, yet morally at least the two ideals stand poles asunder. The Greek view of life had conceived man's happiness to lie in the fullest possible development of all his powers and faculties. Self-realization is the Gospel of Aristotle ; self-sufficiency the Gospel of the Stoic ; and self-sacrifice, when all is said, appears to have appealed to them merely as the noblest consummation of human virtue, a source of conscious and creditable pride, not as the spontaneous outcome of an unreflecting love which discards all thought of self in the service of God or fellow-beings. Here lay the fundamental weakness of the Greek morality ; and to correct it was perhaps the most revolutionary achievement of the new Christian Ethic, in which love became the mainspring and inspiring motive of all right activities. When Christ declared that to seek life was to lose it, and to lose life was to find it, He was replacing the ideal of self-realization by the ideal of self-forgetfulness. And the influence of the new ideal may be illustrated not merely in the early writers of the persecuted Faith, but also down through the Middle Ages in the complete self-abnegation of the monk or friar, in the enthusiasm of the Crusader, or even in the devotion of the ordinary layman to the claims of Mother Church. The spiritual atmosphere of Mediaeval Christendom was something very far removed from Hellenism.

The change of outlook upon life, however, was due in part to something else besides a revolution in moral and religious ideas. For, while the Middle Ages possessed a different and unquestionably higher conception of man's relations to God and to his fellow-men, they had also a very different and much lower conception of the function of the human intellect. A complete severance had, in fact, taken place from the best traditions of Greek thought , and in this there was real loss. It is not so much that men had ceased to study the works of Greek philosophers, for Plato and Aristotle were still a good deal read, albeit in Latin translations. The real trouble was that in reading them men ceased to think for themselves. The reason for this was twofold. In the first place, during the chaos and ignorance of the Dark Ages the tradition of learning had been so nearly lost that, when the threads were again picked up, men clutched at whatever written works survived from the wreck of a more civilized age, and treated them as absolute authorities too sacred to be questioned. The doctrines of Aristotle were accepted as premises from which to argue and draw logical deductions ; but to examine the validity of those premisses was more than anyone dared ; and such an attitude made progress impossible.

In the second place, since education was concentrated

entirely in the hands of a Church which claimed to be the final repository and arbiter of all Truth, it followed that any tendency towards freedom of individual thought was checked at the very source ; and the speculations of the mediaeval schoolmen thus became arid and unfruitful, lacking that vital spirit of inquiry which had been the peculiar genius of the ancient Greeks.

It was not until the latter end of the Middle Ages that this spirit of inquiry was by degrees recovered, and its recovery was largely due to the revival of the interest in Greek. Old volumes which had lain for centuries unnoticed on the shelves of musty libraries were now taken down and conned.[1] Others were brought to Western Europe by Byzantine scholars fleeing from Constantinople before the fury of the Turk. And with this rediscovery of Hellenic literature and, above all, with the renewed study of its great philosophers, there burst upon Christendom the great intellectual upheaval which we call the Renaissance. In the course of that movement the vitalizing power of Greek thought displayed itself in a thousand ways, some good, some bad. Speculation became unfettered. The authority of the Church was challenged ; and the Reformation was the result. As at Athens in the days of Socrates, the accepted traditions of the past went by the board and men launched forth upon the adventurous quest of new truths and new standards, founding a multitude of strange religious sects and propounding a variety of hazardous political theories. Morality suffered. Machiavellian intrigues were dictated by an unlicensed pursuit of self-interest, and (what is always a dangerous symptom) men sought to justify the means they employed by the end they had in view. Meanwhile learning made rapid strides. A new literature sprang up, itself in no small measure influenced by the classical models of the past, Art was revolutionized and a new style of architecture

---

[1] It is worth noting, too, that much Greek scientific knowledge, particularly from the works of Aristotle, found its way back to Europe through the Saracenic civilization of Spain, whither it had been brought from those Arabic sources referred to above.

evolved in imitation of the Greco-Roman. The resumption of scientific inquiry led to discoveries which heralded the Modern Age and led by slow degrees to the Industrial Revolution. The results of the Renaissance in every sphere of life are with us yet ; and the spirit of Hellas works still in the world to-day.

IV. MODERN RESEARCH

But, great as has been the influence of Greece on the thinkers and writers of the last four centuries, it would be an error to suppose that the full range and significance of Hellenism was fully explored even by the greatest scholars among them. From the very outset of the Renaissance there was a tendency to accord an unreflective and un-critical admiration to whatever was classical, and to such an extent has this tendency prevailed that men who were the most erudite masters of the literature of Hellas obtained no real understanding of her art, and were ready to hail as the perfection of Greek style sculpture which in reality was the work of Hellenistic imitators or second-rate Roman copyists. It is little wonder that educated opinion as a whole has tended to treat even Greek literature as little better than an elder sister to the Latin ; and that there was no adequate realization of the enormous gulf which divides Hellas from Rome. It has been reserved, in fact, for the students of our own day to appreciate more truly the contribution of the Greeks to the thought and art of the world. For within the last fifty years new and more scientific methods have been brought to bear on the task of historical research. There has been patient examination and collation of the evidence of original sources, and in particular of the vast number of inscriptions which have recently been brought to light. The excava-tion of many ancient sites has given a new impetus to

---

PLATE XXIV

The interior of the Parthenon looking N.E. to Lyca-bettus, and taken near the spot where once stood the great gold and ivory Colossus made by Pheidias.

INTERIOR OF PARTHENON

CHRONOLOGICAL TABLES
AND SUMMARIES

I. MINOANS AND ACHAEANS

B.C.	Crete.	Greece.	Asia Minor.
4000 to 2300	EARLY MINOAN (1) Stone and bronze tools. (2) Pottery without use of wheel.	Pre-Greek settlements at Tiryns, Corinth, Larissa.	1st city at Troy.
2300 to 1600	MIDDLE MINOAN (1) Powerful dynasties at Cnossos and Phaestos (palaces, frescoes, glazed pottery). (2) Cnossos destroyed by earth-quake (?).	Greeks enter Greece (c. 2000) and become (1) Dorians in Epirus. (2) Achaeans in Thessaly and the south.	2nd city at Troy destroyed c. 2000.
1600 to	LATE MINOAN (1) Cnossos rebuilt on grander scale (throne-room, stairs, drains, etc.).	Mycenae (1) princes buried with rich treasure in shaft-graves. (2) Subsequent princes buried in bee-hive tombs (1500 onwards). Mycenae rebuilt, Lion Gate, etc.	3rd, 4th and 5th cities at Troy. Achaean trade-posts on

? 1300	(2) Cnossos occupied by Mycenaean Greeks.	MYCENAEAN CULTURE dominant in Greece.	western seaboard.
	(3) Cnossos destroyed (?) by Dorians.	Dorian sea-raids on fringe of Mycenaean world (c. 1300–1200).	
1250			Achaeans sack Troy (6th city).
1200		Dorians sack Pylos.	
1150		Dorians sack Mycenae. Dorians overrun Greece (1150 950?).	
1000	[IRON Age begins.]		
750			*Iliad* and *Odyssey* composed by Homer.

II. DORIAN INVASION AND THE MIGRATIONS

I. Dorian Invasion

c. 1300. Cnossos sacked.
c. 1200. Pylos sacked.
c. 1150. Mycenae sacked and collapse of Mycenaean power.

Gradual infiltration of Dorians into Thessaly, Boeotia, Locris, Phocis (*not* Attica), and all Peloponnese except Messenia and Arcadia.
Geometric style of art, distinguished by strong local divergences of craftsmanship, marks the chaos produced by the invasion and decline of Mycenaean culture.

II. Migrations to Asia Minor caused mainly by Dorian pressure :—

(i) Displaced Greeks from Thessaly and Boeotia occupy northern sector (Aeolis).
(ii) Displaced Greeks from the Peloponnese and Attica occupy central sector (Ionia).
(iii) Dorians overflowing from the Peloponnese occupy southern sector (Doris).

III. Formation of Historic States : emerging gradually from Dark Age :—

(i) During eighth century military and political concentration round citadels (*e.g.* Larissa of Argos, Acro-Corinth and Athenian Acropolis) takes place in many plains, but not in Aetolia.
(ii) During 7th and 8th century monarchies gradually replaced by aristocracies. At Athens royal office made elective, and limited in 683 to term of one year. At Sparta kings permanently retained.
(iii) Colonization of Aegean Coasts and Magna Grecia during eighth, seventh and sixth centuries (see next table).

III. COLONIZATION, TRADE AND TYRANNY

N.B.—Originally due to lack of land in mother-states, but leads to commercial enterprise.

A. Era of Colonization (mainly eighth, seventh, sixth centuries).

Mother-States.	Aegean, Black Sea, etc.	Adriatic, etc.
I. ASIA MINOR (due to barrier of Lydia in hinterland)		
Miletus	Cyzicus, 757 ; Abydos, 675 ; Sinope, 800, founds Trapezus, c. 756 ; Naucratis (Egypt), 640.	
Phocaea		Massalia (Gaul), c. 600 ?
II. ISLANDS		
Rhodes		Gela, 688, which founds Acragas, 580.
Thera	Cyrene (N. Africa). 630.	

III. EUBOEA (partly perhaps due to struggle of Chalcis and Eretria
for Lelantine plain at end of eighth century)

Chalcis and *Eretria*	Methone, Pydna, Tor-one, Mende (690), etc., in Chalcidice	Cumae (? 760) ; Catana, 728 ; Leontini, 728 ; Zancle, 715 ; Himera, 648 ; Rhegium, 730

IV. PELOPONNESE, etc.

Megara	Chalcedon, 660 and Byzantium	Sicilian Megara, 728, which founds Selinus, 648
Corinth	Potidaea, 609	Corcyra, 735, which founds Epidamnus
		Syracuse, 735, which founds Camarina, 599
		Anactorium, Leucas, c. 600
Achaea		Croton, 710 ; Sybaris, 721
		Posidonia (Paestum)
Sparta (mainly occupied in con-quest of Messenia)		Taras (Tarentum), 705

N.B.—Dates are mostly approximate.

B. Growth of Wealth

N.B.—Aristocracies of birth replaced gradually by plutocracies.

   (i) Coinage, invented by Lydia, adopted by Ionians (c. 700) :
Euboean and Aeginetan currencies attain vogue in
Aegean c. 680.

  (ii) Wealth of landlords leads to debt and enslavement of
peasantry (cf. Hesiod, eighth-century poet of Boeotia).

 (iii) Competition of slave labour depresses free peasantry.

C. Rise of Tyrants

N.B.—Though unconstitutional rule is obnoxious to Greek sentiment, tyrants gain the support of artisans and traders
against landowning aristocrats, and, by encouraging independence of middle class, pave the way for future democracy.

   I. In Asia Minor, where tyranny provides bulwark against
aggression of Lydia and (later) Persia.

     (*a*) MILETUS *Thrasybulus* (c. 620), the most brilliant of
his era.

     (*b*) SAMOS *Polycrates* (c. 530), ally of Amasis of Egypt and
with a strong navy aims perhaps at hegemony of Aegean.

  II. In Central Greece where tyrants rise as champions of Pre-
Dorian population against oppression of Dorian overlords.

     (*a*) SICYON. Tyranny founded by *Orthagoras* in 660,
carried on by *Cleisthenes* (c. 600–570), who helps to found
Pythian Games at Delphi.

     (*b*) MEGARA. *Theagenes* (c. 640) assists Cylon to attempt
tyranny at Athens.

     (*c*) CORINTH. Tyranny founded by *Cypselus* (657–630),
carried on by *Periander* (625–585), who encourages

'dithyrambic' poetry; plans canal through Isthmus; builds temple.

- (*d*) ATHENS. Tyranny founded by *Pisistratus* (547–527), succeeded by *Hippias* (expelled 510). (See below.)

III. In Sicily where tyranny provides bulwark against Carthaginian menace.

Gelon of Gela (491–478), captures Syracuse and with aid of *Theron* of Acragas defeats Carthaginians at Himera. *Hieron*, his successor (478–467) keeps splendid court, patron of Pindar, etc.

SPARTA

A. Population

- (i) Spartan citizens = Dorian invaders, forbidden to intermarry with other classes. (*a*) ' *Peers* ' (about 4,000, but steadily diminishing, see chapter XV), who can maintain contribution to Messes ; (*b*) ' *Inferiors* ' not possessing full citizen rights (about 20,000).
- (ii) *Perioeci* = out-settlements, especially on coast, of Dorians mixed with Pre-Dorians, who through absence from capital had lost their political rights : chiefly traders and heavily taxed (about 75,000).
- (iii) *Helots* probably = Pre-Dorians enslaved at conquest, working farms of Spartans as serfs (between 200,000 and 300,000).

B. Conquest of Messenia

c. 736– (i) First Messenian War :—Country annexed by Sparta
16   under Theopompus and population reduced to Helot status.

c. 650– (ii) Second Messenian War :—Revolt under *Aristomenes*
30   and long resistance on Mt. Eira. Spartans, fired by Tyrtaeus' poems, recover hold.

C. Lycurgan Reforms (c. 610), called ' Eunomia '

- (i) After Second Messenian War, realizing risk of Helot revolt, Spartans abandon normally luxurious habits and accept strict system of military discipline.
- (ii) Institutions modelled on Cretan methods (see E) introduced perhaps under auspices of mythical Lycurgus.
- (iii) Need for larger army necessitates enfranchisement of more citizens and expansion of three tribes to five.

D. Constitution

- (i) *Dual Kingship*, resulting from early amalgamation of two tribal groups, and hereditary in Agiadae and Eurypontidae families. Royal power confined in peace to priestly functions and membership of Gerousia : in war supreme command.
- (ii) *Gerousia*, or Council of twenty-eight Elders : chosen for life from *noble* families ; originally hold supreme judicial and legislative power : free to override Apella's vote.

(iii) *Apella* or Assembly of fully enfranchised citizens : **not** allowed to debate Gerousia's proposals, but merely **to** vote (normally by acclamation).

(iv) *Five Ephors*

(a) An old office originally of small importance, which under Lycurgan Reform receives wide powers of civil justice and Presidency of Apella.

(b) Chosen annually from *all* citizens by vote of Apella.

(c) By 560 ephors assume virtual control of state, overruling Gerousia, even supervising King's conduct of campaigns and enforcing discipline of Lycurgan System.

E. Lycurgan Discipline

(i) *Crypteia* or Secret Corps of youths for extermination of dangerous Helots.

(ii) Spartan citizens removed from home at 7 and grouped in ' packs ' under prefect (' *eiren* ') : education mainly athletic : endurance fostered by flogging competitions, etc.

(iii) Men allowed no home life (hence unusual independence of Spartan women) ; live in Messes (' *syssitia* ') to which each contributes a fixed portion ; trading forbidden ; iron currency.

F. Foreign Policy

(i) The chief rival of Sparta is *Argos*, which at time of Dorian conquest had become Dorian capital, supplanting Mycenae, and under first king *Temenus* enjoying suzerainty over surrounding Dorian States, Sicyon, Epidauros, Troezen, etc.

(ii) *Pheidon* of Argos (c. 690–650) (a) reasserted this suzerainty (which had been lost during Dark Age), including Megara and Aegina, where he established mint and probably issued Aeginetan currency. (b) Transfers conduct of Olympic games from Elis to Pisa (c. 670). (c) Defeats Spartans, who covet *Thyreatis*, at *Hysiae*, gaining control of eastern coast down to Cythera (668). (d) After Pheidon's death Argive ' Empire ' goes to pieces, the non-Dorian inhabitants of Sicyon, Megara, etc., asserting themselves under leadership of tyrants (see above, III, C. 2).

(iii) *Arcadians of Tegea*, attacked by Sparta with army trained under Lycurgan discipline, but after long war (590–60) are accepted as *subject allies* (in contrast to *annexation* of Messenia).

(iv) Sparta attacks Argos, and after indecisive test of 300 champions, defeats her in pitched battle, and annexes Thyreatis (546).

(v) Sparta extends policy, begun with Tegea, to surrounding states, and by end of sixth century all Peloponnesian States except Achaia and Argos are subject allies of Spartan League, possessing votes in common debates on foreign policy, sending two-thirds of forces to joint campaigns of League, paying no tax except for war purposes.

(vi) Sparta's leadership of Peloponnese greatly strengthened by King Cleomenes (520–489).

ATHENS

A. Early Constitution : Aristocracy of High-born or Eupatrids

(i) Three Archons, chosen from Eupatrids : King Archon (priest), eponymus (justice), polemarch (war).

(ii) High-born Council of Areopagus exercises sovereign power.

(iii) Ecclesia or Assembly of citizens (except landless labourers) has only nominal voice in election or policy.

B. Athens in Seventh Century

c. 632 (i) Owing to poverty of inhabitants and absence of strong artisan class, *Cylon's* attempt at tyranny fails for want of support.

621 (ii) Unwritten law tabulated by *Draco* ; death penalty for theft, etc. ; discrimination between intentional and unintentional homicide ; blood feud replaced by legal process.

(iii) Extortionate methods of rich landowners lead to enslavement of poor peasants.

C. Solon's Reforms

N.B.—Main result to create an artisan class and found commercial greatness of Athens.

I. Economic :
(*a*) Debts of enslaved peasants cancelled.
(*b*) Enslavement for debt illegalized.
(*c*) Legal maximum for expenditure on funerals, etc.
(*d*) Export of home produce (except olive) forbidden.
(*e*) Fathers to teach sons a trade.
(*f*) Foreign artisans encouraged to settle.

II. Political : aiming at balance of power between aristocracy and growing middle class.
(*a*) Power of Areopagus left intact : given function of ' guarding laws '.
(*b*) Citizens of lowest class admitted to Ecclesia.
(*c*) Council of 400 appointed to manage Ecclesia, prepare its business.
(*d*) Code of Law promulgated and popular courts (heliaea) to try cases.

D. Period of Tyranny

I. Rise of Pisistratus.
(*a*) During Solon's absence faction revives.
c. 570 (*b*) Solon on return instigates capture of Salamis from Megara. Pisistratus makes his mark.

(c) While commercial class of ' Coast ' (created by Solon) is struggling with Aristocratic landlords of the ' Plain ', Pisistratus organizes party of poor ' Hillsmen '.

560 (d) Pisistratus voted a bodyguard and seizes power; ejected by Coast and Plain.

559–57 (e) Returns by ruse of disguised Athena and again ejected.

546–27 (f) Strengthened by resources from Mount Pangaeus mines, and friendship with Lygdamis of Naxos, Thebes, Eretria etc, recovers power and reigns till death, 527.

II. Rule of Pisistratus.

(a) Ensures Black Sea supplies by promoting Athenian interests in Hellespont; e.g. encourages *Miltiades* to found settlement on *Chersonese* (559); occupies *Sigeum* (535).

(b) Exploits Thracian gold mines and Attic silver mines at *Laurium*.

(c) Encourages agriculture, especially olive, by loans to small farmers.

(d) By purification of *Delos* asserts Athenian leadership of Ionians.

(e) Increases importance of Panathenaic Festival, reorganizing Homer-recitals, also Dionysiac Festival.

(f) Redecorates Athena's Temple on Acropolis; Enneacrounos aqueduct; Temple of Olympian Zeus begun.

III. Rule of Pisistratus' sons.

527 (a) *Hippias* with *Hipparchus* in power, with splendid court and patronage of poets *Anacreon* and *Simonides*.

514 (b) *Harmodius* and *Aristogeiton* murder Hipparchus.

(c) Hippias becoming tyrannical, exiled nobles plan to oust him.

(d) Delphic oracle, in collusion with *Alcmeonids*, urges intervention of Sparta.

510 (e) Spartan *Cleomenes* expels Hippias; reduces Athens to semi-dependence on Sparta.

508 (f) Democratic movement under Alcmeonid *Cleisthenes* causes nobles to summon Cleomenes, who is successfully resisted.

508 (g) Cleisthenic Constitution begun.

E. Cleisthenes' Reforms (508–7)

(a) To break up clan-system four old tribes replaced by ten tribes composed of *demes* (parishes) widely distributed and forming new basis for election, taxation, etc.

(b) *Boulé* (Council) of 500 (fifty from each tribe), to prepare agenda for Ecclesia and transact current business: committee of fifty (*prytaneis*) in constant session, individual member presiding for one day.

(c) Areopagus retains only vague supervision and guardianship of laws.

(d) Annual ostracism at discretion of Assembly: resulting in ten-year banishment of any man receiving over 6,000 hostile votes; originally a precaution against tyranny, later safety-valve to faction.

(e) Soon after Cleisthenes, **ten generals** (*strategi*) to command contingents of ten tribes. When in 487 choice of archons becomes partially dependent on lot, generals assume wide powers over finance, food-supply, foreign affairs. President of Board becomes virtually Prime Minister of Athens.

F. Relations with Sparta

508 (i) Cleomenes (King of Sparta, 520–489) intervenes unsuccessfully against Cleisthenic democracy.

507 (ii) Cleisthenes appeals for Persian support, but falls into disgrace.

507 (iii) Cleomenes plans invasion of Attica with aid of Boeotia and Chalcis, who are both defeated (Cleruchy at Chalcis) ; and is himself frustrated by objections of Corinthians, who favour Athens as against their chief trade rival Aegina.

504 (iv) Corinth vetoes Cleomenes' proposal to restore tyranny of Hippias.

499 (v) Sparta refuses to assist Ionians in their revolt against Persia (see next chapter).

(?) 494 (vi) Cleomenes crushes Argos at Sepeia, but spares city.

(vii) Disaffection in Peloponnesian League thus crushed ; and in 491 even Athens appeals to Sparta to prevent medism of Aegina.

(viii) Hence general acceptance of Spartan leadership in Persian Wars.

PERSIAN WARS

A. Ionia and Lydia

(i) Commercial prosperity and tyrants' patronage produces great artistic and philosophic activity, especially at Miletus and under Polycrates at Samos (c. 530). (a) *Thales* of Miletus (624–547) student of astronomy, mathematics, philosophy. (b) *Alcaeus* and *Sappho* of Lesbos (c. 600) originate love lyrics. (c) *Pythagoras* of Samos (572–497) settles in Italy and founds school of religious life and mathematico-philosophic inquiry. (d) Hecataeus of Miletus (c. 520) originates historical writing.

(ii) Ionia much influenced by Oriental races, Assyria, Phoenicia, Egypt, and especially Lydia, whence she adopts coinage c. 730.

(iii) Owing to disunion Ionian States (except Miletus) fall under power of *Croesus* of Lydia (560–46) who, as a Philhellene, patronizes Delphi and builds Artemis' Temple at Ephesus.

B. Oriental Empires

(i) EGYPT, though in sixteenth century B.C. extending conquests to Euphrates, gradually weakens by 1200.

(ii) ASSYRIA rises to supremacy c. 1000 ; capital Nineveh ,

cruel military despotism; humbles Egypt and after deporting Northern Israel, threatens Jerusalem (*Sennacherib*) 701.

612 (iii) Assyrian Empire divided between MEDIA and BABYLON, whose king *Nebuchadnezzar* deports Judeans.

c. 550–29 (iv) *Cyrus*, leading mountaineers of PERSIA, supersedes Median dynasty and absorbs all near and middle east. (*a*) Defeats Croesus on River Halys and captures Sardis (546). (*b*) Captures Babylon (539). (*c*) His viceroy *Harpagus* conquers Ionian Greeks (c.543).

529–22 (v) *Cambyses* conquers Egypt (525).

521–486 (vi) *Darius*. (*a*) Organizes Empire into satrapies with trunk roads, courier system, tribute and military levies. (*b*) Expedition into Europe (516); invades Scythia; crosses Danube, but only retains Thracian coast. Serious blow to Persian prestige.

C. Ionian Revolt, due to failure of Scythian expedition and unpopularity of Pro-Persian tyrants

(i) *Histiaeus*, tyrant of Miletus, recalled by Darius to Susa.

499 (ii) *Aristagoras*, his son-in-law and successor at Miletus, fearing failure of his expedition against Naxos will alienate Persian satrap, urges Ionians to revolt in collusion with Histiaeus.

(iii) Aristagoras' mission to Greece procures aid of five *Eretrian* and twenty *Athenian* ships.

498 (iv) Ionians burn Sardis and retire; Athenian ships withdrawn.

494 (v) Revolt, though spreading to Hellespont, Caria and Cyprus, suppressed by defeat of Ionian fleet at *Ladè* and destruction of *Miletus*.

(vi) Fate of Miletus lamented at Athens. Darius plans revenge for sending of the twenty ships.

D. Persian Punitive Expeditions

I. 492. Fleet sent under Darius' son-in-law *Mardonius*, via Thrace; wrecked on *Mount Athos*.

II. 490 (or 491) *Datis* and *Artaphernes* sent (with 140 ships, horse and infantry and ex-tyrant Hippias) viâ Naxos and islands.

(*a*) Sack Eretria and land in Attica near *Marathon*.

(*b*) Some *Alcmeonids*, as leaders of popular party who favour Hippias' return, work in collusion with Persians. Aristocrats, led by *Miltiades* of Chersonese, prepare resistance.

(*c*) Though Spartan help dallies, Athenian with Plataean contingent march to mountains above road from Marathon to Athens.

(*d*) Battle of *Marathon*; Persians, on sign from Alcmeonids, embark cavalry for dash on Athens; Athenian army charge and rout Persian infantry; then march in time to save city.

E. Athens between 490 and 480

489   (i) Miltiades' failure against *Paros* leads to his trial and discredits his party.

     (ii) Alcmeonids return to power, but as leadership of mercantile class passes to *Themistocles*, lose favour ; ostracism of Aristides (482) and others.

488 (or 493) (iii) Themistocles substitutes rock-harbour at *Peiraeus* for old harbour in Phalerum Bay.

487   (iv) War with *Aegina* goes ill until in 482 Themistocles uses surplus on *Laurium* silver-mines to build 200 triremes.

F. The Great Invasion, 480

     (i) *Xerxes* (485–464) prepares huge armament (250,000 troops) bridges Hellespont, cuts canal through Mount Athos.

     (ii) Northern Greeks on Delphic warning waver ; but Sparta, supreme in Peloponnese since defeat of Argos 494, heads resistance and is backed by Athens.

     (iii) Attempt of Greeks to hold pass of *Tempê* (N. Thessaly) outflanked by inland march of Persians.

Aug.   (iv) While Persian fleet is severely mauled at *Artemisium* by storms and Greek attacks, *Leonidas*, with 10,000 Greeks, holds THERMOPYLAE, till taken in rear by Immortals led by traitor Ephialtes.

     (v) Persian detachment marches on Delphi, but is repulsed by mountaineers.

     (vi) While Spartans concentrate on defence of Isthmus, Attica is overrun and Athenians, transporting women, etc. to safety, leave town to invaders.

     (vii) Spartan *Eurybiades* wishes to withdraw Greek fleet from Salamis to Isthmus, but Themistocles forestalls withdrawal by warning Xerxes.

Sep. (viii) BATTLE OF SALAMIS. (*a*) Xerxes overnight sends Egyptians to block western exit of Straits, and posts fleet across eastern exit, landing troops on *Psyttalea*. (*b*) Next morning Persian fleet attacks and is drawn into straits by feigned flight of Greeks. (*c*) On rout of Persian fleet Aeginetans intercept retreat. (*d*) Persians on Psyttalea butchered.

     (ix) Xerxes sails for Hellespont to secure loyalty of Ionian Greeks.

G. Campaign of Plataea, 479

     (i) *Mardonius*, left behind with (?) 150,000 troops, winters in Thessaly.

479 Spring (ii) Intending to secure satrapy over North Greece, Mardonius descends through Boeotia, and after attempt to win Athens by offer of alliance, reoccupies city.

Aug.   (iii) On approach of Spartan *Pausanias* and 100,000 Greeks, Mardonius retires over Mount Cithaeron to Plataea.

     (iv) Battle of PLATAEA :

        (*a*) Greeks on Cithaeron Slopes (Position I) repulse Persian horse.

      (b) Greeks move to plain (Position II), hoping to force battle on favourable ground, but are held on south bank of River Asopus.

      (c) After several days, since their watering parties are harassed by Persian horse and supplies intercepted in passes, Greeks retreat towards mountain.

      (d) Greeks going astray during night retirement (Position III), are attacked at dawn by Persians.

      (e) Spartans with difficulty rout Persian attack, but fail to take camp, till Athenians and other Greeks, after defeating Medising Boeotians, come up to assist ; great slaughter and booty.

  (v) Greek fleet under Spartan *Leotychidas*, inactive since Salamis, venture over to aid of Samos; they land and (479) destroy Persian fleet at *Mycale*, aided by Ionian Greeks, who desert Persians.

DELIAN CONFEDERACY

A. Sparta's Lost Opportunity

    (i) Sparta's supremacy (already well established by aggressive policy of *Cleomenes* (c. 520–489) e.g. at Athens, and his defeat of Argos at *Sepeia* (? 494), gives her undisputed leadership during Persian War.

478 (ii) Spartan opposition to rebuilding of Athenian walls foiled by diplomacy of Themistocles, who also fortifies Peiraeus (Long Walls added 457).

478 (iii) Pausanias, victor of Plataea, liberates Cyprus and Byzantium, but, assuming despotic airs, is deposed 478, and being discovered in intrigue with Persia, is starved to death in sanctuary 471.

   (iv) Sparta lacks initiative to undertake liberation of Ionia.

B. Athens forms Delian Confederacy

479 (i) Athenians expel Persian garrisons from Thrace and Hellespont.

478 (ii) Athenians form Confederacy of Ionians and other Aegean states to resist renewal of Persian aggression.

      (a) Ships provided by Athens and larger islands, e.g. *Samos, Chios, Lesbos*.

      (b) Other states provide tribute, assessed at 460 talents and supervised by *Aristides*.

      (c) Athenian *Hellenotamiae* collect tribute

      (d) Congress of States and League treasury at *Delos* removed to Athens 454.

      (e) Five districts formed for purposes of taxation, 443.

EVENTS BETWEEN 480 AND 434

	Athens and Sparta.	Aegean.	Persia.
			Recapture of *Sestos* (479)
478	Rebuilding of Athens' Walls	FORMATION OF DELIAN LEAGUE	
478	Pausanias recalled from *Byzantium*		Cimon takes *Eion*
475		Cimon attacks *Scyros*	
?473	Sparta beats Argos and Tegea		
?471	Sparta beats Arcadians at *Dipaea*		
471	Exile of Themistocles : death of Pausanias		
?467		*Naxos* reduced	
?466			Cimon defeats Persian fleet and army at *R. Eurymedon*
464	Revolt of the Helots who seize *Ithome*	*Thasos* reduced	
463			
462	Cimon, after rebuff at Ithome, is disgraced. Athens BREAKS WITH SPARTA and joins Argos		Revolt of *Inarus* in Egypt
461	Ostracism of Cimon. Rise of *Pericles* and degradation of Areopagus	Most members of League accept subordinate status; some by force under separate treaties with Athens (except *Lesbos, Chios* and *Samos*)	
459	Athens allies with *Megara*. War against *Corinth* and *Aegina* successfully maintained		Athenian fleet in Egypt
457	Surrender of Aegina. Long Walls completed. Athens, threatened by Spartans, fights indecisively at *Tanagra*, but, by victory of *Oenophyta*, wins *Boeotia*, *Phocis*, *Locris*		
455	Athens settles Helots at *Naupactus* ; **Tol-**mides wins over *Achaea*		

		TREASURY MOVED FROM DELOS TO ATHENS	Loss of Athenian fleet in Egypt
454			
451	Cimon returns Five-year truce with Sparta	Cleruchy at *Naxos*?	Cimon sails to liberate *Cyprus* After Cimon's death PEACE WITH PERSIA
450	Pericles invites Panhellenic Congress		
448	Pericles invites Panhellenic Congress		
447	Athenian Land Empire lost at *Coronea*	Cleruchy at *Andros*? and *Chersonese*	
446	Revolt of *Megara* and *Euboea*		
445	THIRTY YEARS PEACE between Sparta and Athens	Cleruchy at *Histiaea* (Euboea)	
443	Thucydides, conservative opponent of Pericles, ostracized	Pan-Hellenic Colony at *Thurii*	
441		Revolt of Samos (reduced 439)	
'437	Pericles sails to *Black Sea* to secure Crimean corn supply	Colony at *Amphipolis* Cleruchy at *Sinope*? Cleruchy at *Astacus*?	
434			

29

SUMMARY OF ATHENIAN CONSTITUTION

BOULÉ of 500 (50 from each tribe by lot: each 50 forming standing committee for one-tenth of year) prepares agenda for Assembly: deals with foreign embassies, etc.: administers Assembly's resolutions.

ASSEMBLY. Sovereign authority (*a*) initiates legislation on motion of individual (who is liable to penalties for unconstitutional proposals), but passes it on for examination to board chosen from Heliaea; (*b*) decides all questions of policy; (*c*) checks conduct of officials. Executive officials for finance, corn supply, etc.; commanders in war.

GENERALS (10 chosen by direct vote, of whom one presides).

LAW-COURTS. (*a*) *Heliaea* (= whole body of citizens) supervises Assembly's legislative proposals; (*b*) *Jury-Courts* (chosen by lot from panel of voluntary jurors) try civil and criminal cases; (*c*) *Areopagus* tries homicide. ARCHONS (9 chosen by lot from deme nominees) preside over jury-courts and fulfil other unimportant functions.

PERICLEAN AGE

A. Architecture

    (i) Previous history of Acropolis :

        (*a*) Athena's ancient temple near north cliff embellished by Pisistratus.

        (*b*) Destroyed by Persian sack.

        (*c*) New temple begun on more central site, but unfinished owing (?) to Themistocles' fall.

        (*d*) Cimon spends spoils of Eurymedon on terracing south side of hill.

448 (ii) After abortive plan for Pan-Hellenic Conference on rebuilding of temples, Pericles begins *Parthenon* (architect *Ictinus* : sculptor *Phidias*, author of Bronze Athena), dedicated in 438. (Doric Style.)

    (iii) *Propylaea* (mainly Doric) begun 437 at western entrance.

    (iv) Temple of *Nikē* (Ionic) completed c. 435 or 420.

    (v) Ancient image of Athena not transferred to Parthenon, but kept on traditional site near ancient temple, where in c. 420 Nicias builds *Erechtheum* (Ionic).

B. Religion

    (i) Greek gods superimposed on old Minoan cults, of which bestial symbols and rites partly survive.

    (ii) Cult of *Dionysus* (spirit of growth) introduced into Greece from north and from seventh century linked with Demeter and Persephone in *Mysteries of Eleusis*.

    (iii) In sixth century *Orphic* teachers (e.g. Pythagoras fl. 530) gain great prominence and develop mysteries insisting on purification and self-discipline of initiates

C. Poets

    (i) *Stesichorus* of Himera (fl. c. 580) founds choric song and moralizes legend of House of Atreus.

    (ii) *Pindar* of Thebes (522–448) ; conservative and aristocratic ; writes odes on Greek defeat of Persia and on victories of patrons at Olympic games.

    (iii) *Aeschylus* of Athens (525–456) last representative of old conservatism, but profound and original thinker ; *Persae* ; *Prometheus Vinctus* ; Oresteian trilogy *Agamemnon, Coëphori, Eumenides*.

    (iv) *Sophocles* of Athens (496–406) consummate artist ; develops scenery and dramatic technique ; *Oedipus Rex, Oedipus Coloneus, Antigone, Electra*, etc.

    (v) *Euripides* of Athens (c. 480–406) realist in art ; freethinker and reputed atheist ; eventually retires to court of Archelaus of Macedon ; *Medea, Bacchae, Hippolytus*, etc.

D. Sophist Movement

    I. Early Philosophers :

        (*a*) *Thales* of Miletus (624–546) first seeks explanation of natural phenomena.

(b) *Heracleitus* of Ephesus (c. 500) advances theory that all reality is perpetual flux (πάντα ῥεῖ).

(c) *Parmenides* of Elea, S. Italy (c. 500) contends that change is illusory and reality stationary (πάντα μένει).

(d) *Anaxagoras* of Clazomenae, Ionia (500–428) settles at Athens; explains substances as composed of atoms combined by mind (itself, however, corporeal).

(e) *Pythagoras* of Samos (572–497) settles at Croton, S. Italy, where he studies music and mathematics, explaining all phenomena by mystical influence of Number.

II. Fifth Century Sophists :

(i) Since normal education in literature and music ends at 14, the growing desire for political, commercial and forensic efficiency among Athenian democracy leads to demand for further intellectual training.

(ii) Teachers from abroad supply need, charging fees for lectures and causing great unsettlement by rather superficial Individualism.

(a) *Protagoras* of Abdera (485–410) teaches art of citizenship, but propounds individualism (' Man the Measure of all things '.)

(b) *Prodicus* of Ceos (fl. 430) specializes in refinements of speech, synonyms, etc.

(c) *Gorgias* of Leontini (483–376) popularizes stilted, rhetorical style which influences Thucydides.

(d) *Hippias* of Elis (fl. 430) teaches history, geometry, astronomy, grammar, mnemonics, etc.

E. Socrates of Athens (470–399)

(i) ' Converted ' by Delphic oracle, seeks truth by cross-examining neighbours and gathers band of young enthusiasts.

(ii) Holds that Virtue proceeds from Knowledge, and Truth is permanent, not relative.

(iii) Bad effect of New Teaching on some young men (e.g. Alcibiades) leads to strong conservative opposition; e.g. Aristophanes' protest in ' *Clouds* '.

(iv) Conservatives' attack on Pericles and his circle :
  (a) *Anaxagoras* banished for impiety (c. 435 or 450).
  (b) *Phidias* imprisoned for peculation (c. 435).
  (c) Pericles fined (430).

(v) Socrates put to death for ' corrupting the youth ' (399).

PELOPONNESIAN WAR

A. Events leading to War

N.B.—Corinthian Trade threatened by Athens' growing influence.

(i) CORCYRA.

435   (a) During faction struggle in *Epidamnus* (Corcyrean colony) democrats appeal to Corinth whose fleet is beaten by Corcyreans.

    (b) Expecting fresh attack, Corcyra makes defensive alliance with Athens.

    (c) New Corinthian fleet prevented from defeating Corcyreans at *Sybota* by intervention of Athenian ships.

433
432 (ii) POTIDAEA :

    (a) A colony of Corinth, but member of Athenian League; intrigues with Perdiccas of Macedon.

Spring   (b) Athenians order expulsion of Corinthian magistrates and razing of town-walls.

Autumn   (c) On refusal Potidaea besieged (reduced in 430).

Autumn (iii) MEGARA, now ally of Corinth, boycotted by Pericles' order.

432–1 (iv) Corinth persuades Sparta and Congress of Peloponnesian League to declare for war.

431 (v) Diplomatic ultimatum ; Sparta demands expulsion of 'accursed' Alcmeonids. Athens retorts with allusion to Pausanias' death.

Spring (vi) War begun.

    Spartan Alliance : All Peloponnese (except Argos and Achaea), Boeotia, Phocis, Locris, Ambracia.

  Athenian Alliance : Aegean Confederacy, Plataea, Acarnania, Corcyra, and some help from Thessaly.

B.—COURSE OF WAR (431–421).

	Athens and Neighbourhood.	Peloponnese and Boeotia.	North-West Greece and Sicily:	Aegean Empire.
431	Spartan Archidamus invades Attica (May). Athenians raid Megarid	Theban surprise on Plataea foiled (March)		Siege of *Potidaea*
430	Spartans invade Attica Plague in Athens Pericles fined, but re-elected	Athenian fleet under Pericles raids Peloponnese	Phormio at *Naupactus* Peloponnese failure in *Ambracia*	Surrender of Potidaea
429	Plague in Athens Death of Pericles	Spartans combine with Thebans to besiege Plataea	Double victory of Phormio Blockade of Corinthian Gulf complete	
428	Spartans invade Attica Property tax at Athens			Revolt of *Lesbos* Mitylene besieged
427	Spartans invade Attica Rise of Cleon	Capture of Plataea	Laches' mission to Sicily	Surrender of Mitylene
426			Demosthenes' defeat in *Aetolia* and victory at *Olpae*	
425	Spartans invade Attica Cleon gains ascendancy over Nicias	Demosthenes occupies *Pylos*; with Cleon captures 400 Spartans; occupation of Methana and Cythera	Expedition to Sicily detained at *Pylos* Congress of Gela	Allied tribute doubled
424	Aggressive policy of Cleon and Demosthenes Banishment of Thucydides	Threefold operation against Boeotia miscarries; Athenians defeated at *Delium*	Athenians win Oeniadae Athenians capture Port of *Megara* and Cythera	Brasidas in *Chalcidice* Athenians lose *Amphipolis*
423	Negotiations and truce for one year			
422				Battle of *Amphipolis* Cleon and Brasidas killed

421. PEACE OF NICIAS. (*a*) Fifty years' treaty between Athens and Sparta.; (*b*) general restoration of captures. BUT Athens is allowed to retain Port of Megara and refuses surrender of Pylos because Amphipolis is not restored.

INTERLUDE. 421–16

A. Reshuffling of Alliances

421   (i) After Nicias' Peace Athens allies with Sparta.

      (ii) Megara, Boeotia, Corinth alienated by Spartan disregard of their interests.

     (iii) Argos, emerging from neutrality, forms group with Corinth, Elis, Mantinea.

420 (iv) Boeotia having rejoined Sparta, Alcibiades, by duping Spartan envoys, persuades Athens to join Argos.

B. War of Sparta, Boeotia, Tegea v. Argos, Athens, Elis, Mantinea

418   (i) Spartan army catches Argos at disadvantage, but Agis makes truce.

     (ii) Alcibiades persuades Argos to renew war with aid of Athenian contingent.

    (iii) Argo-Athenian army defeated near *Mantinea*.

    (iv) Sparta recovers leadership of Peloponnese.

417   (v) At Athens Alcibiades and Nicias combine for ostracism of *Hyperbolus*.

C. Earlier History of Sicily

   I. CARTHAGINIAN MENACE

      (a) *Gelon* tyrant of Gela (491–78), largely unites Sicily by hegemony over Syracuse and S.E., and alliance with *Theron* of Acragas.

480 (b) In support of exiled tyrant of Himera, Carthaginians under Hamilcar invade Sicily.

      (c) Hamilcar defeated at *Himera* ; peril averted.

474 (d) *Hieron*, Gelon's successor, defeats Etruscans at *Cumae*, thus saving Italian Greeks.

   II. DISCORD IN SICILY

      (a) *Syracuse* (founded by Corinth) heads Dorian group against *Leontini* and cities of Ionian origin.

      (b) Leontini sends *Gorgias* to enlist Athenian support (427).

      (c) Athenian fleet, after detention at Pylos, accomplishes nothing (425).

      (d) At Pan-Sicilian Congress at Gela, *Hermocrates* of Syracuse urges reunion against outside interference (425).

      (e) After Athenian departure Syracuse destroys Leontini (423).

      (f) *Segesta* appeals for Athenian help against Syracuse, and dupes Athenian envoys into recommending expedition (416).

      (g) With support of commercial party Alcibiades carries recommendation.

      (h) Despite alarm over Hermae outrage, expedition (130 triremes and 5,000 hoplites) sails under *Nicias, Alcibiades, Lamachus*.

D. Syracusan Expedition

   I. CAMPAIGN OF 415 :

      (a) Half-hearted reconnaissance of Syracuse loses advantage of surprise.

(b) Alcibiades recalled for trial, but flees to Sparta.
(c) After landing and defeating Syracusans, Nicias retires to winter at Catana.
(d) During winter Syracusan forces organized under Hermocrates.

II. SIEGE OF SYRACUSE.

1st Phase

(a) Athenians rush *Epipolae* and begin circumvallation (414 spring).
(b) Leaving northern arm (AB) unfinished, they turn to capture Syracuse cross-walls at X and at Y (Lamachus killed), and carry southern arm (AC) to harbour.
(c) Spartan *Gylippus* slips through northern gap, bringing reinforcements from Sicily (414 autumn).

2nd Phase

Gylippus carries cross-wall ZZ, so that Athenians are confined to circumvallation lines and camp (late autumn 414).

3rd Phase

(a) Eighty Syracusan ships organized during winter (414–13).
(b) By sea and land attack Syracuse captures Athenian naval base at *Plemmyrium* (413 spring).
(c) Athenian ships forced to move to camp at D.
(d) Arrival of *Demosthenes* with 70 ships and 5,000 hoplites (413 August).

4th Phase

(a) Demosthenes' night attack on Epipolae fails (413 August).
(b) Nicias consents to departure, but is delayed by eclipse (413 August 27).
(c) Indecisive naval action in Great Harbour (September 3).
(d) Attempt to break boom and defeat of Athenian fleet (September 9).
(e) Retreat to *R. Assinarus* ends in total capture (September 18).

PELOPONNESIAN WAR. LAST PHASE

A. Athens' Critical Condition

413 (i) Sicilian disaster means loss of 40,000 men and 240 ships.
413 (ii) Spartans occupy *Decelea*, arresting agriculture, mining and overland communications with Euboea.
413 (iii) Ten Commissioners appointed with wide powers.
(iv) Five per cent. harbour duty substituted for tribute.

B. Revolt of Allies

412 (i) Persian satraps *Tissaphernes* of Lydia and *Pharnabazus* of Phrygia instigate Miletus, Lesbos and other subject allies of Athens to revolt.
412 (ii) Sparta recognizes Persian claim to Ionia, provided satraps finance her fleet.
411 (iii) Though Athens recovers *Lesbos*, blockades *Chios* and secures loyalty of *Samos* democrats, revolt spreads through Southern Ionia and *Rhodes*.
(iv) Athenian fleet stationed at Samos.

C. Revolution of the Four Hundred

1st Phase : Preparations for Reform.

    (a) Attributing Sicilian disaster to ultra-democrats' folly, moderates at Athens incline to constitutional reform 412.

    (b) Agriculturalist-conservative faction, weary of war, especially since Declean occupation, lay plans and form secret clubs (winter 412–11).

    (c) Alcibiades promises to win Tissaphernes round to Athenian side, provided oligarchy is established.

    (d) Officers of fleet at Samos, on Alcibiades' instigation, send *Pisander* to Athens, where proposal is approved, but meets with Tissaphernes' refusal (411 February).

2nd Phase : The Coup d'état.

    (a) *Antiphon*, arch-oligarch, and *Theramenes*, leader of moderates, proceed with plans for reform.

    (b) Assembly at *Colonus* (May, 411) (to which only armed better-class venture) appoints new Council of 400, and arranges for nomination of 5,000 enfranchised citizens (not carried out).

    (c) New Council of 400 ousts old Boulê (411, May).

3rd Phase : Oligarchs' hand revealed.

    (a) Fleet at Samos, refusing to recognize the 400, appoint *Thrasybulus* and Thrasyllus in place of oligarch officers.

    (b) Alcibiades restrains fleet from sailing on Athens.

    (c) Oligarchical members of 400 negotiate with Sparta and begin to build fort at *Peiraeus* (411, June to September).

4th Phase : the counter-revolution.

    (a) *Phrynichus*, prominent oligarch, murdered in Agora (September, 411).

    (b) With Theramenes' approval democrats demolish Peiraeus fort.

    (c) Spartan fleet appears, but sails off to Euboea, which rises in revolt (September, 411).

    (d) 400 deposed ; chief oligarchs flee to Decelea.

    (e) Theramenes' constitution of limited franchise temporarily adopted.

D. Alcibiades' Recall and Fall

    (i) Alcibiades reinstated, but remains with fleet in Ionia.

411 (ii) Spartan *Mindarus*, tired of Tissaphernes' evasions, moves to Hellespont under Pharnabazus' patronage.

411 (iii) Athenian fleet from Samos, under Thrasybulus, joins squadron blockading Byzantium, and defeats Mindarus at *Cynossema*.

410 (iv) Mindarus' fleet annihilated at *Cyzicus*, partly by Alcibiades' reinforcements.

    (v) Fleet's success leads to restitution of Full Democracy, swayed by demagogue *Cleophon*.

408 (vi) Alcibiades, having recovered Byzantium, returns to Athens.

  (vii) *Lysander* improves Spartan fleet, with financial aid of Prince *Cyrus*, who replaces Tissaphernes.

406(viii) Alcibiades commander-in-chief in Ionia; but his lieutenant being defeated at *Notium* during his absence, he is deposed (406).

E. Final Phase

406 (i) Lysander's successor *Callicratidas* defeats *Conon* (Alcibiades' successor) off Lesbos, and blockades him in Mitylene.

406 (ii) New fleet sent from Athens defeats Callicratidas at *Arginusae* (execution of admirals).

(iii) Spartan offer of peace rejected by Cleophon, despite financial exhaustion.

405 (iv) Lysander, reappointed at Cyrus' request, sails to Hellespont and blockades *Lampsacus*.

405 (v) Athenian fleet under Conon annihilated at *Aegospotami* (late summer).

(vi) General revolt of allies (except Samos).

(vii) Spartan terms rejected; but, while Theramenes negotiates at Sparta, blockade and starvation compel surrender (404 April).

Terms :—(*a*) destruction of Long Walls; (*b*) surrender of ships (except twelve) ; (*c*) loss of subject allies ; (*d*) status of subject ally to Sparta.

THE NEW ERA

A. Fourth Century Writers (mainly a Prose Age)

(i) Athenian Philosophers : Plato and Aristotle (see below).

(ii) Athenian Legal Speech Writers :
Lysias, emigrant from Magna Grecia (flor. 403–380) ;
Demosthenes, see below (383–22) ;
Isocrates, pamphleteer (436–338).

(iii) Historians :
Xenophon of Athens (434–354), Hellenic History (continuation of Thucydides) ; memoirs of Socrates and Agesilaus ; Cyropaedia, etc.
Theopompus of Chios (fl. 340), History of Greece.
Timaeus of Sicily (fl. 300), History of Sicily.
Polybius of Megalapolis (205–123), Roman History, and Greek History from 264 B.C.

(iv) Athenian Drama :—*Middle Comedy* (390–335), based largely on parody and ridicule of myths. *New Comedy :* *Menander* (343–291) lifelike presentation of character and adventure, especially love interest ; model for Latin playwrights.

B. Fourth Century Sculptors

More interest in individuality of character than Phidias of Athens (fl. 440) or Polycleitus of Argos (fl. 450) ; but also more affectation of style.
Praxiteles (fl. 360), Hermes at Olympia (extant) ; Aphrodite of Cnidos (numerous copies).

Scopas (fl. 380), worked at Tegea (fragments extant) and on Mausoleum at Halicarnassus.

Lysippus (fl. 340), statues of athletes and portraits of Alexander.

C. Cyrus' Expedition

(i) After death of his father Darius, Cyrus determines on attempt to depose his elder brother *Artaxerxes*.

(ii) Spartan *Clearchus* employed to raise 11,000 Greek mercenaries.

401 spring (iii) With these and 100,000 Asiatic troops Cyrus marches through Asia Minor and Thapsacus towards Babylon.

Summer (iv) Artaxerxes with 400,000 troops meets him outside Babylon at *Cunaxa* where, despite Greeks' success, Cyrus is killed and army dispersed.

400 winter (v) Retreat of 10,000 Greeks.

(a) Clearchus and other generals kidnapped by Tissaphernes.

(b) *Xenophon* and others take the lead and march via Carduchia and Armenia to *Trapezus*.

Spring (vi) Arriving at Byzantium, they serve under Thracian Seuthes and later under Agesilaus. Result : Expedition reveals weakness of Persian Empire and paves the way for Alexander's conquests.

D. Dionysius of Syracuse (405–367)

I. *Rise of Dionysius*

(a) Encouraged by exhaustion of Syracuse and Athens, Carthage renews attack on Sicily.

(b) On appeal from *Segesta* (409), Hannibal sacks *Selinus* and *Himera*.

(c) After a lull *Acragas* is besieged (406) ; Sicilian allies withdraw ; inhabitants escape by night.

(d) Dionysius, denouncing generals' desertion of Acragas, is appointed dictator of Syracuse.

II. *Dionysius and Carthage*

(a) After fall of *Gela* and *Camarina*, Dionysius makes terms with *Hamilcar* (405) ceding south-west of Island.

(b) Dionysius fortifies Ortygia ; builds war-fleet and siege-engines and forms standing army.

(c) Dionysius attempts to oust Carthaginians, taking Motya (398).

(d) Carthaginians attack Syracuse, but are defeated and allowed to depart by Dionysius (397).

(e) Peace terms leave only western extremity to Carthage.

(f) War renewed 383 and 369. Dionysius attacks Lilybaeum : result indecisive.

III. *Dionysius' Empire*

(a) Dionysius conquers Greek towns in toe of *Italy*.

(b) Trading-posts at *Elba, Corsica, Ancona, Adria*, etc.

(c) Alliance with Sparta and Molossi.
(d) Settles Italian mercenaries at *Catana* ; gives *Naxos* to native Sicels.

IV. *Dionysius' Home Policy*
(a) Continues democracy in form.
(b) Heavy taxation for war needs.
(c) Writer of plays ; patron of architects, poets, philosophers (e.g. *Plato* and *Aristippus*).
(d) Suppresses plots by espionage and brutality.
(e) Disregard of Greek sentiment (e.g. enslavement of Plato).

V. *Sicily after Dionysius*
(a) Through weakness of his son *Dionysius II,* and despite efforts of *Dion,* realm falls to pieces.
(b) Petty tyrants arise in Sicilian cities.
(c) *Timoleon* of Corinth with small mercenary force expels tyrants (344) ; checks Carthage ; establishes democracies which form strong federation.

SPARTAN SUPREMACY

A. Lysander and the Aegean
  I. *Aegean States*
  (a) After Aegospotami (405) Aegean cities pass under Spartan control.
  (b) Lysander sets up oligarchic *decarchies* in co-operation with Spartan *harmost* and garrison.
  (c) Tribute of 1,000 talents exacted and employed to hire mercenaries.

  II. *Athens :* 30 Pro-Spartan oligarchs established in power (404 summer) including *Critias* and *Theramenes.*
   (i) *Reign of Terror :*
      (a) Murder of political opponents and rich metics, etc.
      (b) Theramenes procures nomination of 3,000 citizens entitled to fair trial, etc.
      (c) Critias denounces Theramenes (403 January).
   (ii) *Liberation of Athens :*
      (a) *Thrasybulus,* with exiled democrats, occupies *Phyle* (404 December).
      (b) Two unsuccessful attempts of the Thirty to dislodge him (403 January and May).
      (c) Thrasybulus seizes Peiraeus and repels attack, killing Critias (403 summer).
      (d) Spartan Pausanias intervenes, proclaims general amnesty, and withdraws garrison (403 September).
      (e) Full democracy restored.

B. Fall of Lysander
   (i) Fall of Thirty at Athens, followed by overthrow of decarchies in many states, which is not opposed by Sparta.

      (ii) Lysander is deposed (402) and travels to Egypt.
    (iii) Cities of Ionia ceded to Persia, but most Aegean cities retained by Sparta.

C. Agesilaus and Persia

400   (i) When Tissaphernes tries to tighten hold on Ionian cities, Sparta, encouraged by Cyrus' expedition, sends *Thibron* to assist them.

      (ii) Though Thibron carries war into interior and *Dercyllidas* ravages Troad (399), Pharnabazus aids Tissaphernes in checking Spartan success and begins to organize fleet under *Conon*.

    (iii) *Agesilaus*, succeeding to Spartan throne by aid of Lysander, sent to Ionia where he shakes off Lysander's influence ; invades Phrygia (396) ; marches nearly to Sardis (395 spring), and when bought off by Tissaphernes' successor *Tithraustes*, attacks Pharnabazus and pushes inland to Gordium (395 autumn).

394 (iv) Agesilaus recalled by events of Corinthian War.

D. Sparta's Supremacy challenged

I. *Corinthian War*

395   (a) Thebes, Corinth, Argos and Athens, alienated by Spartan selfishness, are egged on by gold of Persian agent Timocrates.

      (b) Thebes heads revolt, repelling Spartan attack and killing Lysander.

      (c) Confederates defeated by Sparta at *Nemea* (394 July) and also by Agesilaus' returning army at *Coronea* (394 August).

      (d) Corinth blockaded by Spartans (391) ; Athenians under *Iphicrates* annihilate Spartan *mora* (390).

II. *Athenian Naval Revival*

      (a) Persian fleet under Athenian *Conon* defeats Spartan fleet under Pisander at *Cnidus* (394).

      (b) Aegean cities expel Agesilaus' garrisons.

      (c) Conon allowed to sail to Athens, where he helps to rebuild Long Walls (393).

      (d) Athens recovers possession of *Lemnos, Imbros, Scyros* and alliance of *Rhodes, Eretria, Byzantium* (389).

E. Sparta recovers with Persian Aid

387   (i) Persians, alarmed by Athenian revival, lend fleet to *Antalcidas*, who, aided by Dionysius of Syracuse, recovers Hellespont.

386   (ii) At Congress of Greek States at *Sardis* satrap dictates terms of *King's Peace*, viz., Persia to retain Ionia ; all Greek states to be independent except Athens' new possessions. (Sparta's rôle is to enforce and interpret the terms.)

D. Sparta's Abuse of her Supremacy

- (i) Agesilaus favours policy of establishing oligarchies in Peloponnesian cities, e.g. *Mantinea* (385) and *Phlius* (381).
- 382 (ii) Spartan expedition to break up Olynthian Confederacy ; Olynthus taken (379).
- 382 (iii) Thebes, already weakened by independence of Boeotia, is surprised by Spartan *Phoebidas*, through treachery of *Leontiades*.
- 379 Dec. (iv) *Melon, Pelopidas* and other exiles recover Thebe by murder of pro-Spartan magistrates ; Spartan garrison withdrawn ; attempts to recapture Thebes frustrated.
- 378 (v) Athens, alienated by attempted surprise of Spartan *Sphodrias*, joins Thebes.
- (vi) Athens appeals to all Greece to join against Sparta ; and under *Callistratus'* guidance increases the scope of her Confederacy, levying a ' contribution ', calling council of allies and refraining from cleruchies.
- 376 (vii) Athenian *Chabrias* defeats Spartan fleet off *Naxos* ; and after peace negotiations foils attempt of Sparta and Dionysius on *Corcyra*.
- 371 (viii) General Congress, meeting at Sparta, frames *Peace of Callias*, declaring independence of all States and pact of non-aggression.
- (ix) *Epaminondas*, Thebes' representative, claims to sign for all Boeotia ; the claim is challenged by Agesilaus.

ASCENDANCY OF THEBES

A. Relations of Thebes to Boeotia

- (i) Boeotian cities, having never coalesced in single state, form Confederacy over which Thebes as leading partner always seeks to extend her control.
- (ii) Sparta, when at enmity with Thebes, always supports independence of Boeotian cities.
- 371 (iii) Hence Agesilaus' objection to Epaminondas' claim to sign for Boeotia (June) and *Cleombrotus'* expedition, which is defeated by Thebans under *Pelopidas* and *Epaminondas* at *Leuctra* (July).

B. Rise of Thebes

- **I. *In Northern Greece***
  - (a) Thebes after Leuctra forms Northern Confederacy, including Phocis, Locris, Aetolia, Euboea.
  - 370 (b) Her chief rival *Jason of Pherae* (Thessaly), retiring, after belated assistance at Leuctra, to plan eastern conquests, is assassinated.
  - (c) Pelopidas attacks Jason's successor *Alexander* of Pherae (369 onwards) ; killed 364, but Thebans overrun Thessaly and invade Macedon.

II. *In Peloponnese, etc.*

371 (a) After Leuctra, pro-Spartan oligarchies at Argos, etc., are assailed by populace.

(b) *Mantinea*, in defiance of Sparta, rebuilds her walls; *Tegea* forms Arcadian Federation.

(c) Arcadia, Argos and Elis join Thebes.

III. *Campaigns of Epaminondas.*

(a) Epaminondas marches into Arcadia; invades Sparta (late 370) and builds fortress on *Mt. Ithome* for Messenians (369 spring).

(b) Epaminondas, on second expedition (369), founds *Megalopolis* as capital of Arcadian League.

(c) On third expedition wins *Achaea* (366), which is soon lost through high-handed policy of Theban government.

(d) Epaminondas leads naval expedition to Propontis and wins over *Byzantium* (364).

IV. *Alienation of Arcadia.*

(a) Pro-Theban terms, brought back by Greek delegates from Susa, alienate Arcadians (367).

(b) Arcadians seize *Olympia* from *Elis*.

(c) Negotiations over Elis lead to attempt of Theban officer to arrest anti-Theban Arcadians (362).

(d) *Mantinea* joins Sparta and Athens, while Tegea remains loyal to Thebes.

V. *Campaign of Mantinea.*

362 (a) Epaminondas marches large northern army to aid Tegea.

(b) Fails to surprise Sparta in absence of Agesilaus' army.

(c) Fails to surprise Mantinea.

(d) In battle of Mantinea, Epaminondas defeats Spartans, Athenians and Mantineans, but is killed.

(e) Theban supremacy collapses.

(f) Sparta lacks funds to recover Messenia (Agesilaus' expedition to Egypt and death, 360).

(g) Arcadian strength declines. Megalopolis dwindles.

C. Athenian Revival

I. *Aegean Confederacy*

(a) Athens extends her control over Aegean; *Timotheus* recovers *Sestos* (365), *Potidaea, Methone* and other Chalcidic towns (365), Euboea (357).

(b) Athenian settlement of cleruchs at *Samos* alienates allies (364).

(c) Financial exhaustion prevents her from re-establishing her control.

II. *Domestic Policy*

(a) Commercial prosperity due to carrying trade and re-working of silver-mines.

(b) Heavy taxation to meet naval needs.

(c) Growing tendency towards socialism, e.g. fee for attendance at Ecclesia 389 (?); *Theoric Fund* to pay for poorer citizens' attendance at festivals.

(d) *Eubulus* (354–50) reorganizes finance, devoting surplus to Theoric Fund, but by economy improving navy, roads and water-supply.

(e) Struggle with Macedon (348–338) prevents building, etc.

(f) *Lycurgus*, by able finance (338–4), restores prosperity and builds stone seats in Theatre and Stadium.

PHILIP OF MACEDON

A. Earlier History of Macedon

(i) *Archelaus*, an enlightened ruler of a savage and backward people ; builder of roads, etc. ; patron of Euripides, etc. d. 399.

(ii) After period of faction *Amyntas* (393–69) succeeds to throne ; is hard pressed by Olynthian League and Illyrian tribes ; but reasserts himself thanks to Sparta's suppression of Olynthus.

(iii) Of his three sons *Alexander* is murdered (368) ; *Perdiccas* killed by Illyrians (359) ; and *Philip* becomes regent for Perdiccas' son (359).

B. Philip establishes Macedonian Power

(i) Having got rid of other claimants to throne, Philip buys off *Paeonians* (358) and defeats Illyrians (358 and 356) with aid of a reorganized army.

(ii) Reorganization of army :

    (a) Cavalry of aristocratic ' Companions ' already efficient.

    (b) Infantry of mercenaries, Macedonians and conquered mountaineers, trained to mobile tactics and use of long ' sarissa '.

357 (iii) Financial resources secured by seizure of *Amphipolis* and Mt. Pangaeus gold mines.

(iv) Seaports secured by seizure of *Pydna* and *Potidaea* (356) and *Methone* (353), while Athens is fully occupied

357–4 with revolt of Chios, Rhodes and Byzantium egged on by *Mausolus of Halicarnassus*.

C. Philip and Phocis

356 (i) Phocians under *Philomelus*, threatened with penalization by Amphictyonic Council under influence of Thebes, seize Delphi and use treasure to hire mercenaries.

354 (ii) Philomelus defeated and killed by Thebans ; *Onomarchus* terrorizes neighbourhood and seizes Thermopylae.

353 (iii) Onomarchus having allied himself to Lycophron of Pherae, the *Larissans* summon Philip's aid.

352 (iv) After defeat and retirement, Philip overcomes Phocians and takes *Pherae* and *Pagasae*.

(v) Philip checked at *Thermopylae* by arrival of Athenian army.

D. Olynthus and Peace of Philocrates

351 (i) Demosthenes, though holding no office, delivers First Philippic.

349 (ii) Philip attacks Chalcidic Confederacy; Athens, being diverted by revolt of Euboea, fails to send troops (except mercenaries under *Chares*) until 348, when they arrive too late to save *Olynthus*.

347 (iii) After attempt to rouse Greeks against Philip, an Embassy of Peace is sent by Athens to Pella, including *Philocrates, Aeschines, Demosthenes*.

346 (iv) During subsequent negotiations Philip takes many forts from Thracian *Cersobleptes* and refuses to ratify terms until within striking distance of Phocis.

(v) Phocian *Phalaecus* sells Thermopylae to Philip, who crushes Phocis and hands it over to Thebes.

346 (vi) Philip gains seat on Amphictyonic Council and presides at Pythian Games.

E. Campaign in Propontis

345–40 (i) Philip keeps away from Greece; campaigns in *Epirus* and *Thrace*.

(ii) Philip's pacific declarations fail to convince Athenians: Demosthenes impeaches Aeschines; tries to rouse Peloponnese; *Phocion* sent to expel Philip's partisans from Euboea.

(iii) On Demosthenes' instigation *Byzantium* and *Perinthus* declare against Philip.

340 (iv) Philip fails to take *Perinthus* and *Byzantium*; defeated by Athenian fleet.

339 (v) Philip turns to successful campaign against *Scythians*; but is wounded by *Triballi*.

F. Chaeronea and Philip's Death

(i) Athens insults Thebes by dedication at Delphi: but Aeschines diverts Amphictyonic Council to punishment of sacrilege of *Amphissans*.

339 (ii) Amphictyons invite Philip's aid against Amphissa.

338 (iii) Philip enters Greece and marches not on Larissa, but to *Elatea* towards Thebes.

Spring (iv) Demosthenes, now supreme, persuades Athenians to ally with Thebans and with them block Philip's passage.

338 Aug. (v) Remaining inactive all summer, Philip manœuvres Greeks back on *Chaeronea* and there defeats them.

(vi) Philip allows Athens immunity from invasion and retention of a few islands, but occupies Thebes, enslaving war-prisoners and exiling anti-Macedonian party.

338 (vii) At Congress of Corinth, Philip founds Pan-Hellenic League, enforcing peace and garrisoning *Thermopylae, Chalcis, Thebes, Corinth*.

337 (viii) At first meeting of League Council, Philip announces expedition against Persia and is voted troops and ships.

(ix) Owing to quarrel *Alexander* and *Olympias* retire from Pella, where in 336 Philip is murdered.

ALEXANDER AND GREECE

A. Before Departure for East

336 (i) News of Philip's death followed by general insurrection ; Alexander, by swift marching, cows resistance and is welcomed by Pan-Hellenic Congress.

335 (ii) Alexander recovers Thrace and makes demonstration across Danube against Scythians.

335 (iii) During Alexander's reduction of Illyrians rumour of his death causes Thebes, egged on by Demosthenes, to attack Macedonian garrison.

335 Oct. (iv) Alexander destroys Thebes, enslaving inhabitants, but waives demand for surrender of Demosthenes, Eubulus and other Athenian agitators.

B. After Departure for East

(i) Greek assistance to expedition very half-hearted.

331 (ii) Sparta leads a revolt, which is crushed by *Antipater*, Alexander's viceroy.

(iii) Alexander's success in East causes wholesale emigration.

324 (iv) Alexander's intention to repatriate exiles causes irritation, especially at Athens.

324 (v) Harpalus, keeper of Alexander's treasure in Persia, absconds to Aegean ; suggests insurrection ; but Athenians arrest him. Owing to peculation of Harpagus' treasure, Demosthenes is exiled.

323 (vi) On news of Alexander's death Demosthenes is recalled and Athens leads revolt.

322 (vii) Revolt of Greeks crushed by Antipater at *Crannon* ; Macedonian garrison posted at Peiraeus. Demosthenes commits suicide.

GREEK PHILOSOPHY AND SCIENCE

A. Philosophy

  I. PLATO (427–347) teaches in *Academy* near Athens.

    (*a*) Develops Socrates' teaching in dialogue form, e.g. Republic, Meno, Crito, Phaedo, etc.

    (*b*) Forms theory of ' Ideas ' which constitute permanent reality and are only dimly reflected in phenomena of visible world.

    (*c*) Devises in *Republic* an ideal state on lines of Spartanlike communism ruled by ' guardians ' educated in higher mathematics and contemplation of Ideas.

  II. ARISTOTLE (384–322) born in *Stagirus* (Chalcidice) ; tutor to Alexander ; teaches in Lyceum, Athens (Peripatetic School).

    (*a*) Treats many subjects, e.g. Poetics, Politics, Ethics and especially Biology.

    (*b*) By strict classification and development of formal

30

logic establishes the methods and terminology employed by subsequent philosophers.

(c) In Ethics develops doctrine of the ' Mean ' as a guide to conduct ; in Politics maintains City-State as the ideal unit.

III. OTHER SCHOOLS, developments of Socratic teaching.

(a) *Cynics* maintain complete independence from all worldly ties ; hence is developed by *Zeno*, a Phoenician from Cyprus (336–264) the *Stoic School*, who hold self-mastery and self-sufficiency to be the source of happiness.

(b) *Cyrenaic School* of *Aristippus* interpret the Good as the Useful and therefore the Pleasurable : hence is developed by *Epicurus* (fl. 300) the doctrine that Pleasure is the source of happiness, but higher pleasures are best.

C. Mathematics

(i) *Thales* of Miletus (624–547) learns practical geometry in Egypt and develops it on theoretical lines.

(ii) *Pythagoras* (572–497) classifies numbers to which he attributes mystic significance ; develops geometry and astronomy ; asserts sphericity of earth.

(iii) *Euclid* of Alexandria (fl. 290) compiles Books of Elements, perfecting proofs of earlier geometricians.

(iv) *Archimedes* (287–212), the most original Greek mathematician ; works on Hydrostatics, Parabola, Trigonometry, etc.

(v) *Eratosthenes* of Cyrene (c. 240) works on Astronomy ; *Apollonius* on Conics (c. 240).

(vi) *Diophantes* of Alexandria (c. 250 A.D.) develops Algebraic notation.

D. Medicine and Biology

(i) *Hippocrates* of Cos (fl. 420) travels to Athens and elsewhere ; his descriptions of cases collected with others in a compilation by Alexandrian students.

(ii) *Aristotle* makes systematic observation and classification of insects, fishes, etc.

(iii) *Theophrastus*, Aristotle's pupil, studies botany.

(iv) During third and second century much learned work at *Alexandria* in all branches of inquiry, especially in dissection and applied science generally. *Heron* (c. 120 B.C.) experiments with steam.

ALEXANDER'S CONQUESTS

A. Conquest of Asia Minor

334 (i) Crosses Dardanelles (April) ; visits Troy ; defeats satraps of Asia Minor at *R. Granicus.*

(ii) Greek towns welcome his re-establishment of democratic constitutions ; *Memnon*, captain of enemies' Greek mercenaries resists at *Miletus* and *Halicarnassus*, but after threatening trouble in Aegean, dies (333).

(iii) Disbanding most of his fleet and leaving main body under *Parmenio* at Ephesus Alexander proceeds with Macedonians along south coast past Mt. Climax.

333 (iv) Strikes up at *Gordium* on main eastern road, where Parmenio rejoins him.

(v) Surprises satrap *Arsames* by seizure of *Mt. Taurus* pass; enters Tarsus.

(vi) Advancing south past Issus, is surprised by *Darius'* appearance in his rear, but turns and defeats him on *R. Pinarus* near *Issus* (333 November).

B. Conquest of Syria and Egypt

333 (i) Alexander, refusing Darius' peace-offers, turns down coast; *N. Syria* and *Phoenicia* submit.

332 (ii) *Tyre* is reduced after siege (January–July) with aid of ships levied from Cyprus and Sidon.

(iii) Palestine and Philistia submit; *Gaza* taken by siege (October).

(iv) Alexander occupies Egypt; chooses site of Alexandria (331) and visits Zeus Ammon.

C. Conquest of East

I. *Central Provinces of Persian Empire* (already well organized under Persian rule).

331 (i) Marches in spring viâ Upper Euphrates and Tigris to neighbourhood of *Arbela*, where he defeats at *Gaugamela* (October) huge oriental host of Darius; enters *Babylon* (October).

(ii) *Susa* entered (December); vast treasure taken.

330 (iii) Despite *Ariobarzanes'* resistance, *Persepolis* taken.

July (iv) Darius, now in power of upstart *Bessus*, overtaken in *Bactria*; slain by followers.

(v) Alexander disbands Greek contingents, re-enlisting some among his Macedonians; trains Orientals in phalanx tactics; discontent of officers; *Philotas'* conspiracy leads to murder of Parmenio.

II. *Outlying Eastern Provinces* (loosely held by Persian kings under local chiefs).

329 (i) Passing through *Kabul* (Afghanistan) and over Hindu Kush subdues *Bactria* (328), where he executes Bessus.

328 (ii) Subdues *Sogdiana* (capital *Samarcand*); marries *Roxana* and founds *Alexandro-eschata* (327).

D. Campaign in India

327 (i) Alexander re-crosses Hindu Kush into Afghanistan (summer).

(ii) While *Hephaestion* descends by *Khyber Pass* to *R. Indus*, Alexander campaigns into mountains towards Chitral (winter).

326 (iii) Joining Hephaestion (spring) subdues *Punjaub*, overcoming *Porus* on *R. Hydaspes*.

(iv) On reaching *R. Hyphasis* troops refuse **to advance** ¡ Alexander consents to retirement.

(v) After march down River Indus (late **autumn**), **main** body sent homewards viâ *Bolan Pass*.

(vi) Alexander continues with picked troops **and** fleet **to** mouth of Indus.

325 (vii) Alexander marches through *Gedrosia* (August–October), rejoining main body near *Kirman*.

(viii) *Nearchus* with fleet sails home viâ Persian Gulf.

E. Reorganization of Empire and Army

324 (i) Flight of *Harpagus* and misgovernment of native governors necessitates disciplinary measures.

(ii) Fusion of races promoted by marriage of army **with** oriental wives.

324 (iii) Drafting of Orientals into phalanx, involving discharge of European veterans, provokes mutiny at *Opis*.

324 (iv) Alexander demands divine honours from Greek States at home.

(v) Embassy from Carthage, Spain, Gaul and Italy with overtures of friendship.

323 (vi) Great preparations at Babylon for expedition to *Arabia*.

(vii) Alexander dies of fever at Babylon, June 13, 323.

F. Alexander's Work and Influence

(i) Finance centralized in hands of treasurer: Harpalus (central provinces), Cleomenes (Egypt).

(ii) Satrap system continued in central provinces ; autonomous Greek democracies allowed in Asia Minor ; old Royal estates kept in Alexander's hands.

(iii) Fusion of races proves a failure.
　(a) Native governors untrustworthy.
　(b) Transplantation of population abandoned.
　(c) Use of natives in phalanx discontinued after Alexander's death.

(iv) Colonies planted in conquered lands.
　(a) Seventy known to have existed.
　(b) Peopled with discharged veterans and emigrants from Europe.
　(c) Town-planning and municipal laws on Greek model.
　(d) Elected magistrates (and possible Councils) under governor appointed by Alexander.

(v) Despite general tendency of colonists to remain aloof from Orientals, Hellenic influences permeate countries of Levant, e.g. effect on Judaism.

(vi) Narrow outlook of Hellenism broadened by contact with other nations.

(vii) Effects of Greek culture in Eastern Mediterranean countries outlast fall of Roman Empire.

HELLENISTIC TIMES AND AFTER

A. Alexander's Successors

(i) Alexander appointed no heir ; Roxana's son born after Alexander's death, eventually killed.

(ii) Alexander's Generals dispute for Empire and after Antigonus' defeat and suicide (301) three permanent kingdoms result.

(a) *Antipater's* son *Cassander* retains Macedonian Europe.

(b) *Ptolemy* and his successors retain Egypt.

(c) *Seleucus* and his successors retain Syria and Mesopotamia, and after 281 such parts of Asia Minor as are not absorbed by Celtic invaders (Galatia) or by independent kingdoms of Pergamum and Pontus.

B. Alexandria and Hellenistic Culture

(i) Alexandria enjoys great prosperity through trade with Arabia and India.

(ii) Ptolemy founds :

(a) ' *Museum* ' or University where great scientific and literary work is done.

(b) *Library*, which encourages great activity of grammarians and commentators.

(iii) Alexandrian literature erudite but not original ; *Callimachus*, epigrammatist, etc. (fl. 250) ; *Apollonius* (fl. 200) ; migrates to Rhodes ; writes epic ' Argonautica ' ; *Theocritus* from Sicily (fl. 280) ; followers of Theocritus, *Bion* and *Moschus*.

(iv) Pergamum and Rhodes develop schools of sculpture ; Athens remains centre of philosophic inquiry.

C. Greece in Third and Second Century B.C.

(i) Though Philip's Pan-Hellenic Union breaks down, states except Athens and Sparta group themselves in two democratic federations :

(a) *Aetolian League* ; founded 323 ; comprises most of northern Greece, Elis and part of Arcadia ; policy militaristic and predatory.

(b) *Achaean League*, founded 281 ; comprises Corinth, Sicyon, Argos, etc. ; owing to its chief founder *Aratus'* fear of Sparta, tends to subservient dependence on *Antigonus of Macedon* ; but after Antigonus' death (218), the soldier *Philopoemon* follows a more independent, but pacific policy.

(ii) Advance of Rome :

(a) After mastering most of Italy, Rome attacks *Tarentum* (281), which, despite assistance of *Pyrrhus* of Epirus, submits in 272.

(b) Sicily, which under *Agathocles* (d. 289) of Syracuse, had kept Carthage at bay, is annexed by Rome after First Punic War (264–41).

(c) During Second Punic War (218–01) Hannibal is backed, though half-heartedly, by *Philip of Macedon*.

(d) In First Macedonian War (200–196) Romans under *Flaminius* defeat Philip's army at *Cynoscephalae* (197), but withdraw after declaring independence of Greece.

(e) In war against *Antiochus* (192–89) Rome conquers all Seleucid provinces in Asia Minor.

(f) Reduces Macedon and converts it into province. (146)

146 (iii) Sparta and Achaean League appeal to Rome to settle quarrel. Roman envoys insulted by Corinth mob. Capture of Corinth by *Mummius*. Greece made subject to Roman governor of Macedonia ; Athens and Sparta allowed to retain autonomy.

D. Influence of Greek Culture on Rome

(i) First contact with Hellenism through cities of South Italy—e.g. dramatist *Livius Andronicus* (240) brought as prisoner from Tarentum.

(ii) Philhellenism spreads among circle of younger Scipio (fl. 150) ; and demand for intellectual training popularizes study of Greek (e.g. Gracchi brothers fl. 135–123) ; young Romans sent to Athens ; Greek much used in speech and writing.

(iii) Latin authors borrow art forms and style from Greek models, especially Hellenistic.

(iv) Unsettling effect of Greek thought shown by Individualism of Late Republic.

(v) Under Empire, need for administrative ability, etc., leads to large employment of Greek secretaries, etc., even in Imperial Civil Service.

(vi) Greek Philosophy, and especially Epicurean and Stoic, much studied.

E. Late Greek Writers.

(i) *Plutarch* of Boeotia (fl. 75 A.D. writes *Lives*, etc.).

(ii) During Cultural Revival under Marcus Aurelius (161–180 A.D.) ; *Lucian*, essayist (fl. 170 A.D.) ; *Galen* of Alexandria (fl. 150 A.D.), greatest medical authority of ancient world.

(iii) *Pausanias* of Asia Minor (fl. 150 A.D.), antiquarian and traveller.

(iv) *Plotinus* of Egypt (204–70 A.D.), Neo-platonist philosopher.

(v) Emperor *Constantine*, having declared Christianity the official religion of State (323 A.D.) Greek culture begins to lose its essential character, except for brief pagan revival under *Julian the Apostate*.

(vii) Byzantine Empire remains home of Greek scholarship, though degenerate, until Turks sack Constantinople (1453) and flight of scholars helps to spread Renaissance in Western Europe.

INDEX